The Grammar

The Grammar Level 1

지은이 Nexus Contents Development Team
펴낸이 임상진
펴낸곳 (주)넥서스

출판신고 1992년 4월 3일 제311-2002-2호 2-14
10880 경기도 파주시 지목로 5
Tel (02)330-5500 Fax (02)330-5555

ISBN 979-11-5752-013-8 54740
979-11-5752-011-4 (SET)

가격은 뒤표지에 있습니다.
잘못 만들어진 책은 구입처에서 바꾸어 드립니다.

www.nexusEDU.kr

The Grammar

Nexus Contents Development Team

Level 1

NEXUS Edu

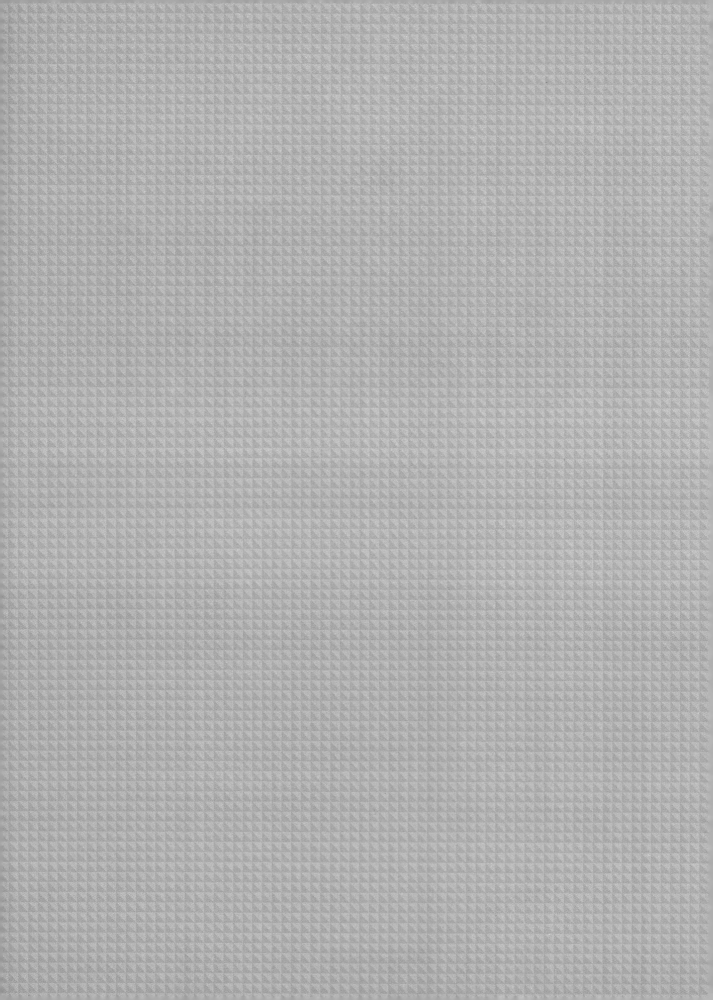

Concise and Core
Grammar Points!

The Grammar Series

Sentence Expansion

기초 문법을 기반으로 문장을 완성,
확장해 가는 학습 방법 적용

Grammar Summary

배운 학습 내용을 차트 및 표로 정리하여
쉽게 암기할 수 있도록 구성

A Variety of Question Types

문법 포인트 확인 ➡ 기초 문법 문제 ➡ 응용 문제 ➡
리뷰 테스트 ➡ 문법 확장 문제 ➡ 종합 문제

Preparation for School Tests

다양한 문제 유형을 통해 내신 대비는 물론
말하기 및 쓰기 실력 향상

Workbook

내신 대비 및 서술형 평가 대비를 위한
충분한 분량의 문제가 수록된 워크북 제공

Concise & Core Grammar

불필요하고 잘 사용하지 않는 문법은 배제하고
핵심적인 부분만을 간결하고 정확하게
예문 중심으로 이해할 수 있도록 구성

Features

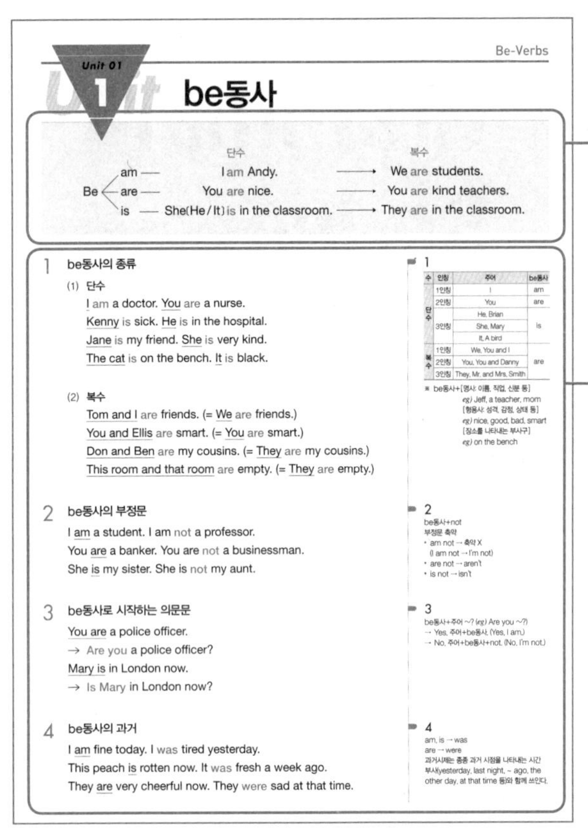

Unit 01

1 be동사

Be-Verbs

	단수		복수
Be — am	I am Andy.	→	We are students.
Be — are	You are nice.	→	You are kind teachers.
Be — is	She(He / It) is in the classroom.	→	They are in the classroom.

1 be동사의 종류

(1) 단수

I am a doctor. You are a nurse.
Kenny is sick. He is in the hospital.
Jane is my friend. She is very kind.
The cat is on the bench. It is black.

(2) 복수

Tom and I are friends. (= We are friends.)
You and Ellis are smart. (= You are smart.)
Don and Ben are my cousins. (= They are my cousins.)
This room and that room are empty. (= They are empty.)

1

수	인칭	주어	be동사
단수	1인칭	I	am
	2인칭	You	are
	3인칭	He, Brian	is
		She, Mary	
		It, A bird	
복수	1인칭	We, You and I	are
	2인칭	You, You and Danny	
	3인칭	They, Mr. and Mrs. Smith	

※ be동사+[명사: 이름, 직업, 신분 등]
eg) Jeff, a teacher, mom
[형용사: 성격, 감정, 상태 등]
eg) nice, good, bad, smart
[장소를 나타내는 부사구]
eg) on the bench

2 be동사의 부정문

I am a student. I am not a professor.
You are a banker. You are not a businessman.
She is my sister. She is not my aunt.

2
be동사+not
부정문 축약
• am not → 축약 X
(I am not → I'm not)
• are not → aren't
• is not → isn't

3 be동사로 시작하는 의문문

You are a police officer.
→ Are you a police officer?
Mary is in London now.
→ Is Mary in London now?

3
be동사+주어 ~? (eg) Are you ~?)
→ Yes, 주어+be동사. (Yes, I am.)
→ No, 주어+be동사+not. (No, I'm not.)

4 be동사의 과거

I am fine today. I was tired yesterday.
This peach is rotten now. It was fresh a week ago.
They are very cheerful now. They were sad at that time.

4
am, is → was
are → were
과거시제는 종종 과거 시점을 나타내는 시간 부사(yesterday, last night, ~ ago, the other day, at that time 등)와 함께 쓰인다.

Concept Note

해당 Unit에서 소개하는 기본 핵심 포인트의 개념과 정의

Grammar Point

문법 포인트 설명: 한글 주석과 영문 예문을 분리하여 문장의 예문 패턴을 집중적으로 비교 분석할 수 있도록 구성

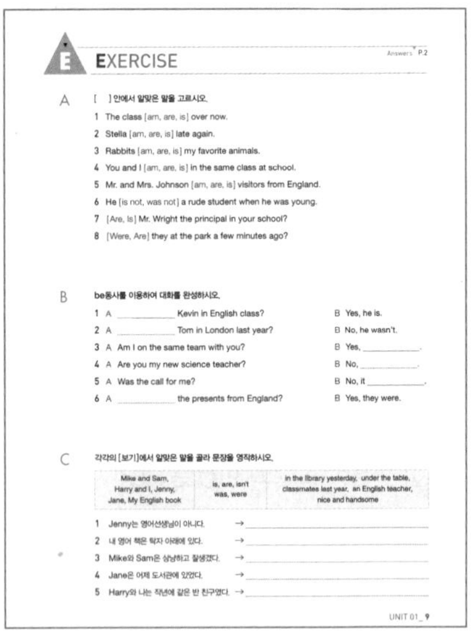

EXERCISE

Answers P.2

A [ ] 안에서 알맞은 말을 고르시오.

1 The class [am, are, is] over now.
2 Stella [am, are, is] late again.
3 Rabbits [am, are, is] my favorite animals.
4 You and I [am, are, is] in the same class at school.
5 Mr. and Mrs. Johnson [am, are, is] visitors from England.
6 He [is not, was not] a rude student when he was young.
7 [Are, Is] Mr. Wright the principal in your school?
8 [Were, Are] they at the park a few minutes ago?

B be동사를 이용하여 대화를 완성하시오.

1 A ________ Kevin in English class? B Yes, he is.
2 A ________ Tom in London last year? B No, he wasn't.
3 A Am I on the same team with you? B Yes, ________.
4 A Are you my new science teacher? B No, ________.
5 A Was the call for me? B No, it ________.
6 A ________ the presents from England? B Yes, they were.

C 각각의 [보기]에서 알맞은 말을 골라 문장을 영작하시오.

Mike and Sam, Harry and I, Jenny, Jane, My English book	is, are, isn't was, were	in the library yesterday, under the table, classmates last year, an English teacher, nice and handsome

1 Jenny는 영어선생님이 아니다. → ________
2 내 영어 책은 탁자 아래에 있다. → ________
3 Mike와 Sam은 상냥하고 잘생겼다. → ________
4 Jane은 어제 도서관에 있었다. → ________
5 Harry와 나는 작년에 같은 반 친구였다. → ________

UNIT 01_ 9

Exercise

배운 내용의 개념과 규칙 등의 확인 연습문제

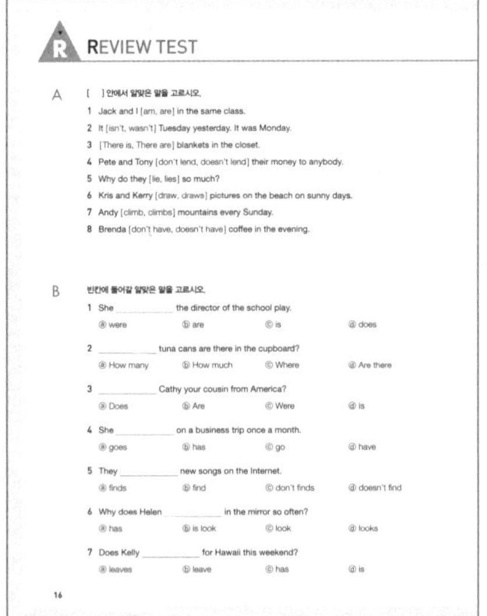

REVIEW TEST

A [ ] 안에서 알맞은 말을 고르시오.

1 Jack and I [am, are] in the same class.
2 It [isn't, wasn't] Tuesday yesterday. It was Monday.
3 [There is, There are] blankets in the closet.
4 Pete and Tony [don't lend, doesn't lend] their money to anybody.
5 Why do they [lie, lies] so much?
6 Kris and Kerry [draw, draws] pictures on the beach on sunny days.
7 Andy [climb, climbs] mountains every Sunday.
8 Brenda [don't have, doesn't have] coffee in the evening.

B 빈칸에 들어갈 알맞은 말을 고르시오.

1 She ________ the director of the school play.
ⓐ were ⓑ are ⓒ is ⓓ does

2 ________ tuna cans are there in the cupboard?
ⓐ How many ⓑ How much ⓒ Where ⓓ Are there

3 ________ Cathy your cousin from America?
ⓐ Does ⓑ Are ⓒ Were ⓓ Is

4 She ________ on a business trip once a month.
ⓐ goes ⓑ has ⓒ go ⓓ have

5 They ________ new songs on the Internet.
ⓐ finds ⓑ find ⓒ don't finds ⓓ doesn't find

6 Why does Helen ________ in the mirror so often?
ⓐ has ⓑ is look ⓒ look ⓓ looks

7 Does Kelly ________ for Hawaii this weekend?
ⓐ leaves ⓑ leave ⓒ has ⓓ is

16

Review Test

각 단원에서 배운 내용을 총 정리하는 장으로 4가지 유형의 문제 형태로 구성. 각각의 문법 포인트를 모아 놓아 전체적으로 구성된 문제풀이를 통해 부족한 부분을 진단

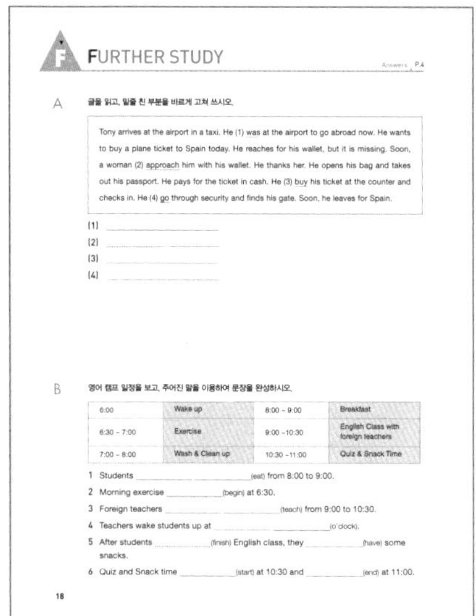

Further Study

짧은 읽기 지문을 통해 각 단원에서 배운 문법 포인트를 체크해 볼 수 있도록 문제 구성. 문법이 확장되어 지문 안에서 잘못된 문장을 수정할 수 있는 능력을 기를 수 있도록 구성

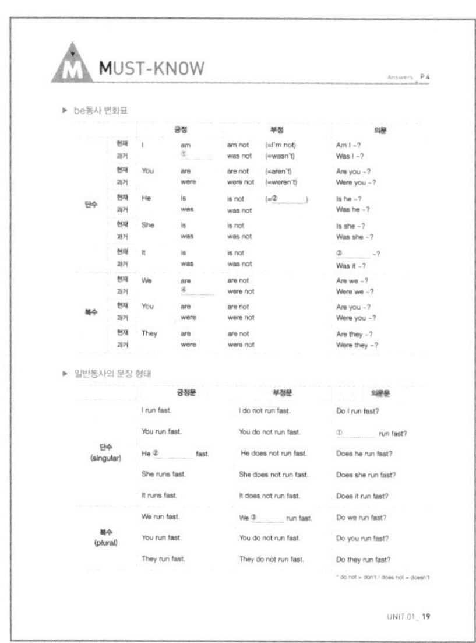

Must-Know

각 단원에서 배운 기본 문법 포인트들을 표로 정리하여 기본적 문법 사항을 놓치지 않도록 구성. 본문에서 다루지 않은 기본 사항과 보충적인 문법 사항을 수록

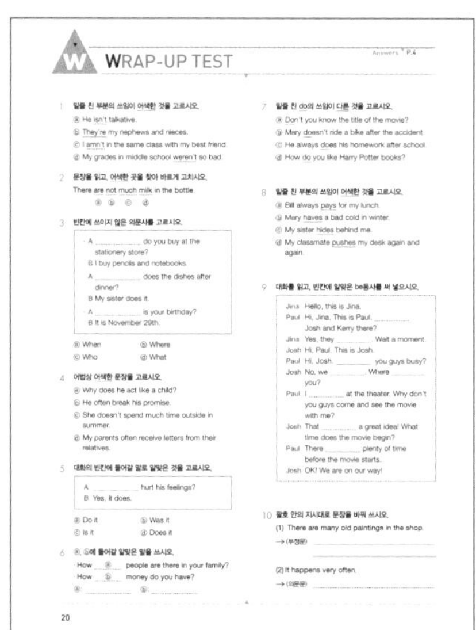

Wrap-up Test

각 단원이 끝나면 내신형 문제를 통해 앞에서 배운 문법 포인트를 확인할 수 있도록 구성. 문법을 종합적으로 정리할 수 있으며, 학교 시험에서 많이 출제되는 서술형 문제로 구성되어 있어 내신을 완벽하게 대비할 수 있도록 구성

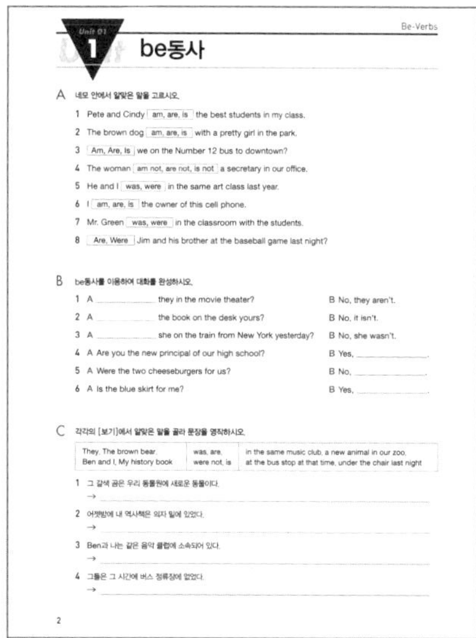

Workbook

기초 문법 확인 문제 외에도 내신 완벽 대비를 위한 객관식, 서술형 문제를 유닛별로 구성하여 자기주도학습을 할 수 있도록 구성

Contents

The Grammar

1
Level

be동사와 일반동사

1 be동사
2 일반동사
3 일반동사의 부정문과 의문문
4 의문사가 있는 의문문 / There is (are)

be동사

	단수		복수
Be — am	I am Andy.	→	We are students.
Be — are	You are nice.	→	You are kind teachers.
Be — is	She(He/It) is in the classroom.	→	They are in the classroom.

1 be동사의 종류

(1) 단수

I am a doctor. You are a nurse.
Kenny is sick. He is in the hospital.
Jane is my friend. She is very kind.
The cat is on the bench. It is black.

(2) 복수

Tom and I are friends. (= We are friends.)
You and Ellis are smart. (= You are smart.)
Don and Ben are my cousins. (= They are my cousins.)
This room and that room are empty. (= They are empty.)

1

수	인칭	주어	be동사
단수	1인칭	I	am
	2인칭	You	are
	3인칭	He, Brian	is
		She, Mary	
		It, A bird	
복수	1인칭	We, You and I	are
	2인칭	You, You and Danny	
	3인칭	They, Mr. and Mrs. Smith	

※ be동사+[명사: 이름, 직업, 신분 등]
eg) Jeff, a teacher, mom
[형용사: 성격, 감정, 상태 등]
eg) nice, good, bad, smart
[장소를 나타내는 부사구]
eg) on the bench

2 be동사의 부정문

I am a student. I am not a professor.
You are a banker. You are not a businessman.
She is my sister. She is not my aunt.

2
be동사+not
부정문 축약
- am not → 축약 X
  (I am not → I'm not)
- are not → aren't
- is not → isn't

3 be동사로 시작하는 의문문

You are a police officer.
→ Are you a police officer?
Mary is in London now.
→ Is Mary in London now?

3
be동사+주어 ~? (*eg)* Are you ~?)
→ Yes, 주어+be동사. (Yes, I am.)
→ No, 주어+be동사+not. (No, I'm not.)

4 be동사의 과거

I am fine today. I was tired yesterday.
This peach is rotten now. It was fresh a week ago.
They are very cheerful now. They were sad at that time.

4
am, is → was
are → were
과거시제는 종종 과거 시점을 나타내는 시간 부사(yesterday, last night, ~ ago, the other day, at that time 등)와 함께 쓰인다.

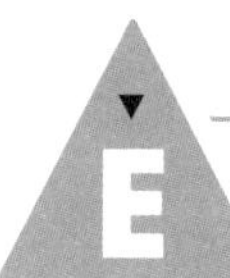

EXERCISE

Answers P. 2

A

[ ] 안에서 알맞은 말을 고르시오.

1 The class [am, are, is] over now.

2 Stella [am, are, is] late again.

3 Rabbits [am, are, is] my favorite animals.

4 You and I [am, are, is] in the same class at school.

5 Mr. and Mrs. Johnson [am, are, is] visitors from England.

6 He [is not, was not] a rude student when he was young.

7 [Are, Is] Mr. Wright the principal in your school?

8 [Were, Are] they at the park a few minutes ago?

B

be동사를 이용하여 대화를 완성하시오.

1 A __________ Kevin in English class? B Yes, he is.

2 A __________ Tom in London last year? B No, he wasn't.

3 A Am I on the same team with you? B Yes, __________.

4 A Are you my new science teacher? B No, __________.

5 A Was the call for me? B No, it __________.

6 A __________ the presents from England? B Yes, they were.

C

각각의 [보기]에서 알맞은 말을 골라 문장을 영작하시오.

Mike and Sam, Harry and I, Jenny, Jane, My English book	is, are, isn't was, were	in the library yesterday, under the table, classmates last year, an English teacher, nice and handsome

1 Jenny는 영어선생님이 아니다. → __________

2 내 영어 책은 탁자 아래에 있다. → __________

3 Mike와 Sam은 상냥하고 잘생겼다. → __________

4 Jane은 어제 도서관에 있었다. → __________

5 Harry와 나는 작년에 같은 반 친구였다. → __________

Unit 01 2 일반동사

1·2인칭, 복수 — I / You / They/We — live in London, England.

3인칭 단수 — She/He lives in Seoul, Korea. / The rabbit/It lives in the mountain.

> 일반동사
> 주어의 동작이나 상태를 나타냄
> go (가다)
> sleep (자다)
> love (~을 사랑하다)
> eat (~을 먹다)

1 일반동사의 종류

(1) 동사+목적어 (O)
I like science.
You hate math.

(2) 동사+목적어 (X)
We swim.
They walk.

(3) 동사+목적어 (O) 또는 (X)
The boys sing.
The boys sing a Christmas song.

2 일반동사의 변화 (3인칭 단수)

(1) 대부분의 일반동사+s
My sister reads fashion magazines every weekend.
My brother drinks a lot of milk.
Susan writes a letter to Roy every Sunday.

(2) -sh, -ch, -s, -x, -z, -o로 끝나는 동사+es
She finishes her work at 6 o'clock.
James watches sports news all the time.
He passes every test.
Bill fixes computers very well.
My father goes on a business trip every month.

(3) 〈자음+y〉로 끝나는 동사: -y를 -i로 고치고+es
My sister, Mary, studies Chinese every Sunday.
She copies newspapers every morning.

(4) 〈모음+y〉로 끝나는 동사:+s
Tom plays the flute very well.
He enjoys the music class.

1
(1) 목적어를 필요로 하는 동사
like (~을 좋아하다)
hate (~을 싫어하다)
want (~을 원하다)
(2) 목적어가 필요 없는 동사
swim (수영하다)
walk (걷다)
go (가다)
(3) 목적어가 필요, 또는 필요 없는 동사
sing (노래하다)
(~을 노래하다)

2
※ 1인칭, 2인칭, 복수 → 동사 변화 없음

(1) eat → eats
sleep → sleeps
dance → dances
come → comes

(2) wash → washes
catch → catches
fix → fixes
do → does
buzz → buzzes

(3) fly → flies
cry → cries

(4) buy → buys
stay → stays

cf) 불규칙 변화: have → has
I have a fever, and she has a fever, too

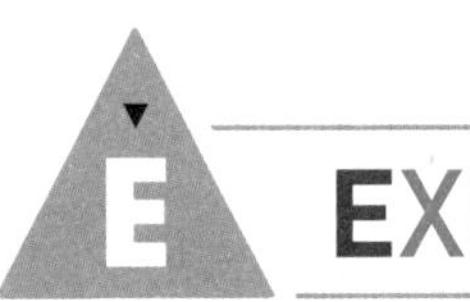

EXERCISE

Answers P.2

A

[ ] 안에서 알맞은 말을 고르시오.

1 Walter [drink, drinks] a lot of water when he is flying.

2 My father [fly, flies] to New York regularly.

3 Paul and his brother [speak, speaks] English very well.

4 Susan [catch, catches] a cold every winter.

5 Jake [enjoy, enjoys] ice cream for dessert.

6 My grandparents [have, has] a farm in the countryside.

7 The girl [practice, practices] the flute every day.

8 He always [fix, fixes] his friends' bikes.

B

주어진 말을 이용하여 현재시제 문장을 완성하시오.

1 Mike ______________(wear) a T-shirt and jeans on weekends.

2 The woman ______________(take) a taxi to the subway station.

3 Terry always ______________(buy) used books at online bookstores.

4 My friend ______________(have) his own car.

5 Amy ______________(wash) the dishes after dinner.

6 Pete always ______________(worry) about his weight.

7 Pat's father ______________(teach) math in high school.

8 He ______________(play) tennis with his sister on Saturdays.

C

밑줄 친 부분을 바르게 고쳐 쓰시오.

1 Eric's hair is quite long. It reach his shoulders. ______________

2 She always pay for everything when we get together. ______________

3 Many children bites their fingernails. ______________

4 Lauren and her husband knows a lot about plants. ______________

5 Mark always tell a lie to his friends. ______________

6 My brother collect coins from many countries for a hobby. ______________

일반동사의 부정문과 의문문

부정문	I do not like dogs.	She does not like cats.
긍정문	I like cats.	She likes dogs.
의문문	Do you like cats?	Does she like cats?

1 일반동사의 부정문

(1) 주어(1·2인칭, 복수)+do not+동사원형

I take a bus to school.

My friends do not take a bus to school. They take the subway.

(2) 주어(3인칭 단수)+does not+동사원형

Mark travels to his hometown every holiday.

He does not travel alone.

My mother reads a novel every night.

She does not read a magazine.

1

(1) 주어가 1인칭, 2인칭, 복수일 때

(2) 주어가 3인칭 단수(she, he, it)일 때

※ do not = don't
does not = doesn't

2 일반동사의 의문문

(1) Do+주어+동사원형 ~?

I drink a lot of water every day.

→ Do you drink a lot of water every day?

-Yes, I do. / No, I don't.

They play tennis every Sunday.

→ Do they play tennis every Sunday?

-Yes, they do. / No, they don't.

(2) Does+주어+동사원형 ~?

He knows Erica's address.

→ Does he know Erica's address?

-Yes, he does. / No, he doesn't.

It barks a lot every night.

→ Does it bark a lot every night?

-Yes, it does. / No, it doesn't.

2

(1) I, You, They

(2) She, He, It

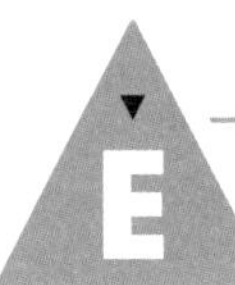

EXERCISE

Answers P.2

A 물음에 알맞은 응답을 연결하시오.

1 Do you like Italian food? •		• (a) No, I don't. I don't know it.
2 Does your brother study economics? •		• (b) Yes, I do. I like it very much.
3 Do Jack and Jill live together? •		• (c) No, she doesn't.
4 Does she learn Japanese? •		• (d) Yes, they do.
5 Do you know her birthday? •		• (e) Yes, he does.

B 밑줄 친 부분을 바르게 고쳐 쓰시오.

1 Do he often invite his friends to his house? ____________

2 Does your father likes soccer? ____________

3 Does Jane and Bob sometimes go to Paris? ____________

4 Does Harry sends text messages to his friends? ____________

5 Henry don't throw garbage on the street. ____________

6 Nancy and her boyfriend doesn't study very hard. ____________

7 My aunt does not cooks well. ____________

C 괄호 안의 지시대로 문장을 완성하시오.

1 You have lunch at the school cafeteria. (의문문)

→ ______________________ at the school cafeteria?

2 He brushes his teeth before he goes to bed. (부정문)

→ ______________________ before he goes to bed.

3 Does this store sell coffee and hot dogs? (긍정문)

→ ______________________ coffee and hot dogs.

4 His uncle arrives at 7 from Seattle. (의문문)

→ ______________________ at 7 from Seattle?

5 My brother and I love chocolate. (부정문)

→ ______________________ love chocolate.

Unit 01 4 의문사 있는 의문문 / There is[are]

Wh-words	Where is my book?	It is on the desk.
	What does she do?	She works at a bank.
There is / are	There is a book on the desk. (There is+단수 명사)	There are books on the desk. (There are+복수 명사)

1 의문사가 있는 의문문

(1) 의문사+be동사

A Who is she? B She is my grandmother.

A What is this? B It is my cell phone.

A Where are you? B I'm at the airport.

A Why are you in a hurry? B I am late for school.

(2) 의문사+do동사+주어+일반동사

A When do you go swimming?

B I go swimming on Monday.

A What does she learn in the P.E. class?

B She learns yoga.

> 1
> 의문사+동사+주어
> • who (누구) - 사람을 물어볼 때
> • what (무엇) - 사물, 동물
> • where (어디) - 장소
> • why (왜) - 이유
> • when (언제) - 시간, 때
> • how (어떻게) - 방법, 상태
> *eg)* How is your class?
> - It is great.
>
> ※ 의문사로 시작하는 의문문에는 yes나 no로 답하지 않는다.

2 There is(are)

(1) There is(was)+단수, There are(were)+복수

There is a coin in my wallet.

There was a big frog in the pond.

There are two walnuts on the plate.

There were many cows on my uncle's farm.

(2) Is(Are) there ~?, How many(much) ~?

Is there a bench in your garden?

Are there many students in the club?

A How many boys are there in your family?

B There are two boys in my family.

A How much water is there in the bucket?

B There is a little water in the bucket.

> 2
> (1) There is (was)+단수 명사
> : ~가 있다 / 있었다
> There are (were)+복수 명사
> : ~들이 있다 / 있었다
> ※ 이때 there는 따로 해석하지 않는다.
>
> (2) How many+셀 수 있는 명사 (복수 명사)
> How much+셀 수 없는 명사 (단수 명사)
> ※ [Unit 8 명사와 관사] 참조
>
> ※ **Is(Are) there ~?의 대답**
> Is(Are) there ~?
> → Yes, there is(are).
> → No, there isn't(aren't).
>
> ※ There is / are **부정**
> There is / are
> There was / were +not

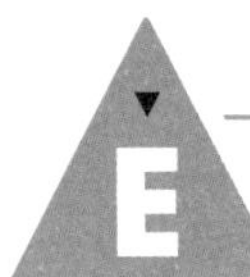

EXERCISE

Answers P.2

A

[ ] 안에서 알맞은 말을 고르시오.

1 When does your dad [come, comes] home?

2 How [are, do] you open this window?

3 Who [is, does] the man over there?

4 There [is, are] a fly in my soup!

5 There [is, are] many guests at my party, so I need more food.

6 There [was, were] a new student in his seat.

7 There [was not, were not] much space between the two buildings.

B

밑줄 친 부분을 바르게 고쳐 쓰시오. 틀리지 않았다면, O표 하시오.

1 When does she goes to London? ______________

2 There is many tourists at the beach. ______________

3 Where do their classrooms? ______________

4 How many candies were there in the box yesterday? ______________

5 Are there any football games last week? ______________

6 Were there a good restaurant near here ten years ago? ______________

7 What are you do on Sundays? ______________

C

괄호 안의 지시대로 문장을 완성하시오.

1 Kate and Bill feed the fish in the pond. (When 의문문)

→ ______________________ the fish in the pond?

2 Your brother takes flute lessons. (Where 의문문)

→ ______________________ flute lessons?

3 There is a polar bear at the zoo. (부정문)

→ ______________________ at the zoo.

4 There are many students in the playground. (How many 의문문)

→ ______________________ in the playground?

5 There is a lot of juice in the bottle. (How much 의문문)

→ ______________________ in the bottle?

REVIEW TEST

A

[ ] 안에서 알맞은 말을 고르시오.

1 Jack and I [am, are] in the same class.

2 It [isn't, wasn't] Tuesday yesterday. It was Monday.

3 [There is, There are] blankets in the closet.

4 Pete and Tony [don't lend, doesn't lend] their money to anybody.

5 Why do they [lie, lies] so much?

6 Kris and Kerry [draw, draws] pictures on the beach on sunny days.

7 Andy [climb, climbs] mountains every Sunday.

8 Brenda [don't have, doesn't have] coffee in the evening.

B

빈칸에 들어갈 알맞은 말을 고르시오.

1 She ____________ the director of the school play.

ⓐ were ⓑ are ⓒ is ⓓ does

2 ____________ tuna cans are there in the cupboard?

ⓐ How many ⓑ How much ⓒ Where ⓓ Are there

3 ____________ Cathy your cousin from America?

ⓐ Does ⓑ Are ⓒ Were ⓓ Is

4 She ____________ on a business trip once a month.

ⓐ goes ⓑ has ⓒ go ⓓ have

5 They ____________ new songs on the Internet.

ⓐ finds ⓑ find ⓒ don't finds ⓓ doesn't find

6 Why does Helen ____________ in the mirror so often?

ⓐ has ⓑ is look ⓒ look ⓓ looks

7 Does Kelly ____________ for Hawaii this weekend?

ⓐ leaves ⓑ leave ⓒ has ⓓ is

C 주어진 말을 이용하여 현재시제 문장을 완성하시오.

1 Your T-shirt is really nice. It ______________(look) good on you.

2 How ______________ you ______________(commute), by subway or by bus?

3 Glen ______________(write) mystery novels.

4 Does Lisa ______________(want) a glass of water?

5 We usually ______________(order) a combination pizza.

6 Jenny ______________ ______________(not, wait) patiently for her friends.

7 Mr. and Mrs. Jones ______________ ______________(not, take) a nap in the afternoon.

D 밑줄 친 부분을 바르게 고쳐 문장을 다시 쓰시오.

1 Who are your favorite actor?

→ ____

2 My friends and I goes to a concert today.

→ ____

3 Danny study a lot of subjects.

→ ____

4 Isn't Sarah at her grandmother's thirty minutes ago?

→ ____

5 He prefer cookies for snacks, but I prefer chocolate.

→ ____

6 When does his flight arrives?

→ ____

7 My father and I do not washes our car when it rains or snows.

→ ____

F FURTHER STUDY

Answers P.4

A

글을 읽고, 밑줄 친 부분을 바르게 고쳐 쓰시오.

Tony arrives at the airport in a taxi. He (1) was at the airport to go abroad now. He wants to buy a plane ticket to Spain today. He reaches for his wallet, but it is missing. Soon, a woman (2) approach him with his wallet. He thanks her. He opens his bag and takes out his passport. He pays for the ticket in cash. He (3) buy his ticket at the counter and checks in. He (4) go through security and finds his gate. Soon, he leaves for Spain.

(1) ______________________

(2) ______________________

(3) ______________________

(4) ______________________

B

영어 캠프 일정을 보고, 주어진 말을 이용하여 문장을 완성하시오.

6:00	Wake up	8:00 ~ 9:00	Breakfast
6:30 ~ 7:00	Exercise	9:00 ~10:30	English Class with foreign teachers
7:00 ~ 8:00	Wash & Clean up	10:30 ~11:00	Quiz & Snack Time

1 Students ____________ ____________(eat) from 8:00 to 9:00.

2 Morning exercise ____________(begin) at 6:30.

3 Foreign teachers ____________ ____________(teach) from 9:00 to 10:30.

4 Teachers wake students up at ____________ ____________(o'clock).

5 After students ____________(finish) English class, they ____________(have) some snacks.

6 Quiz and Snack time ____________(start) at 10:30 and ____________(end) at 11:00.

MUST-KNOW

Answers P.4

▶ be동사 변화표

			긍정		부정		의문
단수	현재 과거	I	am ① ______	am not was not	(=I'm not) (=wasn't)		Am I ~? Was I ~?
	현재 과거	You	are were	are not were not	(=aren't) (=weren't)		Are you ~? Were you ~?
	현재 과거	He	is was	is not was not	(=② ______)		Is he ~? Was he ~?
	현재 과거	She	is was	is not was not			Is she ~? Was she ~?
	현재 과거	It	is was	is not was not			③ ______ ~? Was it ~?
복수	현재 과거	We	are ④ ______	are not were not			Are we ~? Were we ~?
	현재 과거	You	are were	are not were not			Are you ~? Were you ~?
	현재 과거	They	are were	are not were not			Are they ~? Were they ~?

▶ 일반동사의 문장 형태

	긍정문	부정문	의문문
단수 (singular)	I run fast.	I do not run fast.	Do I run fast?
	You run fast.	You do not run fast.	① ______ run fast?
	He ② ______ fast.	He does not run fast.	Does he run fast?
	She runs fast.	She does not run fast.	Does she run fast?
	It runs fast.	It does not run fast.	Does it run fast?
복수 (plural)	We run fast.	We ③ ______ run fast.	Do we run fast?
	You run fast.	You do not run fast.	Do you run fast?
	They run fast.	They do not run fast.	Do they run fast?

* do not = don't / does not = doesn't

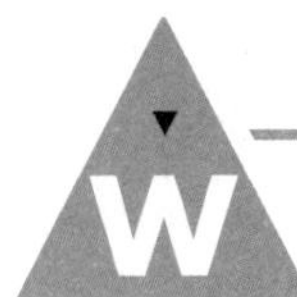

WRAP-UP TEST

Answers P.4

1 밑줄 친 부분의 쓰임이 어색한 것을 고르시오.

ⓐ He isn't talkative.

ⓑ They're my nephews and nieces.

ⓒ I amn't in the same class with my best friend.

ⓓ My grades in middle school weren't so bad.

2 문장을 읽고, 어색한 곳을 찾아 바르게 고치시오.

There are(ⓐ) not(ⓑ) much(ⓒ) milk(ⓓ) in the bottle.

3 빈칸에 쓰이지 않은 의문사를 고르시오.

· A _______ do you buy at the stationery store?
B I buy pencils and notebooks.

· A _______ does the dishes after dinner?
B My sister does it.

· A _______ is your birthday?
B It is November 29th.

ⓐ When ⓑ Where

ⓒ Who ⓓ What

4 어법상 어색한 문장을 고르시오.

ⓐ Why does he act like a child?

ⓑ He often break his promise.

ⓒ She doesn't spend much time outside in summer.

ⓓ My parents often receive letters from their relatives.

5 대화의 빈칸에 들어갈 말로 알맞은 것을 고르시오.

A _______ hurt his feelings?
B Yes, it does.

ⓐ Do it ⓑ Was it

ⓒ Is it ⓓ Does it

6 ⓐ, ⓑ에 들어갈 알맞은 말을 쓰시오.

· How __ⓐ__ people are there in your family?

· How __ⓑ__ money do you have?

ⓐ: _______ ⓑ: _______

7 밑줄 친 do의 쓰임이 다른 것을 고르시오.

ⓐ Don't you know the title of the movie?

ⓑ Mary doesn't ride a bike after the accident.

ⓒ He always does his homework after school.

ⓓ How do you like Harry Potter books?

8 밑줄 친 부분의 쓰임이 어색한 것을 고르시오.

ⓐ Bill always pays for my lunch.

ⓑ Mary haves a bad cold in winter.

ⓒ My sister hides behind me.

ⓓ My classmate pushes my desk again and again.

9 대화를 읽고, 빈칸에 알맞은 be동사를 써 넣으시오.

Jina Hello, this is Jina.
Paul Hi, Jina. This is Paul. _______ Josh and Kerry there?
Jina Yes, they _______. Wait a moment.
Josh Hi, Paul. This is Josh.
Paul Hi, Josh. _______ you guys busy?
Josh No, we _______. Where _______ you?
Paul I _______ at the theater. Why don't you guys come and see the movie with me?
Josh That _______ a great idea! What time does the movie begin?
Paul There _______ plenty of time before the movie starts.
Josh OK! We are on our way!

10 괄호 안의 지시대로 문장을 바꿔 쓰시오.

(1) There are many old paintings in the shop.

→ (부정문) _______________

(2) It happens very often.

→ (의문문) _______________

동사의 시제

1 현재시제 / 현재진행형

2 현재진행형 (부정문, 의문문, 불가동사)

3 과거시제 / 과거진행형

4 미래시제

현재시제 / 현재진행형

현재시제 I walk to school every day.

현재진행형 I am walking to school now.
→ be+동사원형+-ing

1 현재시제

(1) I go to bed at 11 o'clock every night.
My brother studies a world map every weekend.

(2) The Eiffel Tower lies in Paris.
Whales are mammals.

(3) She is nervous because of the exam.
They like horror movies very much.

(4) My flight leaves at 8 o'clock.
He starts for Seoul on July 15th.

1

(1) 일상적인 습관, 반복적인 일
(2) 일반적인 사실, 변하지 않는 진리
(3) 현재의 감정 및 기호
(4) 출발, 도착(start, leave, arrive, reach)의 의미를 지닌 동사의 현재형이나 현재진행형이 가까운 미래를 나타내는 시간 표현과 함께 쓰여 미래를 의미한다.

2 현재진행형

(1) I am cleaning my room now.
My friends are waiting for me.

He is using the copy machine now.
She is smiling at him.

Ben is running on the playground.
My classmate is hitting his desk now.

The dog is lying down on the grass.
The plant is drying out now.

(2) He is taking driving lessons these days.
Max is studying French this year.

(3) Jeff is coming over to my house tonight.
I am visiting my parents in Rome next week.

2

현재진행형: be+V-ing
(1) 현재 진행되고 있는 동작
(2) 일시적으로 지속되는 일
(3) 가까운 미래의 일
[UNIT 2, 4. 미래시제] 참조

※진행형 만드는 법

• 동사+-ing	learn - learning fly - flying tell - telling
• -e로 끝나는 동사 : e빼고 -ing	give - giving take - taking make - making
• 〈단모음+단자음〉으로 끝나는 동사 : 자음 하나 더+-ing	set - setting put - putting run - running
• -ie로 끝나는 동사 : ie를 y로 고치고 -ing	lie - lying die - dying tie - tying

EXERCISE

Answers P.5

A

[ ] 안에서 알맞은 말을 고르시오.

1 Water [boils, is boiling] at 100 degrees.

2 The hands of a clock [go, are going] around twice a day.

3 Mandy [likes, is liking] to have a party with her family.

4 I [travels, am traveling] to Korea next spring.

5 A stem [carries, is carrying] water from the roots.

6 I usually [brush, am brushing] my teeth and then wash my face.

7 My sister [take, is taking] the first train tomorrow morning.

B

주어진 말을 이용하여 문장을 완성하시오.

1 The famous musical "Cats" ____________(run) at the ABC Theater once a year.

2 The tailor ____________(make) a blue suit for my party now.

3 The Seine River ____________(flow) through Paris.

4 Ricky's mom ____________(call) him every weekend because he lives alone in Taiwan.

5 He ____________(leave) for London tomorrow morning.

6 Ice cream ____________(taste) good especially on a very hot day.

7 My sister ____________(set) the table for dinner every night.

C

괄호 안의 지시대로 문장을 완성하시오.

1 He is singing many old pop songs on the street now. (현재시제)
→ He ____________ many old pop songs on the street every day.

2 My brother is going to the swimming pool now. (현재시제)
→ My brother ____________ to the swimming pool on Wednesdays.

3 He ties his shoes every day. (현재진행형)
→ He ____________ his shoes right now.

4 She usually writes very long letters to her friend. (현재진행형)
→ She ____________ a very long letter to her friend now.

현재진행형(부정문, 의문문, 불가동사)

현재진행형	Fred is packing his luggage.
(의문문)	Is Fred packing his luggage?
(부정문)	No, he is not packing his luggage.
현재진행형 (불가동사)	(X) Jeff is not liking Emma.
	→ Jeff does not like Emma.

1 현재진행형의 부정문과 의문문

(1) John is not riding his bicycle. He is walking now.
Kate is not feeding her dog. She is watching TV now.

(2) A Are you going to the gym now?
B Yes, I am. / No, I'm not.

A What is he doing now?
B He is sleeping.

2 진행형을 만들 수 없는 표현

(1) 감정동사
(O) I hate oysters.
(X) I am hating oysters.

(2) 감각동사
(O) This soup smells good.
(X) This soup is smelling good.

(3) 인식동사
(O) He knows the truth.
(X) He is knowing the truth.

(4) 소유동사
(O) She has a laptop computer.
(X) She is having a laptop computer.

(5) 기타
(O) I need a stapler.
(X) I am needing a stapler.

1

(1) **부정문**
be동사+not+V-ing

(2) **의문문**
(의문사+)be동사+주어+V-ing ~?

※ 의문사로 시작하는 의문문은 Yes나 No로 대답하지 않는다.

2

(1) **감정동사**
eg) like, hate, love 등

(2) **감각동사**
eg) see, hear, smell, taste, sound, feel 등

(3) **인식동사**
eg) know, understand 등

(4) **소유동사**
eg) have, belong to 등

(5) **기타**
eg) want, need, exist 등

※ have가 eat이나 spend의 뜻일 때는 진행형 가능
eg) He is having a good time.
= spending
She is having lunch.
= eating

EXERCISE

Answers P.5

A

[ ] 안에서 알맞은 말을 고르시오.

1 I [take, am taking] my dog to the vet once a month.

2 Kelly [doesn't want, is not wanting] sandwiches for lunch.

3 [Is, Are] they making cookies for the party in the kitchen?

4 Allen [hates, is hating] rats and insects.

5 Are Don and Frank [follow, following] us?

6 He [doesn't, is not] chatting on the Internet now. He is studying.

7 Students [has, are having] hamburgers and drinks in the park right now.

B

밑줄 친 부분을 바르게 고쳐 쓰시오. 틀리지 않았다면 O표 하시오.

1 This uniform <u>is belonging to</u> Jack. ________________

2 Are your sisters <u>cook</u> lunch right now? ________________

3 Stella <u>doesn't cutting</u> tomatoes into slices in the kitchen now. ________________

4 I <u>am knowing</u> a lot about Scotland. ________________

5 Is she <u>singing</u> in the church choir now? ________________

6 He <u>is has</u> brunch with his girlfriend at the restaurant now. ________________

C

괄호 안의 지시대로 문장을 완성하시오.

1 Bell and Thomas are working in the same company. (의문문)

→ ____________ Bell and Thomas ____________ in the same company?

2 She is feeding the doves at the children's park now. (현재시제 긍정문)

→ She ____________________ the doves at the children's park every Sunday.

3 Jack is not driving his old car to work these days. (현재시제 부정문)

→ Jack ____________________ his old car to work every day.

4 Sarah asks Jacob many questions about computers. (현재진행형)

→ Sarah ____________________ Jacob many questions about computers now.

5 I don't water the plants in the garden. (현재진행형 부정문)

→ I ____________________ the plants in the garden now.

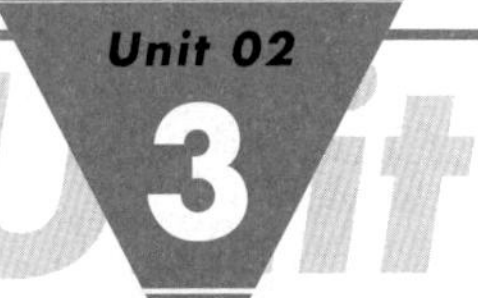

과거시제 / 과거진행형

현재 I live in Seoul now. We see him every weekend.

(규칙 변화) (불규칙 변화)

과거 I lived in Suwon last year. We saw him last weekend.

> 과거시제
> 과거의 상태나 과거에 일어난 일을 나타냄. 종종 과거 시점을 나타내는 어구(yesterday, last night, ago 등)와 같이 쓰임

1 과거시제

(1) 규칙 변화

He always helps me a lot.
He helped me a lot yesterday.

My sister changes her hairstyle so often.
She changed her hairstyle again last week.

I study American history as my major.
I studied Korean history two years ago.

(2) 불규칙 변화

I go to school with Jack.
I went to school alone yesterday.

Noah usually makes action movies.
He made a horror movie last summer.

My sister usually comes home early.
She came home very late last night.

They usually put cheese on a hamburger.
They put bacon on a hamburger yesterday.

2 과거시제의 부정문과 의문문

My mother sent me beautiful roses yesterday.
She did not send me tulips.

Did she send you flowers?
→ Yes, she did. / No, she didn't(did not).

3 과거진행형

I was writing a letter when you called me.
What were you doing in the kitchen?

1

과거형 동사 변화

(1) 규칙변화

• 동사원형+ed	help - helped walk - walked open - opened
• e로 끝나는 동사+d	love - loved close - closed use - used
• 〈자음+y〉로 끝나는 동사: -y를 -i로 바꾼 후+ed	study - studied cry - cried
• 〈모음+y〉로 끝나는 동사+ed	play - played pray - prayed
• 〈단모음+단자음〉으로 끝나는 동사+자음 하나 더+ed	stop - stopped clap - clapped

(2) 불규칙변화

• A-B-C형: go - went - gone / take - took - taken
• A-B-B형: make - made - made / find - found - found
• A-B-A형: come - came - come / run - ran - run
• A-A-A형: put - put - put / shut - shut - shut / cost - cost - cost

2

• 부정문
did not(didn't)+동사원형

• 의문문
Did+주어+동사원형 ~?

3

was / were + V-ing
: 과거 어느 시점에 진행되고 있는 동작이나 상태

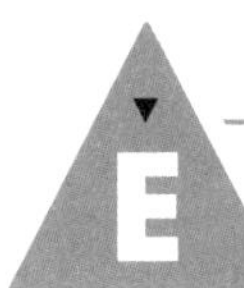

EXERCISE

Answers P.5

A

[　] 안에서 알맞은 말을 고르시오.

1 Bill [dropped, drops] out of Harvard in 1992.

2 When did Elizabeth [become, became] the queen of England?

3 Last week, John took care of his son when he [doesn't, didn't] go to work.

4 [Were you, Did you] tell the rumor to Helen last night?

5 We [meet, met] for the first time in 2000.

6 I [live, lived] in Canada for three years when I was a child.

7 Alice [did come not, did not come] to school yesterday. She was very sick.

8 My brother [grew, grows] ten centimeters when he was fifteen.

B

주어진 말을 이용하여 문장을 완성하시오.

1 The two World Wars ____________(destroy) many cities in Europe.

2 He ____________(buy) a box of chocolate for me last night.

3 I hit my brother, and he ____________(cry) a lot yesterday.

4 What did your father ____________(teach) in high school?

5 John Pemberton, a druggist, ____________(invent) Coca-Cola in 1885.

6 Henry Ford ____________(build) his first car with bicycle wheels in 1896.

7 My aunt ____________(give) me a cell phone for my birthday present last year.

C

[보기]에서 알맞은 말을 골라 어법에 맞게 바꿔 대화를 완성하시오.

Word Bank	know	tell	milk	like

Tim　My grandfather (1) ____________ me interesting stories about his childhood last night.

Nancy　That sounds interesting. Which did you like most?

Tim　I (2) ____________ the stories about his growing up on a farm.

Nancy　A farm?

Tim　Yes. I didn't (3) ____________ that.

Nancy　Really?

Tim　Yes. It was interesting. He said he (4) ____________ cows when he was a child.

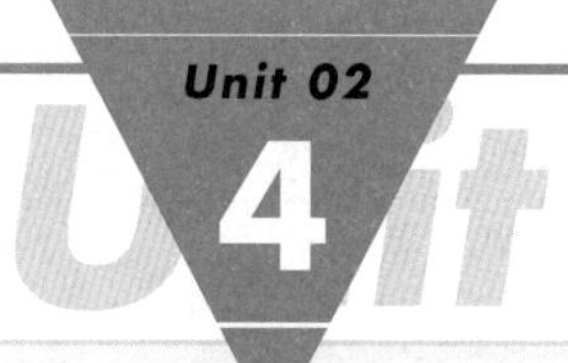

Unit 02 4 미래시제

현재 I go jogging alone every morning.

미래 My friend will go jogging with me tomorrow morning.

I am going to go jogging with him tomorrow morning.

> 미래시제
> 종종 미래를 나타내는 부사구 (soon, tomorrow, tonight, next week 등)와 함께 쓰여 미래 사실을 나타냄

1 미래시제 (will / be going to)

(1) My parents will be back tomorrow.
(= My parents are going to be back tomorrow.)

The new department store will open next week.
(= The new department store is going to open next week.)

(2) I will lose 10 kilograms this year.
I will go there by noon.
I will do my homework after dinner.

> 1
> will(be going to)+동사원형
> (1) 미래의 일
> (2) 말하는 사람의 의지를 나타낼 때
>
> *cf)* 근거가 확실한 미래 예측에는 will보다 be going to가 더 자연스럽다.
> *eg)* Look at the clouds! It is going to rain.
> Watch out! The vase is going to fall.

2 미래시제의 부정문

I will not watch TV tonight.
(= I'm not going to watch TV tonight.)

Bill won't listen to my advice.
(= Bill is not going to listen to my advice.)

> 2
> 주어+will not+동사원형
> (= be동사+not going to)
> 축약형태: will not → won't
> 주어+will → 주어'll

3 미래시제로 쓰이는 현재 / 현재진행형

(1) If it snows tomorrow, I will wear a coat.
I will buy you lunch when she comes.
Tom will continue his studies after he graduates.

(2) The train is arriving soon.
They are leaving for Sydney this week.
Is he coming back to Seoul tomorrow?

> 3
> (1) 현재시제로 미래 표시
> : 시간, 조건의 뜻을 가진 부사절에서 미래시제 대신 현재시제를 사용
> (2) 현재시제와 현재진행형으로 미래 표시
> : come, go, leave, arrive 등의 동사가 가까운 미래를 나타내는 부사구(soon, this week, this year, tonight, tomorrow 등)와 함께 쓰이는 경우

EXERCISE

Answers P.5

A

[ ] 안에서 알맞은 말을 고르시오.

1 Fred [will buy, will buys] a digital camera.

2 Mary will [is, be] at the meeting with us this afternoon.

3 I [will not, am not] going to answer the phone.

4 We will [are, stay] at home if it rains tomorrow.

5 She [won't move, will move not] to another state until she graduates.

6 Dan's secretary [will, is] going to take messages for him.

7 They [will, are] make a TV commercial for the perfume.

B

밑줄 친 부분을 바르게 고쳐 쓰시오.

1 What <u>are</u> you do this summer vacation? ______________

2 Will he <u>builds</u> a one-hundred story building in this town? ______________

3 I <u>will see not</u> the dolphin show this time. ______________

4 Which apartment will she <u>rents</u> next month? ______________

5 How long <u>do</u> they going to stay in Austria? ______________

6 I will buy you a nice dinner if I <u>will win</u> the game this Sunday. ______________

C

주어진 말을 이용하여 문장을 완성하시오.

1 We go to the Han River to enjoy inline skating on Sundays. (be going to)

→ We ______________ to the Han River to enjoy inline skating tomorrow.

2 His flight arrives at 10 o'clock. (be V-ing)

→ His flight ______________ at 10 o'clock.

3 There is a special yoga class on Fridays. (will)

→ There ______________ a special yoga class next Friday.

4 I will quit my part-time job next month. (be going to, not)

→ I ______________ my part-time job next month.

5 Are you going to pick me up after work tonight? (will)

→ __________ you __________ me up after work tonight?

REVIEW TEST

A

[ ] 안에서 알맞은 말을 고르시오.

1 I [eat, ate, am eating] a chicken salad and onion soup for lunch yesterday.

2 My plane [departs, departed, was departing] at 7:00 tomorrow morning.

3 Americans [eat, ate, were eating] black-eyed peas every New Year's Day for good luck.

4 She [has, have, is having] blue eyes and long, wavy blond hair.

5 I can't answer the phone. I [take, took, am taking] a shower now.

6 I [am going, will, will not] to grow some plants in the garden.

7 Philip [studies, studied, is studying] physics when he was in college.

B

빈칸에 들어갈 알맞은 말을 고르시오.

1 Did you ______________ my CDs on the desk?

ⓐ moved ⓑ were moving ⓒ move ⓓ be moving

2 Kathy ______________ about the history of volcanoes.

ⓐ isn't know ⓑ doesn't know ⓒ didn't knew ⓓ will be know

3 What ______________ after you graduate from college?

ⓐ are you do ⓑ were you ⓒ are you going to ⓓ will you do

4 Our teacher got angry because no one ______________ to the lesson.

ⓐ will listen ⓑ is listening ⓒ did listening ⓓ was listening

5 What were you doing when I ______________ the room?

ⓐ entered ⓑ am entering ⓒ will enter ⓓ enter

6 Nancy will take us to the space museum after we ______________ our homework.

ⓐ will finish ⓑ finished ⓒ were finishing ⓓ finish

7 My classmates ______________ a good time at the beach now.

ⓐ were having ⓑ are having ⓒ will be have ⓓ had

C

[보기]에서 알맞은 말을 골라 어법에 맞게 바꿔 문장을 완성하시오.

Word Bank	reply	make	watch	know	close	save	leave

1 Peter __________ a model airplane for his little brother now.

2 She __________ to your e-mail when she comes back from her business trip.

3 The store opens at 9 am and __________ at 10 pm on weekdays.

4 Alicia __________ money all the time.

5 Now I __________ the correct answer to this math problem.

6 My friends visited my blog and __________ New Year's messages.

7 My friend and I __________ the final game tomorrow.

D

밑줄 친 부분을 바르게 고쳐, 문장을 다시 쓰시오.

1 My father and I will drove to Chicago tomorrow for a motor show.

→ __________

2 After he repairs my bike, I treated him to dinner downtown.

→ __________

3 Who is goes to the grocery store this weekend?

→ __________

4 I tell my mother about the accident last night.

→ __________

5 We were talk about the science project when the teacher came in.

→ __________

6 She is very disappointed if you don't come to the party tonight.

→ __________

7 We really are needing desks and chairs in the computer lab.

→ __________

F FURTHER STUDY

Answers P.6

A 글을 읽고, 밑줄 친 부분을 바르게 고쳐 쓰시오.

> Ladies and gentlemen, this is your captain speaking. Welcome aboard Flight 293 to Paris. We (1) <u>will takes off</u> in about 15 minutes. Please fasten your seat belt, sit back, and relax. We (2) <u>will be fly</u> at thirty-five thousand feet and expect to land in an hour and a half. According to the weather forecast, the weather at our destination (3) <u>was</u> good. So, we (4) <u>going to</u> have a smooth and uneventful flight. Please don't forget to turn off your cell phone. Thank you and enjoy your flight.

(1) ______________

(2) ______________

(3) ______________

(4) ______________

B Cathy의 일정을 보고, 주어진 말을 이용하여 문장을 완성하시오.

• Cathy's Summer Holiday Schedule •

Today's Date: May 3rd

Last Year (In Alaska)	This Year (In Las Vegas)
July 1st~3rd: Sea Kayaking July 4th~6th: Ice Climbing July 7th~8th: Summer Dog Sledding July 9th~10th: Glacier Trekking	August 2nd: Natural History Museum August 3rd: Hoover Dam August 4th~5th: Grand Canyon August 6th: Red Rock Canyon

1 Last year, Cathy ____________(travel) in Alaska for ____________ days. On the first day, she ____________(go) sea kayaking.

2 On the last day in Alaska, she ____________(go) glacier trekking and ____________ (have) a great time.

3 This year, she ____________(be going to) visit Las Vegas and will spend ____________ days there.

4 On August 3rd, she is going to ____________(visit) the Hoover Dam and ____________(take) pictures.

5 Also, she will visit the Grand Canyon for ____________ days and ____________(stay) in a nice hotel.

Answers P.7

▶ 동사변화표

현재	과거	과거분사	현재	과거	과거분사
am, is/are	was / were	been	keep (유지하다)	kept	kept
become (~되다)	① ______	become	know (알다)	⑫ ______	known
begin (시작하다)	began	begun	learn (배우다)	learned	learned
believe (믿다)	believed	believed	leave (떠나다)	left	left
blow (불다)	blew	blown	lend (빌려주다)	lent	lent
break (부수다)	② ______	broken	let (시키다)	let	let
bring (가져오다)	brought	brought	lie (거짓말하다)	⑬ ______	lied
build (짓다)	built	built	lie (눕다)	lay	lain
buy (사다)	bought	bought	live (살다)	lived	lived
call (부르다)	called	called	lose (지다)	⑭ ______	lost
carry (운반하다)	carried	carried	make (만들다)	made	made
catch (잡다)	③ ______	caught	marry (결혼하다)	married	married
choose (고르다)	chose	chosen	meet (만나다)	met	met
come (오다)	came	come	move (움직이다)	moved	moved
cost (비용이 들다)	cost	cost	open (열다)	opened	opened
cry (울다)	④ ______	cried	order (명령하다)	ordered	ordered
cut (자르다)	cut	cut	pay (지불하다)	⑮ ______	paid
destroy (파괴하다)	⑤ ______	destroyed	play (놀다)	played	played
do (하다)	did	done	put (놓다, 두다)	put	put
draw (그리다)	drew	drawn	read (읽다)	⑯ ______	read
drink (마시다)	⑥ ______	drunk	ride (타다)	rode	ridden
drive (운전하다)	drove	driven	run (뛰다)	ran	run
eat (먹다)	⑦ ______	eaten	sell (팔다)	sold	sold
enjoy (즐기다)	enjoyed	enjoyed	send (보내다)	sent	sent
fail (실패하다)	failed	failed	set (두다)	set	set
fall (떨어지다)	⑧ ______	fallen	sing (노래하다)	⑰ ______	sung
feel (느끼다)	⑨ ______	felt	sit (앉다)	sat	sat
fight (싸우다)	fought	fought	solve (풀다)	solved	solved
fill (채우다)	filled	filled	speak (말하다)	spoke	spoken
find (찾다)	found	found	stay (머물다)	stayed	stayed
finish (끝내다)	finished	finished	stop (멈추다)	⑱ ______	stopped
fix (고치다)	fixed	fixed	study (공부하다)	studied	studied
fly (날다)	flew	flown	swim (헤엄치다)	swam	swum
give (주다)	⑩ ______	given	take (잡다, 취하다)	⑲ ______	taken
go (가다)	went	gone	tell (말하다)	told	told
grow (자라다)	grew	grown	think (생각하다)	thought	thought
hear (듣다)	⑪ ______	heard	try (노력하다)	tried	tried
help (돕다)	helped	helped	wake (깨다, 깨우다)	woke	woken
hold (쥐다)	held	held	worry (걱정하다)	worried	worried
hurt (다치게 하다)	hurt	hurt	write (쓰다)	⑳ ______	written

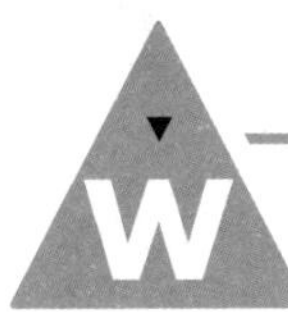

WRAP-UP TEST

Answers P.7

1 밑줄 친 부분이 어색한 것을 고르시오.

ⓐ She is chopping tomatoes and onions.
ⓑ She is mixing tomatoes and onions.
ⓒ She is baking bread in the kitchen.
ⓓ She is friing potatoes.

2 빈칸에 들어갈 알맞은 말을 고르시오.

> She ___________ some money from Carrie yesterday.

ⓐ will borrow ⓑ borrowed
ⓒ borrows ⓓ is borrowing

3 문장을 읽고, 어색한 곳을 찾아 바르게 고치시오.

If Cathy spreads my secret, I tell everybody her math score.
(ⓐ If Cathy / ⓑ spreads / ⓒ tell / ⓓ her math score)

4 동사의 연결이 어색한 것을 고르시오.

ⓐ set - set ⓑ begin - began
ⓒ fly - flied ⓓ leave - left

5 주어진 문장을 부정문으로 바르게 바꾼 것을 고르시오.

> They bought the blue shirt yesterday.

ⓐ They bought not the blue shirt yesterday.
ⓑ They did not buy the blue shirt yesterday.
ⓒ They did not bought the blue shirt yesterday.
ⓓ They do not bought the blue shirt yesterday.

6 어법상 어색한 문장을 고르시오.

ⓐ Honesty is the best policy.
ⓑ You are attending the meeting on Friday.
ⓒ Kent will not going to help his sister.
ⓓ When did the Korean War start?

7 밑줄 친 부분의 쓰임 올바른 것을 고르시오.

ⓐ This big house is belonging to Donald.
ⓑ I was needing bandages when I broke my wrist.
ⓒ John is liking his sister a lot.
ⓓ He is having dinner at the fancy restaurant now.

8 대화를 읽고, 빈칸에 들어갈 수 없는 것을 고르시오.

> A Did you ___________ last weekend?
> B Yes, I did.

ⓐ visit your grandparents
ⓑ do house chores
ⓒ write a letter to me
ⓓ took a nap

[9-10] 글을 읽고, 물음에 답하시오.

> Youtube.com is a popular web site. People share music, TV shows, and other media on the site. Soon, it (A) will sharing some of its profits with its members. I am a member, so I (B) get some money from YouTube, too.

9 (A) will sharing을 바르게 고쳐 쓰시오.

10 (B) get을 알맞은 형태로 바꿔 쓰시오.

동사의 완료형

1 현재완료 (계속)

2 현재완료 (완료, 경험, 결과)

3 과거완료와 미래완료

Unit 03
1
Unit

현재완료 (계속)

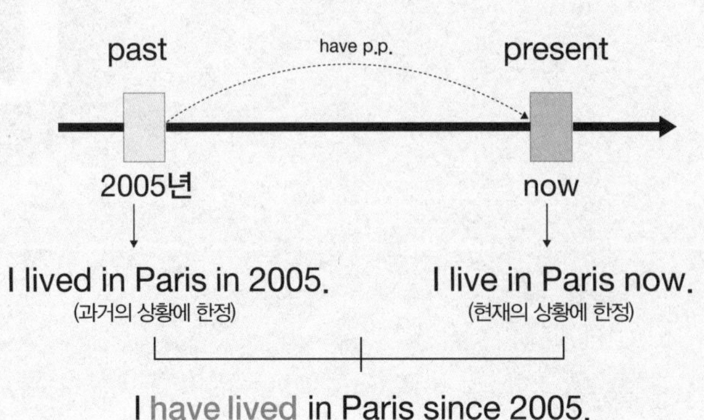
past
have p.p.
present
2005년
now
I lived in Paris in 2005.
(과거의 상황에 한정)
I live in Paris now.
(현재의 상황에 한정)
I have lived in Paris since 2005.

현재완료: have[has]+p.p.
과거의 상황이 현재까지 연결되는 상황에 사용 (현재의 사실에 더 중점을 두는 표현)

1 과거부터 현재까지 지속되는 상황이나 행동 (since, for 등과 함께)

I started playing tennis five years ago.
I still play tennis now.
→ I have played tennis for five years.

She started her project in 2005.
She still works on her project now.
→ She has worked on her project since 2005.

A How long have you stayed in this city?
B I have stayed in this city for two weeks.

1
계속: (지금까지 계속) ~해왔다

※현재완료(계속)와 자주 쓰이는 어구:
• for+기간 (~동안)
eg) for two days/weeks/years
• since+시점 (~이래로)
eg) since 2000, since I was born

2 현재완료와 함께 쓰는 시간 부사 (지속된 상황)

I have learned about his philosophy for one year.
(X) I have learned about his philosophy in 2006.
I learned about his philosophy in 2006.

I have read the story since I was young.
(X) I have read the story two weeks ago.
I read the story two weeks ago.

cf) 현재완료에 쓰이는 과거분사 변화: have(has)+p.p.

A-A-A	cut - cut - cut	set - set - set
A-B-A	come - came - come	run - ran - run
A-B-B	live - lived - lived	find - found - found
A-B-C	eat - ate - eaten	see - saw - seen

2

※ 완료시제는 과거의 특정 시점을 나타내는 어구들(yesterday, last year, ago)과 함께 쓸 수 없다.
(X) I have done it yesterday.
(O) I did it yesterday.

• **현재완료의 축약형**
I have=I've
She/He has=She's/He's
(He is = He's와 혼동 주의)
• **부정문:** have(has) not p.p.
• **의문문:** Have(Has)+주어+p.p. ~?
→ Yes, 주어+have(has).
→ No, 주어+haven't(hasn't).

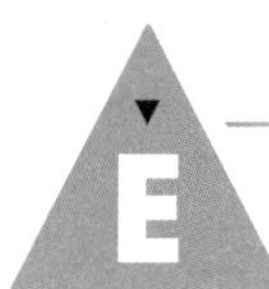

EXERCISE

Answers P.7

A

[ ] 안에서 알맞은 말을 고르시오.

1 I [live, have lived] in Seoul since I was three years old.

2 He [met, has met] Rachel in Italy two years ago.

3 Many people [visited, have visited] the Louvre Museum in Paris last year.

4 My mother [studied, has studied] Chinese for 7 months until now.

5 Josh [has listened, listened] to classical music since he was six.

6 Jennifer has driven her own car [since, for] 2002.

7 How long [have, do] you been here?

B

주어진 말을 이용하여 문장을 완성하시오.

1 I have ______________(read) an English novel since Tuesday.

2 The architect has ______________(design) buildings for 30 years.

3 I have 600 bottle caps from all over the world. I have ______________(collect) them since 1999.

4 How long have you ______________(know) each other?

5 They ______________(complete) the experiment an hour ago.

6 What have they ______________(eat) in the mountain for a month?

7 Has she ______________(be) in Korea since 2005?

C

주어진 말을 이용하여 문장을 완성하시오.

1 Jane started studying French six years ago, and she still studies French.
→ She ______________ ______________(study) French for six years.

2 I joined a tennis club in 2006, and I am still a member of the club.
→ I ______________ ______________(be) a member of the tennis club since 2006.

3 I started reading comic books at 9 o'clock, and I am still reading comic books.
→ I ______________ ______________(read) comic books since 9 o'clock.

4 Kelly bought a computer three years ago, and she still uses the computer.
→ Kelly ______________ ______________(use) the computer since she bought it.

현재완료 (완료, 경험, 결과)

계속	We have known each other for five years. (계속 ~해 오고 있다)
완료	He has already finished his homework. (~를 (이미) 끝마쳤다)
경험	I have met him once before. (~한 적이 있다)
결과	He has gone to Italy. (~해버렸다. 그 결과 지금 …하다) (= He is not here now.)

1 과거에 시작된 상황이나 상태가 현재에 완료 (just, already, yet 등과 함께)

I started my research three months ago. And I finished it just now.
→ I have just finished my research.
cf) I finished my research three months ago.

There were many apples in the box last week, but I ate all of them.
→ I have already eaten all of the apples in the box.
cf) I ate all of the apples yesterday.

> 1
> **동작/상황의 완료: (지금 막) ~했다**
> 과거에 시작된 동작이나 상황이 막 완료되었을 때 사용
>
> **동작/상황의 완료와 자주 쓰이는 어구**
> just, already, yet 등의 부사
> *eg)* have+ [just / already] +p.p.

2 과거부터 지금까지의 경험 표현 (ever, never, before, once 등과 함께)

We have seen the movie before.
I have never met the president.
We haven't bought CDs recently.

Have you ever been to Canada?
How many times have you read the novel?

> 2
> **경험: ~한 경험이 있다**
> 빈도부사 및 횟수를 나타내는 표현(ever, never, before, once, twice, recently 등)과 함께 쓰인다.
>
> *cf)* When으로 물어보는 의문문은 특정한 시점을 물어보는 것이므로 완료형을 쓰지 않는다.
> A: When did you meet him?
> B: I met him last year.

3 과거 상황이 현재에 미치는 결과 암시

Dan went to L.A. last year.
(Dan may be in L.A. now, or he may have come back. We don't know.)
Dan has gone to L.A.
(Dan went to L.A., and he is not here now.)

He lost his digital camera last month.
(He may find it now. We don't know.)
He has lost his digital camera.
(He lost it, and he does not have it now.)

> 3
> **결과: ~해버렸다, (그 결과) 지금은 …하다**
> 과거의 일이 현재에 영향을 미치는 경우 사용
> *cf)* 과거시제는 과거의 상황(사실)에만 한정

EXERCISE

Answers P.8

A

[ ] 안에서 알맞은 말을 고르시오.

1 I [have met, have meet] the president twice.

2 Mr. Lee [have interviewed, has interviewed] the prime minister three times so far.

3 Kevin's girlfriend [has gone, has went] to Australia.

4 I have [seen never, never seen] a UFO.

5 Have you [ever been, been ever] to the Eiffel Tower?

6 My father [has lost, has lose] his briefcase at the airport before.

7 How many times [you have read, have you read] his poem?

B

주어진 말을 이용하여 문장을 완성하시오.

1 I rode a motorcycle for the first time in my life yesterday.

→ I ____________ (ride) a motorcycle only once.

2 Bob doesn't live in New York anymore. He moved to Boston yesterday.

→ Bob ____________ (move) to Boston.

3 Mr. and Mrs. Johnson don't speak Spanish. They will take their first lesson tonight.

→ Mr. and Mrs. Johnson ____________ (never, study) Spanish before.

4 I lost my cell phone in the library last week. I don't have it now.

→ I ____________ (lose) my cell phone.

5 Christine takes cooking lessons once a week. She made her first cake last week. This week she made her second cake.

→ Christine ____________ (make) two cakes so far.

6 Jim's sister is in Australia now. She went there a week ago.

→ Jim's sister ____________ (go) to Australia.

C

밑줄 친 부분을 바르게 고쳐 쓰시오.

1 Sweden never lost to England in the World Cup since 1968. ____________

2 According to this bus schedule, the last bus have just gone. ____________

3 I have meet Susan when I was ten years old. ____________

4 They do not have exchanged all of their dollars for euros yet. ____________

5 How many times have you ask her on a date so far? ____________

Unit 03
3

과거완료와 미래완료

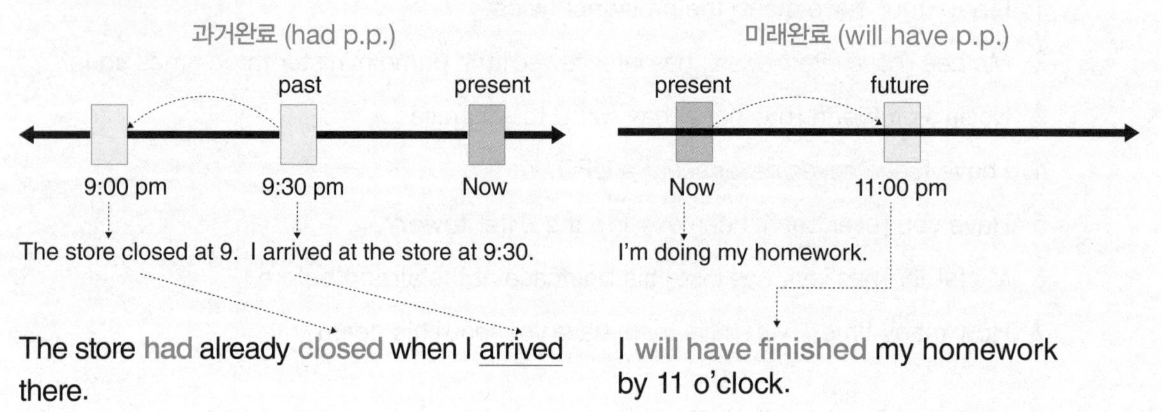
과거완료 (had p.p.)
past
present
9:00 pm
9:30 pm
Now
The store closed at 9. I arrived at the store at 9:30.
The store had already closed when I arrived there.
미래완료 (will have p.p.)
present
future
Now
11:00 pm
I'm doing my homework.
I will have finished my homework by 11 o'clock.

1 과거완료 (had p.p.)

Sean had lived in Paris for 5 years before he died.
Brad had already left his house when I called him.
Ann had seen a koala when she was in Australia.
Lenny had finished the project before I called him.

cf) 대과거
She saw me after I had seen her.

1
과거완료: 과거의 정해진 기준 시점 이전부터 과거의 기준 시점까지

현재완료: 어느 과거 시점부터 현재의 기준 시점까지

cf) 대과거: 과거에 일어난 어떤 일보다 먼저 일어난 일을 시간상으로 구분할 때 사용

2 미래완료 (will have p.p.)

I will have finished taking the final examination by 11 o'clock.
In 6 months, he will have studied in middle school for 3 years.
The musical will have started by the time he comes here.

2
미래완료: 미래의 어떤 시점에 완료되거나 지속되는 일을 표현. 보통 미래의 기준 시점을 나타내는 부사구와 함께 쓰인다.

3 과거완료, 미래완료의 의문문과 부정문

Had you finished the project before I called you?
→ No, I had not〔never〕 finished it before you called me.

Will you have finished the test by 4 o'clock?
→ No, I will not have finished it by 4 o'clock. I will have finished it by 5 o'clock.

3
• **과거완료**
의문: Had+주어+p.p. ~?
부정: had not〔hadn't〕 p.p.

• **미래완료**
의문: Will+주어+have p.p. ~?
부정: will not〔won't〕 have p.p.

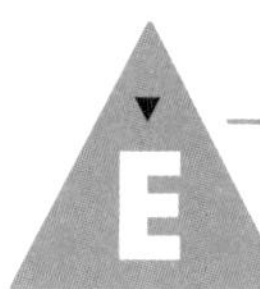

EXERCISE

Answers P.8

A

[ ] 안에서 알맞은 말을 고르시오.

1 Kenny [had, have] lived in Japan before he went to high school.

2 They [had, will have] already moved when I returned to this country.

3 We [have, will have] learned about photography for three years by next week.

4 The class [has, had] already started when I arrived at school.

5 I [had, will have] finished reading this book around 5 o'clock tomorrow.

6 By the time Korea hosts the Winter Olympics, it [had, will have] built many new facilities.

B

주어진 말을 이용하여 과거완료 또는 미래완료 문장을 완성하시오.

1 The model house ____________________(burn) down, so we had to build it again.

2 Eric's mom ____________________(already, cook) dinner before he got home.

3 Kate ____________________(teach) history for many years before she taught geography.

4 Susie ____________________(memorize) the word list by tomorrow.

5 Ken ____________________(pass) the last course by the end of this year.

6 I ____________________(be) in Canada for six months by the time you visit me next month.

C

주어진 문장을 참고하여, 문장을 완성하시오.

1 Michael quit university in 2013. I enrolled in university in 2014.

→ Michael ____________________ university when I enrolled in university.

2 Kelly heard the rumor about Sarah yesterday. I told Kelly about the rumor this morning.

→ Kelly ____________ already ____________ the rumor about Sarah when I told her about it.

3 He finished his presentation at 3:00. I entered the meeting room at 3:15.

→ He ____________________ his presentation when I entered the meeting room.

4 I have read 90 books so far. I will read ten more books by the end of the year.

→ I ____________________ 100 books by this year.

5 She has sold three cards. She will sell seven more cards tonight.

→ She ____________________ ten cards by tomorrow.

REVIEW TEST

A

[ ] 안에서 알맞은 말을 고르시오.

1 How long [have, are] you known Bill Gates?

2 I [have visited, will have visited] Germany four times when I go there again tomorrow.

3 Jinny [had already eaten, has already eaten] all the cookies when I came home.

4 Have you seen my wallet? I [not have seen, have not seen] it since Friday.

5 Scott [will be, has been] a musician for 7 years.

6 We helped Susan because she [hasn't finished, hadn't finished] her homework.

7 Where [have you been, will you been] this afternoon?

B

빈칸에 들어갈 알맞은 말을 고르시오.

1 I ____________ my favorite CD a few days ago.

ⓐ lose ⓑ lost ⓒ have lost ⓓ had lost

2 English ____________ many words from other languages for many years.

ⓐ borrow ⓑ is borrowing ⓒ has borrowed ⓓ will have borrowed

3 I ____________ my Chinese friends to my house party the other night.

ⓐ invite ⓑ invited ⓒ have invited ⓓ will have invited

4 They ____________ 100 more houses for homeless people by next year.

ⓐ build ⓑ built ⓒ have built ⓓ will have built

5 My friends ____________ a surprise party for me when I entered the classroom.

ⓐ prepares ⓑ had prepared ⓒ has prepared ⓓ will have prepared

6 By next Sunday, I ____________ all the invitation cards to everyone.

ⓐ send ⓑ sent ⓒ have sent ⓓ will have sent

7 Ellie ____________ her father's car before he got up this morning.

ⓐ had washed ⓑ has washed ⓒ washes ⓓ will have washed

C

[보기]에서 알맞은 말을 골라 어법에 맞게 바꿔 문장을 완성하시오.

Word Bank	hear	sleep	lose	stay	win	give	have

1 It was reported that two people __________ __________ their lives in the accident.

2 Have you __________ about his new film?

3 His soccer team __________ __________ every match before they lost last week's match.

4 My sister bought a present for me, but she __________ __________ it to me yet.

5 I __________ __________ this terrible headache since I came back from the trip.

6 It is Sunday today. We __________ __________ __________ here for a week by next Saturday.

7 Wake up now! You __________ __________ for over 16 hours.

D

밑줄 친 부분을 바르게 고쳐, 문장을 다시 쓰시오.

1 She loses her key so she is waiting for her mom outside.

→ ______________________________

2 Martin is sleeping now. He has slept on the sofa for 3 o'clock.

→ ______________________________

3 How many times have you rode a horse so far?

→ ______________________________

4 I practice writing essays for almost three years before I took the entrance test.

→ ______________________________

5 We have studied all the verb tenses by the end of next week.

→ ______________________________

6 I don't know Mark at all. I have ever met him before.

→ ______________________________

7 By the end of this class, he will have makes great progress in English grammar.

→ ______________________________

FURTHER STUDY

Answers P.9

A 글을 읽고, 밑줄 친 부분을 바르게 고쳐 쓰시오.

(1) I <u>have find</u> some interesting stories about Christmas tree lights. Before Edison (2) <u>invents</u> the electric light, people had used candles to decorate their Christmas trees. Edison's assistant, Edward Johnson, (3) <u>has created</u> the idea of electric tree lights in 1882, and Edison developed the first electric Christmas tree lights. Edison invented a set of 80 bulbs and decorated a Christmas tree with those bulbs. A lot of people around the world (4) <u>enjoy</u> electric Christmas tree lights since then.

(1) ______________________

(2) ______________________

(3) ______________________

(4) ______________________

B 표를 보고, 주어진 말을 이용하여 문장을 완성하시오.

three years ago	Now	one month later
I moved to China. I studied Chinese. I met my boyfriend in China.	I still live in China. I study English. I still date my boyfriend.	I will live in Singapore. I will study French. I will marry my boyfriend.

1 I ______________________(live) in China __________ three years.

2 I ______________________(live) in China now.

3 I ______________________(study) Chinese three years ago.

4 I ______________________(study) French one month later.

5 I ______________________(date) my boyfriend for about four years by the end of next year.

6 I ______________________(marry) my boyfriend next month.

MUST-KNOW

Answers P.10

▶ 시제에 따른 동사 형태

	단순 형태	진행 형태	완료 형태
현재	give	am(are/is) giving	have(has) ① ________
과거	gave	② ________	had given
미래	will give	will be giving	③ ________

▶ 동사의 다양한 시제

1 과거시제 – 단순 과거 I **watched** a movie last night.
– 과거진행형 I **was watching** a movie when you called me.

2 현재시제 – 단순 현재 She always **wears** short skirts.
– 현재진행형 She **is wearing** a short skirt now.

3 미래시제 – will / be going to He **will** leave tomorrow.
He **is going to** leave tomorrow.
– 현재시제로 미래 표현 He will not leave if it **snows** tomorrow.
– 현재진행형으로 미래 표현 He **is leaving** on September 3rd.

4 완료 – 현재완료 Kelly **has** not **finished** dinner yet.
– 과거완료 Kevin **had** already **finished** dinner when I arrived.
– 미래완료 They **will have finished** dinner by 8 tonight.

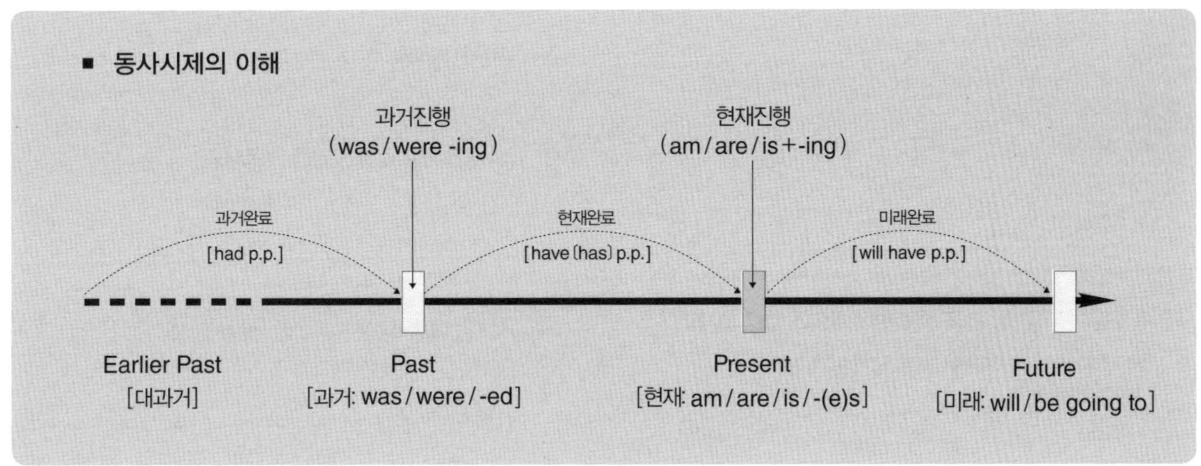

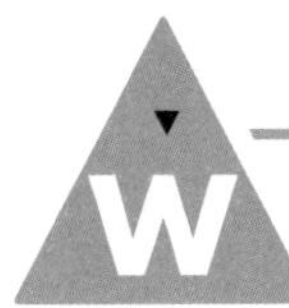

WRAP-UP TEST

Answers P.10

1 밑줄 친 부분의 쓰임이 어색한 것을 고르시오.

ⓐ This little boy has drawn 100 pictures since he was 4.

ⓑ I have just read the newspaper.

ⓒ They have grew vegetables in the backyard.

ⓓ Kate has spread the rumor.

2 빈칸에 들어갈 알맞은 단어를 쓰시오.

· Mike has repaired the car ___ⓐ___ 3 hours in the garage.
· I have worked as a sales manager ___ⓑ___ 2000.

ⓐ: ⓑ:

3 현재완료의 쓰임이 다른 하나를 고르시오.

ⓐ Have you ever tried Turkish ice cream?

ⓑ I have flown the Concorde to Athens once.

ⓒ He and his son have just planted ten apple trees.

ⓓ I have never thrown trash on the streets or sidewalks.

4 빈칸에 들어갈 말이 바르게 연결된 것을 고르시오.

· When I arrived at the party, Jane wasn't there. She __________ already.
· When I arrived at the party, Jane wasn't there. So I __________ an hour ago.

ⓐ have left - had left

ⓑ had left - left

ⓒ had left - have left

ⓓ had left - had left

5 두 문장이 같은 뜻이 되도록 빈칸에 알맞은 말을 쓰시오.

Sue forgot his name, and she still can't remember it.

→ Sue ____________________ his name.

6 [보기]에서 알맞은 말을 골라 어법에 맞게 바꿔 문장을 완성하시오.

wear	raise	steal	hide

(1) The thief ____________________ ten books in the library so far.

(2) He ____________________ for three hours under the bed before the thief went away.

(3) I ____________________ a Kimono once. It was uncomfortable.

(4) She will ____________________ wild orchids for one year by next month.

7 문장을 읽고, 어법상 어색한 곳을 찾아 바르게 고치시오.

How many(ⓐ) times(ⓑ) have(ⓒ) you rode(ⓓ) a horse so far?

[8-10] 글을 읽고, 물음에 답하시오.

I (A)[have been, have gone] to Cleveland, Ohio many times. It is an amazing city with many interesting museums. I visited an unusual museum on Lake Erie when I was in Cleveland. The museum ___(B)___ a submarine during World War II before it became a museum, so it sits in the water. (C) 그 박물관은 많은 관광객을 끌어들이고 있어.

8 (A)에서 알맞은 말을 고르시오.

9 (B)에 들어갈 알맞은 말을 고르시오.

ⓐ were ⓑ had been

ⓒ have been ⓓ is

10 주어진 말을 이용하여 (C)를 영작하시오.
(attract, many tourists)

The museum ____________________.

조동사

1 조동사 (능력, 허가, 요청, 제안)

2 조동사 (의무, 금지, 충고, 과거의 습관)

3 조동사 (추측, 가능성)

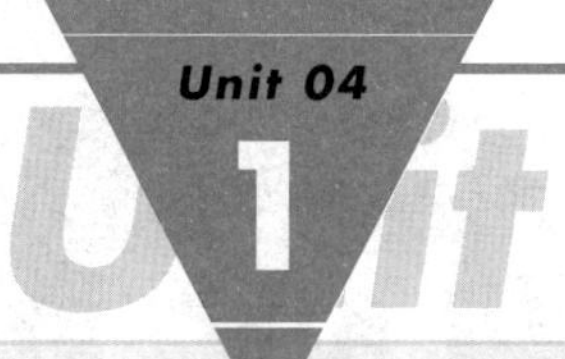

조동사 (능력, 허가, 요청, 제안)

현재동사	Shawn sings a Spanish song.
조동사 (능력)	He can sing a Spanish song.
(허가)	You may sing a Spanish song at the party.
(요청, 제안)	Could you sing a Spanish song for the guests?

조동사
동작이나 상태를 의미하는 동사를 도와 그 동사만으로 표현하기 어려운 상세한 의미(허가, 추측, 요청, 의무 등)를 나타내는 동사

1 조동사의 특징

(O) He can climb a rope ladder very well.
(X) He can climbs a rope ladder very well.

He cannot climb on the roof. (cannot = can't)
Can he climb on the roof?

> 1
> **조동사+동사원형**
> 부정문: 조동사+not+동사원형
> 의문문: 조동사+주어+동사원형 ~?

2 능력: can

I can fix my computer.
(= I am able to fix my computer.)
I could climb trees very well when I was little.
(= I was able to climb trees very well when I was little.)
I will be able to buy a new house next year.

> 2
> **~할 수 있다**
> ※ 조동사 두 개를 연달아 쓸 수 없다.
> (X) will can → (O) will be able to

3 허가: can, may

You can stay as long as you want.
You may go home if you don't feel well.

Can I have some more bread? I am still hungry.
Could I have some more, please?
May I have some water, please?

> 3
> **~해도 좋다, ~해도 될까요?**

4 요청, 제안: can, could, will, would, may, shall

Can you lend me $5?
Could you pick them up on your way home?

Will you give me a call before you leave?
Would you close the door, please?

Shall we dance?
Shall we go?

> 4
> **~해 주시겠어요?, ~할까요?**
> (shall은 영국식 표현)
>
> ※더 공손한 표현
> can → could
> will → would

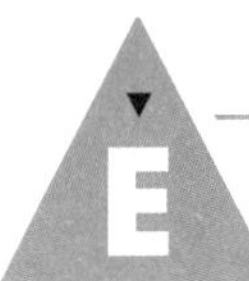

EXERCISE

Answers P.10

A

[ ] 안에서 알맞은 말을 고르시오.

1 You may [takes, took, take] a nap if you are sleepy.

2 [Can, Does, Will] he be able to remove the computer virus?

3 What can Bob [do, does, did] with these balloons?

4 He [won't, can be able to, will not be] bring his car tomorrow.

5 [Could, Will be able to, Are you able] you give me a glass of soda pop?

6 Were you [can, shall, able to] do a handstand when you were a child?

B

[보기]에서 알맞은 말을 고르고, 주어진 조동사를 이용하여 문장을 완성하시오.

Word Bank	read	experience	go	play	treat

1 Steve likes music. He ________________(can) the guitar.

2 I am studying medicine now. I will ________________(be able to) patients someday.

3 You ________________(may) to the party with your friends tonight.

4 Jenny ________________(cannot) Japanese well. She started learning it last week.

5 They ________________(be able to) Korean culture when they came here last year.

C

괄호 안의 지시대로 문장을 바꿔 쓰시오.

1 Mike has recently taken a cooking class. So he can cook for himself. (미래시제로)

→ Mike has recently taken a cooking class. So ______________________________.

2 Please turn up the volume a little bit! (Can you ~? 형으로)

→ ______________________________

3 Will you say your name once more, please? (더 공손한 표현으로)

→ ______________________________

4 Let's start our meeting now. (Shall ~? 형으로)

→ ______________________________

5 He can rent DVDs on the Internet. (be able to 의문문으로)

→ ______________________________

Unit 04

Unit 2 조동사 (의무, 금지, 충고, 과거의 습관)

금지, 의무 — You must come back by 10 o'clock. (must → ~해야 한다)

충고 — You look pale. You had better see a doctor. (had better → ~하는 것이 좋다)

과거의 습관 — When I had a dog, I would take him for a walk to the park. (would → ~하곤 했다)

1 의무, 금지: must, have to, should

Our school has a dress code.
You must wear a school uniform.
(= You have to wear a school uniform.)

You must not wear jeans at school.
cf) You don't have to wear a uniform.

You should fasten your seat belt when you drive.
You should not speak impolitely to your mother.

> 1
> ~해야 한다 (must > should)
> must의 과거: had to
> must의 미래: will have to
> - must는 과거, 미래형이 없으므로 have to를 사용한다.
>
> ※ 주의
> must not: ~하지 말아야 한다(금지)
> *cf)* don't have to: ~할 필요 없다(불필요)

2 충고: had better, should

James is waiting for you.
You had better hurry, or he will get angry.
You had better not make any excuses.

There will not be enough seats in the restaurant.
You should reserve seats. You should not go without a reservation.

> 2
> • ~하는 것이 좋다
> (그렇게 하지 않으면 문제가 생길 것이라는 의미가 포함된 강한 충고)
> had better의 부정: had better not

3 과거의 습관: would, used to

On sunny days, we would go up the hill.
Sandra used to eat meat, but now she eats only vegetables.
Whenever my father was angry, my sister would hide behind me.
My father used to go fishing on Sundays. (But not anymore)

cf) (O) This place used to be a chocolate factory. (상태)
(X) This place would be a chocolate factory.

(O) I used to have a red car. (상태)
(X) I would have a red car.

> 3
> • would: 과거의 습관 (동작)
> • used to: 과거의 습관 (동작, 상태)
> (지금은 그렇지 않다는 의미를 포함)

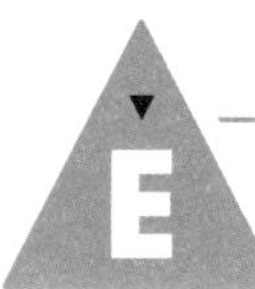

EXERCISE

Answers P.10

A

[ ] 안에서 알맞은 말을 고르시오.

1 I [must, may] go now. It's too late.

2 You [don't have to, must not] carry a heavy book if you buy an e-book.

3 You [might, had better] ask him first before you use his computer.

4 You [should, would] be polite and respectful to your elders.

5 Paul [had to, must] take care of his mother because she was sick.

6 Whenever I was sad, I [should, would] call my best friend and talk about my problem.

7 I [used to, would] have many dolls, but I don't have them anymore.

B

[보기]에서 알맞은 말을 골라 문장을 완성하시오.

Word Bank	would	must	must not	don't have to

1 You ________________ follow the traffic signals.

2 Sam ________________ work out in the gym whenever he felt blue.

3 The trip is optional, so you ________________ go if you're busy.

4 When you are in class, you ________________ send text messages.

C

괄호 안의 지시대로 문장을 완성하시오.

1 Charles must pay a $100 fine because of the speeding ticket. (과거시제로)
→ Charles ________________ a $100 fine because of the speeding ticket.

2 There is a big tree in our garden. (used to 이용하여 과거의 상태로)
→ There ________________ a big tree in our garden.

3 She made the same mistake again. Her boss is very angry. (had better 부정문으로)
→ She ________________ the same mistake again. Her boss is very angry.

4 You have to bring your towel to the gym. (부정문으로)
→ You ________________ your towel to the gym.

5 My brother would sleep on the sofa in the living room. (현재의 습관으로)
→ My brother ________________ on the sofa in the living room from time to time.

조동사 (추측, 가능성)

추측, 가능성 (불확실)	There might be a snowstorm tomorrow. (might → ~일지도 모른다)
(확신)	He must be tired now. He walked for 3 hours. (must → ~임에 틀림없다)
조동사+have p.p.	I should have helped the old lady. (should have helped → ~했어야 했다 (그런데 하지 못했다))

1 추측, 가능성

(1) 불확실한 추측, 가능성: may, might, could

A I haven't seen Danny these days.
B He may〔might〕 be very busy with his work.

A Where is Kelly?
B I'm not sure. She could be in the library.

(2) 확신을 나타내는 추측: must, cannot

A There's someone at the door.
B It must be Sam. He told me he would come by.

A George stole the money.
B It can't be true! He is a very honest man!

2 과거의 추측이나 심경: 조동사+have p.p.

A Where did you put the stapler?
B Did you check the drawer? I might have put it in there.

A Hey! Be careful. You could have hit me!
B Oh, I am really sorry.

A Have you heard? Aaron cheated on the test!
B He cannot have done such a thing.

A It was a terrible movie.
B I agree. We should have seen a different one.

A Sally got a perfect score on the exam.
B I know! She must have studied very hard.

1

(1) 불확실한 추측, 가능성
~일 수도 있다

※ might는 may의 과거가 아니다. may보다 확신이 덜 한 경우 might를 쓴다.
※ 추측의 may는 It is possible that ~으로 바꿔 쓸 수 있다.

(2) 확신을 나타내는 추측
• must: ~임이 틀림없다
• cannot: ~일 리가 없다

2

조동사+have p.p.

may have p.p. might have p.p.	~이었을지도 모른다
could have p.p.	~이었을 수도 있다 (가능할 뻔했으나 일어나지 않음)
cannot have p.p.	~이었을 리가 없다
should have p.p.	~했어야 했다 (실제로 하지 않아서 매우 유감임을 표현)
shouldn't have p.p.	~하지 말았어야 했다 (실제로 해서 매우 유감임을 표현)
must have p.p.	~이었음이 틀림없다 (과거의 일에 대한 확실한 추측)

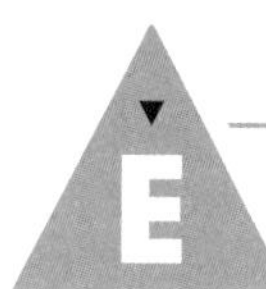

EXERCISE

Answers P.11

A

[ ] 안에서 알맞은 말을 고르시오.

1 He doesn't look very well. He [must, have to] be sick.

2 He [can't, may] be the criminal. The police found his fingerprints on the victim's car.

3 This painting [can't, must not] be a fake. I got it directly from the artist.

4 She didn't call me last night. She [might, could] have forgotten my phone number.

5 Someone [cannot, must] have fixed the clock. It works well now.

6 Luckily, he put out the fire quickly. The damage [should, could] have been much worse.

7 I'm hungry. I [should, might] have eaten something before school started.

B

[보기]에서 알맞은 말을 골라 문장을 완성하시오.

Word Bank			
	may snow	must have hurt	must be
	may have left	should have made	

1 He has a bandage on his finger. He ________________ his finger.

2 It's getting cold. It ________________ tonight.

3 The restaurant is full. We ________________ a reservation yesterday.

4 There ________________ something wrong with my phone. I can't hear you well.

5 I can't find my wallet. I ________________ it at home.

C

우리말과 같은 뜻이 되도록 주어진 단어와 조동사를 이용하여 문장을 완성하시오.

1 그가 그 책을 원래의 자리에 돌려놓았을지도 몰라. (put back)
→ He ________________________ the book in its original place.

2 Corey가 그 가격에 자신의 트럭을 팔았을 리가 없어. (sell)
→ Corey ________________________ his truck for that price.

3 그녀는 돈을 모두 옷 사는 데 썼음이 틀림없어. (spend)
→ She ________________________ all the money on clothes.

4 왜 그렇게 늦게 집을 나왔어? 기차를 놓칠 뻔 했잖아. (miss)
→ Why did you leave home so late? We ________________________ the train.

5 숙제에 대해 선생님께 여쭤봤어야 했는데. (ask)
→ I ________________________ my teacher about the homework.

REVIEW TEST

A

[ ] 안에서 알맞은 말을 고르시오.

1 You [don't have to, must not] pay now. You can send a check later.

2 I [used to, can] do it myself. It looks very easy.

3 You [must not, don't have to] be late for class again.

4 Class is finished. You [would, may] leave now.

5 She looks so tired. She [had better, used to] go home and get some rest.

6 Whenever it was sunny, Sandra [would, should] go wind surfing.

7 I broke my father's antique china vase. I [should, might] have been more careful.

B

빈칸에 들어갈 알맞은 말을 고르시오.

1 She __________ get a job after she passed the exam.

ⓐ have to ⓑ must ⓒ was able to ⓓ were able to

2 They __________ live here, but they moved to another city.

ⓐ will ⓑ may ⓒ used to ⓓ should

3 You __________ go there alone. You should take someone.

ⓐ can ⓑ should ⓒ will ⓓ had better not

4 My parents __________ be very tired after their trip to New Zealand.

ⓐ could have ⓑ has to ⓒ is able to ⓓ must

5 You __________ stay here tonight if you want, but you must leave tomorrow.

ⓐ may ⓑ will not ⓒ used to ⓓ have to

6 You __________ skip meals. It is bad for your health.

ⓐ may ⓑ should not ⓒ would not ⓓ should

7 I __________ be able to meet you next Friday because I have another appointment.

ⓐ will not ⓑ had to ⓒ used to ⓓ cannot

C [보기]에서 알맞은 말을 골라 문장을 완성하시오.

Word Bank	don't have to	would	might	is able to	must	had better

1 When my sister couldn't fall asleep, I ____________ sing a lullaby for her. (과거 습관)

2 You ____________ bring your umbrella. It'll be rainy in the afternoon. (조언)

3 John ____________ speak five different languages. (능력)

4 I ____________ wear my school uniform today. I can wear casual clothes. (불필요)

5 She ____________ be very ill. She has never missed a class before. (확실한 추측)

6 She didn't answer the phone. She ____________ have been in the meeting. (과거의 불확실한 추측)

D 밑줄 친 부분을 바르게 고쳐, 문장을 다시 쓰시오.

1 He won't is able to move into his uncle's apartment.
→ ______________________________

2 You don't have to worry about the fruit. I can picks up some from the market.
→ ______________________________

3 I don't have the book right now, but you might can borrow it from Angie.
→ ______________________________

4 Be careful! You might fall down. You had to hold the handrail.
→ ______________________________

5 Joe looked upset. He must heard the gossip.
→ ______________________________

6 Will you took my dog for a walk? I don't have enough time now.
→ ______________________________

7 He failed the test. He might have studied harder for the exam.
→ ______________________________

F FURTHER STUDY

Answers P.12

A 글을 읽고, 밑줄 친 부분을 바르게 고쳐 쓰시오.

It is March 7th today. My mother's birthday is coming soon. Last year on her birthday, my father wasn't home because he (1) <u>have to</u> go on a business trip to Taiwan. My brother and I were also on a field trip during the whole week, so we (2) <u>can't</u> make it to her birthday party, either. She (3) <u>could</u> have felt very sad. This year, again, my father may not spend time with us on her birthday. He may go on another business trip somewhere. So, my brother and I are planning to buy special gifts for our mother this year. And we might (4) <u>made</u> seaweed soup and bake some cookies for her.

(1) ______________________

(2) ______________________

(3) ______________________

(4) ______________________

B [보기]에서 알맞은 조동사를 고르고, 주어진 말을 이용하여 문장을 완성하시오.

Word Bank	will	can	cannot	have to	must not

1 2 3 4 5

1 The road is very slippery, so you ______________________(speed). (속도를 내지 말아야 한다)

2 If you go this way, you ______________________(the entrance). (입구를 찾을 수 있다)

3 If you drive over the 40 mile per hour speed limit, you ______________________ (get a ticket). (교통위반 딱지를 뗄 것이다)

4 You ______________________(here). (여기에 주차할 수 없다)

5 If you see this traffic sign, you ______________________(slow down) and watch for kids. (속도를 줄여야 한다)

▶ 조동사별 쓰임

can/could	능력, 허락, 추측, 요청 등	He **can** make a model airplane very well. (능력 = be able to) You **can** go now. (허락) She **could** be a little late. (추측) **Could** you make me a sandwich? (요청)
may/might	허락, 요청, 추측 등	**May** I take a day off tomorrow? (허락) You **might** need my help. (추측)
shall/should	의무, 충고, 제안 등	We **should** not speak loudly in the library. (의무) **Shall** we go now? (제안)
will/would	미래, 의지, 요청, 과거의 습관(would) 등	I **will** go to a concert tomorrow. (미래) I **will** not tolerate his behavior this time. (의지) **Will** you go with me? (요청) We **would** play hide-and-seek when we were young. (과거의 습관)
must	의무, 추측 등	You **must** do your homework before you come to class. (의무 = have to) He **must** be late again. (추측)

▶ 공손함의 정도

can < may	**Can** I take a message?	**May** I take a message?
can < could	**Can** you give me an example?	**Could** you give me an example?
will < would	**Will** you fill out this form?	**Would** you fill out this form?

▶ 확신의 정도

	긍정문 (affirmative)	부정문 (negative)
100% 사실	Larry **is** at home.	Larry **isn't** in the hospital.
강한 확신	Larry **must** be at home.	Larry **can't** be in the hospital.
불확실한 추측	Larry **may** be at home. Larry **might** be at home. Larry **could** be at home.	Larry **may not** be in the hospital. Larry **might not** be in the hospital.

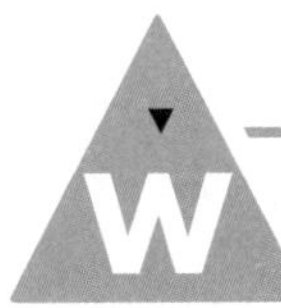

WRAP-UP TEST

Answers P.12

1 대화를 읽고, 밑줄 친 부분과 바꾸어 쓸 수 있는 것을 고르시오.

> A May I use your phone?
> B Of course, but you should not use it too long.

ⓐ Do ⓑ Should
ⓒ Might ⓓ Can

2 문장을 읽고, 어색한 곳을 찾아 바르게 고치시오.

Seven prisoners could(ⓐ) escaped(ⓑ) from(ⓒ) the jail and run away(ⓓ).

3 밑줄 친 must의 쓰임이 다른 것을 고르시오.

ⓐ You must not press this red button.
ⓑ They must tell the police the truth.
ⓒ Many students failed the history test. It must be very hard.
ⓓ A car can hit you. You must cross the street at the crosswalk.

4 어법에 맞는 문장을 고르시오.

ⓐ He can invents a bulb for saving energy.
ⓑ Jack had not better give up exercising every day.
ⓒ The plane will has to take off on time.
ⓓ The little boy might get lost on the street.

5 밑줄 친 can의 쓰임이 같은 것끼리 묶은 것을 고르시오.

> ① The rat can go through the maze very fast.
> ② Can I borrow the book from the library?
> ③ Can you give me some advice to get up early?
> ④ Do you think he can find the ring?
> ⑤ Can you tell me the way to the post office?
> ⑥ You can choose two cups from ten.

ⓐ ①④, ②⑥, ③⑤ ⓑ ①②, ④⑥, ③⑤
ⓒ ①④, ②③, ⑤⑥ ⓓ ①⑥, ②⑤, ③④

6 빈칸에 알맞은 말을 쓰시오.

· There ___ⓐ___ be something wrong with my phone. I can't hear you. (~임이 틀림없다)
· It ___ⓑ___ be a lie. He never lies. (일 리가 없다)

ⓐ: ⓑ:

7 [보기]에서 알맞은 단어를 골라 문장을 완성하시오.

don't have to	must have	should	used to

(1) There ______________ be a fancy restaurant around City Hall.
(2) He ______________ moved the heavy boxes. He is very kind.
(3) You ______________ wear a formal dress to attend the party. You can wear casual clothes.
(4) You ______________ brush your teeth before you go to sleep.

8 주어진 말과 조동사를 이용하여 문장을 영작하시오.

(1) 나는 그와의 약속을 지켜야 했는데. (지키지 않았다.) (keep the promise with him)
→ ______________________________

(2) 그가 그런 일을 했을 리가 없다. (do such a thing)
→ ______________________________

[9-10] 글을 읽고, 물음에 답하시오.

> My parents (A) will can buy a new car next month. They have saved for it for a couple of years. They used to have a nice car, but they ___(B)___ scrap it five years ago after they had a car accident. Dad may buy a blue car because it is his favorite color.

9 (A)를 바르게 고치시오.

10 (B)에 들어갈 알맞은 말을 고르시오.

ⓐ had to ⓑ could
ⓒ might ⓓ had better

부정사

1 to부정사의 역할

2 to부정사의 의미상 주어 / 부정

3 부정사의 기타 쓰임

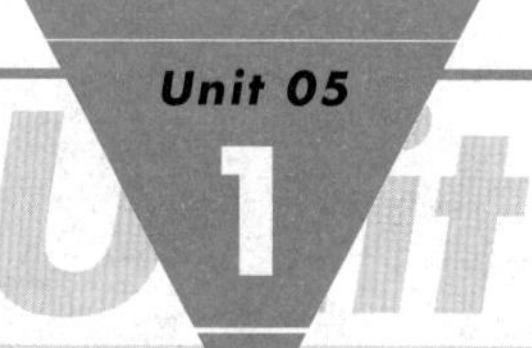

to부정사의 역할

명사 역할	I want to visit Disneyland. (→~것을)
형용사 역할	I wanted something to read. (→~할)
부사 역할	We went to the bookstore to buy comics. (→~하기 위하여)

to부정사: to+동사원형
동사의 성격을 가지고 있으면서 (동작/상태 표시, 목적어를 가질 수 있음) 문장 내에서 명사, 형용사, 부사처럼 사용

1 명사 역할

(1) To eat mushrooms is good for your health.
(= It is good for your health to eat mushrooms.)

(2) My hope is to have my own company.
His dream is to ride in a spaceship.

(3) I want to write a novel.
I decided to make a new plan.

2 형용사 역할

I want something to drink.
He brought some bread to eat.

cf) She needs paper to write on.
He has many good friends to play with.

3 부사 역할

(1) We went to the supermarket to buy orange juice.
Kelly doesn't eat fried foods (in order) to lose weight.

(2) Michelle grew up to be a famous golfer.
He worked hard, only to fail.

(3) My parents were surprised to see my bad grades.
He was happy to get together with his friends.

(4) You must be crazy to say so.
I was stupid to tell her my secrets.

(5) Chinese characters are hard to learn.
This liquid medicine is easy to take.

1
명사적 쓰임: ~하는 것
(1) 주어(Subject)
(2) 보어(Complement)
(3) 목적어(Object)
: to부정사를 목적어로 사용하는 동사
- want, hope, wish, like 등
※[MUST-KNOW] 참조

※to부정사가 주어로 사용되는 경우보다 가주어 it을 사용해 바꾸거나, 동명사(-ing) 형태로 쓰이는 경우가 많다. [Unit 6 참조]

2
형용사적 쓰임: ~할, ~하는
- 명사 뒤에서 수식

cf) to부정사+전치사
• live in a house
→ a house to live in
• write on paper
→ paper to write on
• play with friends
→ friends to play with

3
부사적 쓰임: 동사, 형용사 수식
(1) 목적: ~하기 위해서 (= in order to)
(2) 결과: ~해서 (그 결과) …되다
~했지만(그 결과) …되었다(only to fail)
(3) 감정의 원인: ~해서
(4) 판단의 근거: ~하는 걸 보니, 하다니
must / can't] V…+to V (~하는 것을 보니)
(5) ~하기에

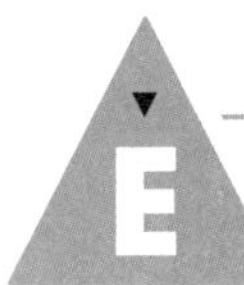

EXERCISE

Answers P.13

A

밑줄 친 to부정사를 쓰임에 따라 명사적 "N", 형용사적 "A", 부사적 "Ad"로 구분하시오.

1 I went to California to visit my cousin. ______

2 His dream is to build his own house. ______

3 She wants something to read while she is on the train. ______

4 To clean my room is my responsibility. ______

5 Her mother gave her some toys to play with. ______

6 I was happy to see you. ______

B

[보기]에서 쓰임이 같은 to부정사를 고르시오.

(a) He studied hard to be a doctor.
(b) It is hard to climb mountains.
(c) I'm planning to make a schedule for the field trip.
(d) She didn't have anything to do.
(e) He was happy to see her again.

1 It is not common to see shooting stars. ______

2 I need a box to put these school materials in. ______

3 He was excited to receive his teacher's praise. ______

4 I want to be an engineer. ______

5 They called the restaurant to book a table. ______

C

[보기]에서 알맞은 말을 골라 어법에 맞게 문장을 완성하시오.

Word Bank	become	eat	watch	buy	pass

1 They were excited ______ the game.

2 ______ a better language learner, you should read a lot.

3 He wants ______ a ring for his girlfriend.

4 I'm hungry. Do you have anything ______?

5 She was happy ______ the test.

Unit 05

Unit 2 to부정사의 의미상 주어 / 부정

주어가 같을 때 I want ~+I exercise every morning. (same)
주어 탈락
→ I want to exercise every morning.

주어가 다를 때 I want ~+They exercise every morning. (different)
목적격으로
→ I want them to exercise every morning.
의미상 주어

to부정사의 의미상 주어
- 문장의 주어와 to부정사의 주어가 같을 때: 의미상 주어 필요 없음
- 문장의 주어와 to부정사의 주어가 다를 때: 목적격 사용

1 to부정사의 의미상 주어

(1) I want to eat vegetables. (I – to eat)
His mother wants to go there. (His mother – to go)

I want him to eat vegetables. (him – to eat)
His mother wants him to go there. (him – to go)

(2) It is necessary to read a lot of books. (people – to read)
It is necessary for her to read a lot of books. (her – to read)

It is fun to wear a wig. (people – to wear)
It is fun for him to wear a wig. (him – to wear)

It was nice of him to clean his brother's room. (him – to clean)
It was kind of them to save the poor cat. (them – to save)

1
(1) 문장의 주어 또는 to부정사 앞에 나온 목적격이 의미상 주어가 된다.

(2) 'it ~ to부정사' 구문의 의미상 주어
- for+목적격: 〈for+목적격〉을 주어로 해석 (easy, difficult, possible 등)
→ It is difficult for+목적격+to V
- of+목적격: 앞에 사람을 칭찬하거나 비판하는 의미가 형용사가 나올 때 (kind, nice, wise, stupid, foolish 등)
→ It is nice of 목적격+to V

2 to부정사의 부정

I told you to keep the file. It's useful.
→ I told you not to keep the file. It's useless.

I told the taxi driver to go faster.
→ I told the taxi driver not to go faster.

It is stupid of her to believe Jerry.
→ It is stupid of her not to believe Jerry.

2
not+to부정사

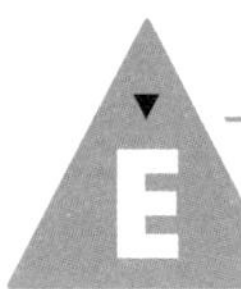

EXERCISE

Answers P.13

A

[ ] 안에서 알맞은 말을 고르시오.

1 Leo's mother wants [him, his] to date Ally again.

2 It is difficult [of her, for her] to have a part-time job and be a college student.

3 He warned his daughter [not to use, to not use] her credit card.

4 My family wants [me, mine] to attend school in the U.S.

5 It is kind [of you, for you] to help me with my math homework.

6 She asked him [doesn't close, not to close] the window.

B

괄호 안에 주어진 말을 **to**부정사의 의미상 주어로 하여 문장을 완성하시오.

1 I didn't want to make excuses about copying from the Internet. (they)
→ I didn't want ________________ to make excuses about copying from the Internet.

2 Susan wants to live in the school dormitory. (her little sister)
→ Susan wants ________________ to live in the school dormitory.

3 It is important not to waste time. (you)
→ It is important ________________ not to waste time.

4 It was foolish to spend so much money on the game. (he)
→ It was foolish ________________ to spend so much money on the game.

5 He wants to use the color pink. (she)
→ He wants ________________ to use the color pink.

C

밑줄 친 부분을 바르게 고쳐 쓰시오.

1 It is nice <u>for you</u> to come and help me. ________________

2 It is hard <u>me</u> to write an essay in English. ________________

3 The old man told <u>to him</u> not to throw away the bottles. ________________

4 I tried <u>to not think</u> about my mistakes in the exam. ________________

부정사의 기타 쓰임

의문사+to부정사 We haven't decided what to eat for lunch.

too ~ to ... You are too young to travel alone. (→ too+형용사+to부정사)

원형부정사 My sister made me clean her room. (→ 사역동사+목적어+원형부정사)

1 의문사 + to부정사

I don't know what to say.
(= I don't know what I should say.)

Please tell me how to get to the subway station.
(= Please tell me how I should get to the subway station.)

I can't decide where to go.
(= I can't decide where I should go.)

> 1
> what to do (무엇을 해야 할지)
> how to swim (어떻게 수영해야 할지)
> when to meet (언제 만나야 할지)
> where to go (어디로 가야 할지)
> whom to go with (누구와 가야 할지)
>
> 의문사+to부정사
> = 의문사+주어+should+동사원형
> (to부정사의 의미상 주어)

2 too ~ to ... / 형용사[부사]+enough to ~

(1) I am too young to see that movie.
(= I am so young that I can't see that movie.)

Amy is too tired to finish the race.
(= Amy is so tired that she can't finish the race.)

(2) He is smart enough to go to medical school.
(= He is so smart that he can go to medical school.)

She speaks English well enough to be an interpreter.
(= She speaks English so well that she can be an interpreter.)

> 2
> (1) too ~ to V ...
> : 너무 ~해서 ...할 수 없다
> = so ~ that+주어+can't ...
>
> (2) **형용사[부사]+enough+to V**
> : ~할 만큼 (충분히) ...하다
> = so ... that+주어+can ~
>
> *cf)* enough의 위치
> • enough+명사+to V
> I had enough money to buy a new stereo.
> • 형/부+enough+to V
> She is wise enough to solve the problem.

3 원형부정사

(1) Julia made her little brother clean her room.
My teacher let me read my poem to the class.

(2) I heard someone knock on the door.
We saw our teacher leave the classroom.

cf) Tom helped me (to) carry my luggage.

> 3
> **원형부정사**
> 사역/지각동사+목적어+원형부정사
> (1) 사역동사: make, have, let 등
> (2) 지각동사
> • 보다: see, watch, look at
> • 듣다: hear, listen to
> • 느끼다: feel
>
> *cf)* help는 원형부정사와 to부정사 모두 쓸 수 있다(주로 원형부정사 사용).

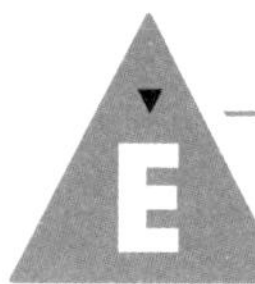

EXERCISE

Answers P.13

A

[ ] 안에서 알맞은 말을 고르시오.

1 Could you tell me [what to meet, where to meet] her?

2 Let us [to find, find] a cute birthday present for her.

3 I don't know [how to solve, what to solve] this math problem.

4 My dad made me [to fix, fix] my sister's bicycle.

5 I saw the teacher [to put, put] the student's cell phone in her pocket.

6 She is [old enough, enough old] to see the soap opera.

7 I was too sleepy [concentrate, to concentrate] on the class.

B

밑줄 친 부분을 바르게 고쳐 쓰시오.

1 I didn't know how contact her. ____________________

2 His office was to difficult too find. ____________________

3 I heard someone to scream in the dark. ____________________

4 Could you tell me where should sit? ____________________

5 It was warm to enough take off my coat. ____________________

6 Mom made me to wash my sneakers. ____________________

7 Let me introduced my family to you. ____________________

C

두 문장이 같은 뜻이 되도록 문장을 완성하시오.

1 He is too old to walk by himself.

= He is ________ ________ that he ________ ________ by himself.

2 My dog is smart enough to find the way home.

= My dog is ________ ________ that he ________ ________ the way home.

3 I am so sick that I can't go to school today.

= I am ________ ________ ________ ________ to school today.

4 His father is so wise that he can encourage his son's musical talents.

= His father is ________ ________ ________ ________ his son's musical talents.

REVIEW TEST

A

[ ] 안에서 알맞은 말을 고르시오.

1 We saw many people [to walk, walk] fast on the street.

2 This watch is [too, enough] expensive for me to buy.

3 He had his son [run, to run] to the store to get some milk.

4 He needs a friend [play, to play] with.

5 She promised [not to be, to be not] angry with me again.

6 Jake wants to know [how talks, how to talk] to girls.

7 It was difficult [of her, for her] to follow the main idea of the conversation.

B

빈칸에 들어갈 알맞은 말을 고르시오.

1 They have practiced hard enough ___________ this game.

ⓐ to win ⓑ win ⓒ won ⓓ for winning

2 They couldn't decide ___________ her for her birthday.

ⓐ what give ⓑ what to give ⓒ what she gives ⓓ what she should give

3 It is kind ___________ to show me the way to the train station.

ⓐ your ⓑ for you ⓒ of you ⓓ to you

4 My teacher let me ___________ costumes for the school play.

ⓐ design ⓑ designed ⓒ to design ⓓ are designing

5 These days, I'm learning ___________ the guitar.

ⓐ how to play ⓑ what to play ⓒ when to play ⓓ who to play

6 I have something ___________ with you about your grade.

ⓐ discuss ⓑ discussed ⓒ to discuss ⓓ discussing

7 The doctor advised ___________ to work out regularly.

ⓐ mine ⓑ of me ⓒ my ⓓ me

C

[보기]에서 알맞은 말을 골라 어법에 맞게 바꿔 문장을 완성하시오.

Word Bank	wear	eat	make	give	run	tell	live

1 Let me ____________ you a little about my school life.

2 I didn't know what ____________ my brother for Christmas.

3 I never intended ____________ you angry.

4 Are you looking for a place ____________?

5 I saw a big truck ____________ the red light at the crosswalk.

6 This cheese smells too strong for me ____________.

7 It is our school's rule for students ____________ a uniform.

D

밑줄 친 부분을 바르게 고쳐, 문장을 다시 쓰시오.

1 He is strong too to move these boxes.

→ ______________________________

2 She gave me a red pen to write on.

→ ______________________________

3 I want to have some chocolate to help relieving my stress.

→ ______________________________

4 The coach made all the players to run around the stadium track.

→ ______________________________

5 David is enough brave to bungee jump.

→ ______________________________

6 He decided be a soccer player when he was seven.

→ ______________________________

7 It was unwise for you to criticize your friend like that.

→ ______________________________

F FURTHER STUDY

Answers P.15

A 글을 읽고, 밑줄 친 부분을 바르게 고쳐 쓰시오.

Cooking is one of my favorite hobbies, and I cook lunch for my family every Sunday. Last Sunday, my parents wanted me (1) make some spaghetti with tomato sauce. My father wanted to have garlic bread, too. However, there was no garlic bread at home, and I didn't have (2) time enough to buy garlic bread at the bakery next to our house. So, I had my little brother (3) to buy garlic bread while I was boiling the spaghetti noodles. My parents helped me prepare for lunch and (4) setting the picnic table in the backyard. It was very pleasant to have lunch with all my family members.

(1) ______________________

(2) ______________________

(3) ______________________

(4) ______________________

B 우리말과 같은 뜻이 되도록 주어진 단어와 to부정사를 이용하여 문장을 완성하시오.

1 영어 문법은 한국인들이 배우기에 쉽지 않다. (Koreans, learn)

→ English grammar is ____.

2 이 자전거는 타기에는 너무 작다. (ride)

→ This bike is ____.

3 그녀의 딸은 같이 놀 강아지를 원한다. (a puppy, play with)

→ Her daughter ____.

4 이 홀은 약 100명 정도를 수용할 수 있을 만큼 넓다. (large, accommodate, about 100 people)

→ This hall is ____.

5 선생님은 우리에게 언제 리포트를 내야 하는지 알려주시지 않았다. (hand in, the report)

→ The teacher didn't tell us ____.

Answers P.15

▶ to부정사를 목적어로 취하는 동사들

동사+to V	예문
want	Fred wants **to be** a movie director.
hope	They hope **to go** to an Italian restaurant.
plan	Sandra plans **to enter** the university of Florida.
mean	I didn't mean **to scare** you.
decide	She decided **to give** him another chance.
expect	Tim expected **to see** the president.
promise	He promised **to study** harder.
intend	I intended ① ________(return) the book right away.
agree	We agreed ② ________(put off) the meeting.
refuse	He refused ③ ________(comment) on the incident.

▶ 동사원형을 목적어로 쓰는 동사들

동사 종류		예문
사역 동사	make	My father made me **clean** the toilet.
	have	I had my brother **answer** the phone.
	let	My mother let us **go** to the party last weekend.
지각 동사	see	I saw him **hide** something behind his back.
	watch	I heard my baby brother **cry** in his room.
	hear	She felt her house **shake** last night.
	feel	*지각동사의 경우, 목적격보어로 진행형을 쓸 수도 있다. (그 시점에서의 진행 의미를 강조할 때)

■ **문장 전체를 꾸며주는 to부정사**

(1) to begin with (우선, 먼저, 처음에)
eg) To begin with, I don't like her hairstyle.

(2) to be short (간단히 말하면, 요컨대)
eg) To be short, we don't have enough time before the deadline.

(3) to be sure (확실히, 물론)
eg) Trust, to be sure, is one of the most important things between friends.

(4) to tell the truth (사실을 말하자면)
eg) To tell the truth, I love her.

(5) to be frank with you (솔직히 말하자면)
eg) To be frank with you, I totally forgot about the appointment.

(6) so to speak (말하자면)
eg) My English teacher is, so to speak, a walking dictionary.

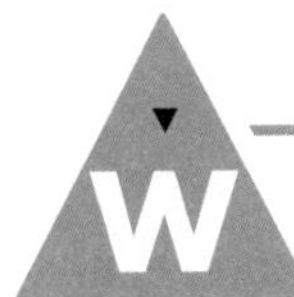

WRAP-UP TEST

Answers P.15

1 빈칸에 들어갈 알맞은 말을 고르시오.

My hope is ____________ all around the world.

ⓐ travel ⓑ travels

ⓒ traveled ⓓ to travel

2 대화를 읽고, 어색한 곳을 찾아 바르게 고치시오.

A My mom's birthday is(ⓐ) tomorrow. I don't know what to buy(ⓑ) for her(ⓒ).

B What does she want have(ⓓ)?

3 빈칸에 들어갈 알맞은 말을 쓰시오.

· That's very kind ___ⓐ___ you to help me move this table.

· It is hard ___ⓑ___ me to find the way with this map.

ⓐ: ⓑ:

4 어법상 어색한 문장을 고르시오.

ⓐ The department store is a good place to go shopping.

ⓑ Could you tell me how to use this copy machine?

ⓒ He agreed to not attend the meeting.

ⓓ To skip meals is bad for your health.

5 주어진 문장의 밑줄 친 부분과 쓰임이 같은 것을 고르시오.

He studied hard to be a doctor.

ⓐ My dream is to be a famous actor.

ⓑ I decided not to buy carnations for Mother's Day.

ⓒ I have many people to invite to my birthday party.

ⓓ He went to the store to buy some milk.

6 빈칸에 to를 쓸 수 있는 것을 고르시오.

ⓐ He had me ______ spread the false rumor.

ⓑ We heard the cat ______ scratch the door with its claws.

ⓒ The boy went home early to help his mom ______ clean the house.

ⓓ He felt something ______ move under his bed.

7 우리말과 같은 뜻이 되도록 주어진 말을 이용하여 문장을 완성하시오.

나는 지진에 대한 기사를 찾으려고 지난 신문을 살펴보았다.

= I looked through old newspapers __________ the article about earthquakes. (find)

8 두 문장의 의미가 통하도록 문장을 완성하시오.

(1) The concert hall is so huge that it can hold 1,000 people.

= The concert hall is ____________________ ____________________.

(2) He is too tired to concentrate on this work.

= He is __________ tired __________ ____________________.

(3) To exercise regularly is very important for me.

= It ____________________ to ____________________.

[9-10] 글을 읽고, 물음에 답하시오.

Henry the eighth was King of England in the 16th century. He is famous for having six wives. People did not want the King ___(A)___ their daughter to be his wife because his wives had very short and unhappy lives, but they didn't have any choice ___(B)___. If the King chose their daughter, they had to allow her ___(C) be___ his wife.

9 (A), (B)에 알맞은 말을 고르시오.

ⓐ to choose - to make ⓑ choose - to make

ⓒ choose - make ⓓ to choose - make

10 (C)에 주어진 동사를 어법에 맞게 바꿔 쓰시오.

동명사

1 동명사의 역할

2 동명사의 의미상 주어 / 부정

3 동명사 / to부정사를 쓰는 동사

동명사의 역할

→동사 →동명사(동사의 성격+명사의 역할)

동명사 We like traveling together.

주어 역할 Helping the poor is not easy for them.

보어 역할 Their job is helping the poor.

목적어 역할 They enjoy helping the poor.

> 동명사(V-ing)
> 동사의 성격(동작/상태를 나타내며, 목적어를 가질 수 있음)을 가지고 있으면서도 문장 안에서 명사처럼 쓰임

1 주어 역할을 하는 동명사

Playing is important for kids.
Playing computer games is one of my hobbies.

Walking is good for our health.
Walking in the forest makes us feel free.

> 1
> **주어: ~하는 것은, ~하는 것이**
> 주어로 쓰이는 동명사: 항상 단수 취급
> Reading is fun.
> Reading magazines is fun.

2 목적어 역할을 하는 동명사

(1) I finished washing the dishes.
I don't mind changing seats with you.
Do you like playing football?

(2) Thank you for lending me your umbrella.
I'm proud of being Korean.
This cat is good at catching mice.

> 2
> **목적어: ~하는 것을**
> (1) 타동사의 목적어
> : finish, mind, like, enjoy+-ing
> (2) 전치사의 목적어

3 보어 역할을 하는 동명사

His dream is becoming a pilot.
Her hobby is listening to classical music.
My goal is becoming an expert in economics.

cf) ① 동명사 vs. ② 현재진행형

① His hobby is cooking. (~하는 것이다)
② He is cooking in the kitchen now. (~하는 중이다)

① My job is taking pictures.
② I am taking pictures now.

> 3
> **보어: ~하는 것이다**
> *cf)* be+-ing
> ~하는 것이다 (동명사)
> His hobby is collecting coins.
> (=)
> ~하는 중이다 (진행형)
> He is collecting coins now.
>
> ※ 동명사 만드는 법은 Unit 2의 "진행형 만드는 법" 참조

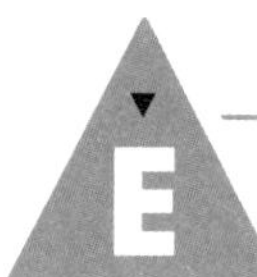

EXERCISE

Answers P.16

A

[ ] 안에서 알맞은 말을 고르시오.

1 Having a pet [is, are] good for your mental health.

2 He is a businessman, but his dream was [to being, being] a lawyer.

3 I am really sorry for [disturb, disturbing] you when you are busy.

4 Telling lies about one's grades [make, makes] me really angry.

5 My sister enjoys [talking, to talk] about celebrities.

6 I love [wears, wearing] jeans and a white T-shirt.

7 One of my wishes is [winning, won] a full scholarship to a good university.

8 Lisa spends a lot of money on [decorate, decorating] her house.

B

밑줄 친 -ing를 쓰임에 따라 동명사 "G", 현재분사 "P"로 구분하시오.

1 Her bad habit is biting her nails. ______

2 My dog is biting the old slippers. ______

3 The girl is playing the flute on the stage. ______

4 My little brother's hobby is playing with toy soldiers. ______

5 One of his chores is doing the laundry for his mom. ______

6 Ron is doing his homework in the library. ______

C

괄호 안의 지시대로 문장을 완성하시오.

1 I walked by a bakery. It makes my mouth water. (주어 역할)

→ ______________________ makes my mouth water.

2 I listen to pop music. I like it very much. (목적어 역할)

→ I like ______________________ very much.

3 When she was a child, she wanted to become a detective. (주어 역할)

→ ______________________ was her childhood dream.

4 She helped me clean the classroom. I thanked her. (목적어 역할)

→ I thanked her for ______________________.

5 Jim is a teacher. He teaches history at a public school. (보어 역할)

→ Jim's job is ______________________ at a public school.

동명사의 의미상 주어 / 부정

주어가 같을 때 — same: I like+I read comic books.
(의미상 주어는 문장의 주어와 같음)
→ I like reading comic books.

주어가 다를 때 — different: I like+They sing pop songs.
(의미상 주어는 소유격으로)
→ I like their singing pop songs.

1 동명사의 의미상 주어

Do you mind opening the window?
Do you mind my opening the window?

I will stop surfing the Internet at night.
I will stop his surfing the Internet at night.

▶ 1
동명사의 의미상 주어는 원칙적으로 소유격이나, 실제 구어체에서는 목적격을 쓰는 경우도 많다.
eg) I don't mind you opening the door.

2 동명사의 부정

My bad habit is not doing my homework on time.
I can't forgive his not telling me the truth.

▶ 2
not+동명사

3 동명사 구문

I go shopping with my mom every weekend.
My brother goes fishing with my father once a month.

Henry is busy preparing for the exam now.
She was busy making copies of the document.

I look forward to seeing you again.
We look forward to going on a field trip tomorrow.

This program prevents others from accessing your files.
The rule will prevent students from cheating with their cell phones.

I feel like eating out tonight.
The test is over. I feel like going to a movie.

▶ 3

go -ing	~하러 가다
be busy -ing	~하느라 바쁘다
look forward to -ing	~하는 것을 기대하다 (여기서 to는 전치사)
prevent(stop) ~from -ing	...가 ~하는 것을 막다
feel like -ing	~하고 싶다

※기타 동명사 구문은 [MUST-KNOW] 참조

EXERCISE

Answers P.16

A

[ ] 안에서 알맞은 말을 고르시오.

1 We went [camp, camping] on the beach last summer vacation.

2 The teacher felt sorry for [not helping, helping not] him more.

3 Do you mind [I, my] interrupting you while you are speaking?

4 The programmer can prevent users [of adding, from adding] new software.

5 The security guard stopped [her, hers] from shouting in the hospital.

6 She is busy [to arrange, arranging] for the meeting.

7 I look forward [to go, to going] back to Korea this September.

B

밑줄 친 동사를 동명사로 바꿔 대화를 완성하시오.

1 Mr. and Mrs. Powell <u>visit</u> art museums once a week.
→ Do they like ____________ art museums?

2 Sam's uncle <u>climbs</u> mountains every weekend.
→ Does he enjoy ____________ mountains?

3 My two brothers hardly ever <u>clean</u> their rooms.
→ Do they avoid ____________ their rooms?

4 Wendy always <u>goes</u> shopping with her friends.
→ Does she enjoy ____________ shopping with her friends?

5 Paul never <u>eats</u> pizza. It makes him sick.
→ Does he dislike ____________ pizza?

C

밑줄 친 부분을 바르게 고쳐 쓰시오.

1 I like <u>he</u> driving me to school. ____________

2 We are looking forward to <u>hear</u> from you. ____________

3 She prefers <u>eating not</u> late in the evening. ____________

4 I feel like <u>to take</u> a walk in the park. ____________

5 I have been busy <u>prepare</u> for the math competition these days. ____________

동명사 / to부정사를 쓰는 동사

동명사만 쓰는 동사	I enjoy going to the zoo. (X) I enjoy to go to the zoo.
to부정사만 쓰는 동사	I want to discuss the plan with you. (X) I want discussing the plan with you.
동명사 vs. to부정사	He stopped eating French fries for his health. He stopped to eat pizza for lunch.

1 동사+동명사 (V–ing)

We finished feeding the ducks.
Did you enjoy meeting people at the party?
I miss living with my grandmother.
I don't mind your using my cell phone.

> 1
> enjoy, miss, finish, mind, avoid, give up, quit, postpone, consider+V-ing

2 동사+to부정사 (to V)

She wanted to explain the game's rules to me.
Did Matthew hope to see you again?
I have decided to live on campus.
My father promised to come home early.

> 2
> want, hope, wish, plan, seem, mean, decide, promise, pretend, fail+to V

3 동명사와 to부정사를 목적어로 갖는 동사

(1) 의미가 같은 경우

I began learning hip-hop dancing last month.
(= I began to learn hip-hop dancing last month.)
I hate swimming in the sea.
(= I hate to swim in the sea.)

(2) 의미가 다른 경우

forget
- 미래: Don't forget to buy some potatoes when you go to the grocery store.
- 과거: I will never forget meeting the president.

try
- 노력: He tried to persuade his mother, but he failed.
- 시도: Jerry tried writing with his left hand just for fun.

> 3
> 동명사와 to부정사를 동시에 쓸 수 있는 동사
> (1) 의미가 같은 경우
> love, like, hate, begin, start, continue 등
> (2) 의미가 다른 경우
> forget, remember, stop, try 등
> *eg)*
> • forget[remember]
> – to V: (앞으로) ~할 것을 잊다[기억하다]
> – -ing: (과거에) ~한 것을 잊다[기억하다]
> • try
> – to V: ~하려고 애쓰다, 노력하다
> – -ing: (시험 삼아) ~해 보다
> ※ [MUST-KNOW] 참조

EXERCISE

Answers P.16

A

[ ] 안에서 알맞은 말을 고르시오.

1 She gave up [to find, finding] her lost cell phone.

2 I didn't mean [to hurt, hurting] your feelings.

3 The politician promises [to increase, increasing] education spending.

4 Would you mind [to answer, answering] some questions for me?

5 Michael quit [to complain, complaining] about the food at the school cafeteria.

6 Peter planned [to bring, bringing] a picnic lunch for his best friend, Sam.

B

주어진 말을 어법에 맞게 바꿔 문장을 완성하시오.

1 On my way home, I stopped ______________(play) computer games at the PC room.

2 I stopped ______________(play) computer games and ran home after reading my mom's text message.

3 To improve her concentration, she tried ______________(study) while listening to classical music.

4 It was a horrible scene. She tried ____________________________(not, think) about it.

5 He forgot ______________(buy) some ice cream on sale last week, so he bought more today.

6 He forgot ______________(buy) a present for his girlfriend for their anniversary.

C

주어진 말을 어법에 맞게 바꿔 문장을 완성하시오.

1 I stopped ______________(ride) my bike to avoid ______________(hit) people.

2 He seemed ______________(be) a liar, but he pretended ______________(be) honest.

3 Did you finish ______________(write) your report? I want ______________(watch) the video with you.

4 I promised ______________(help) her fix the table, but I forgot ______________(bring) my hammer.

5 They started ______________(paint) the house at 8 am today, but they failed ______________(finish) painting it.

REVIEW TEST

A

[ ] 안에서 알맞은 말을 고르시오.

1 Nancy enjoys [going, to go] skiing in winter.

2 Jack decided [not making, not to make] Jim a member of his baseball team.

3 I haven't considered [applying, to apply] to any private universities.

4 She has to avoid [giving, to give] a quick answer in order not to make a mistake.

5 Remembering people's names [is, are] difficult.

6 I'm sorry for [not to keep, not keeping] my promise.

7 Susan is busy [selecting, to select] songs for the fashion show.

B

빈칸에 들어갈 알맞은 말을 고르시오.

1 The movie was so sad that I felt like ________.

ⓐ cry ⓑ to cry ⓒ crying ⓓ be crying

2 Albert will ________ in Nepal this Sunday and come back in a month.

ⓐ go trek ⓑ go to trek ⓒ goes trek ⓓ go trekking

3 ________ too much fast food is bad for our health.

ⓐ To ate ⓑ Eating ⓒ To eating ⓓ Eat

4 They must remember ________ their homework by next week.

ⓐ finished ⓑ finishing ⓒ to finish ⓓ finish

5 The citizens are trying to prevent the mayor from ________ a new City Hall.

ⓐ build ⓑ building ⓒ to build ⓓ be building

6 My teacher postponed ________ us the project until we have finished our exams.

ⓐ to be given ⓑ to give ⓒ giving ⓓ give

7 Jordan ________ his bag for his trip to Egypt now.

ⓐ pack ⓑ were packing ⓒ is packing ⓓ is packed

C [보기]에서 알맞은 말을 골라 어법에 맞게 바꿔 문장을 완성하시오.

Word Bank	sleep	forgive	watch	go	close	look	graduate

1 I was angry with her, but I decided ________________ her mistakes.

2 ________________ from school at the top of my class is my goal this year.

3 We spent a lot of time ________________ for a good restaurant.

4 I will never forget ________________ the wonderful fireworks last night.

5 I feel like ________________ to the cinema tonight.

6 Remember ________________ the windows before you go out.

7 She tried not ________________ in class, but she started to doze as soon as the teacher started the lesson.

D 밑줄 친 부분을 바르게 고쳐, 문장을 다시 쓰시오.

1 They wish organizing a schedule for the club's activities.

→ ____

2 His staying in Seoul make me happy.

→ ____

3 My sister continued take care of the children in the orphanage for a year.

→ ____

4 This town is very famous for make noodles with rice.

→ ____

5 My hobby is to collecting news articles in my scrapbook.

→ ____

6 They finished to present the report at 2 pm.

→ ____

7 Eat protein is necessary for muscle growth.

→ ____

Answers P.17

A 글을 읽고, 밑줄 친 부분을 바르게 고쳐 쓰시오.

We all (1) <u>want living</u> long and healthy lives. We can do many things for our health. Let me give you five tips to help you maintain good health. First, (2) <u>stop to eat</u> too much fat. Second, try to eat more fruits and vegetables every day. Third, don't (3) <u>forget drinking</u> enough water each day. Water is important for every system in the body! Fourth, remember to exercise regularly. Even walking ten minutes three times a week will help you feel better. Finally, (4) <u>give up to eat</u> too late at night. Remember to do these things and you won't have to see your doctor very often.

(1) ____________________

(2) ____________________

(3) ____________________

(4) ____________________

B 우리말과 같은 뜻이 되도록 주어진 단어와 동명사를 이용하여 문장을 완성하시오.

1 많이 웃는 것은 좋은 약이다. (laugh, a lot)

→ ____________________ good medicine.

2 이 잡지를 읽는 것이 어떻게 다이어트를 해야 할지 가르쳐 줄 것이다. (magazine)

→ ____________________ will teach you how to diet.

3 학생들의 주된 불만은 영문법을 공부하는 것이 지루하다는 것이다. (study, English grammar, boring)

→ A principal complaint of students is that ____________________.

4 내게 있어 가장 어려운 일은 아침에 일찍 일어나는 일이다. (get up early)

→ The most difficult thing for me is ____________________.

Answers P.18

▶ 동명사를 목적어로 취하는 동사

동사+V-ing	예문
enjoy	The little girl enjoys **riding** a horse.
finish	She finished **drawing** a portrait of her mother.
quit	My father quit **smoking** last month.
avoid	He avoided **meeting** his friends.
give up	Tony gave up **taking** swimming lessons.
put off	They put off ① ___________(deliver) my air conditioner.
(=postpone)	= They postponed ② ___________(deliver) my air conditioner.
consider	She is considering ③ ___________(change) her job.
mind	Do you mind ④ ___________(hold) this door for me?

▶ 동명사와 to부정사를 목적어로 취하는 동사

동사	동사+V-ing	동사+to V
stop	Kevin stopped **talking** when he entered the library. (말하는 것을 멈추었다)	Kevin stopped **to ask** a question to the librarian. (질문하기 위해서 멈추었다) *cf)* 부사적 쓰임
try	I tried **taking** vitamin C for my cold. (시험 삼아 비타민 C를 먹어보았다)	I tried **to solve** the puzzle. (퍼즐을 풀려고 애썼다)
forget	I forgot **printing** out the report for the class. (출력했다는 것을 잊어버렸다)	Don't forget **to print** out the report! (출력하는 것을 잊어버리지 마라)
remember	My dad didn't remember **buying** me a watch last year. (산 것을 기억하지 못했다)	Remember **to buy** me a present during your visit to Europe! (살 것을 기억해라)

■ 동명사를 사용한 구문

(1) It is no use -ing (~해봐야 소용없다) = It is useless to V
eg) It is no use complaining to the teacher. (= It is useless to complain to the teacher.)

(2) There is no -ing (~하는 것은 불가능하다) = It is impossible to V
eg) There is no getting these CDs for free. (= It is impossible to get these CDs for free.)

(3) cannot help -ing (~하지 않을 수 없다) = cannot but + 동사원형
eg) We couldn't help paying the extra charge. (= We couldn't but pay the extra charge.)

(4) have trouble -ing (~하는 데 어려움이 있다)
eg) I sometimes have trouble going to sleep.

(5) On -ing (~하자마자)
eg) On seeing me, she held my hands.

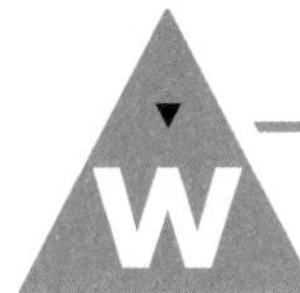

WRAP-UP TEST

Answers P.18

1 빈칸에 들어갈 말이 바르게 짝지어진 것을 고르시오.

> · _________ fireworks is very exciting.
> · The house started _________ suddenly.

ⓐ Seeing - burning
ⓑ To seeing - burning
ⓒ See - to burn
ⓓ To see - burn

2 문장을 읽고, 어법상 어색한 곳을 찾아 바르게 고치시오.

> Mary is afraid of sleep alone in her big house.

3 밑줄 친 부분의 쓰임이 다른 것을 고르시오.

ⓐ We are drawing our portraits.
ⓑ Matt's hobby is playing ice hockey.
ⓒ My favorite activity is making cookies.
ⓓ His dream is becoming a famous basketball player like Michael Jordan.

4 어법상 어색한 문장을 고르시오.

ⓐ The teacher delayed going on a picnic.
ⓑ Kate always misses traveling Eastern Europe.
ⓒ Jim quit eating snacks at night to lose weight.
ⓓ They were lost. They stopped to drive to ask for directions.

5 짝지어진 문장이 의미가 같은 것을 고르시오.

ⓐ He stopped borrowing books from the library.
= He stopped to borrow books from the library.
ⓑ She continued dancing to Christmas carols.
= She continued to dance to Christmas carols.
ⓒ Tom didn't remember to turn off the light.
= Tom didn't remember turning off the light.
ⓓ Jim tried to catch fish with a bamboo stick.
= Jim tried catching fish with a bamboo stick.

6 밑줄 친 부분이 바르게 쓰인 것을 고르시오.

ⓐ Mike failed passing the entrance exam.
ⓑ She didn't mean scaring you.
ⓒ I'm interested in arrange flowers.
ⓓ Dad prevents my brother from going outside.

7 [보기]에서 단어를 골라 어법에 맞게 바꿔 쓰시오.

> go　　send　　slide　　discover

(1) The road was very slippery. My friend and I kept _________ on the road.
(2) Sorry, I don't feel like _________ to the cinema with you.
(3) She tried _________ new facts about extinct animals, and she couldn't.
(4) I received the same message from him twice. Probably, he forgot _________ me the message.

8 우리말과 같은 뜻이 되도록 주어진 말을 이용하여 문장을 완성하시오.

나는 새 해리 포터 책을 읽는 것을 기대하고 있다.
(look forward to)

= I am _______________________
the new Harry Potter book.

[9-10] 글을 읽고, 물음에 답하시오.

> (A) 내가 우리 휴가 계획을 바꿔도 괜찮겠니? I would like to visit Mt. St. Helens in Washington. It erupted in 1980. I hope ___(B)___ the amazing changes in the landscape since then. It seems ___(C)___ many people.

9 (A)를 영작하시오.

= Do you mind _________ _________ our vacation plan?

10 (B), (C)에 들어갈 말이 바르게 연결된 것을 고르시오.

ⓐ to see - to attract ⓑ see - to attract
ⓒ to see - attract ⓓ see - attract

분사와 수동태

1 분사의 종류 및 의미
2 분사의 쓰임
3 수동태의 개념과 형태
4 여러 가지 수동태

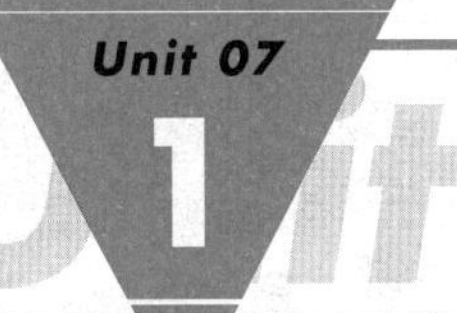

분사의 종류 및 의미

동사	분사	명사를 꾸며주는 형용사 역할
smile (웃다)	smile+ing: 현재분사 (웃고 있는)	The smiling girl is my niece. (능동)
injure (상처를 입히다)	injure+ed: 과거분사 (상처를 입은)	He treated the injured workers. (수동)

1 현재분사: 능동 (~하고 있는, ~하는)

Look at the dancing girl.
The crying woman is Susan.
I saw a frightening movie last night.

> 1
> 현재분사(V-ing)
> : 능동, 진행의 의미

2 과거분사: 수동 (~하게 된)

Wind is blowing from the opened windows.
The broken vase is my mother's.

> 2
> 과거분사(V-ed)
> : 수동, 완료의 의미
> [수동태 Unit7, 3] 참조

3 감정을 나타내는 분사

(1) 주어가 사물일 때 (~한 기분이 들게 하는)

The opera was boring. (→ the boring opera)
(X) The opera was bored.
The news was surprising. (→ the surprising news)
The result was disappointing.
The movie was exciting.

(2) 주어가 사람일 때 (~한 기분이 드는)

The boy was surprised. (→ the surprised boy)
The girl was shocked. (→ the shocked girl)
I was embarrassed by my mistakes.
He is interested in making web pages.

■ 동명사(①/②)와 현재분사

① Look at the sleeping bag. (The bag for sleeping) (동명사)
Look at the sleeping cat. (The cat is sleeping.) (현재분사)
② Her hobby is making cards. (Her hobby = making cards) (동명사)
She is making cards now. (She → making) (현재분사)

> 3
> 감정을 나타내는 분사들
> • boring - bored
> • exciting - excited
> • shocking - shocked
> • surprising - surprised
> • interesting - interested
> • disappointing - disappointed
> ※ [MUST-KNOW] 참조

cf) 주어가 사람일 때
• Mary is bored. (Mary가 지루해한다. - 지루함을 느끼는 Mary)
• Mary is boring. (Mary는 지루하다. - 사람을 지루하게 만드는 Mary)

• 동명사
① 명사 앞: 용도 (~하는 데 이용되는)
② 주어, 목적어, 보어 역할

• 현재분사: 진행 (~하고 있는)

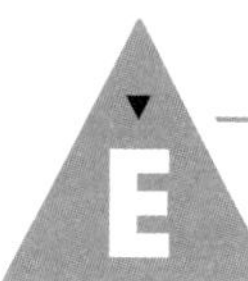

EXERCISE

Answers P.18

A

[ ] 안에서 알맞은 말을 고르시오.

1 Those five hours of classes were really [tiring, tired].

2 Peter doesn't eat [boiling, boiled] silk worms because they smell bad.

3 Riding a roller coaster is [thrilling, thrilled] and [exciting, excited].

4 The [laughing, laughed] girl is my cousin. She is very nice.

5 Jinny was [satisfying, satisfied] with the result of the test.

6 There was a [breaking, broken] car in front of his house.

7 We watched the ants [carrying, are carried] bread crumbs into their holes.

B

밑줄 친 부분을 참고하여 문장을 완성하시오.

1 Tom went to the swimming pool an hour ago. He is ____________ now.

2 He is opening the door. The door is ____________ now.

3 She went to a dance party. She is ____________ now.

4 The story interests me a lot. I learned a lot from this ____________ story.

5 She was excited after she saw the movie. It was an ____________ movie.

6 Who broke this window? Mom will be very angry to see this ____________ window.

C

밑줄 친 -ing를 쓰임에 따라 동명사 "G", 현재분사 "P"로 구분하시오.

1 I saw a shocking program on air pollution. ____________

2 It was a very boring detective story. ____________

3 Did she stop doing the project? ____________

4 My favorite hobby is going fishing. ____________

5 I read a detective story last night. It was really interesting. ____________

6 He insisted on playing outside instead of studying. ____________

분사의 쓰임

현재분사 The shining stars are beautiful.

현재분사구 The stars shining in the sky are beautiful.

과거분사 This is the given information.

과거분사구 This is the information given last week.

1 분사가 단독으로 명사를 꾸밀 때: 명사 앞

Look at the crying girl.
The fixed bike is mine.
The lost dog is mine.

> 1
> 분사가 단독으로 명사를 꾸밀 경우
> : 분사+명사

2 분사에 수식어구가 붙을 경우: 명사 뒤

Look at the girl crying in the playground.
The bike fixed by Fred is mine.
The dog lost in the park is mine.

> 2
> 분사에 추가적인 어구가 붙어서 명사를 꾸밀 경우:
> 명사+분사

3 주어를 설명할 때: 동사 뒤

His car is amazing.
The rumor was shocking.
The school trip was exciting.

> 3
> **주어를 보충 설명**
> • shocking rumor (충격적인 소문)
> • exciting school trip (신 나는 수학여행)
> • bored Susan (지루한 Susan)
> • tired Fred (피곤한 Fred)

4 목적어를 설명할 때: 목적어 뒤

I saw a boy. He was dancing.
→ I saw a boy dancing.
Sue heard her name. Her name was called.
→ Sue heard her name called.

> 4
> **목적어를 보충 설명**
> • 능동
> • 수동

■ **분사구문** (Unit 12 부사절 참조)

Since I felt dizzy, I lay down on the sofa.
→ Feeling dizzy, I lay down on the sofa.

As he was disappointed, he frowned.
→ (Being) Disappointed, he frowned.

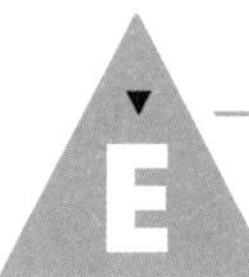

EXERCISE

Answers P.19

A

[ ] 안에서 알맞은 말을 고르시오.

1 Don't go close to the [bark, barking] dog!

2 The sweater [folding, folded] nicely is my younger sister's.

3 I saw the thief [running, ran] down the road.

4 The woman [sitting, sat] on the bench is my teacher. Let's go and say hello.

5 The bicycle [stole, stolen] in front of the school was my best friend's.

6 My friend's explanation was very [confusing, confused] to me.

7 Fred felt someone [pulling, are pulling] his shirt.

B

주어진 말을 이용하여 문장을 완성하시오.

1 The car ______________(park) next to that red one is hers.

2 The audience was ______________(amuse) by the tricks of the cute puppies.

3 Let's ask Jimmy ______________(sit) behind you.

4 Jake doesn't look good these days. He looks ______________(worry) about something.

5 You should report your ______________(lose) baggage to the police right away.

6 I saw Tom ______________(fix) his car in the driveway.

C

밑줄 친 부분을 바르게 고쳐 쓰시오.

1 A stone rolling gathers no moss. ______________

2 We were very exciting at the Halloween party. ______________

3 Dana was boring and wanted to go home early. ______________

4 The found jacket in the library is Jerry's. ______________

5 My little brother is frightening of the dark. ______________

6 The police found the diamond ring taking in the robbery. ______________

Unit 07

3 수동태의 개념과 형태

능동
(행위자 중심)

The reporter wrote the article.
주어 동사 목적어

① The article
② The article was written
③ The article was written by the reporter.

수동
(동작을 당한 사람이나 사물 중심)

be+p.p. by+행위자

능동태
행동을 한 행위자에 초점을 맞춤

수동태
주어가 어떠한 행위를 당한 경우나 발생된 사건(결과)에 초점

1 문장 종류에 따른 수동태

(1) 긍정문

The security guard closes the gate at 9 pm.
→ The gate is closed by the security guard at 9 pm.

My dog bit a little child last night.
→ A little child was bitten by my dog last night.

They will send this parcel tomorrow.
→ This parcel will be sent (by them) tomorrow.

(2) 부정문

The students do not elect the class president.
→ The class president is not elected by the students.

Anthony did not make the calendar.
→ The calendar was not made by Anthony.

(3) 의문문

Did he build the house in 2013?
→ He built the house in 2013.
→ The house was built by him in 2013.
→ Was the house built by him in 2013?
cf) When was the house built by him?

1
수동태 만드는 법
① 원래 문장의 목적어를 → 주어로
② 동사를 → be동사+p.p.
③ 주어를 → by+목적격

※ 조동사(can, will 등) 문장의 수동태
: 조동사 + be+p.p.
We can cancel the meeting.
→ The meeting can be canceled (by us).

(3) 의문문의 수동태 만들기
① 평서문으로
② 수동태로
③ 의문문으로
→ 의문사가 있는 의문문으로 만들기

2 〈by+행위자〉를 쓰지 않는 경우

French and English are spoken (by Canadians) in Canada.
His flight was canceled because of the storm.
My car was stolen last night.

2
〈by+행위자〉를 쓰지 않는 경우
• 행위자가 일반적인 사람인 경우
• 행위자를 나타내지 않아도 분명한 경우
• 행위자를 알 수 없거나 중요하지 않을 때

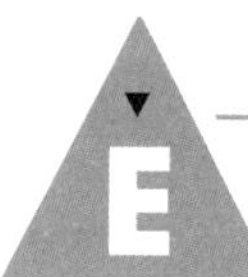

EXERCISE

Answers P.19

A

[ ] 안에서 알맞은 말을 고르시오.

1 The guests [served, were served] many kinds of Chinese dishes at the party.

2 My room [cleaned, was cleaned] by my sister yesterday.

3 The problem [was solving, was solved] by Jack.

4 He [orders, is ordered] a tuna sandwich for his son once a week.

5 Was the exam [taking, taken] by John this afternoon?

6 Your scores will [report, be reported] at the end of the class.

7 The roof [was damaging, was damaged] again because of the hurricane.

B

밑줄 친 부분을 바르게 고쳐 쓰시오.

1 Many people <u>shocked</u> by that news. ______________

2 Pizza will <u>delivered</u> to you at 7. ______________

3 The cell phone <u>is repaired</u> at the service center yesterday. ______________

4 The homework should <u>be did</u> by Bob, not his mother. ______________

5 His hair <u>cut</u> by the barber last night. ______________

6 Children <u>are bring</u> by their parents on their first day of school. ______________

C

주어진 문장을 수동태 문장으로 바꿔 쓰시오.

1 Julie paints her fingernails every weekend.
→ Julie's fingernails ______________ by her every weekend.

2 A shoplifter stole a box of chocolate from the store.
→ A box of chocolate ______________ from the store by a shoplifter.

3 Our cook will develop a new menu soon.
→ A new menu ______________ by our cook soon.

4 The committee will hold a meeting tomorrow.
→ A meeting ______________ by the committee tomorrow.

5 Did the principal present the award to the student?
→ ______________ the award ______________ to the student by the principal?

여러 가지 수동태

목적어가 두 개일 때 James teaches ① us ② physics.

①을 주어로 → We are taught physics by James.
②를 주어로 → Physics is taught to us by James.

1 목적어가 두 개일 때

(1) 사람, 사물 목적어 모두 주어로 쓰는 경우

Jack sends her roses every week.
→ She is sent roses by Jack every week.
→ Roses are sent to her by Jack every week.

Robert told me an interesting story.
→ I was told an interesting story by Robert.
→ An interesting story was told to me by Robert.

(2) 사물 목적어를 주로 주어로 쓰는 경우

He wrote me a letter.
→ A letter was written to me by him.
Tom bought her a book.
→ A book was bought for her by Tom.

1
(1) 대부분의 4문형 동사(give, send, show, teach, tell 등): 사물 목적어가 주어가 될 경우, 사람 목적어 앞에 to를 씀
(2) make, buy, get, cook 등 일부 4문형 동사: 사람 목적어 앞에 for를 씀

※ 사람 목적어 앞에 of를 쓰는 동사: ask, inquire
eg) Ann asked ① him ② a question.
① → He was asked a question by Ann.
② → A question was asked of him by Ann.

2 by 이외의 전치사를 사용하는 경우

She was surprised at the test result.
I was disappointed with the test score.
We are interested in learning history.
The cake is covered with white chocolate.
The desk is made of pine wood.
The wine is made from French grapes.

2
- be satisfied with (~에 만족하다)
- be surprised at (~에 놀라다)
- be amazed at (~에 놀라다)
- be pleased with (~에 기뻐하다)
- be scared of (~을 두려워하다)
- be worried about (~에 대해 걱정하다)
- be disappointed with (~에 실망하다)
- be known to (~에게 알려져 있다)
- be interested in (~에 흥미가 있다)
- be covered with (~로 덮여있다)
- be filled with (~로 가득 차다)
- be made of / be made from (~로 만들어져 있다)

※ be made of (재료의 성질이 유지될 때)
be made from (재료의 성질이 변할 때)

3 수동태가 불가능한 동사

Chris has a wonderful garden.
(X) A wonderful garden is had by Chris.
My boyfriend resembles Brad Pitt.
(X) Brad Pitt is resembled by my boyfriend.

3
have(가지고 있다), lack, resemble, belong 등의 상태 동사는 수동태 불가

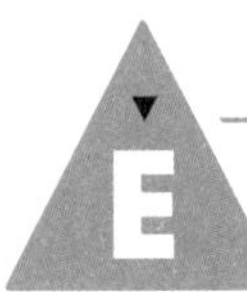

EXERCISE

Answers P.19

A

[ ] 안에서 알맞은 말을 고르시오.

1 The third little pig had a house made [of, from] bricks.

2 Yogurt is made [on, from] milk.

3 We were surprised [to, at] his sudden appearance.

4 The trees over the hill are covered [on, with] snow.

5 She was amazed [at, for] his ability to study for a long time.

6 I was disappointed [with, to] their poor service.

B

밑줄 친 부분을 바르게 고쳐 쓰시오.

1 The red cell phone is belonged to me. ______________

2 A cake was made to the guest by the baker. ______________

3 This pudding can be made for flour and eggs. ______________

4 A new backpack will be bought to me. ______________

5 She is interested at biology, not math. ______________

6 Pictures of the suspects shown to me by the police. ______________

C

주어진 문장을 수동태 문장으로 바꿔 쓰시오.

1 Kim told me a strange story about Susie.

→ I ______________________________ about Susie by Kim.

2 Brian teaches us English.

→ English ______________________________ by Brian.

3 Ted made me a paper crane.

→ A paper crane ______________________________ by Ted.

4 My mom cooked us fried rice.

→ Fried rice ______________________________ by my mom.

5 He gave his son a strawberry cake.

→ A strawberry cake ______________________________ by him.

REVIEW TEST

A [ ] 안에서 알맞은 말을 고르시오.

1 Lisa is reading a [fascinating, fascinated] novel.

2 The book was [reading, read] by millions of people.

3 The witch has a [breaking, broken] mirror.

4 His notebook was filled [with, at] small drawings, not lecture notes.

5 The school festival [canceled, was canceled] because of the rain.

6 Our principal's speech yesterday morning was [moving, moved].

7 An apple tree will [plant, be planted] by John.

8 Students [giving, given] afternoon detentions behave better the next day.

* detention: (벌로서) 방과 후 학교에 남게 함

B 빈칸에 들어갈 알맞은 말을 고르시오.

1 David's talk was ____________ and interesting.

ⓐ entertain ⓑ entertaining ⓒ entertained ⓓ being entertained

2 They didn't prepare any food. I was disappointed ____________ that.

ⓐ from ⓑ with ⓒ of ⓓ in

3 The boys are ____________ in front of the girls.

ⓐ standing ⓑ stood ⓒ standed ⓓ be stood

4 The computer ____________ by Max.

ⓐ not fixed ⓑ not was fixed ⓒ fixed ⓓ was not fixed

5 The novel ____________ in French was really difficult for me to read.

ⓐ wrote ⓑ written ⓒ writing ⓓ written being

6 Too many questions were asked ____________ at the meeting.

ⓐ on me ⓑ for me ⓒ of me ⓓ at me

7 I have a book about the 200 most ____________ hotels in the world.

ⓐ charm ⓑ charming ⓒ charmed ⓓ charms

Answers P.19

C 주어진 말을 이용하여 문장을 완성하시오.

1 The Egyptian pyramids were ____________(make) of stone.

2 Are you ____________(satisfy) with the test result?

3 The movie I saw yesterday was really ____________(touch).

4 He finished running 4 kilometers, but he didn't look ____________(exhaust) at all.

5 The research will ____________(present) by Sally at the conference tomorrow.

6 Look! Fred is shaking his leg again! It is very ____________(annoy).

D 밑줄 친 부분을 바르게 고쳐, 문장을 다시 쓰시오.

1 He was very exciting to see his friend in Korea.

→ ____________________

2 She was not satisfied at my explanation for being late.

→ ____________________

3 Mike is resembled his father.

→ ____________________

4 The patient will schedule for surgery in the morning by the doctor.

→ ____________________

5 We were all surprising and horrified when we saw the horror movie.

→ ____________________

6 Here is a list of the top ten most embarrassed fashion trends.

→ ____________________

7 The news was shocking. We were interested at the news.

→ ____________________

F FURTHER STUDY

Answers P.20

A 글을 읽고, 밑줄 친 부분을 바르게 고쳐 쓰시오.

You might hear people (1) said that it will bring bad luck if you open an umbrella indoors. I am (2) worrying whenever I open my umbrella in the house by mistake. Does it really cause bad luck? Or is it just a meaningless superstition? Actually, it is one of the most common superstitions and, like many others, it has its background story. When umbrellas were first (3) inventing, they were very huge. So, when a huge umbrella was (4) opening indoors, it might hurt family members or break something in the house. Now it is understandable why people had to create that superstition.

* superstition 미신 * meaningless 의미 없는

(1) ______________________

(2) ______________________

(3) ______________________

(4) ______________________

B 표를 보고, 수동태 또는 능동태 문장을 완성하시오. (수동태는 행위자도 쓸 것)

Name	Job	Masterpiece	Year
Alexander Graham Bell	Inventor	Telephone	1876
John Logie	Inventor	Television	1926
The Beatles	English Rock Band	*Yesterday*	1960s
Dan Brown	Writer	*Da Vinci Code*	2003
Chris Columbus	Director	*Harry Potter and the Sorcerer's Stone*	2001

1 The telephone ______________________(invent) in 1876.

2 *The Da Vinci Code* ______________________(write) in 2003.

3 *Yesterday* ______________________(sing) in the 1960s.

4 John Logie ______________________(invent) in 1926.

5 *Harry Potter and the Sorcerer's Stone* ______________________(direct) in 2001.

Answers P.21

▶ 감정을 나타내는 현재분사 / 과거분사

현재분사 (-ing)	과거분사 (-ed)	예문
amazing (놀라운)	amazed (놀란)	Did Tom win? It's ① ________!
annoying (짜증나게 하는)	annoyed (짜증난)	I was ② ________ because of flies.
boring (지루하게 하는)	bored (지루한)	The lecture was very ③ ________.
confusing (혼란시키는)	confused (혼란스러운)	I can't solve this ④ ________ problem.
disappointing (실망시키는)	disappointed (실망스러운)	He is ⑤ ________ with himself.
embarrassing (당황하게 하는)	embarrassed (당황한)	What an ⑥ ________ event!
exciting (신 나게 하는)	excited (신이 난)	The ⑦ ________ people clapped loudly.
frightening (겁나게 하는)	frightened (겁이 난)	He was ⑧ ________ of the dark.
interesting (흥미를 주는)	interested (흥미 있는)	She told me an ⑨ ________ story.
moving (감동을 주는)	moved (감동한)	It was a ⑩ ________ speech.
satisfying (만족스럽게 하는)	satisfied (만족한)	She is ⑪ ________ with her new record.
shocking (충격을 주는)	shocked (충격을 받은)	It was a ⑫ ________ music video.
surprising (놀라게 하는)	surprised (놀란)	They were ⑬ ________ at the news.
tiring (지치게 하는)	tired (지친)	This work is very ⑭ ________.
worrying (걱정하게 만드는)	worried (걱정하는)	Jake is ⑮ ________ about his health.

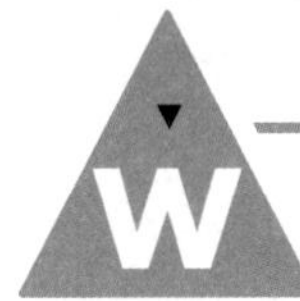

WRAP-UP TEST

Answers P.21

1 밑줄 친 ⓐ, ⓑ를 어법에 맞게 바꿔 쓰시오.

· The boy ⓐ sit on the bench is reading a book.

· ⓑ Break glass can be very dangerous.

ⓐ: ⓑ:

2 주어진 문장을 수동태 문장으로 바꿔 쓰시오.

Many young boys admire the beautiful actress.

→The beautiful actress ____________________

____________________________________.

3 두 문장의 뜻이 통하도록 분사를 이용하여 문장을 완성하시오.

The puppy is very cute. The puppy is held by the girl.

= The puppy ________________________ is very cute.

4 밑줄 친 부분의 쓰임이 다른 하나를 고르시오.

ⓐ A running car suddenly stopped.

ⓑ Collecting stamps is her hobby.

ⓒ His boring class makes students yawn.

ⓓ My teacher always gives us puzzling quizzes.

5 어법상 어색한 문장을 고르시오.

ⓐ My brother is disappointed with his birthday present.

ⓑ This oak tree was planted by my grandfather.

ⓒ These paintings are resembled with Monet's.

ⓓ The thieves were arrested.

6 수동태의 형태가 잘못된 것을 고르시오.

ⓐ The fruit basket was put on the table.

ⓑ Students are excited about the field trip.

ⓒ The problem has been solved by a clever student.

ⓓ A pencil is made by cedar wood and carbon.

7 대화를 읽고, 빈칸에 들어갈 말이 바르게 짝지어진 것을 고르시오.

A How was the movie? Was it ____________?

B Not at all. I was really ____________.

ⓐ boring - interesting

ⓑ bored - interested

ⓒ bored - interesting

ⓓ boring - interested

8 주어진 말을 이용하여 문장을 완성하시오.

(1) The movie about Christ was really ____________. (touch)

(2) Her eyes were ____________ with tears. (fill)

[9-10] 글을 읽고 물음에 답하시오.

> The statue of Cupid is really (A) interesting. The popular statue (B) visits by many people. Cupid (C) is known as the god of love. My brother visited there last year. He (D) pretended to shoot an arrow like Cupid. He took many photos of it. He still keeps (E) 그 조각상과 같이 찍은 사진들 at that time. They make him smile every time he sees them.

9 (A), (B), (C), (D) 중 어법상 어색한 것을 고르시오.

10 (E)를 바르게 영작한 것을 고르시오.

ⓐ the photos taking with the statue

ⓑ taking the photos with the statue

ⓒ taken the photos with the statue

ⓓ the photos taken with the statue

명사와 관사

1 명사(I)
2 명사(II)
3 관사

명사 (I)

셀 수 있는 명사	Mark put a vase on the table. Sally bought vases for her friends.
셀 수 없는 명사	The cup on the table is full of water. Karen moved to London.

명사
사람, 사물, 장소 등의 이름

1 명사의 종류

(1) 셀 수 있는 명사

There is a blackboard in the classroom.
There are a lot of roses in the garden.

My family goes hiking every Sunday.
They go skiing with their families often.

(2) 셀 수 없는 명사

Max likes Susan very much.
Paul lives in London, England.

Do you take sugar in your coffee?
Water is essential for us to live.

Love is hugging. Friendship is helping each other.

1
(1) 셀 수 있는 명사
- 사물, 장소: blackboard, cup, boy, school 등
- 집합체: family, class, police 등

(2) 셀 수 없는 명사
- 고유한 이름: London, England, Max, Susie 등
- 물질, 사물: water, oil, sugar, butter, air, money, time 등
- 보이지 않는 추상적 개념: happiness, love, friendship, luck 등

2 셀 수 있는 명사의 단수/복수

(1) 단수형: a/an+명사

I found a scrapbook in the attic.
I bought an orange at the supermarket.

(2) 복수형

[규칙 변화]

There are thirty-five chairs in my classroom.
Put the potatoes in these boxes.
I got a lot of toys and candies for my birthday.

[불규칙 변화]

Two young men and five children are watching TV.
My baby sister has two teeth and two feet.
I went fishing with my dad, and we caught six fish.
They saw two deer in the forest.

2
(1) 단수
- a+자음 *eg)* a cap, a basket
- an+모음[a, e, i, o, u]발음으로 시작하는 명사
  eg) an apple, an orange

(2) 복수
[규칙 변화] 명사+-(e)s
※ [MUST-KNOW] 참조

cf) 규칙 변화 예외
- piano → pianos / zoo → zoos
  safe → safes / roof → roofs 등
- 한 쌍으로 된 명사: 복수
  glasses, pants, scissors 등
  eg) Where are my glasses?
- -s로 끝나는 학과명, news 등: 단수
  economics, mathematics 등
  eg) Economics is not an easy subject.

[불규칙 변화]
child → children / foot → feet
fish → fish / deer → deer 등

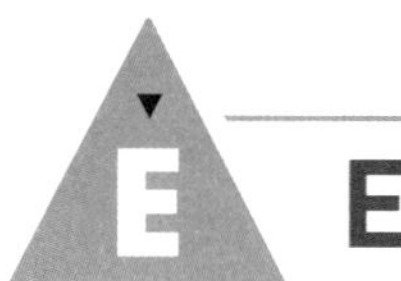

EXERCISE

Answers P.21

A

[ ] 안에서 알맞은 말을 고르시오.

1 Vicky bought a lot of [tomato, tomatoes] on her way home.

2 His family lives in [a Vancouver, Vancouver], Canada.

3 I don't put [a salt, salt] in my soup.

4 We have two [pianos, pianoes] in our house.

5 The [memories, memorys] of true friendship will last forever.

6 I have 28 [toothes, teeth] in my mouth.

7 The socks in the drawer [is, are] my sister's.

B

주어진 말을 이용하여 문장을 완성하시오.

1 My ____________(glass) need to be fixed.

2 The king had six ____________(wife) in his palace.

3 Those ____________(box) are for the Christmas presents.

4 Greg bought me two ____________(puppy) on my birthday.

5 The ____________(boy) enjoy learning English on the Internet.

6 We saw three ____________(deer) on the mountain last weekend.

7 Jack has ten ____________(goose) and five ____________(ox) on his farm.

8 Please put the socks on the baby's ____________(foot).

C

밑줄 친 부분을 바르게 고쳐 쓰시오. 틀리지 않았다면 O표 하시오.

1 We have lots of snows in winter. ____________

2 Mathematic is really fun to study. ____________

3 There are two car in the garage. ____________

4 There are a lot of dish in the sink. ____________

5 Do you have some times to talk with me? ____________

6 There were several pictures on the wall. ____________

7 In elementary school, my teachers were all woman. ____________

명사 (Ⅱ)

셀 수 없는 명사 I drink milk every day.

I drink three cartons of milk every day.

셀 수 없는 명사
물질을 담을 수 있는 용기나 세는 단위를 사용하여 센다.

1 셀 수 없는 명사를 세는 단위

Robin has ordered a cup of coffee.
She offered me two cups of tea.

Greg wanted a spoonful/spoon of sugar.
Put three spoonfuls/spoons of olive oil into the pot.

I want to eat a slice of pizza.
My brother eats five slices of cheese every day.

1
셀 수 없는 물질명사는 a cup of, a spoonful/spoon of, a piece of와 같은 단위 표현과 함께 써서 수량을 표시한다.

- a glass of water (한 잔의 물)
  two glasses of water
- a pound of meat (1파운드 고기)
  two pounds of meat
- a loaf of bread (빵 한 덩어리)
  two loaves of bread

※ [MUST-KNOW] 참조

2 some, any, much, a lot of

Sue gave some chalk to her teacher.
There isn't any salt in the shaker.
We don't have much rain during winter.
Jack drinks a lot of grape juice every day.

cf) We have many sandwiches to share.
There are a lot of students in the playground.

2
셀 수 없는 물질명사의 양을 나타낼 때는 some/any(약간), much = a lot of/lots of (많은)를 사용한다.

cf) 셀 수 있는 명사의 막연한 수를 나타낼 때에도 some/any, many = a lot of/lots of가 쓰인다.

3 명사의 격

(1) 주격과 목적격

The teacher has a lot of cookies for us.
I bought some flowers from a little girl.

(2) 소유격(~의)

My father's car is black.
Pete's hair is very short and yellow.
Where is the boys' room?

The buttons of my jacket are too big.
I can't remember the title of the book.

3
(1) 주격 (~은/는/이/가)
목적격 (~을/를)

(2) 소유격
- 명사+'s: 생물인 경우
  (s로 끝나는 명사는 ' 만 붙임)
- of+명사: 무생물인 경우
  (단, 시간, 거리, 가격, 무게를 나타낼 때는 무생물에 's를 붙인다. *eg)* today's weather / one dollar's worth)

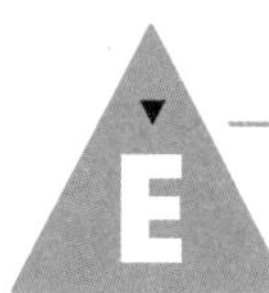

EXERCISE

Answers P.22

A

[　] 안에서 알맞은 말을 고르시오.

1 My father usually drinks some [wine, wines] with his meal.

2 Fred asked me to buy three loaves of [bread, breads].

3 Could you put some [sugar, sugars] in my coffee?

4 Timmy gave me [much, many] candies for the kids.

5 They don't have [much, many] homework to do today.

6 I need a [sheet, loaf] of paper to write on.

7 We ordered three [piece, pieces] of cake at the restaurant.

8 Those books aren't mine. They are [of Karen, Karen's].

B

[보기]에서 알맞은 말을 골라 주어진 조건을 참고하여 문장을 완성하시오.

Word Bank	a bottle of	a carton of	a piece of	a cup of	a glass of

1 Can I have ________________ Coke, please? (콜라 1잔)

2 He wants to buy ________________ wine. (포도주 3병)

3 My teacher made me bring ________________ chalk. (분필 1개)

4 I need ________________ flour to make cookies. (밀가루 4컵)

5 She buys ________________ milk at the supermarket every morning. (우유 3팩)

C

밑줄 친 부분을 바르게 고쳐 쓰시오. 틀리지 않았다면 O표 하시오.

1 Sandy didn't borrow <u>many</u> money from me. ________________

2 My uncle bought ten pounds of <u>beefs</u> for us. ________________

3 I will show you my <u>sisters's</u> rooms. ________________

4 <u>Today's</u> weather is sunny and warm. ________________

5 My teacher told us two <u>story</u> in the class. ________________

6 Harry gave a <u>pairs</u> of socks to Cathy. ________________

7 We don't have <u>any</u> time to do it. ________________

관사

명사와 관사

a/an+셀 수 있는 명사

There is a basket on the table.

There are many oranges in the basket.

the+단수/복수 명사

I ate one of the oranges.

관사를 쓰지 않는 경우

My brother goes to bed around 11 o'clock.

1 부정관사 a/an

He has a dictionary and two books in his backpack.
Can I borrow a pen?
The bus goes 80 km an hour.
A dog is a faithful animal.

> 1
> a/an의 쓰임
> ① 하나의, 한 개의 = one
> ② 무리 중에서 (아무거나) 하나
> ③ ~마다, ~당 = per
> ④ 종족 전체를 대표하는 대표명사
> (= Dogs are faithful animals.)

2 정관사 the

(1) I bought a book and a CD for her.
The book was $10, and the CD was $12.
I saw a young boy at McDonald's.
The boy was eating a hamburger.

(2) Would you close the door, please?
Put those files on the table.

(3) Look at the cat over there!
Read the sentences on page 56.

(4) The sun was shining brightly in the sky.
Listen! Martin is playing the piano.
He is the tallest student in our school.
Today is the second day of the school trip.

> 2
> the의 쓰임
> (1) 앞에서 말한 것을 다시 말할 때
> (2) 서로 알고 있는 것을 말할 때
> (3) 수식어의 꾸밈을 받아 의미가 한정될 때
> (4) 기타
> • 하나밖에 없는 것
> *eg)* the sun, the earth, the moon, the sky
> • 악기 이름 앞
> *eg)* play the violin (piano)
> • 형용사 최상급 앞 (Unit 10 참조)
> • 서수 앞

3 관사를 쓰지 않는 경우

Let's play volleyball together.
Can I talk about this after lunch?
I usually go to school by bus.
My family goes to church on Sundays.
cf) We went to the church to meet our friends.

> 3
> 관사를 쓰지 않는 경우
> ① 운동경기 이름 앞: play golf
> ② 식사 이름 앞
> ③ by+교통수단
> : by train, by taxi, by plane
> (take a taxi 등에는 a를 쓴다.)
> ④ go to+school (bed / church)
> *cf)* go to church: 예배 보러 가다
> go to the church: 교회 건물에 (친구 만나러) 가다

EXERCISE

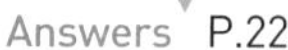

Answers P.22

A

[ ] 안에서 알맞은 말을 고르시오.

1 There is a comic book on his desk. [A, An, The] comic book is Jane's.

2 Jay had [a, an, the] ice cream cone for dessert.

3 I have [a, an, the] idea for the potluck party.

4 My aunt works at the White House, so she often sees [a, an, the] President.

5 Kerry lent me [a, an, the] interesting book to read.

6 Jerry took [a, an, the] taxi not to be late for the test at school.

7 Please show me [a, an, the] book on the top shelf.

B

a, an, the, ø 중에서 알맞은 것을 골라 문장을 완성하시오.

1 What time do you usually go to ____________ bed?

2 We have ____________ lunch at 12:30.

3 Can you bring me ____________ dictionary on my desk?

4 She is playing ____________ guitar in the living room now.

5 I try to review English vocabulary at least twice ____________ week.

6 Is there ____________ empty locker for the new student?

C

밑줄 친 관사와 쓰임이 같은 것을 [보기]에서 고르시오.

Example

(a) I saw a beautiful dress. I'd like to buy the dress.
(b) Do you know the man standing next to Kate?
(c) A man is walking on the street with a dog.
(d) He can make fifteen model planes a day.

1 He raises a monkey in his house. ____________

2 The motorboat can go 120 kilometers an hour. ____________

3 He has a ring in his hand. The ring is made of gold. ____________

4 The box on the shelf was empty. ____________

REVIEW TEST

A

[ ] 안에서 알맞은 말을 고르시오.

1 Can you pass me [a, the] scissors on the desk?

2 There were many [child, children] in this kindergarten last year.

3 I don't have [much, many] money to buy those game CDs.

4 I believe health is [the, ø] most important factor for happiness in life.

5 [An, The] Earth is the third planet from the Sun in our solar system.

6 Ellie enjoys playing [ø, the] badminton in the school yard.

7 Politics [is, are] not an interesting subject to me.

8 [Jacobs, Jacob's] trousers are too tight for him.

B

빈칸에 들어갈 알맞은 말을 고르시오.

1 How about ____________ cake for dessert?

ⓐ a carton of ⓑ many ⓒ a glass of ⓓ a piece of

2 There is ____________ umbrella in the big basket.

ⓐ a ⓑ some ⓒ an ⓓ two

3 I saw two ____________ run across the kitchen counter.

ⓐ mouse ⓑ mice ⓒ mouses ⓓ mices

4 Economics ____________ his major when he was a college student.

ⓐ was ⓑ were ⓒ is ⓓ are

5 What time do you usually go to ____________?

ⓐ the work ⓑ works ⓒ a work ⓓ work

6 I have visited more than fifteen ____________ so far.

ⓐ city ⓑ citys ⓒ cities ⓓ the city

7 She buys two bottles of ____________ every day.

ⓐ grape juice ⓑ waters ⓒ cheese ⓓ eggs

C

a, an, the, ø 중에서 알맞은 것을 골라 문장을 완성하시오.

1 I want ____________ kiwi juice instead of milk.

2 My cousin plays ____________ violin in his school orchestra.

3 ____________ red hat in the shop window looks great.

4 Shall we go out for ____________ lunch?

5 How long does it take to go to the art museum by ____________ bus?

6 How many hours do you sleep ____________ day?

D

밑줄 친 부분을 바르게 고쳐, 문장을 다시 쓰시오.

1 The President lives in a White House.

→ ______________________________

2 My family visits the orphanage once the month.

→ ______________________________

3 Your gloves is hanging on the clothes rack.

→ ______________________________

4 It was a first day of the food festival in our town.

→ ______________________________

5 Jake bought ten pound of meat for the dinner party.

→ ______________________________

6 I need a article about the exhibition in Hong Kong.

→ ______________________________

7 My brother and I don't usually have the breakfast.

→ ______________________________

FURTHER STUDY

Answers P.23

A 글을 읽고, 밑줄 친 부분을 바르게 고쳐 쓰시오.

Whenever I visit (1) an Italy, I am fascinated by the sidewalk cafes. Many (2) Italian enjoy talking with friends there. They have conversations about various things in life such as culture, art, films, food, and sports. I would like to have some (3) a juice and dessert with them. Another attraction might be anniversaries of historical (especially medieval) events with costume parades. Most Italian towns (4) was founded many centuries ago, so everywhere in Italy, there is a battle or a historical event to celebrate.

* medieval: 중세의 * costume: (민속) 의상

(1) ____________________

(2) ____________________

(3) ____________________

(4) ____________________

B 표를 보고, 주어진 정보를 이용하여 문장을 완성하시오.

Name	Things to do	Where to go	How to go
Angela	buy water (6, bottle)	supermarket	by car
Ben	attend a meeting	Beijing, China	by plane
Donald	buy bread (2, loaf)	bakery	by bike
Edward	meet Christine	City Hall	on foot

1 Angela will go to the supermarket by car to buy ____________________.

2 This Sunday, Ben will go to ____________________ to attend a meeting. He will go there ____________________.

3 Donald will go to the bakery by bike and buy ____________________.

4 Edward will go to City Hall to meet Christine. He will go there ____________________ because it is near his home.

MUST-KNOW

Answers P.23

▶ 셀 수 있는 명사의 복수형 변화

규칙 변화		불규칙 변화	
animal - animals boat - boats color - ① ______ tree - trees potato - potatoes box - ② ______ church - churches dish - dishes	bus - ③ ______ city - cities fly(파리) - ④ ______ boy - boys key - ⑤ ______ guy - guys leaf - leaves wife - ⑥ ______	child - ⑦ ______ foot - feet goose - geese man - ⑧ ______ mouse - mice ox - oxen tooth - teeth woman - women	piano - pianos person - people deer - deer series - series sheep - ⑨ ______ roof - roofs cliff - cliffs safe(금고) - ⑩ ______
(1) 대부분 명사: -s를 붙임 (2) -x, -o, -ch, -sh, -s로 끝나는 명사: -es를 붙임 (3) 〈자음+y〉로 끝나는 명사: -y 대신 -ies를 붙임 (4) 〈모음+y〉로 끝나는 명사: -s만 붙임 (5) -f, -fe로 끝나는 명사: -f나 -fe대신 -ves를 붙임		* 규칙성이 없음: 형태가 일정하지 않게 변하거나, 변하지 않고 그대로 복수형으로 사용	

▶ 셀 수 없는 물질명사를 세는 단위

단위	물질명사
a cup of	tea, hot chocolate, coffee 등의 따뜻한 음료 *eg)* a cup of coffee
a glass of	water, orange juice, milk, wine 등의 차가운 음료 *eg)* a glass of water
a piece of a slice of	cake, chalk, cheese, pizza 등의 덩어리로 된 것을 조각으로 나눈 것 *eg)* a piece of cake, a piece of chalk, a slice of cheese
a spoonful/spoon of	sugar, salt, flour, butter, olive oil 등의 양념류 *eg)* a spoonful/spoon of sugar
기타	**a bottle of** water[wine, beer] **a sheet(piece) of** paper **a kilo of** bacon **a loaf of** bread **a pound of** beef **a carton of** milk

1 Rick bought ① ______________ bread. (세 덩어리)

2 I drink two cups of coffee every day. (두 잔)

3 Cindy loves cheese. She eats five slices of cheese at a time. (다섯 장)

4 Put two spoonfuls/spoons of olive oil into the pot. (두 숟가락)

5 Can you give me ② ______________ water, please? (열 병)

6 We need one hundred sheets(pieces) of paper. (백 장)

7 My mom asked me to buy ③ ______________ pork. (3파운드)

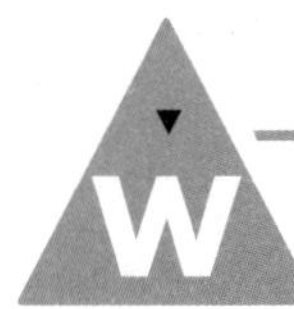

WRAP-UP TEST

Answers P.24

1 명사의 단수, 복수형이 잘못 짝지어진 것을 고르시오.

ⓐ tree - trees ⓑ wife - wives
ⓒ tomato - tomatos ⓓ goose - geese

2 빈칸에 들어갈 말이 바르게 연결된 것을 고르시오.

· You are ______ first person to arrive here.
· The Concord flew about 2,400 km ______ hour.

ⓐ a - an ⓑ the - an
ⓒ the - the ⓓ a - the

3 대화를 읽고, 어법상 어색한 곳을 찾아 바르게 고치시오.

A How many(ⓐ) people(ⓑ) are in your class?
B There are(ⓒ) seven man and six woman(ⓓ).

4 어법상 어색한 문장을 고르시오.

ⓐ The Earth goes around the Sun.
ⓑ I'll stay seven days in Paris, France.
ⓒ Today I had to go to school early.
ⓓ I borrowed a book. A book is *Gone with the Wind*.

5 어법상 올바른 문장을 고르시오.

ⓐ Susan bought much juices at the supermarket.
ⓑ Please don't put any sugar in my coffee.
ⓒ I need two piece of paper to write an essay.
ⓓ Ben likes to eat meats with vegetables.

6 셀 수 없는 명사를 모두 고르시오.

money	star	class	peace
bread	sheep	Jones	foot

7 밑줄 친 우리말을 소유대명사를 이용하여 영작하시오.

A Your bag is nice.
B Thank you, but it's 내 것이 아니야.
→ ______________________

8 [보기]에서 단어를 골라 해석을 참고하여 문장을 완성하시오.

bottle slice pound loaf

(1) Cut ____________ of bread into 8 pieces. (빵 한 덩어리)

(2) Put ____________ of cheese on each plate. (치즈 다섯 조각)

(3) To make steaks for three people, first prepare ____________ of beef. (쇠고기 3 파운드)

(4) Set the table and open ____________ of wine. (와인 한 병)

[9-10] 글을 읽고, 물음에 답하시오.

___(A)___ live in the sea and swim like fish, but they are not fish. Why are whales mammals? First, like all mammals, whales are warm-blooded. Fish are cold-blooded. Second, whales breathe ___(B)___ through lungs, but fish take in water through gills to breathe. Finally, whales give birth to babies that drink their mother's milk. Fish lay ___(C)___, and their mother does not feed them.

*gill: 아가미

9 (A)에 들어갈 알맞은 말을 고르시오.

ⓐ A whale ⓑ The whale
ⓒ An whale ⓓ Whales

10 (B)와 (C)에 들어갈 말이 바르게 짝지어진 것을 고르시오.

ⓐ air - egg ⓑ airs - eggs
ⓒ air - eggs ⓓ an air - eggs

대명사

1 인칭 / 지시 / 의문대명사

2 소유 / 재귀대명사

3 부정대명사 (I)

4 부정대명사 (II)

인칭 / 지시 / 의문대명사

(고유)명사 Steve is my best friend.

(인칭)대명사
- 주격 He is very diligent.
- 소유격 His hobby is playing the guitar.
- 목적격 I gave him the guitar.

대명사
사람이나 사물 등을 대신해서 쓰는 말로 인칭대명사, 지시대명사, 의문대명사, 소유대명사, 재귀대명사 등이 있다.

1 인칭대명사

I got my first cell phone last month. My mom bought it for me.
You should hurry. Your mother will give you a ride.
He loves his dog. It brings him joy and happiness.
She is very kind to her friends. They like her.
It is Tom's coat. Its color is red. He always wears it.
We must meet our client at the hotel. He's waiting for us.
You should do your best. Then, I will tell you the answer.
They will be here soon. I'll give their photos to them.

cf) 비인칭주어
It is 7 o'clock now. / It is Monday, June 7th.
It is snowy today. / It is very dark in here.
It is a little over 400 km from Seoul to Busan.

2 지시대명사

This is a postcard from Canada, and that is a parcel from Brazil.
These are roses, and those are tulips.
cf) Look at this cat! It's lovely.

3 의문사

Who left the door open?
Whose cell phone is this? (= Whose is this cell phone?)
Who(m) do you go camping with? (= With whom do you go camping?)

Which is better for you, tea or coffee?
Which do you like better?

What is your favorite day of the week?
What does he have in his hand?

1
사람, 사물, 동물을 대신하여 쓰는 대명사

주격	소유격	목적격
I	my	me
you	your	you
he	his	him
she	her	her
it	its	it
we	our	us
you	your	you
they	their	them

※소유격 its와 it's(= it is의 축약형) 혼동 주의!

- 시간 / 날짜, 요일
- 날씨 / 명암
- 거리

→ it을 사용

※비인칭주어 it은 '그것'이라고 해석하지 않는다.

2
이것, 저것 등 지시할 때 쓰는 대명사
- this(단수) / these(복수)
  : 가까이 있는 사람이나 물건
- that(단수) / those(복수)
  : 멀리 있는 사람이나 물건

cf) 명사 앞에 쓰여 '이 ~, 저 ~'의 뜻으로도 쓸 수 있다.

3
누구, 어떤 것, 무엇 등을 물어볼 때 사용하는 대명사

주격	소유격	목적격
who	whose	whom
which	-	which
what	-	what

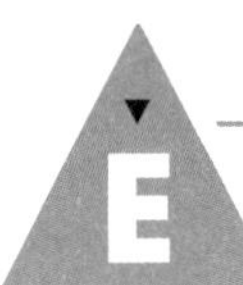

EXERCISE

Answers P.24

A

[ ] 안에서 알맞은 말을 고르시오.

1 I like [your, him, us] hairstyle and hair color.

2 The teacher punished [they, their, them] for being late.

3 Mike has told [we, our, us] the secrets of his success.

4 Cathy has studied hard for [she, her, hers] math test.

5 [My, They, Him] cousin will come to L.A. to visit me.

6 Adam posted some photographs on [he, his, him] blog.

7 Rick's car is brand new. [It is, They are] really cool.

8 [Those, That] paper cups in the cabinet were prepared for the party.

9 [This, It] is three blocks from here to the subway station.

10 What day is [that, it] today?

B

밑줄 친 부분을 대명사로 바꿔 문장을 완성하시오.

1 My father is a comedian. → ________ is very funny.

2 My friend, Jennie, is from Australia. → ________ speaks English.

3 I have four snakes. I love my snakes. → They are my pets. I love ________.

4 These shoes are very colorful. → ________ are not very expensive.

5 The price of this computer is reasonable. → ________ size is very small.

6 What do your aunt and uncle do? → ________ work at a department store.

7 Sally and I have been friends for 10 years. → ________ are best friends.

C

의문사를 이용하여 대화를 완성하시오.

1 A ________ is your job? B I am a florist.

2 A ________ are they? B They are my friends, Jake and Harry.

3 A ________ one is your book? B The small one with the red cover.

4 A ________ is your favorite actor? B My favorite actor is Jim Carrey.

5 A ________ does your mother do? B She is an English teacher.

6 A ________ eraser is on the floor? B It is Jim's.

Unit 2 소유 / 재귀대명사

소유대명사 It is my purse. = It's mine.
It is not her purse. = It's not hers.

재귀대명사 He said to himself, "I can do it!"
I did the math homework by myself.

1 소유대명사

This pen is not mine. (=my pen) Is it yours? (= your pen)
I showed him my photos, and he showed me his. (= his photos)
I couldn't find my cell phone, so Julie lent me hers. (= her cell phone)
Which seats are ours? (= our seats)
We told them about our plan, but they wouldn't tell us about theirs. (= their plan)

1
〈소유격+명사〉를 대신하여 사용하는 대명사

소유격	소유대명사
my	mine
your	yours
his	his
her	hers
its	-
our	ours
your	yours
their	theirs

2 재귀대명사

(1) 목적어가 주어와 같을 때 (생략할 수 없음)
She hurt herself during the game.
Take care of yourself.
He always talks about himself.

(2) 강조를 위해 (생략 가능)
Just leave it. I'll clean it (myself).
The President (himself) visited the hospital to comfort the injured citizens.

2
'~ 자신'의 뜻으로, 주어와 동일한 사람/사물이 목적어로 올 때, 혹은 강조를 위해 쓰이는 재귀대명사

인칭	재귀대명사
I	myself
you	yourself
he	himself
she	herself
it	itself
we	ourselves
you	yourselves
they	themselves

3 재귀대명사의 관용적 표현

(1) He went home by himself.
She baked all the cakes for the party by herself.
The lid opened of itself.
I was almost beside myself because of him.
Between ourselves, I think Larry is mean.

(2) Help yourself to dessert.
Enjoy yourself at the party!
Make yourself at home while you're staying here.

3
(1) 전치사+재귀대명사
- by oneself (홀로, 혼자서)
- of itself (저절로)
- beside oneself (제정신이 아닌)
- between ourselves (우리끼리 얘긴데)

(2) 기타 관용적 표현
- help yourself (to~) (~을 마음껏 먹다)
- enjoy oneself (즐거운 시간을 보내다)
- make yourself at home (편안하게 있다)

EXERCISE

Answers P.24

A

[ ] 안에서 알맞은 말을 고르시오.

1 These are not our bags. [Yours, His, Ours] are made of leather.

2 I put my file in the red folder. Put [her, yours, him] in the green folder.

3 Jane borrowed my pen because she lost [hers, her, him].

4 I think this is your cell phone. Isn't it [his, yours, hers]?

5 Sam got his report card, but I didn't get [mine, their, your].

6 His car is very unique. He told us about [our, his, him].

7 They haven't eaten all of their snacks. Maybe we can have some of [ours, mine, theirs].

B

[보기]에서 알맞은 말을 골라 문장을 완성하시오.

Word Bank	myself	yourself	himself	herself	ourselves	yourselves

1 Jake's mother said to me, "Make ____________ at home."

2 I stopped ____________ before telling her about the surprise party.

3 We don't need your help. We can do it ____________.

4 He was sitting by ____________ in one corner of the cafe.

5 I told her to believe in ____________ and do her best in the speech competition.

6 Did you guys make this model house for ____________?

C

주어진 해석을 참고하여 문장을 완성하시오.

1 I fought with my best friend. I was ____________ ____________. (제정신이 아닌)

2 You are a grown-up, so you should do it ____________ ____________. (혼자서)

3 The bird cage opened ____________ ____________. (저절로)

4 Let's keep this information ____________ ____________. (우리끼리의 얘기로, 비밀로)

부정대명사 (Ⅰ)

Some labs are in the basement of this building.
All of the workers in the building work from 9 am to 6 pm.
Every researcher wears a white gown.
Each gown has many pockets.

> 부정대명사
> 구체적으로 정해지지 않은 불특정한 대상을 지칭하는 대명사

1 some/any+단수 또는 복수

Some are good.
Some are bad.
I have some presents for you.
Do you want some kiwi juice?
I don't have any question(s).
Do you have any money to pay the bill?

> 1
> some / any+단수 또는 복수
> • 막연한 수량을 의미(다소, 얼마간)
> • 셀 수 있는 / 없는 명사에 모두 사용
>
> ※ some: 긍정문, 권유하는 의문문에 사용
> any: 부정문, 의문문, 조건문에 사용

2 all, every, each

(1) All items are 50% off.
All the students are polite.
All (of) the students are polite.

(2) Every student has his or her own merits.
She goes to the bookstore every Saturday.

(3) Each student was introduced to the principal.
Santa gave each child a hug.
cf) Each of the students has a different personality.

> 2
> (1) • all+복수 명사 → 복수 취급
> • all (of) the / 소유격+명사일 때 → of는 생략 가능
>
> (2)(3) every / each+단수 명사 → 단수 취급
>
> *cf)* each of+복수 명사 → 단수 취급

3 both, either/neither

(1) The reporters interviewed both twin boys.
Both (of) the twins have dimples on their cheeks.

(2) A: What do you want, coffee or tea?
B: Either is fine with me.

(3) I don't take after either of my parents.
(= I take after neither of my parents.)

> 3
> (1) both+복수 명사: ~ 둘 다 → 복수 취급
>
> (2) either+단수 명사: (둘 중 어느) 하나
> neither+단수 명사: 둘 다 ~아닌
> → 모두 단수 취급
>
> *cf)* either A or B / neither A nor B → B에 일치
>
> (3) not+either → neither

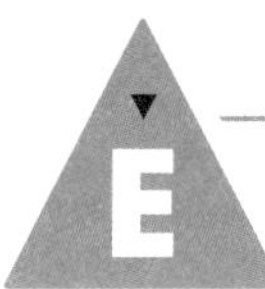

EXERCISE

Answers P.24

A

[ ] 안에서 알맞은 말을 고르시오.

1 [Every, Both] student has to clean the classroom floor.

2 He bought [some, any] flowers for his mother on Mother's Day.

3 [Every, All] children under 16 must go to school.

4 [Both, Every] bus is equipped with a first-aid kit.

5 Is there [some, any] space in your locker for my books? Mine is full.

6 [Both, Each] student has to take a yearly physical examination to check for health problems.

7 Both are unacceptable to me. I will not take [either, neither] of them.

B

[보기]에서 알맞은 말을 골라 문장을 완성하시오.

Word Bank	all	every	both	some	any	neither	either

1 ____________ my mom and dad majored in English literature.

2 ____________ girl has her own style.

3 ____________ the kids are playing on the playground.

4 I will go to the school dance with ____________ of them, Bill or Larry.

5 I need ____________ advice from the teacher about my future.

6 Fred doesn't have ____________ plan for the next summer vacation.

7 I can believe ____________ Tom nor Jane. They are not trustworthy.

C

밑줄 친 부분을 바르게 고쳐 쓰시오. 틀리지 않았다면 O표 하시오.

1 We paid attention to his every <u>words</u>. ____________

2 I don't have any <u>coins</u> to put in the vending machine. ____________

3 <u>Any</u> were pleased with their test results, but others weren't. ____________

4 All the people <u>was</u> horrified at the scene. ____________

5 Each <u>book</u> is introduced with a short summary. ____________

6 All of her <u>bag</u> are handmade. ____________

부정대명사 (Ⅱ)

요소가 둘인 경우 ◎ one ◎ the other

요소가 셋인 경우 ◎ one ◎ another ◎ the other

제한된 범위 안에서 ◎ one ◎◎◎◎... the others (하나는, 그 나머지는)

◎◎... some ◎◎◎◎... the others (몇몇은, 그 나머지는)

불특정 그룹 ◎◎◎◎ ... ◎◎ ◎◎◎ ◎◎... some others (몇몇은, 다른 몇몇은)

1 one, another, (the) other

(1) One (= People) should keep quiet in the library.
I lost my pen, so I bought a new one (= pen).
cf) I lost my pen, and I couldn't find it (= the lost pen).

(2) This bag is too big. Please show me another (= bag).
cf) We've known one another (= each other) for ten years.

(3) Jack is smarter than the other students.
Some students like math, but others (= other students) hate it.

> I have two pens! One is blue, and the other is red.
> One of my students prefers action movies, and the others prefer romantic comedies.
> I have three vases. One is green, another is red, and the other is black.

1
(1) one: ① 불특정한 일반인
② 같은 종류의 사람이나 사물

※one과 it의 차이 주의!
one: 같은 종류의 아무거나 하나
it: 앞에서 언급한 바로 그 것

(2) another: (같은 종류의) 또 다른 것
(3) other: 다른 (것, 사람)

• one, the other
(둘 중에) 하나는, 다른 하나는
• one, the others
(여러 개 중에) 하나는, 나머지 다른 것은
• one, another, the other
(셋 중에) 하나는, 다른 하나는, 나머지 하나는

2 most, no

(1) Most people are worried about their weight.
I have visited most countries in Europe.
Most of my paintings are portraits.

(2) There was no e-mail in my mailbox. (= not any)
No pets are allowed in this building.

2
(1) most: 대부분의 ~
(2) no: 아무 ~도 (아닌)
= not a, not any

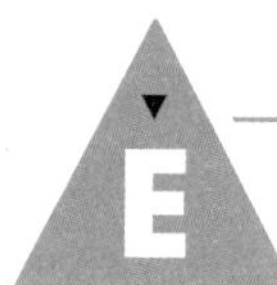

EXERCISE

Answers P.25

A

[ ] 안에서 알맞은 말을 고르시오.

1 I bought an eraser yesterday, but I lost [one, it] this morning.

2 [Most, One] should respect other people.

3 There are two flights to Rome. One is at 9 am, and [other, the other] is at 2 pm.

4 We have known [each other, the other] for almost 5 years.

5 Some students helped the teacher clean up, and [the others, another] didn't help.

B

[보기]에서 알맞은 말을 골라 문장을 완성하시오.

Word Bank	one	another	the other	one another	most	no

1 The teacher's question was too hard, and ____________ one could answer it.

2 They bought two small cakes. One was delicious, but ____________ was not.

3 ____________ readers of this book are very intelligent.

4 They have the same preferences, but they are different from ____________.

5 ____________ should always do one's best at everything.

6 There are three rooms in my house. One is mine, ____________ is my brother's, and the other is my parents'.

C

우리말과 같은 뜻이 되도록 문장을 완성하시오.

1 나의 반 친구들 중 한 명은 매우 키가 크고, 나머지 다른 친구들은 키가 작다.

→ ____________ of my classmates is very tall, and ____________ are short.

2 상자 안에 있는 몇 개의 오렌지는 신선하지만, 그 나머지는 썩었다.

→ ____________ of the oranges in the box are fresh, but ____________ are rotten.

3 어떠한 언어도 배우기에 쉽지 않다.

→ ____________ languages are easy to learn.

REVIEW TEST

A

[ ] 안에서 알맞은 말을 고르시오.

1 Ben visited [both, either] Germany and Italy during the summer vacation.

2 The door opened [of itself, from itself] at midnight.

3 The question is too hard for [us, ours] to solve by ourselves.

4 I can't believe the socks are [my, mine]. They are very stinky.

5 Every [child, children] is ready to listen to the tape.

6 Jim bought a nice scarf. He will give [one, it] to Julie tomorrow.

7 You will earn [some, any] money if you get a part-time job.

B

빈칸에 들어갈 알맞은 말을 고르시오.

1 ____________ takes about 5 hours to get there.

ⓐ There ⓑ What ⓒ It ⓓ This

2 Are there ____________ candles in the drawer? The light is out.

ⓐ both ⓑ either ⓒ each ⓓ any

3 Your explanation of the accident does not agree with ____________.

ⓐ your ⓑ hers ⓒ their ⓓ my

4 Help ____________ to the dessert.

ⓐ itself ⓑ myself ⓒ ourselves ⓓ yourself

5 He has two daughters. One is a nurse, and ____________ is a teacher.

ⓐ another ⓑ other ⓒ the other ⓓ others

6 ____________ must think about one's mistakes first before blaming others.

ⓐ Every ⓑ One ⓒ Each ⓓ Either

7 Some people admire other people, and ____________ are admired.

ⓐ one ⓑ other ⓒ others ⓓ the other

C [보기]에서 알맞은 말을 골라 문장을 완성하시오.

Word Bank	another	any	it	all	herself	his	the others

1 Shelly managed to carry all her books home by ____________.

2 I don't have ____________ complaints about my school.

3 ____________ of the tickets were sold out when we arrived.

4 Some of my classmates were studying, and ____________ were talking.

5 This skirt is too tight. Can you show me ____________?

6 Kenny always expects me to pay for ____________ meals.

7 ____________ is 4 miles to the nearest post office.

D 밑줄 친 부분을 바르게 고쳐, 문장을 다시 쓰시오.

1 My father and I go to watch a baseball game every weekends.
→ ____

2 Do it yours. I don't have enough time to help you.
→ ____

3 There are three balls. One is for me, another is for Daniel, and others is for Jake.
→ ____

4 Every girl in my school are expected to wear a skirt.
→ ____

5 Some birds sat on eggs in theirs nests.
→ ____

6 I found this cool links about cartoons on my friend's blog.
→ ____

7 Whom left the door open?
→ ____

FURTHER STUDY

Answers P.26

A 글을 읽고, 밑줄 친 부분을 바르게 고쳐 쓰시오.

(1) Ones of the most popular souvenirs among visitors to Ireland is a shillelagh. A shillelagh is a walking stick, and people used it for fighting and protecting (2) himself at country fairs in the nineteenth century. It is long and made of hardwood. Shillelaghs used to be made of oak, but these days (3) it is made of holly, ash, or blackthorn wood instead of oak. When you go to Ireland, you should purchase a shillelagh carefully because (4) any shops sell short and fake ones.

* souvenir: 기념품 a shillelagh: (아일랜드) 곤봉 holly: 서양호랑가시나무
ash: 서양물푸레나무 blackthorn: 산사나무

(1) ______________________

(2) ______________________

(3) ______________________

(4) ______________________

B 우리말과 같은 뜻이 되도록 주어진 말을 이용하여 문장을 완성하시오.

1 그는 자신의 나이에 비해서 약하다. (weak, for one's age)

→ ____

2 아이들은 자기들끼리 논다. (children, play among)

→ ____

3 목성에 생물체가 있나요? (there, any life, on Jupiter)

→ ____

4 공항까지 얼마나 걸리나요? (how long, take, get, to the airport)

→ ____

5 나는 두 명의 남동생이 있다. 한 명은 키가 크고, 다른 한 명은 작다. (have, two brothers, tall, and, short)

→ ____

Answers P.26

▶ 인칭대명사 정리

수	인칭	주격	소유격	목적격	소유대명사	재귀대명사
단수	1	I	my	me	① ______	myself
	2	You	your	you	② ______	yourself
	3	He	③ ______	him	his	himself
		She	her	her	hers	herself
		It	its	it	-	④ ______
복수	1	We	our	⑤ ______	ours	ourselves
	2	You	your	you	yours	⑥ ______
	3	They	their	them	theirs	themselves

▶ 부정대명사 정리

부정대명사		예문
each, every	단수 취급	Each of them has a role in the school play. Every mother ① ______(know) her child's habits very well.
either, neither	단수 취급	Either of these two tickets is yours. Neither of the boys ② ______(be) diligent.
some of+명사 all of+명사 most of+명사	뒤에 나오는 명사의 수에 따라 단수/복수 취급	Some of my friends have part-time jobs. Stir well until all of the sugar is dissolved. Most of your information ③ ______(be) correct.
one, the other	(2개 중에서) 하나는, 나머지 하나는	I have two hamburgers. One is for my brother, and ④ ______ is for my sister.
one, another, the other	(3개 중에서) 하나는, 다른 하나는, 나머지는	I have three best friends. One, Linda, is talkative, ⑤ ______, Sally, is cute, and the other, Julia, is timid.
some, the others	(제한된 수에서) 일부는, 나머지는	Look at these puppies! Some are black, and ⑥ ______ are white.
one another = each other	서로	The girls are talking seriously to one another. (= The girls are talking seriously to each other.)

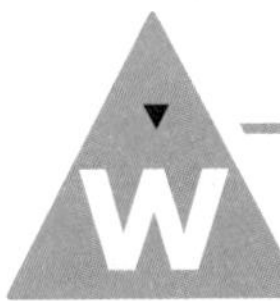

WRAP-UP TEST

Answers P.26

1 빈칸에 공통으로 들어갈 알맞은 말을 쓰시오.

· __________ is getting darker and darker.

· __________ is 10 minutes to 7.

· __________ was stormy yesterday.

2 밑줄 친 one의 쓰임이 다른 것을 고르시오.

ⓐ One should respect the elderly.

ⓑ I have only one bag, and I have lost it.

ⓒ No one is allowed to open this door.

ⓓ You prefer the blue car, but I like the black one.

3 대화를 읽고, 어색한 곳을 찾아 바르게 고치시오.

A Mom, I can't find(ⓐ) my gloves. Have you seen them(ⓑ)?

B Are these your(ⓒ) or your brother's(ⓓ)?

4 어법상 어색한 문장을 고르시오.

ⓐ She repaired the car herself.

ⓑ You should have faith in yourself.

ⓒ He didn't come to the meeting. He was beside himself.

ⓓ They are visiting us this weekend. I'll reserve hotel rooms for themselves.

5 밑줄 친 부분의 쓰임이 어색한 것을 고르시오.

ⓐ All of the trees in the mountain have burnt.

ⓑ Would you like some tea with that cake?

ⓒ Some of pages are torn, and others have been scribbled on.

ⓓ He wrote two books. One is about his life and other is about his accomplishments.

6 빈칸에 알맞은 말을 모두 고르시오.

__________ student will have a room in the dormitory.

ⓐ Some ⓑ Every

ⓒ Each ⓓ Either

7 주어진 표현을 이용한 문장으로 바꿔 쓰시오.

Jane didn't give me any advice. James didn't give me any advice. (neither of)

→ ______________________________

8 [보기]에서 알맞은 단어를 골라 문장을 완성하시오.

whose	who	which	whom

(1) I made chocolate and strawberry cakes. __________ would you like to have?

(2) I saw you at the gallery. __________ did you go with?

(3) There is a new bicycle in the backyard. __________ bicycle is it?

(4) __________ painted the fence?

[9-10] 글을 읽고, 물음에 답하시오.

Shrews are very small mammals, only growing up to three inches long. They have brown or gray fur. (A) They fur becomes lighter in the summer and darker in the winter. They eat small insects or small amounts of seeds or fruits. It is very hard to see them. Fortunately, my friend and I saw one in the living room last night. My friend wanted to catch ___(B)___, but I stopped him before he could do that because shrews are not harmful.

*shrew: 뾰족뒤쥐

9 (A)를 어법에 맞게 고치시오.

10 (B)에 들어갈 알맞은 말을 고르시오.

ⓐ them ⓑ it

ⓒ him ⓓ one

형용사와 부사

1 형용사
2 부사
3 비교급과 최상급 (규칙, 불규칙)
4 비교급과 최상급 (기타)

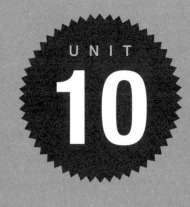

형용사

명사 수식　Kevin is a kind boy. 〈형용사+명사〉

주어 설명　He is kind to his classmates. 〈보어 역할〉

> 형용사
> 사람이나 사물의 성질, 상태 등을 묘사하는 데 쓰이는 품사. 명사를 직접 수식하거나, 주어 또는 목적어를 보충 설명

1 형용사의 역할

(1) It was a fantastic party.
I'm looking for a big green bag.

(2) Would you like something cold to drink?
Is there anything bad about animal rights?

(3) The class was interesting.
We found the class enjoyable.

1
(1) 형용사+명사
(2) -thing+형용사
(3) 주어, 목적어를 보충 설명

2 여러 가지 형용사 형태

He is a very responsible and reliable employee.
What a wonderful world! I am very cheerful.
Some careless students wrote on the classroom wall.
My little brother is very energetic and talkative.
It's a lovely day, isn't it?
The basketball game was thrilling, but I felt tired when I got home.

2
(1) -able, -ible: 가능성
(2) -ful: 가득함
(3) -less: ~가 없는
(4) -ous, -ish, -y, -ic, -ive 등: 성질
(5) 명사+ly형
eg) lovely, friendly
(6) 분사형 형용사 (-ing / -ed)
-ing형: exciting, boring, surprising 등
-ed(p.p.)형: excited, bored, surprised 등
※ [MUST-KNOW] 참조

3 수량을 나타내는 형용사

(1) How many people are there in the pool?
There are few boys in the pool.
There are a few girls in the pool.
There are not many adults in the pool.

(2) How much oil is there in the bottle?
There is little oil in the bottle.
There is a little oil in the bottle.
There is not much oil in the bottle.

(3) I bought some plates.
I don't need any plates.
I have a lot of plates.

Can I have some water?
Do you have any flour?
I drink a lot of water every day.

3

셀 수 ○	few 거의 없는 (부정) a few 조금 있는 (긍정) many 많은
셀 수 ×	little 거의 없는 (부정) a little 조금 있는 (긍정) much 많은
셀 수 ○/× 모두 가능	some 약간의 (주로 긍정문에) any 약간의 (주로 부정, 의문문에) a lot of = lots of 많은

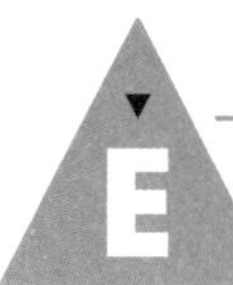

EXERCISE

Answers P.27

A

[ ] 안에서 알맞은 말을 고르시오.

1 I heard a [loud, loudly] noise in the hallway.

2 [A lot of, Much] people run along the riverside every morning.

3 I don't usually drink [few, much] water.

4 These boxes are very [heavy, heavily].

5 He is very shy, so he has [little, few] friends.

6 I've learned [something new, new something] about him.

7 We don't have [some, any] money right now.

8 Harry is good at math. He only missed [a little, a few] questions on the test.

B

밑줄 친 부분을 바르게 고쳐 쓰시오. 틀리지 않았다면 O표 하시오.

1 There aren't <u>some</u> mistakes on your test. ____________________

2 Andrew didn't do <u>wrong anything</u>. It was all my fault. ____________________

3 Most of my classmates are <u>friendly</u>. ____________________

4 Willy couldn't stand her <u>selfish</u> attitude. ____________________

5 There were not <u>much</u> people in the waiting room. ____________________

6 Free online games are not <u>excited</u>. ____________________

7 I'm going to buy a <u>little</u> books for my brother. ____________________

C

우리말과 같은 뜻이 되도록 주어진 말을 배열하시오.

1 fun / is / girl / Tina / and / cute / a (Tina는 귀엽고 재미있는 소녀이다.)

→ ____

2 a few / there were / the classroom / in / students (교실 안에는 학생들이 몇몇 있었다.)

→ ____

3 delicious / looking for / something / the girl / is (그 소녀는 맛있는 무언가를 찾고 있다.)

→ ____

부사

동사 수식 I entered the house quietly.

형용사 수식 This ice cream is really delicious.

다른 부사 수식 Mike practices the piano very hard.

문장 전체 수식 Strangely, there was no one on the street.

부사
동사, 형용사, 다른 부사, 문장 전체를 수식하는 품사

1 부사의 역할

(1) Chris runs fast. Sandra walks slowly.

(2) My parents got very angry.

cf) My score is good enough to pass the test.

(3) He is late for school too often.

(4) Fortunately, no one was hurt in the accident.

1
(1) 동사 수식
(2) 형용사 수식: 부사+형용사
cf) 형용사+enough
(3) 다른 부사 수식
(4) 문장 전체 수식
(부사의 위치가 자유로운 편)

2 부사의 형태

(1) 형용사+ly형

He worried deeply about his grades.

He couldn't understand the science class clearly.

(2) -ly를 붙였을 때 뜻이 변하는 경우

He worked very hard. He could hardly move a finger.

I came late again. I haven't seen him lately.

(3) 형용사와 부사의 형태가 같은 경우

The early bird catches the worm. (형용사)

I get up early in the morning. (부사)

2
(1) 형용사+ly → 부사 (deeply, clearly)
cf) 명사+ly → 형용사 (lovely, friendly)

(2)

형용사 = 부사	부사
hard (딱딱한 / 열심히)	hardly (거의 ~않다)
late (늦은 / 늦게)	lately (최근에)
high (높은 / 높게)	highly (대단히, 몹시)

(3) 형태가 같은 형용사와 부사
: fast, slow, early, late, hard

3 빈도를 나타내는 부사

100%	Kevin is always kind to me.
	Cindy usually gets up at 7 o'clock.
	She often goes to school on foot.
	I sometimes go to the movies.
	He rarely smiles at me.
0%	I never tell a lie.

3
빈도부사의 위치
• be동사 / 조동사+빈도부사
• 빈도부사+일반동사

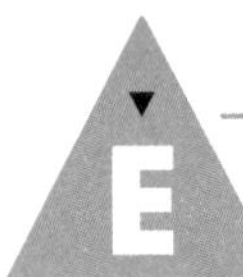

EXERCISE

Answers P.27

A

[ ] 안에서 알맞은 말을 고르시오.

1 She looked at his cell phone [envious, enviously].

2 She is a [hard, hardly] worker.

3 Tom came home very [late, lately] last night.

4 Kevin gets along [well, good] with everyone.

5 Please walk [quiet, quietly] in the hallway.

6 I [eat sometimes, sometimes eat] fast food.

7 We [usually have, have usually] a school festival in the spring.

8 Jake is a sleepyhead. He [is often, often is] late for school.

B

[보기]에서 알맞은 말을 골라 문장을 완성하시오.

Word Bank	dangerously	loudly	carefully	highly	easily

1 You will be able to solve this problem ____________. It's not difficult at all.

2 Ben always plays music too ____________.

3 She was ____________ competitive and wanted to win.

4 We should take him to a hospital. He is ____________ ill.

5 Students must check their exams ____________ before they turn them in.

C

주어진 부사를 적절한 위치에 넣어 문장을 다시 쓰시오.

1 Swimming is called the perfect exercise. (often)

→ ______________________________

2 Do you have a lot of homework? (usually)

→ ______________________________

3 I have been to Scotland. (never)

→ ______________________________

4 The woman drove her car fast. (too)

→ ______________________________

Unit 10

Unit 3 비교급과 최상급 (규칙, 불규칙)

	규칙 변화	불규칙 변화
원급	Your writing is neat.	My history teacher is good.
비교급	It is neater than mine. (원급+-er)	He is better than my math teacher.
최상급	It is the neatest in the class. (원급+-est)	He is the best teacher in my school.

비교급
두 가지 대상을 비교할 때

최상급
여러 가지 대상 가운데 '가장 ~한 것'을 나타낼 때

1 규칙 변화

(1) -er / -est를 붙이는 경우

This red bag is cheap.
This red bag is cheaper than the yellow one.
This red bag is the cheapest one in the store.

I usually get up early in the morning.
I get up earlier than my brother.
I get up earliest among my family members.

(2) more / most를 붙이는 경우

Robin is a successful businessman.
Robin is a more successful businessman than Daniel.
Robin is the most successful businessman in America.

Mary talks loudly.
Mary talks more loudly than Sally.
Mary talks most loudly of all the students.

2 불규칙 변화

(1) John bakes cookies very well.
He bakes cookies better than his sister.
However, his mom bakes cookies (the) best in his family.

(2) The service of the restaurant was bad.
The music of the restaurant was worse than the service.
The food was the worst of all.

1

비교급/최상급 만드는 법

(1) -er/-est를 붙이는 경우
- 단어+-er/-est
  (-e로 끝날 땐 -r/-st만 붙임)
- 〈자음+y〉로 끝나는 단어
  : -y를 -i로 고치고 -er/-est를 붙임
- 〈단모음 + 단자음〉으로 끝나는 단어
  : 자음을 하나 더 붙이고 -er/-est를 붙임

※ 부사의 최상급에는 원칙적으로 the를 붙이지 않는다.

(2) more/most를 붙이는 경우
- 3음절 이상의 단어
- 일부 2음절 단어

※ 비교급 + than ~: ~보다 더 …하다
※ the+최상급+of 복수 명사 / in 장소나 단체를 나타내는 단수 명사 : ~ 중에서 가장 …한
eg) of all the boys, of five members, in my family, in our class 등

※ [MUST-KNOW] 참조

2

불규칙 변화

뜻	원급	비교급	최상급
좋은	good/well	better	best
나쁜	bad/ill	worse	worst
많은	many/much	more	most
적은	little	less	least
늦은	late	later	latest
순서가 나중인	late	latter	last

EXERCISE

Answers P.27

A

[　] 안에서 알맞은 말을 고르시오.

1 Which do you like [well, better, best], this one or that one?

2 It's [warm, warmer, the warmest] today than yesterday.

3 This seat is [dirty, dirtier, the dirtiest] than that one.

4 It is [pretty, prettier, the prettiest] ring in the store.

5 His speaking ability was [bad, worse, worst] than his knowledge of English grammar.

6 Seoul is [big, bigger, the biggest] city in Korea.

7 Stanley has [much, more, the most] expensive clothes among his friends.

B

밑줄 친 부분을 바르게 고쳐 쓰시오. 틀리지 않았다면 O표 하시오.

1 Mercury is the most small planet in our universe. ____________

2 I go to bed latter than my parents. ____________

3 My computer is least expensive than his. ____________

4 Jimmy is the taller boy in my class. ____________

5 Could you please speak more quietly? ____________

6 This is the thinest cell phone in Korea. ____________

7 Typing is always more quick than handwriting. ____________

C

주어진 말을 이용하여 문장을 완성하시오.

1 TV documentaries are ____________(educational) than dramas.

2 She likes pizza ____________(good) than hamburgers.

3 Winter is ____________(cold) season of the year.

4 The Nile River is ____________(long) than the Amazon River.

5 People ____________(easily) forget bad things than good things.

6 I will make ____________(funny) movie in the world.

7 After she entered high school, she got ____________(busy) than before.

비교급과 최상급 (기타)

She is as careful as Jake.

열등비교 → She is less careful than Jake.
|| She is not so careful as Jake.

우등비교 → She is more careful than Jake.
↓ 강조 She is much more careful than Jake.

1 기타 비교급과 최상급 표현

(1) His wife looked a lot older than him.
This sandwich is much more delicious than I expected.

(2) Used CDs are usually less expensive than new ones.
(= New CDs are usually more expensive than used ones.)

(3) It is getting warmer and warmer these days.
My classmates and I are getting closer and closer.

(4) The more I spend time with him, the more I like him.
The harder I study, the better my grades will get.

(5) The customer service is better than I expected.
The solution was much easier than I thought.

(6) He has one of the cutest dogs in the world.
She is the most beautiful woman (that) I've ever seen.

1

(1) **비교급 강조 부사**
: much, even, still, far, a lot+비교급

(2) **열등비교**
: less ~ than …: …보다 덜 ~하다

(3) **비교급** and **비교급**
: 점점 더 ~하다

(4) the **비교급** ~, the **비교급** …
: 더 ~할수록 더 …하다

(5) **비교급+**than**+절(주어+동사)**
: (주어)가 ~한 것보다 더 …한
eg) than I thought, than I expected 등

(6) **최상급 표현**
• one of the+최상급+복수 명사
: 가장 ~한 (명사) 중의 하나
• 최상급+(that)+주어+have ever p.p.
: (주어)가 지금까지 ~한 것 중 가장 …한

2 원급을 이용한 비교 표현

(1) Today is as cold as yesterday.
He speaks Spanish as well as his Spanish friends.

(2) Skateboarding is not as difficult as skiing.
(= Skateboarding is less difficult than skiing.)
(= Skiing is more difficult than skateboarding.)

(3) This apple pie is twice as big as that pumpkin pie.
His computer is three times as expensive as mine.

(4) Try to run as fast as you can!
(= Try to run as fast as possible!)
I brought as many books as I could.
(= I brought as many books as possible.)

2

(1) as **원급** as …: …**만큼 ~하다**

(2) A is not so(as)**+원급+**as B
: A는 B만큼 ~하지 않다
= A is less+원급+than B
= B is+비교급+than A

(3) **배수사+**as**+원급+**as ~
: ~의 (몇 배)로 …한

(4) as**+원급+**as**+주어+**can
: (주어)가 할 수 있는 한 ~하게
= as+원급+as possible: 가능한 ~하게

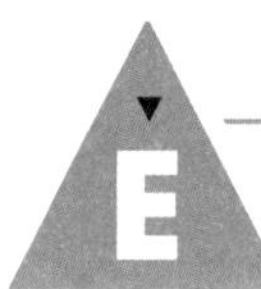

EXERCISE

Answers P.28

A

[ ] 안에서 알맞은 말을 고르시오.

1 It will be rainy. It's getting [dark, darker] and darker.

2 The harder they study, [the better, the best] scores they will get.

3 Danny is [as smartly as, as smart as] Timothy.

4 Her new novel was [not as, as not] amazing as people say.

5 He is a [very, much] better person than you think.

6 The express train is [twice as fast as, two so fast as] the regular one.

7 Ninety percent is [good, the best] score I've ever gotten on a math test.

B

밑줄 친 부분을 바르게 고쳐 쓰시오.

1 Try to eat as slowly as possibly. ____________

2 The faster you complete the task, the many points you get. ____________

3 His pocket money is twice much as mine. ____________

4 Living with food allergies is not as easier as you might think. ____________

5 This comic book is much least interesting than I expected. ____________

6 He is one of the lazy men I've ever met. ____________

C

우리말과 같은 뜻이 되도록 주어진 말을 이용하여 문장을 완성하시오.

1 우리가 함께 있으면 있을수록, 우리는 더 행복해질 것이다. (long, happy)

→ ____________ we stay together, ____________ we will be.

2 낮이 점점 짧아지고 있다. (short)

→ The daytime is becoming ____________.

3 그 남자는 내가 생각했던 것보다 나이 들지 않았다. (old)

→ The man is ____________ I thought.

4 그 미국 문화 수업은 내가 들은 수업 중 가장 힘든 수업이다. (hard, take)

→ The American culture class is ____________.

5 우리 집은 저 집의 두 배만큼 크다. (large)

→ My house is ____________ that house.

REVIEW TEST

A

[　] 안에서 알맞은 말을 고르시오.

1 The little boy speaks English very [good, well].

2 He is selfish. So his relationships with his friends are [terrible, terribly].

3 Women live [the longest, longer than] men.

4 This job is [a lot more, very much] difficult than my previous job.

5 His lecture was [informative certainly, certainly informative].

6 Teaching requires as much effort [than, as] learning.

7 Try to concentrate in class as [long, longer] as possible.

B

빈칸에 들어갈 알맞은 말을 고르시오.

1 They are not ____________ workers.

ⓐ diligent　ⓑ diligently　ⓒ diligence　ⓓ more diligent

2 He scored ____________ than we expected.

ⓐ bad　ⓑ worse　ⓒ worse that　ⓓ the worst

3 Millet expressed nature in a ____________ way than other artists.

ⓐ peaceful　ⓑ peacefully　ⓒ as peaceful　ⓓ much more peaceful

4 He is ____________ guy in our team.

ⓐ intelligent　ⓑ more intelligent　ⓒ most intelligent　ⓓ the most intelligent

5 I could answer the questions ____________ than before because the quiz wasn't difficult.

ⓐ easy　ⓑ easier　ⓒ more easily　ⓓ as easily

6 It will take three times as ____________ money as you think.

ⓐ many　ⓑ more　ⓒ much　ⓓ most

7 She looks ____________ depressed than last night.

ⓐ little　ⓑ less　ⓒ least　ⓓ the least

Answers P.28

C

주어진 말을 이용하여 문장을 완성하시오.

1 The book is terrible. It is ____________(bad) book I've ever read.

2 The faster you drive, ____________(much) fuel you will use.

3 After the storm, today's sea is much ____________(calm) than yesterday's.

4 Solar energy is one of ____________(clean) fuels for heating.

5 Fortunately, we made ____________(few) mistakes than we had thought.

6 Computers are getting ____________ and ____________(cheap) thanks to the development of new technology.

7 The distance from my office to the factory was ____________(far) than I thought.

D

밑줄 친 부분을 바르게 고쳐, 문장을 다시 쓰시오.

1 Bella is the nicest <u>girls</u> I've ever known.

→ ________________________________

2 We are <u>terrible</u> sorry for this inconvenience.

→ ________________________________

3 The red shirt looks <u>well</u> on you than the white one.

→ ________________________________

4 Riding a motorcycle is not as easy <u>than</u> riding a bike.

→ ________________________________

5 Teresa and I <u>often can</u> see these plays on Broadway.

→ ________________________________

6 The dentist was <u>two</u> as busy as usual, so I couldn't make an appointment.

→ ________________________________

7 Drinking too <u>many</u> Coke is bad for your health.

→ ________________________________

FURTHER STUDY

Answers P.29

A 글을 읽고, 밑줄 친 부분을 바르게 고쳐 쓰시오.

According to some studies, if students learn to play musical instruments, they tend to get (1) good test scores than others. So many American parents (2) strong encourage their children to learn to play musical instruments. They (3) choose usually from band instruments, stringed instruments, and the piano. If students can play band instruments, they (4) often can participate in school marching bands and perform at football games or in parades. If they learn stringed instruments such as the violin or the cello, they can participate in school and community orchestra programs.

(1) ______________

(2) ______________

(3) ______________

(4) ______________

B 표를 보고, [보기]와 같이 문장을 완성하시오.

• Used Car List •

Vehicles	Price
Z3 (BMW)	$13,000
Explorer (Ford)	$4,500
Sonata (Hyundai)	$11,000
Camry (Toyota)	$8,500
S40 (Volvo)	$8,500

Example The Z3 is the most expensive car in the list. (expensive)

1 The Camry is ______________ ______________ than the Sonata. (expensive)

2 The Explorer is ______________ ______________ car in the list. (cheap)

3 The S40 is ______________ ______________ ______________ the Camry. (expensive)

4 The Sonata is ______________ than the Z3. (cheap)

MUST-KNOW

Answers P.29

▶ 형용사를 만드는 접미사

접미사	형용사 예			
-able / ible	response	- ① ______	flex	- flexible
	wash	- washable	believe	- ② ______
-ful	beauty	- beautiful	use	- ③ ______
-less	care	- careless	use	- ④ ______
-ous	danger	- ⑤ ______	fame	- famous
	vary	- ⑥ ______	courage	- courageous
	anxiety	- anxious	curiosity	- ⑦ ______
-y	health	- ⑧ ______	wealth	- wealthy
-ic	base	- basic	history	- ⑨ ______
-ive	act	- active	create	- ⑩ ______
-al	culture	- ⑪ ______	music	- musical
	globe	- ⑫ ______	fate	- fatal
-ical	type	- ⑬ ______	history	- historical
-ern	east	- eastern	west	- ⑭ ______
	south	- ⑮ ______	north	- northern
-ly	friend	- friendly	love	- ⑯ ______

▶ 비교급과 최상급 정리

(1) 형용사와 부사의 원급+(e)r/(e)st

short	- ① ______	- ② ______
long	- longer	- longest
small	- smaller	- smallest
large	- ③ ______	- ④ ______
nice	- ⑤ ______	- ⑥ ______

(2) 〈단모음+단자음〉: 끝자음+er/est

big	- ⑦ ______	- ⑧ ______
hot	- ⑨ ______	- ⑩ ______
thin	- thinner	- thinnest

(3) 〈자음+y〉: -y를 -i로 고치고 er/est

busy	- ⑪ ______	- ⑫ ______
early	- earlier	- earliest
pretty	- prettier	- prettiest
happy	- ⑬ ______	- ⑭ ______

(4) 일부 2음절어, 대부분의 3음절어 이상의 형용사나 부사: more, most를 붙임

famous	- ⑮ ______	- ⑯ ______
useful	- more useful	- most useful
beautiful	- more beautiful	- most beautiful
interesting	- ⑰ ______	- ⑱ ______

(5) 불규칙변화

good / well	- better	- best
bad / ill	- ⑲ ______	- ⑳ ______
many / much	- more	- most
few	- fewer	- fewest
little	- ㉑ ______	- ㉒ ______
old	- ㉓ ______	- oldest
	- ㉔ ______	- eldest
far	- farther	- farthest
	- further	- furthest

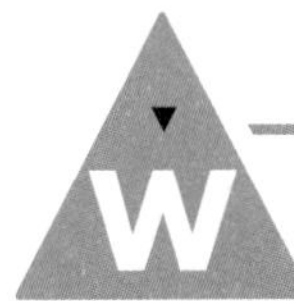

WRAP-UP TEST

Answers P.29

1 원급, 비교급, 최상급의 연결이 어색한 것을 고르시오.

ⓐ bad - worse - worst
ⓑ little - less - least
ⓒ thin - thinner - thinnest
ⓓ busy - busyer - busyest

2 대화를 읽고, 어색한 곳을 찾아 바르게 고치시오.

A Mom, I'm really thirsty. I need cold something to drink.
B Look inside the refrigerator.

3 어법상 어색한 문장을 고르시오.

ⓐ My math scores are getting higher and higher.
ⓑ Your book is twice as thicker as hers.
ⓒ The more you have, the more you have to give.
ⓓ Tina is the most beautiful girl I've ever seen.

4 밑줄 친 부분의 쓰임이 어색한 것을 고르시오.

ⓐ They hardly ever win a game.
ⓑ Have you met him lately?
ⓒ Eagles fly highly.
ⓓ The train arrived early.

5 빈칸에 들어갈 말이 바르게 연결된 것을 고르시오.

· I have ________ things to do.
· There is ________ salt left.
· I received the ________ gifts in my family.

ⓐ much - few - least
ⓑ many - little - fewest
ⓒ a little - few - fewer
ⓓ a few - little - less

6 주어진 문장을 참고하여 문장을 완성하시오.

Times Square is crowded.

(1) 비교급 Times Square is ________________ ________________ than Central Park.

(2) 최상급 Times Square is ________________ ________________.

7 짝지어진 문장의 의미가 다른 것을 고르시오.

ⓐ Daniel is not as fast as Robin.
 = Daniel is faster than Robin.
ⓑ Swim as fast as possible.
 = Swim as fast as you can.
ⓒ She dances the ballet well.
 = She is a good ballerina.
ⓓ Danny is less clever than Tony.
 = Tony is cleverer than Danny.

8 [보기]에서 알맞은 부사를 골라 영작하시오.

always	usually	sometimes

(1) Noah는 항상 아침을 거른다. (skip)

→ ________________

(2) 너는 주말에 주로 무엇을 하니? (do, on the weekend)

→ ________________

(3) 너의 충고는 때때로 매우 도움이 돼. (advice, be, helpful)

→ ________________

[9-10] 글을 읽고, 물음에 답하시오.

(A) 영어에서 가장 긴 단어를 들어 본 적이 있나요? It refers to a lung disease and is made of 45 letters. It called "pneumonoultamicroscopicsilicovolcanoconiosis." But we don't use this word. The ____(B)____ are considered to be "I" or "a." These two words are always used in our daily life.

9 (A)를 영작하시오.

→ Have you ever heard ________________ in English?

10 (B)에 들어갈 알맞은 말을 고르시오.

ⓐ shortest words ⓑ shorter words
ⓒ short words ⓓ most short words

전치사

1 장소 / 방향 전치사
2 시간 전치사
3 기타 전치사

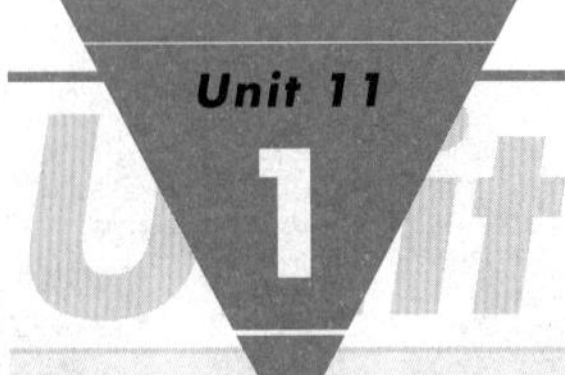

장소, 방향 전치사

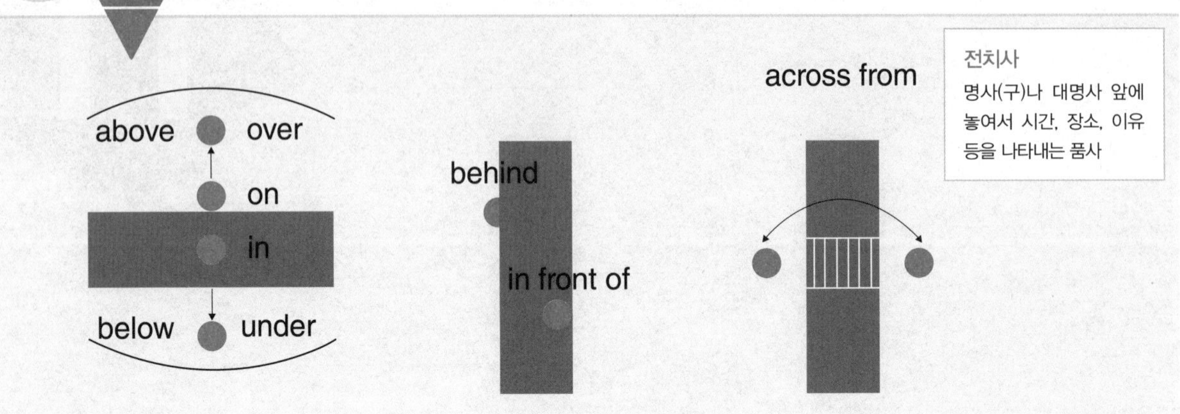

전치사
명사(구)나 대명사 앞에 놓여서 시간, 장소, 이유 등을 나타내는 품사

1 위치, 장소 전치사

(1) There are a lot of photos on the table.
Raise your hands over your head.
Glasses are on the shelf above the sink.
Groundwater runs under the ground.
The kitchen is directly below my room.

(2) Let's put the wastebasket in front of the mirror.
The bookshelf is behind the chair.

(3) The bakery is between 7th and 8th Streets.
There is a beautiful house among the trees.

(4) The bank is across from the stationery store.

(5) There is a candy store next to the post office.

(6) Movie tickets are in the box.
The grocery store is at the corner.
There is a squirrel near the oak tree in the park.

1

(1)
- on: ~ 위에
- over: ~ 너머에, ~ 위에
- above: ~ 위에
- under: ~ 아래에
- below: ~ 아래에

(2)
- in front of: ~ 앞에
- behind: ~ 뒤에

(3)
- between A and B: A와 B 사이에
- among: ~ 사이에

(4)
- across from: ~ 건너편에, 반대편에

(5)
- next to(=beside, by): ~ 옆에

(6)
- in: ~ 안에
- at: ~에
- near: ~ 가까이에

2 방향 전치사

(1) This train goes from Seoul to Busan.
We walked slowly toward the building.

(2) The snake is going into the pot.
He took a pen out of his pencil case.

(3) His grades are going up these days.
I sprained my ankle while walking down the stairs.

2

(1)
- from ~ to: ~로 부터 …로
- toward: ~로 향하여

(2)
- into: ~안으로
- out of: ~밖으로

(3)
- up: 위로
- down: 아래로

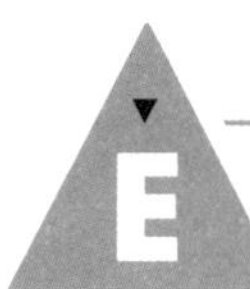

EXERCISE

Answers P.30

A

[ ] 안에서 알맞은 말을 고르시오.

1 The boy is climbing [at, up] the rope in the playground.

2 Sarah has her math class [between, among] English and music.

3 Don't jump [out of, in] the window. It's very dangerous.

4 He reached [into, among] his locker to get his books.

5 There is a pond [near, over] my house that is full of frogs.

6 Hang that picture [on, above] the sofa.

7 In Korean schools, second-year classrooms are usually [in, below] third-year classrooms.

B

in, on, at 중에서 알맞은 것을 골라 대화를 완성하시오.

1 A Is Karen ____________ the entrance? B Yes, she is.

2 A Where is Norway ____________ the map? B Here it is.

3 A Rocky, where are you? B I am ____________ the bathroom.

4 A Where is the leftover pizza? B It is ____________ the refrigerator.

5 A Someone is ____________ the door. B Do you know who it is?

6 A Look at the picture ____________ the wall. B Wow. It was painted by Gogh.

C

괄호 안의 해석을 참고하여 문장을 완성하시오.

1 There's something ________________ your back. (너의 등 뒤에)

2 The piano is ________________ the cabinet. (진열장 옆에)

3 He just got back ________________ Singapore. (싱가포르로부터)

4 There are gifts for you ________________ the Christmas tree. (크리스마스 나무 밑에)

5 The man was waiting for me ________________ the terminal. (터미널 앞에서)

6 The hospital is ________________ from the parking lot. (주차장 건너편에)

7 Hurry! That was the second bell! Get ________________ the classroom. (교실 안으로)

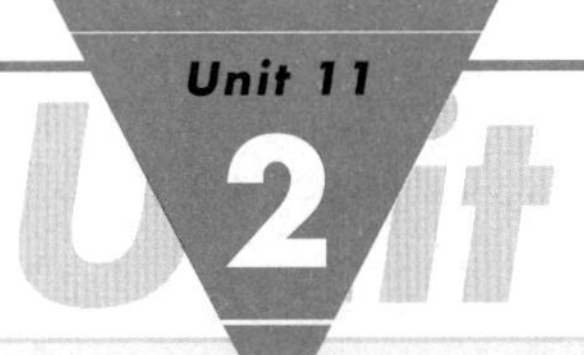

시간 전치사

He will be 14 years old in 2022.

He will enter middle school in March 2022.

The first day of school is on March 2nd.

His first class starts at 8 o'clock.

1 시간 전치사 (I)

(1) in+연도, 계절, 월 등
Amy first went to Europe in 2006.
I always go scuba diving in summer.
Chris will visit Germany in July.

(2) on+날짜, 요일, 특정한 날 등
We will go on a picnic on September 20th.
Andrew has a dental appointment on Monday.
I want to get many presents on Children's Day.

(3) at+시각, 하루의 때 등
I can meet you at 3 o'clock.
These days, my father comes home at midnight.

2 시간 전치사 (II)

(1) You should come back before dinner.
We can go to see a movie after school.

(2) Let's meet in front of the bank around〔about〕 4.

(3) He will not sleep during the exam period.
They will stay for 3 months.

(4) You have to finish it by tomorrow.
We waited for him until 5.

(5) I take my tennis lesson from 5 to 7.
I haven't met him since last year.
I'll be there in 2 hours.

1

(1) in+연도, 계절, 월 등

cf) in the morning / in the afternoon / in the evening

(2) on+날짜, 요일, 특정한 날 등
eg) on Christmas Day, on Easter Day

(3) at+시각, 하루의 때 등
eg) at noon, at night

2

(1)
• before: ~전에
• after: ~후에

(2)
• around(=about): (몇 시) 경에, 즈음에

(3)
• during, for: ~동안

※during과 for의 구별
• during+어떤 일이 일어난 때(when)를 나타내는 명사
eg) during summer vacation
during winter
• for+지속된 기간 (how long)
eg) for 3 months
for a week

(4)
• by: ~까지(**완료** 기한을 의미)
• until: ~까지(특정 시점까지의 **계속**을 의미)

(5)
• from ~ to: ~부터 …까지
• since: ~이래로 (계속) (현재완료와 함께 쓰임)
• in: ~후에

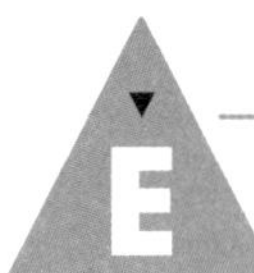

EXERCISE

Answers P.30

A

[ ] 안에서 알맞은 말을 고르시오.

1 My family goes skiing at Yongpyung Resort [in, on, at] winter.

2 My birthday is [in, on, at] March 27th.

3 My father always wants to eat something [in, on, at] midnight.

4 I leave for a trip to France [in, on, at] Friday night.

5 My class begins [in, on, at] 9 am.

6 We often climb Mt. Dobong [in, on, at] Sundays.

7 He used to call me [in, on, at] noon.

B

[보기]에서 알맞은 말을 골라 문장을 완성하시오.

Word Bank	for	until	during	since	around	by

1 I always wake up ____________ sunrise. (해가 뜰 무렵에)

2 It was raining ____________ midnight. (한밤중까지–계속)

3 I have lost contact with her ____________ graduation. (졸업 이후로)

4 You have to pay attention ____________ class. (수업시간 동안)

5 I will do my best to finish them ____________ September. (9월까지–완료)

6 Mark thought about the matter ____________ a moment. (잠시 동안)

C

괄호 안의 해석을 참고하여 문장을 완성하시오.

1 People who go to church eat eggs ______________________. (부활절에)

2 You should come back home ______________________. (여섯 시까지)

3 I will meet Joanna late ______________________. (오후에)

4 You should finish this report ______________________. (크리스마스 전에)

5 He hasn't been to school ______________________. (5일 동안)

6 I have to work ______________________ to 5 pm. (오전 9시부터)

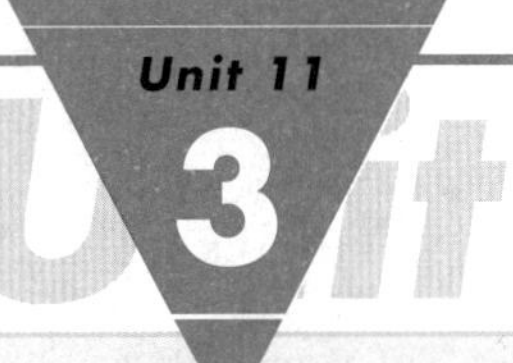

기타 전치사

수단, 도구	목적, 이유	장소, 방향
• with: ~로, ~를 가지고 • by+교통수단: ~로, ~를 타고	(1) • for: ① ~를 위해 ② (목적지)~를 향해 (2) • for: ~ 때문에 • with: ~ 때문에, ~로	around along through • around: ~주위에 • along: ~를 따라 • through: ~를 통과하여

1 수단, 도구

I painted my chair with this brush.
Can I go there by subway?

> 1
> • with: ~로, ~를 가지고
> • by+교통수단: ~로, ~를 타고
> (by taxi, by plane, by subway)
>
> *cf)* on foot: 걸어서

2 목적, 이유

(1) 목적

She brought an apple for the teacher.
He wore a nice suit for his job interview.
Are you leaving for London tonight?

(2) 이유

Thank you for coming to see me.
I have been busy with work.

> 2
> (1) • for: ① ~를 위해
> ② (목적지)~를 향해
>
> (2) • for: ~ 때문에
> • with: ~ 때문에, ~로

3 기타 전치사

The dog was running around the house.
Every weekend, I ride my bike along the Han River.
My phone call got cut off when we went through the tunnel.

Would you like to go shopping with me?
Happy birthday to you!
The letter was not written by me.
How did you know about the secret?
I have a great book on pop singers.
I bought the calendar for just $3.

> 3
> • around: ~주위에
> • along: ~를 따라
> • through: ~를 통과하여
> • with: ~와 함께
> • to: ~에게
> • by: ~에 의해
> • about, on: ~에 관한
> • for: ~의 가격에

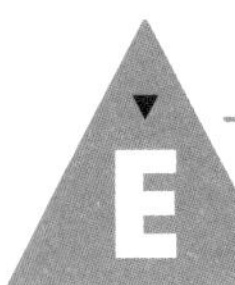

EXERCISE

Answers P.30

A

[ ] 안에서 알맞은 말을 고르시오.

1 Molly and I took a walk [through, around] the beautiful lake.

2 He is talking [with, along] the school counselor about his future.

3 I'll sell my old bike to you only [with, for] $10.

4 I'm sorry [to, for] talking in class.

5 I had to wait long to go [through, around] customs at the airport.

6 Wipe up the spilled juice [with, for] this paper towel.

B

[보기]에서 알맞은 말을 골라 문장을 완성하시오.

Word Bank	by	through	around	with	for	about

1 Come and sit ______________ the campfire. (캠프파이어 주위로)

2 What was the TV program ______________? (무엇에 대한)

3 We will throw a surprise party ______________ Julie. (Julie를 위한)

4 This is one of the most famous paintings ______________ Picasso. (Picasso에 의한)

5 The little kid had no one to play ______________, so she seemed lonely. (함께 놀)

6 He drove his first car ______________ the streets of Munich. (Munich 거리를 통과하여)

C

괄호 안의 해석을 참고하여 문장을 완성하시오.

1 I had no cash so I paid for my books ______________________________. (카드로)

2 It will take 2 hours to go there ______________________________. (기차로)

3 What do you do ______________________________? (너의 건강을 위해)

4 What happened ______________________________ last night? (그들에게)

5 Cut the paper ______________________________. (이 선을 따라)

6 I'll write ______________________________ for the writing assignment. (내 여름 방학에 관해)

REVIEW TEST

A

[ ] 안에서 알맞은 말을 고르시오.

1 My little brother likes to see movies [about, for] aliens.

2 I should study for the midterm exam [during, at] the holidays.

3 They will stay with us [by, until] this October.

4 According to a superstition, walking [under, after] a ladder brings bad luck.

5 I have been studying English [for, at] 8 years.

6 Jordan is very popular [in, among] the students in his class.

7 I went to the festival [by, with] my girlfriend last week.

B

빈칸에 들어갈 알맞은 말을 고르시오.

1 He will come back to Seoul ____________ two weeks.

ⓐ out of ⓑ between ⓒ during ⓓ in

2 I bought some flowers ____________ your grandmother.

ⓐ for ⓑ between ⓒ by ⓓ on

3 Have you ever read a book written ____________ Tolstoy?

ⓐ among ⓑ by ⓒ above ⓓ into

4 My brother and I were born ____________ January.

ⓐ among ⓑ on ⓒ at ⓓ in

5 The man sat silently on the chair ____________ the table.

ⓐ into ⓑ in ⓒ from ⓓ beside

6 Would you please stop by my office ____________ 5?

ⓐ in ⓑ around ⓒ on ⓓ from

7 The little girls are practicing ballet ____________ the huge mirror.

ⓐ in ⓑ on ⓒ in front of ⓓ among

C [보기]에서 알맞은 말을 골라 문장을 완성하시오.

Word Bank	into	on	for	near	about	at	with

1 Please study hard ___________ your future!

2 I started learning English ___________ a year ago.

3 Turn right ___________ the corner.

4 My family goes to church ___________ Sundays.

5 Do not go ___________ the dog when it's eating something.

6 John put his pencil back ___________ his pencil case.

7 The new girl in the class played ___________ her hair.

D 밑줄 친 부분을 바르게 고쳐, 문장을 다시 쓰시오.

1 What should I pack for my backpacking trip with India?

→ ___________________________

2 Almost every day among June to August, I went to the gym to work out.

→ ___________________________

3 You should give your paper from me before class.

→ ___________________________

4 He took off his coat and laid it down above the sofa.

→ ___________________________

5 I saw a cat playing for a small ball near the door.

→ ___________________________

6 I want you to buy some snacks at the store across of the school entrance.

→ ___________________________

7 Kelly visited New York during the winter vacation. She went there with train.

→ ___________________________

FURTHER STUDY

Answers P.31

A 글을 읽고, 밑줄 친 부분을 바르게 고쳐 쓰시오.

Every Sunday, I wake up early (1) at the morning and go jogging around my town for an hour with my dog. After jogging, I go to the beautiful park near the river (2) on my town and watch people playing soccer. On my way back (3) up my place, I drop by a small coffee shop across from the park and enjoy coffee there. In the afternoon, I usually spend time relaxing or watching TV. Sometimes I go to watch a movie (4) between my friends.

(1) ____________________

(2) ____________________

(3) ____________________

(4) ____________________

B 우리말과 같은 뜻이 되도록 주어진 말을 이용하여 문장을 완성하시오.

1 매 식사 후에 이를 닦아야 한다. (brush one's teeth, every meal)
→ You should ______________________________.

2 나는 도서관에서 두 시간 동안 공부했다. (the library, two hours)
→ I studied ______________________________.

3 Richard, 정오 전에 네 숙제를 제출해야 한다. (hand in, noon)
→ Richard, you have to ______________________________.

4 나는 저녁에 중식당에서 그를 만날 것이다. (a Chinese restaurant)
→ I'll meet him ______________________________.

5 계단을 내려올 때 조심해라. (come, the stairs)
→ Be careful when ______________________________.

Answers P.32

▶ 전치사별 쓰임과 예시

전치사	쓰임
in	〈장소: ~안에〉 - in the room, in the office, in a cafe, in my bag, in the box 〈시간: 계절, ① ________, 월〉 - in summer, in 2007, in July, in the morning, in the afternoon, in the evening 〈시간: ② ________〉 in 2 hours, in 15 minutes, in 30 seconds
on	〈장소: ③ ________, ~표면에〉 - on the table, on the shelf, on the hill, on the wall 〈시간: 날짜, ④ ________, 특정한 날〉 - on March 20th, on Sunday, on Monday, on Christmas Day, on Easter Day
at	〈장소: ~에 (특정한 지점)〉 - at school, at home, at the corner, at the bus stop 〈시간: 하루의 때〉 - at noon, at night, at midnight
to	〈방향: ~로〉 - go to school, to the east, from New York to Seattle 〈대상: ⑤ ________〉 - Happy birthday to you!, Give it to him. 〈시간: ~(시) 전〉 - You should come back at a quarter to nine. (9시 15분 전 = 8시 45분)
by	〈장소: ~옆에 (=beside, next to)〉 - sit by me, by him, by her, by the house 〈시간: ⑥ ________ (완료의 기한)〉 - by 10 o'clock, by 7, by this week, by tomorrow 〈수단: ~로〉 - by bus, by car, by train, by ship, by airplane *cf)* on foot
for	〈방향: ~을 향하여〉 - leave for Paris, head for America 〈시간: ⑦ ________〉 - for 3 days, for 2 months, for a week, for a long time 〈목적: ⑧ ________〉 - for you, for her, for his birthday present

▶ 주의해야 할 전치사의 쓰임

last Friday afternoon: last 앞에는 전치사를 잘 쓰지 않는다.

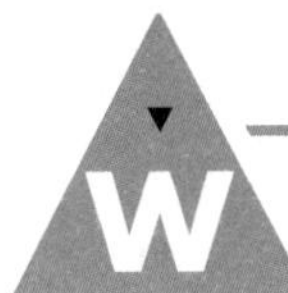

WRAP-UP TEST

Answers P.32

1 빈칸에 공통으로 들어갈 전치사를 고르시오.

· I have been ______ a small car for 6 hours.

· The plane is taking off ______ 5 minutes.

ⓐ on ⓑ in

ⓒ at ⓓ into

2 글을 읽고, 어색한 부분을 찾아 바르게 고치시오.

Among many people, she could find me easily. I was on red pants and walked with my dog along the street.

3 어법상 어색한 문장을 고르시오.

ⓐ The plane is above the clouds.

ⓑ There are many living things under the sea.

ⓒ They had a big parade in Independence Day.

ⓓ You should pack your bag before lunch.

4 밑줄 친 부분의 쓰임이 어색한 것을 고르시오.

ⓐ She went to Japan with ship.

ⓑ What do you usually do after school?

ⓒ He has done research on pollution.

ⓓ They are very busy with gardening.

5 빈칸에 들어갈 말이 바르게 연결된 것을 고르시오.

· Our house was built ______ my grandfather.

· The boy made a nice card ______ his mother.

· We have studied in the library ______ 7 am.

ⓐ by - by - from ⓑ with - to - for

ⓒ by - for - since ⓓ with - for - since

6 밑줄 친 to의 쓰임이 다른 것을 고르시오.

ⓐ Please give it to me.

ⓑ What happened to you?

ⓒ They go to the park every morning.

ⓓ Can you tell me how to get to the drug store?

7 두 문장이 같은 뜻이 되도록 문장을 완성하시오.

We set up our tent next to the oak tree.

= We set up our tent ______ the oak tree.

8 우리말과 같은 뜻이 되도록 문장을 완성하시오.

(1) 너는 10시까지 집에 들어와야 해.

= You should come home ______ ten.

(2) 우리는 서로를 오랫동안 보지 못했다.

= We haven't seen each other ______ a long time.

[9-10] 글을 읽고, 물음에 답하시오.

While I was in the Netherlands, I went to the Van Gogh museum. He painted __(A)__ 1,000 paintings during his life. I could see his famous paintings like "Sun Flowers" and "Starry Night" at the museum. I learned that he lived __(B)__ Gauguin in Arles. After Gauguin had left him, he cut off his ear.

9 (A)에 들어갈 알맞은 말을 고르시오.

ⓐ about ⓑ by

ⓒ for ⓓ below

10 (B)에 들어갈 알맞은 전치사를 쓰시오.

접속사와 절

1 등위접속사

2 명사절을 이끄는 종속접속사

3 부사절을 이끄는 종속접속사

4 부사절의 축약 (분사구문)

등위접속사

단어+단어 Seoul and London are my favorite cities.

구+구 I like playing the violin and learning foreign languages.

문장+문장 He went into the store, and his dog waited outside.

> 등위접속사
> 서로 대등한 관계인 단어와 단어, 구와 구, 문장과 문장을 연결하는 품사

1 and, but, or, so

(1) He did his homework but didn't clean his room.
Kelly enjoyed the trip, but her husband didn't.

(2) Which one would you like, coffee or green tea?
cf) You or your sister has to come.
You should get some rest or go to see a doctor.
Did you bring your lunch or do you want to eat out?

(3) I was tired, so I went to bed early.
I got a bad score, so I didn't tell my mom.

> 1
> (1) but: 그러나
> (2) or: 또는
> *cf)* 〈A or B〉가 주어로 올 때는 둘 중 B에 동사를 맞춘다.
> *eg)* He or you have to go.
> (3) so: 그래서 (문장을 연결)

2 명령문+and / or ~

Hurry and you will be able to get there on time.
(= If you hurry, you will be able to get there on time.)

Hurry or you will be late for school.
(= If you don't hurry, you will be late for school.)
(= Unless you hurry, you will be late for school.)

> 2
> • 명령문+and: ~해라, 그러면 (= If you ~: ~한다면)
> • 명령문+or: ~해라, 그렇지 않으면 (= If you don't ~: ~하지 않는다면) (= Unless you ~: ~하지 않는다면)

3 한 쌍으로 쓰이는 접속사

Both Tom and Susan wear glasses.
Whales are not fish, but mammals.
He is not only handsome, but (also) generous.
Let's study together either in the library or at my house.
Neither my parents nor my teacher was happy about my grade.

> 3
> • both A and B: A와 B 둘 다
> → 주어는 A+B: 복수 취급
> • not A but B: A가 아니고 B
> • not only A but also B: A뿐만 아니라 B도
> • either A or B: A나 B 둘 중 하나
> • neither A nor B: A, B 둘 다 ~ 아닌
> → 주어는 B: B에 동사를 맞춤

EXERCISE

Answers P.32

A

[ ] 안에서 알맞은 말을 고르시오.

1 I like playing computer games [so, and] chatting online.

2 I ran to school, [but, so] I was still late for class.

3 Do you have a question [so, or] a comment about the lecture?

4 He found his coat, [but, or] his hat was gone.

5 It is getting dark, [or, so] we have to leave now.

6 I was busy yesterday, [or, so] I couldn't see him.

7 The ball rolled into the road, [and, or] a car hit it.

8 Please call me [but, or] e-mail me as soon as possible.

B

두 문장의 의미가 통하도록 **and** 또는 **or**를 이용하여 문장을 완성하시오.

1 If you go straight for one block, you will find the building.
→ Go straight for one block ____________ you will find the building.

2 If you don't stop making that noise, I will complain to the teacher.
→ Stop making that noise ____________ I will complain to the teacher.

3 If you don't tell the truth, she will be very upset.
→ Tell the truth ____________ she will be very upset.

4 If you bring your membership card, you can get a discount.
→ Bring your membership card ____________ you can get a discount.

C

접속사를 이용하여 문장을 완성하시오.

1 Kevin is good at both math ____________ English.

2 Jasmine is not only beautiful, ____________ very smart.

3 She can study either at home ____________ in the library.

4 Harrison is not a singer ____________ an actor.

5 I make it a rule neither to borrow ____________ to lend money.

6 She likes to watch movies both at home ____________ in the theater.

Unit 12

2 명사절을 이끄는 종속접속사

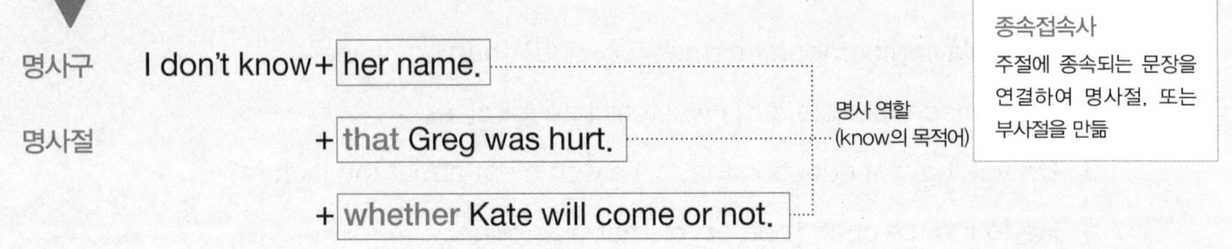

종속접속사
주절에 종속되는 문장을 연결하여 명사절, 또는 부사절을 만듦

1 that

(1) 주어 역할

That he is late for school is uncommon.

(→ It is uncommon that he is late for school.)

(2) 목적어 역할

I know (that) buses are always crowded at rush hour.

She believes (that) she is the prettiest in the class.

He thinks (that) his face is too long.

(3) 보어 역할

The point is that the store closes at 9.

The problem is that he doesn't like vegetables.

(4) 동격

I heard the news that Paul had a car accident.

She is trying to hide the fact that she is very sick.

▶ 1

(1) **주어 역할: ~하는 것은**
that절이 주어로 나오는 경우에는 가주어 it을 주어로 대신하고 that절을 뒤로 옮기는 것이 자연스럽다. (It ~ that)

(2) **목적어 역할: ~하는 것을**
: know, think, believe 등
이때의 접속사 that은 생략 가능하다.

(3) **보어 역할: ~하는 것이다**

(4) **동격: ~라는**
that절 내용이 the news, the fact와 동격이다.

2 if / whether

I don't know if he will come (or not).

(= I don't know whether he will come (or not).)

I wonder if they can use the Internet at home (or not).

She has to decide whether she will stay (or not).

■ 간접의문문

I don't know. + What does she want?
→ I don't know what she wants.

She didn't tell me. + Where did she buy it?
→ She didn't tell me where she bought it.

▶ 2

if (~ or not)= whether (~ or not): ~인지 아닌지: 동사의 목적어로 쓰임

cf) whether (~or not)절은 명사처럼 주어, 보어로 쓸 수 있다. 단, if절은 주어로 쓸 수 없다.

※ **간접의문문**: 의문문이 다른 문장 안에서 명사절로 쓰임
(1) 의문사 있는 간접의문문
I don't know what I want.
when he comes.
(2) 의문사 없는 간접의문문
if/whether+주어+동사(+or not)
I don't know if/whether I want it.
he comes.

cf) 의문사+do you think+주어+동사
do you believe
Where do you think she bought it?

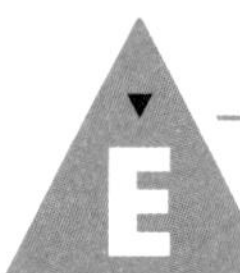

EXERCISE

Answers P.32

A

[ ] 안에서 알맞은 말을 고르시오.

1 I believe [if, that] the boy broke the window.

2 The question is [that, whether] she will agree or not.

3 I wonder [if, that] she ate six slices of pizza last night.

4 His mother knows [that, whether] he is playing computer games.

5 He doesn't care [that, whether] you like him or not.

6 No one can deny the fact [if, that] smoking is harmful.

7 I don't remember [if, what] Mark turned in his report.

B

"It ~ that"구문을 이용하여 문장을 완성하시오.

1 She keeps asking questions. It is stressful.

→ It is stressful ______________________________.

2 We exercise regularly. It is very important.

→ It is very important ______________________________.

3 Karen always wins first prize. It is amazing.

→ It is amazing ______________________________.

C

간접의문문을 완성하시오.

1 Who is he? I don't remember.

→ I don't remember ______________________________.

2 Where was Harry going? She didn't know.

→ She didn't know ______________________________.

3 How did you solve the math problem? I really want to know.

→ I really want to know ______________________________.

4 Why did you leave early? Everybody was curious.

→ Everybody was curious ______________________________.

5 Can he finish the work by 10? I am not sure.

→ I am not sure ______________________________.

Unit 12

Unit 3 부사절을 이끄는 종속접속사

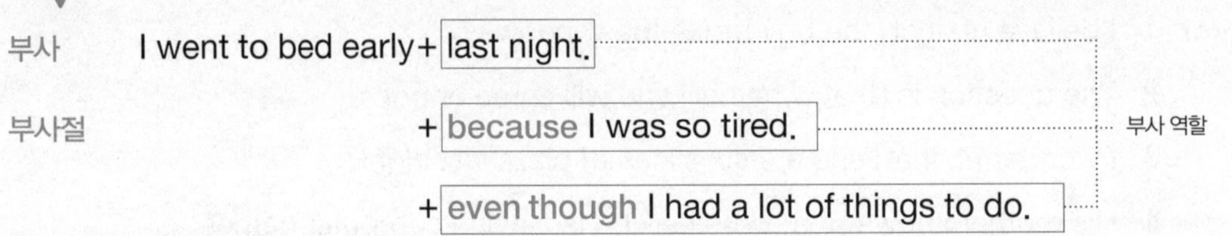

부사
I went to bed early+ last night.
부사절
+ because I was so tired.
+ even though I had a lot of things to do.
부사 역할

1 조건

Be confident first, if you want to speak English well.
He will be there unless it rains.
(= He will be there if it does not rain.)

1
if / unless (= if not)
: 만약 ~라면 / 만약 ~이 아니라면

※조건 부사절에서는 현재형으로 미래시제를 나타낸다.
(O) I will not go out if it rains tomorrow.
(X) I will not go out if it will rain tomorrow.

2 이유

He is in a hurry because the class begins in a minute.
cf) We didn't go out because of the cold weather.

Since it was cold outside, we didn't go out.
As it was raining all day, few people visited the amusement park.

2
because, as, since: 왜냐하면

cf) because+절 (주어+동사)
because of+명사구/대명사구

3 양보

I went to school, (even) though I was very sick.
Although it didn't look fresh, it tasted sweet.
He helped her, even though he was very busy at that time.

3
though, although, even though
: ~임에도 불구하고

4 시간

When school is over, we will go to the gym.
She was crying as I entered the classroom.
My brother ate the pizza while I was sleeping.
You can keep my book until I need it again.
I'll buy some popcorn before the movie starts.
I arrived at the airport after my flight took off.
I have been interested in animations since I was little.

4
- when, as: ~할 때
- while: ~하는 동안, ~하는 중에
- until (=till): ~할 때까지
- before: ~하기 전에
- after: ~한 후에

※시간 부사절에서는 현재형으로 미래시제를 나타낸다.
(O) She will finish her homework before he comes.
(X) She will finish her homework before he will come.

- since: ~ 이후로, 이래로 (현재완료와 함께 쓰임)

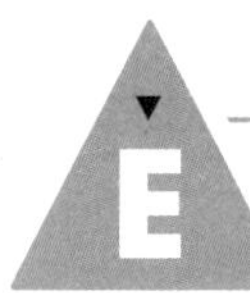

EXERCISE

Answers P.32

A

[ ] 안에서 알맞은 말을 고르시오.

1 [If, Unless] you don't arrive on time, we won't be allowed to enter the show.

2 [As, If] I like peaches, my grandfather picked some for me on his farm.

3 [If, Unless] you take good notes, you can't do well on the test.

4 The man tried to save her, [even though, unless] it was very dangerous.

5 I can't buy a cell phone [because, though] I don't have any money now.

6 I usually drink a glass of milk [although, before] I go to bed.

7 We are going to stay here [because of, until] the meeting ends.

8 [When, While] you get there, you should send me an e-mail.

B

밑줄 친 부분을 바르게 고쳐 쓰시오. 틀리지 않았다면 O표 하시오.

1 My mother will pick you up after she will finish her work. ____________

2 You have to keep exercising until you lose 10 pounds. ____________

3 I regret not visiting my relatives until I was in Tokyo. ____________

4 He has gained a lot of experience since he came here. ____________

5 Don't eat snacks in the classroom if you bring enough for everyone. ____________

6 I can't focus on studying because the hot weather. ____________

C

두 문장의 의미가 통하도록 주어진 접속사를 이용하여 문장을 완성하시오.

1 I woke up late, so I was late for school. (because)

→ I was late for school ______________________________.

2 Unless he leaves early, he can't arrive on time. (if)

→ ______________________________, he can't arrive on time.

3 I made some mistakes, but I still got an A. (though)

→ ______________________________, I still got an A.

Unit 12

Unit 4 부사절의 축약 (분사구문)

접속사, 주어 탈락

부사절 As he felt happy, he smiled at her.

분사구문 Feeling happy, he smiled at her.

분사구문
현재분사를 활용하여 부사절을
부사구로 간단히 만든 구문으로
주로 문어체에서 사용

1 분사구문의 종류

(1) 시간, 때

When he graduated from school, he moved to Japan.
→ Graduating from school, he moved to Japan.

(2) 이유

Since I felt dizzy, I lay down on the sofa.
→ Feeling dizzy, I lay down on the sofa.
As he was disappointed, he said nothing.
→ (Being) Disappointed, he said nothing.

(3) 조건

If you turn to the next page, you can see the test.
→ Turning to the next page, you can see the test.

(4) 동시동작(상황)

While he was crossing the road, he talked to Julie on the phone.
→ (Being) Crossing the road, he talked to Julie on the phone.

cf) 주어가 다를 때

Since the plant was dry, I watered it.
→ The plant being dry, I watered it.

1
접속사의 종류에 따라 시간, 이유, 조건 등의 의미를 나타냄
- 시간: when, as, after, before
- 이유: as, because, since
- 조건: if
- 동시상황: while, and

분사구문 만들기
① 접속사 생략
② 주어 생략
③ 동사는 현재분사(-ing)로
(단, being으로 시작하는 경우, being을 생략하기도 한다.)

※경우에 따라 접속사를 생략하지 않고 그대로 남겨 두기도 한다.
eg) While studying English,
I listened to the music.

cf) 주어가 다를 때는 주절의 주어를 남겨둔다.

2 분사구문의 부정

Since he did not arrive on time, he missed his flight.
→ Not arriving on time, he missed his flight.

Because I didn't know him well, I didn't invite him.
→ Not knowing him well, I didn't invite him.

2
분사구문의 부정: Not (Never)+분사 (-ing/-ed)

EXERCISE

Answers P.33

A

[ ] 안에서 알맞은 말을 고르시오.

1 Though she [being, was] tired, she cooked for us.

2 [Been, Being] young, he doesn't think carefully before he acts.

3 [Find, Finding] the clue, we solved the mystery.

4 If she [reading, reads] the book, she can get a good grade.

5 After you [finish, will finish] dinner, you have to wash the dishes.

6 [Not winning, Winning not] the game, we walked away disappointed.

B

두 문장이 같은 뜻이 되도록 [ ] 안에서 알맞은 접속사를 고르시오.

1 Leaving the house, he locked the door.
= [As, Though] he left the house, he locked the door.

2 Failing math, he needed some help from his friend.
= [Although, Since] he failed math, he needed some help from his friend.

3 Coming early, we still won't be able to see her.
= [Even though, While] we come early, we still won't be able to see her.

4 Arriving at the store to buy a board game, he called me.
= [If, When] he arrived at the store to buy a board game, he called me.

5 Not sitting straight at your desk, you can get back pain.
= [If, Though] you don't sit straight at your desk, you can get back pain.

C

두 문장의 의미가 통하도록 분사구문을 이용하여 문장을 완성하시오.

1 When we stood in front of the house, we saw a ghost.
→ ____________________, we saw a ghost.

2 As we were very scared, we hugged each other.
→ ____________________, we hugged each other.

3 If you buy two of them, you will get one free.
→ ____________________, you will get one free.

4 After I finished my homework, I watched a movie.
→ ____________________, I watched a movie.

REVIEW TEST

A

[ ] 안에서 알맞은 말을 고르시오.

1 I thought [that, though] he was innocent, but he wasn't.

2 We don't know [what, when] they will arrive.

3 Ryan has visited many palaces [since, when] he arrived in Seoul.

4 You can't watch TV [if, unless] you clean your room.

5 There's nothing I can do [since, until] the weather clears up.

6 Wanda goes to ballet class on Thursdays, [but, or] I go there on Fridays.

7 You should not talk [until, while] you are eating something.

B

빈칸에 들어갈 알맞은 말을 고르시오.

1 It snowed a lot last night, ____________ I'm going skiing.

ⓐ if　ⓑ unless　ⓒ so　ⓓ though

2 Today, it was rainy in the morning ____________ sunny in the afternoon.

ⓐ but　ⓑ if　ⓒ or　ⓓ so

3 I am in a hurry ____________ the train leaves in a moment.

ⓐ but　ⓑ because　ⓒ after　ⓓ although

4 We should turn off our cell phones ____________ we go into the theater.

ⓐ so　ⓑ or　ⓒ before　ⓓ though

5 Which computer do you want, this one ____________ that one?

ⓐ and　ⓑ or　ⓒ because　ⓓ if

6 Eric's baby brother wants to have both a toy car ____________ a robot.

ⓐ but　ⓑ so　ⓒ and　ⓓ or

7 ____________ he was sitting in front of the heater, he still felt very cold.

ⓐ Because　ⓑ As　ⓒ Until　ⓓ Although

Answers P.33

C

[보기]에서 알맞은 말을 골라 문장을 완성하시오.

Word Bank	or	if	unless	because	though	after	where

1 I want to go with you ____________ you don't mind.

2 Mary took her sister to the play ____________ it is for all ages.

3 You will get sicker and sicker ____________ you go to the hospital.

4 Patrick has lost his dog, and he doesn't know ____________ it is.

5 Please call me as soon as possible, ____________ leave me a message.

6 Beethoven still composed music ____________ he went deaf.

7 ____________ he is very young, he can speak English fluently.

D

밑줄 친 부분을 바르게 고쳐, 문장을 다시 쓰시오.

1 He won't believe me unless I will give him the evidence.

→ ______________________________

2 Although it is a sudden request, they didn't complain at all.

→ ______________________________

3 Kelly doesn't remember what did she yesterday.

→ ______________________________

4 Being wake up early, we weren't late for school.

→ ______________________________

5 You will not pass the exam, if you study hard.

→ ______________________________

6 Unless you enter the concert hall, you should check your seat number.

→ ______________________________

7 Because it's new, this lap top computer doesn't function properly.

→ ______________________________

FURTHER STUDY

Answers P.34

A 글을 읽고, 밑줄 친 부분을 바르게 고쳐 쓰시오.

Returning home, I found the front door open. Since I definitely remembered (1) what I had locked the door on my way out, I became afraid that my place had been robbed. I froze and listened. (2) Hear nothing, I decided to go in and see what was going on. (3) Because I entered the house, I saw that nothing had been taken or broken. I started to feel better. Then I heard noises coming from the bathroom. Someone was in it. I wondered (4) that was going on in there. After several seconds, the door was opened, and I saw a familiar face – my brother! He had dropped by to visit me. He needed to go to the bathroom badly, so he had rushed and not closed the front door properly.

(1) ______________________

(2) ______________________

(3) ______________________

(4) ______________________

B 우리말과 같은 뜻이 되도록 주어진 말을 이용하여 문장을 완성하시오.

1 네가 전화했을 때 나는 수학 공부를 하고 있었다. (when, call)
→ ______________________, I was studying math.

2 비록 비가 심하게 오고 있지만 우리는 가야 한다. (although, rain, heavily)
→ ______________________, we have to go.

3 나는 Mike가 학교를 그만두었다는 소문을 들었다. (that, quit, the school)
→ I heard the rumor ______________________.

4 우리는 여기 이사 올 때까지 강아지 한 마리를 키웠다. (until, move)
→ We raised a puppy ______________________.

5 만약 숙제를 다 끝내지 않으면, 너는 우리와 같이 갈 수 없다. (unless, finish one's homework)
→ You can't come with us ______________________.

Answers P.34

▶ 접속사의 종류

종류	예
등위접속사	for (왜냐하면) and (그리고) but (그러나) or (또는) yet (그러나) so (그래서)
종속접속사	(1) 시간, 때: ① ____________, since, as, while, until, before, after (2) 원인: ② ____________, since, as (3) 조건: ③ ____________, unless (4) 양보: even though, although, though
상관접속사	(1) A and B: A와 (그리고) B (2) not A but B: A가 아니라 B (3) either A or B: A 또는 B (4) neither A nor B: A도 B도 아닌 (5) not only A but also B: A뿐만 아니라 B도

▶ 절(clause)의 종류

종류		예문
명사절	[접속사/의문사] (1) that (2) if / whether (3) 의문사	(1) It is true that freedom is very precious. (2) I wonder if she is okay now. I don't care whether she comes or not. (3) I don't understand what he said.
부사절	[접속사/분사구문] (1) 시간 (2) 이유 (3) 조건 (4) 양보	(1) When he visited me, I was doing my homework. (2) As he asked me to call, I called him last night. (3) If you want to meet him, you should e-mail him first. (4) Though I was very tired, I finished my homework.
형용사절	[관계대명사] (1) who (2) which (3) that 〈Unit 13 관계대명사 참조〉	(1) I like the girl who sits next to me. (2) I like sandwiches which have thick slices of ham and cheese. (3) We see the dog and the boy that are coming to us.

WRAP-UP TEST

Answers P.34

1 빈칸에 들어갈 말이 순서대로 짝지어진 것을 고르시오.

> · I called her _______ she didn't answer me.
> · I can't go out _______ my mom comes home.
> · _______ they were very tired, they kept practicing.

ⓐ but - until - Although
ⓑ so - while - Although
ⓒ but - until - If
ⓓ so - while - If

2 문장을 읽고, 어색한 곳을 찾아 바르게 고치시오.

The baseball game was called off because the heavy rain and strong wind.

3 어법상 어색한 문장을 고르시오.

ⓐ Since I got up late, I took a taxi.
ⓑ I was very curious why was she angry at me.
ⓒ We drink a glass of water before we have a meal.
ⓓ Even though the doctor advised him to exercise, he didn't.

4 두 문장이 같은 뜻이 되도록 문장을 완성하시오.

(1) If you take this pill, you will feel better.
→ Take this pill _________ you will feel better.
(2) Unless you take an umbrella, you will get wet.
→ Take an umbrella _________ you will get wet.

5 빈칸에 공통으로 들어갈 말을 쓰시오.

· There is no hope ___________ my mom will forgive me.
· It is unbelievable ___________ she made the same mistake.
· Our plan is ___________ we teach each subject to each other.

6 밑줄 친 when의 쓰임이 다른 하나를 고르시오.

ⓐ Call me when you need my help.
ⓑ When I arrived at the bus stop, the bus had already gone.
ⓒ I used to be good at running when I was young.
ⓓ We asked the box office when the movie would start.

7 밑줄 친 부분을 분사구문으로 바꾸시오.

Since he didn't study hard, he didn't do well on the finals.
→ ______________________________, he didn't do well on the finals.

8 빈칸에 알맞은 상관접속사를 써 넣으시오.

(1) Edison invented ___________ the radio and the phonograph.
(2) Neither my husband ___________ I reserved a hotel.

[9-10] 글을 읽고, 물음에 답하시오.

> Many people have heard about St. Patrick's Day, but they have never heard about St. Patrick. (A) When he was young, he was captured by Irish warriors and was made a slave. Later the English youth escaped. ___(B)___ he became a Christian priest, he returned to Ireland and brought Christianity to the people there.

9 (A)를 분사구문으로 바꾸시오.

10 (B)에 들어갈 알맞은 말을 고르시오.

ⓐ Unless ⓑ Until
ⓒ After ⓓ If

관계사

1 관계대명사
2 관계대명사의 쓰임
3 관계대명사의 특별 용법
4 관계부사

관계대명사

사람인 경우	사물인 경우
I know a girl.+She has curly hair.	I bought a computer.+It is brand-new.
대명사 역할	대명사 역할
I know a girl+who has curly hair.	I bought a computer+which is brand-new.
접속사 역할	접속사 역할
I know a girl who has curly hair.	I bought a computer which is brand-new.

1 관계대명사의 역할 (접속사+대명사)

I don't like the man. + He is wearing a hat.
→ I don't like the man who is wearing a hat.

The tree is a palm tree. + It grows in the tropical climate.
→ The tree is a palm tree which grows in the tropical climate.

2 관계대명사의 선행사

선행사	관계대명사	예문
사람	who	I have a friend who is talkative. (선행사: a friend)
사물, 동물	which	Eat the food which is on the dining table. (선행사: the food)
모두 포함	that	We are watching two cats and three kids that are playing in the playground. (선행사: two cats and three kids)

(1) 선행사가 사람일 때
I have a friend who is very nice to everybody.
Can you see the student that is talking to the teacher?

(2) 선행사가 사물 및 동물일 때
She has a cell phone which has a digital camera.
I bought a dog that has curly hair.

(3) 여러 가지 선행사
I saw a boy and a dog that were walking in the park.
He was the only one that was interested in the election.
It is the most beautiful flower that I have ever seen.

1
관계대명사
두 문장을 연결해주는 「접속사+대명사」의 역할

2
선행사: 관계사절이 수식하는(설명하는) 명사
(1) 사람: who, that
(2) 사물: which, that
(3) 여러 가지 선행사: that
- 사람+사물
- 최상급/서수, the only, the very, the same, -thing+명사일 때 who나 which보다는 that을 주로 쓴다.
- (x) 전치사+that / (x) of that

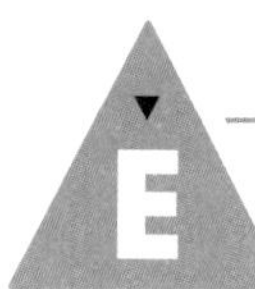

EXERCISE

Answers P.35

A

[ ] 안에서 알맞은 말을 고르시오.

1 I have never met a person [which, who] likes cold weather as much as you do.

2 She has a brother and a sister [which, who] have dimples on their cheeks.

3 Nancy visited an apple orchard [which, who] is 100 years old.

4 I'll take the idea [that, who] you have agreed with each other.

5 I want to date someone [which, who] is outgoing and humorous.

6 The police found the dog and the young boy [who, that] were lost in my town.

B

밑줄 친 부분을 바르게 고쳐 쓰시오. 틀리지 않았다면 O표 하시오.

1 She met a guy which was very cute and handsome. ______

2 I need to catch the school bus who leaves at 7 o'clock. ______

3 We visited a museum that is located in downtown Sydney. ______

4 Did you bring the dog whose is barking outside? ______

5 I want to do something of that we all can enjoy together. ______

6 He decided to sell the car who has been driven for two years. ______

C

두 문장을 관계대명사를 이용하여 한 문장으로 바꿔 쓰시오.

1 I always ask my friend. He is good at math.

→ ______

2 Korea has many cities. They are modern.

→ ______

3 He rescued a little girl. She was drowning.

→ ______

4 You are the only person. You can help me.

→ ______

5 She will bring something. It will make you surprised.

→ ______

관계대명사의 쓰임

주격 Henry has a girlfriend. She is studying in Italy.

= Henry has a girlfriend who is studying in Italy.

목적격 I met the magician. I saw him in the movie.

= I met the magician whom I saw in the movie.

소유격 He is washing his dog. Its name is Rocky.

= He is washing his dog whose name is Rocky.

1 주격 (~은 / 는 / 이 / 가)

James called the person who had left a message.
He wants to go to a high school which has a dorm.
We talked to the girl that was the team leader.

선행사	관계대명사의 격		
	주격	목적격	소유격
사람	who	who(m)	whose
사물/동물	which	which	whose (of which)
모두 포함	that	that	-

1
주격: 관계대명사+동사

2 목적격 (~을 / 를)

I don't like the man (whom) I met at the party.
Frank gave me the watch (which) I wanted to buy.
She pointed at the picture (that) you mentioned.

cf) She is the person (whom) I have been looking for.
(= She is the person for whom I have been looking.)
This is the dog (which) I must take care of.
(= This is the dog of which I must take care.)

2
목적격: 관계대명사+주어+동사
→ 관계대명사 생략 가능
※목적격 관계대명사 whom을 who로도 쓸 수 있다.

cf) 전치사의 목적어가 되는 관계대명사
: 〈전치사+관계대명사〉순으로 올 때는 관계대명사를 생략할 수 없다.

3 소유격 (~의)

He has a sister. Her school is in London.
→ He has a sister whose school is in London.

He has a notebook. Its cover is yellow.
→ He has a notebook whose cover is yellow.

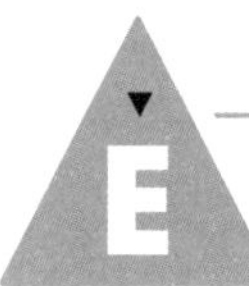

EXERCISE

Answers P.35

A

[ ] 안에서 알맞은 말을 고르시오.

1 She enjoys comic books [which, who] are written in English.

2 We know that man [who, whose] is talking to Susan.

3 Ricky is the only person [who, whose] birthday is in July.

4 He likes the dog [that, who] is in the pet shop.

5 I have a lovely friend [whom, whose] everybody likes.

6 They purchased a picture [that, whose] everyone wanted to have.

7 I finished the courses [for which, for whom] I signed up.

8 He is a man [which, whom] I really wanted to meet.

B

밑줄 친 부분을 바르게 고쳐 쓰시오.

1 He can order anything <u>who</u> he wants. ______________

2 Let's ask the boy <u>which</u> is sitting on the bench. ______________

3 I was the only member <u>whose</u> came to the monthly meeting. ______________

4 My friend has a cat <u>that</u> eyes are blue and gray. ______________

5 We received calendars <u>who</u> are full of beautiful pictures. ______________

6 She has a boyfriend <u>which</u> goes to Cornell University. ______________

7 I like the English teacher <u>which</u> every student likes. ______________

C

밑줄 친 부분을 선행사로 하여 관계대명사를 이용한 문장으로 바꿔 쓰시오.

1 I have <u>a friend</u>. His sister goes to Harvard University.

→ ______________________________

2 There is <u>a book</u>. It is very similar to mine.

→ ______________________________

3 Every Sunday, he visits <u>his grandmother</u>. She really enjoys cooking.

→ ______________________________

4 This is <u>the first event</u>. Charles has planned it.

→ ______________________________

5 This is <u>a brand-new TV</u>. We bought it yesterday.

→ ______________________________

관계대명사의 특별 용법

제한적 용법 Mary has a son who is a famous actor.
(유명한 배우인 아들이 하나 있다는 뜻으로 아들이 총 몇 명인지 알 수 없음)

계속적 용법 Mary has a son, who is a famous actor.
(아들이 하나 밖에 없는데, 그 아들이 유명한 배우라는 뜻)

1 제한적 용법과 계속적 용법

Jim has a brother who is a fireman.
Jim has a brother, who is a fireman.
(= Jim has a brother, and he is a fireman.)

I bought a car which has a wonderful car stereo.
I bought a car, which was stolen the next day.
(= I bought a car, and it was stolen the next day.)

cf) (X) He moved to a new house, that has a garden.

1
제한적(한정적) 용법
- 선행사+관계(대명사)절
- 관계절을 먼저 해석한 후, 선행사를 해석하는 것이 자연스럽다.

계속적 용법
- 쉼표(,)+관계대명사 = 접속사+대명사
- 앞 문장을 보충 설명

cf) 관계대명사 that은 계속적 용법에 쓰이지 않는다. (X) , that

2 절 전체를 선행사로 받는 계속적 용법

I bought a car, which made my mom angry.
= and it (it = that I bought a car)

She invited the man, which was generous of her.
= and it (it = that she invited the man)

2
앞의 절 전체를 선행사로 받는 계속적 용법의 관계대명사는 which이다.

■ 관계대명사 that vs. 종속접속사 that
: that 앞에 선행사가 있으면 관계대명사, 없으면 접속사이다. 단, 동격 접속사에 주의하자.

- 관계대명사 Look at the girl that (who) is eating a hot dog.
  This is the apple pie that (which) I made.
- 접속사 I know that she loves me.
  That she won the lottery is unbelievable.
  (= It is unbelievable that she won the lottery.)

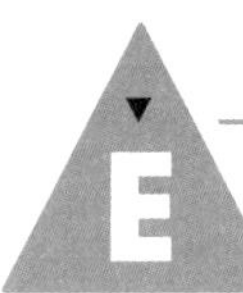

EXERCISE

Answers P.35

A 선행사에 밑줄을 그으시오.

1 I have two sisters, who are studying at Seoul National University.

2 She has a brother who lives in Africa.

3 He bought sneakers, which didn't fit his feet.

4 Jennifer bought a skirt which is blue and white.

5 Yesterday I broke some windows, which made my teacher angry.

6 Yesterday I broke some windows which had been replaced last week.

7 The salesperson visited a house, which was a waste of time.

8 The salesperson visited a house which was next to the shopping mall.

B 우리말과 같은 뜻이 되도록 빈칸에 알맞은 관계대명사를 써 넣으시오.

1 나는 일본 애니메이션에 대한 보고서를 읽었다.

→ I read the report ____________ was about Japanese animation.

2 그녀는 우주비행사로서 받아들여진 최초의 여성이었다.

→ She was the first woman ____________ was accepted as an astronaut.

3 나는 어젯밤에 그에게 전화했는데, 그것은 실수였다.

→ I called him last night, ____________ was a mistake.

4 Van Gogh는 세계에서 가장 유명한 화가 중 한 명인데, 그는 1890년에 죽었다.

→ One of the most famous artists in the world is Van Gogh, ____________ died in 1890.

C 밑줄 친 that을 접속사는 "C", 관계대명사는 "R"로 구분하시오.

1 This is the house that we live in. ____________

2 I know that the coach cares about the team. ____________

3 They carried several boxes that looked very heavy. ____________

4 It was amazing that we found each other in the crowd. ____________

5 The truth is that he is innocent. ____________

6 We wanted to join the team that won the championship last year. ____________

관계부사

관계대명사 This is the house which my friend lives in.

in which

관계부사 This is the house where my friend lives.

관계부사 = 전치사+관계대명사
접속사와 부사(구)의 역할을 하며 관계대명사처럼 선행사를 꾸며주지만, 대명사 역할 대신, 부사 역할을 함(시간, 장소, 이유, 방법)

1 where: 장소

This is the cafe. Rick first met Jinny in the cafe.
→ This is the cafe in which Rick first met Jinny.
→ This is the cafe where Rick first met Jinny.

This is the hospital. I was born in the hospital.
→ This is the hospital where (= in which) I was born.

※ 관계부사의 종류

	선행사	관계부사
장소	the place, the city, the house 등	where
시간	the time, the day, the year 등	when
이유	the reason: 생략 가능	why
방법	the way나 how 중 하나만 써야 함	how

2 when: 시간

2013 was the year. We first met in that year.
→ 2013 was the year in which we first met.
→ 2013 was the year when we first met.

It was fall. We went hiking together in fall.
→ It was fall when (= in which) we went hiking together.

3 why: 이유

Tell me the reason. You were late for the reason.
→ Tell me the reason for which you were late.
→ Tell me (the reason) why you were late.

3
※ the reason은 선행사로 잘 쓰이지 않는다.

4 how: 방법

Tell me how you solved this problem.
(= Tell me the way you solved this problem.)

Tell me the way. You solved this problem in the way.
→ Tell me the way (in which) you solved this problem.
→ Tell me how you solved this problem.

4
※방법을 나타내는 how는 the way와 함께 쓸 수 없다.
(X) Tell me the way how you passed the exam.

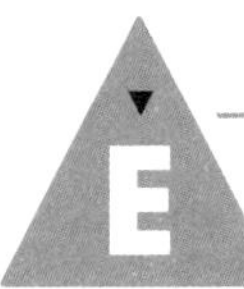

EXERCISE

Answers P.36

A

[ ] 안에서 알맞은 말을 고르시오.

1 The school [when, where] I graduated had a swimming pool.

2 Yesterday was the day [where, when] she had an interview for entering the university.

3 He didn't let anyone know [the way, which] he got into the building.

4 Sleeping in class is [how, why] he was sent to the principal's office.

5 The man is sitting in the office [where, how] my father used to work.

6 That was the time [how, when] everyone took off.

7 Does she understand [why, where] she failed the test?

8 I don't know [how, where] anyone can operate this old copier.

B

빈칸에 **where, when, how** 중 알맞은 것을 써 넣으시오.

1 Have you been to the park ______________ the new statue is?

2 The day ______________ we left for Europe was a cold, rainy day.

3 Can you tell me ______________ we can get to the National Art Museum?

4 This is ______________ my mother taught me English last year.

5 That was the week ______________ my brother from Hong Kong stayed here.

6 He found the room ______________ the meeting will be held.

C

[보기]와 같이 관계부사를 이용한 문장으로 바꿔 쓰시오.

Example The hotel wasn't very clean. We stayed there.
→ The hotel where we stayed wasn't very clean.

1 The circus was closed down. We saw some clowns there.

→ ____

2 2013 was the year. My team won the championship then.

→ ____

3 Tell me the way. You made the cake in the way.

→ ____

4 I can tell the reason. Matt painted his house red for the reason.

→ ____

REVIEW TEST

A

[ ] 안에서 알맞은 말을 고르시오.

1 I wrote a letter to my friend [who, whose] lives in Oregon, America.

2 I had to help the person [which, whose] car had broken down.

3 I visited the village [where, why] my father was born.

4 He is the person [whom, whose] I talked about.

5 Would you tell me [how, the way how] you got an A in the course?

6 She didn't write down the date on [which, why] they are arriving.

7 Tina is the only person [that, which] makes me pleased.

B

빈칸에 들어갈 알맞은 말을 고르시오.

1 His sister bought a dog ____________ is one month old.

ⓐ who ⓑ which ⓒ whose ⓓ about which

2 We have an English teacher ____________ hometown is London.

ⓐ who ⓑ whose ⓒ which ⓓ that

3 I know the city ____________ Jessy lives.

ⓐ who ⓑ whose ⓒ which ⓓ where

4 He calls his sister ____________ he likes the most.

ⓐ which ⓑ whose ⓒ whom ⓓ for which

5 Amy wants to have the same cat ____________ Susie has.

ⓐ who ⓑ of which ⓒ whose ⓓ that

6 Jack bought a house ____________ roof is blue.

ⓐ whom ⓑ that ⓒ which ⓓ whose

7 Kenny helped a girl and a puppy ____________ were lost.

ⓐ who ⓑ which ⓒ that ⓓ what

C

[보기]에서 알맞은 말을 골라 문장을 완성하시오.

Word Bank	, who	who	, which	which	that	whose	why

1 The girl ____________ is sitting on the seashore is my sister.

2 He was not the first winner ____________ I expected.

3 My friend, Amy ____________ lives next door, made a cake for me yesterday.

4 She bought a necklace ____________ is made of white gold.

5 Would you mind telling me the reason ____________ you are calling?

6 We saw a big fish ____________ fins look like a butterfly's wings.

7 Stockholm ____________ is the capital of Sweden, is one of the most crowded museum-towns in the world.

D

밑줄 친 부분을 바르게 고쳐, 문장을 다시 쓰시오.

1 This is the first time who I have won a prize.

→ ________________________________

2 He loves that girl whose is wearing glasses.

→ ________________________________

3 Somebody hit my brother, who made me mad.

→ ________________________________

4 My mom bought a computer which color is black.

→ ________________________________

5 Those colored pencils, which is blue, are my sister's.

→ ________________________________

6 I'll never forget the day why I first met you.

→ ________________________________

7 My grandmother lent me a book who has the recipe.

→ ________________________________

FURTHER STUDY

Answers P.37

A 글을 읽고, 밑줄 친 부분을 바르게 고쳐 쓰시오.

When I turned six, I got a pet (1) whose had curly, white fur and long ears. It was my birthday present, a two-month-old puppy. I named it Harry. I was very happy to have Harry, but soon I realized (2) which it was hard work to raise a pet. My mom said Harry was my pet and not hers! So she neither fed nor cleaned him. I would learn to be responsible. She wrote me a list of the things (3) who I had to do. Besides feeding and cleaning him, I had to take him for walks every weekend. And when he was ill, I took him to the vet, (4) whom takes care of sick animals.

(1) ______________

(2) ______________

(3) ______________

(4) ______________

B 우리말과 같은 뜻이 되도록 관계사와 주어진 말을 이용하여 문장을 완성하시오.

1 Paul은 청바지를 입고 있는 형과 함께 놀고 있다. (wear, blue jeans)
→ Paul is playing with his brother ______________.

2 나는 큰 정원이 있는 집에서 살고 싶다. (a big garden)
→ I want to live in a house ______________.

3 스쿨버스가 일찍 왔는데, 나를 놓고서 떠날 뻔 했다. (come, early)
→ My school bus, ______________, almost left without me.

4 나는 그 시험이 연기된 이유를 모르겠다. (be postponed)
→ I don't know the reason ______________.

5 나는 그에게 다음 버스가 도착할 시간을 알려주었다. (the next bus, will, arrive)
→ I told him the time ______________.

Answers P.37

▶ 관계대명사

선행사	관계대명사	관계대명사의 격		
		주격	목적격	소유격
사람	who	who	③ ________	④ ________
사물, 동물	which	② ________	which	whose [of which]
모두 포함	① ________	that	that	없음

▶ 관계부사

선행사		관계부사	전치사+관계대명사
장소	the place, the city, the house 등	① ________	in which (on / at 등)
시간	the time, the day, the year 등	② ________	in which (on / at 등)
이유	the reason: 주로 생략	③ ________	for which
방법	(the way): how와 같이 쓸 수 없음	④ ________	in which

cf) 관계부사를 〈전치사+관계대명사〉로 바꿀 때는 앞에 나오는 선행사에 따라 전치사가 달라진다.

▶ 접속사 that vs. 관계대명사 that

	접속사 that	관계대명사 that
주어	**That** we met Super Junior on the street was a miracle. (= It was a miracle **that** we met Super Junior on the street.)	I met singers **that** are popular in Korea. **(= who)**
목적어	I believe **that** she loves me. I think **that** she is very beautiful.	This is the apple pie **that** I made. **(= which)**
보어	The truth is **that** coffee is addictive. The point is **that** I can't do anything without you.	
비교	※앞에 선행사가 없다. ※접속사 that은 that을 제외해도 뒤에 따라오는 문장이 완벽하다.	※앞에 선행사가 있다. ※관계대명사 that은 접속사이면서 뒤 문장의 주어나 목적어이기 때문에 뒤에 오는 문장이 미완성 문장이다.

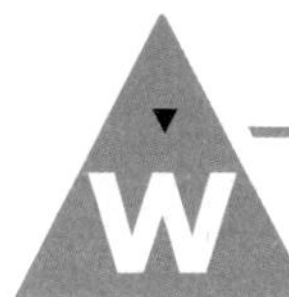

WRAP-UP TEST

Answers P.37

1 빈칸에 알맞은 말을 고르시오.

Where is my bike? It used to be next to your car.
= Where is my bike ___________ used to be by your car?

ⓐ who ⓑ whose
ⓒ which ⓓ what

2 빈칸에 들어갈 말이 바르게 연결된 것을 고르시오.

· The doctor ___________ I wanted to meet was on a holiday.
· I know a man ___________ job is writing journals.
· They couldn't forget the day ___________ their son was born.

ⓐ which - whose - when
ⓑ that - whose - which
ⓒ who - whose - which
ⓓ whom - whose - when

3 어법상 어색한 문장을 고르시오.

ⓐ I couldn't find the room where the meeting was held.
ⓑ Amy, who is my friend, won first prize.
ⓒ Please show me the way how you made a cup of cappuccino.
ⓓ Today I saw the most beautiful woman that I'd ever seen.

4 [보기]의 밑줄 친 that과 쓰임이 같은 것을 고르시오.

He can buy you anything that you want to have.

ⓐ The book that you were looking for was found in the attic.
ⓑ She told us the news that six prisoners had escaped from the jail.
ⓒ Let me introduce that man drinking a glass of wine.
ⓓ She doesn't believe that he graduated from law school.

5 우리말과 같은 뜻이 되도록 주어진 말을 이용하여 문장을 완성하시오.

야구는 내가 가장 즐기는 스포츠이다. (enjoy)
→ Baseball is the sport ___________ ___________ most.

6 밑줄 친 관계사의 쓰임이 어색한 것을 고르시오.

ⓐ I don't understand which she complains.
ⓑ She is the girl whom I wanted to meet.
ⓒ He was the first person that arrived here.
ⓓ August 23rd is the day when she was born.

7 문장을 읽고, 어색한 부분을 찾아 바르게 고치시오.

The house where burned last year will be rebuilt in one year.

8 문장을 읽고, 공통으로 들어갈 단어를 쓰시오.

· He bought a red dress ___________ fits his wife perfectly.
· ___________ do you want try on, blue pants or black pants?

[9-10] 글을 읽고, 물음에 답하시오.

Do you know ___(A)___ Will Rogers was so popular in the U.S. in the early 1900s? Here are the reasons. He was an Indian and cowboy whose credo was "I never met a man ___(B)___ I didn't like." He was a movie star who appeared in more than 50 movies. During his lifetime, he traveled around the world three times. He also wrote six books. He was a family man who was very close to his wife, Betty, and their four children.

*credo: 신조

9 (A)에 들어갈 알맞은 말을 고르시오.

ⓐ which ⓑ why
ⓒ when ⓓ how

10 (B)에 들어갈 알맞은 관계대명사를 쓰시오.

가정법 및 화법

1 가정법

2 가정법 (과거완료, 기타 가정법)

3 화법 / 부가의문문

가정법

단순조건 (가능한 현실)	If you fall here, you will get hurt. (→ Maybe you will get hurt.)
가정법 과거 (현실의 반대)	If I were very rich, I would buy an island. (→ As I am not very rich, I don't buy an island.)

가정법
일반적인 인칭이나 시제에 따른 법칙에 따르지 않고, 특정한 동사(과거)를 이용하여 사실과 반대되거나, 실현 불가능한 일을 가정하는 표현

1 단순조건: 실현 가능

If+주어+동사 현재형 ~, 주어+조동사 (will, can 등)+동사원형 ~

If you study hard, you will pass the exam.
If Sara leaves early, I will be very sad.
If it rains tomorrow, we will stay home.
If you put your hands in the hot water, you will get burned.

1
실현 가능한 경우와 과학적 사실을 주로 표현
: 만약 ~한다면 …할 것이다

2 가정법 과거: 실현 가능하지 않음

If+주어+ [be동사: were / 일반동사: 과거형] ~, 주어+조동사(would, could 등)+동사원형 ~

If I were a bee, I would sting his arm.
(= As I am not a bee, I don't sting his arm.)

If I were a boss, I could hire him right away.
(= As I am not a boss, I can't hire him right away.)

If he were strong, he could lift the weight.
(= As he is not strong, he can't lift the weight.)

If I had a bigger house, I would invite all my friends.
(= As I don't have a bigger house, I don't invite all my friends.)

If she knew the truth, she would tell him.
(= As she doesn't know the truth, she doesn't tell him.)

2
실현 불가능한 경우나 현재와 반대되는 상황을 표현: 만약 ~라면, ...할 텐데

※be동사는 were를 사용. 단 회화체에서는 was도 사용 가능.

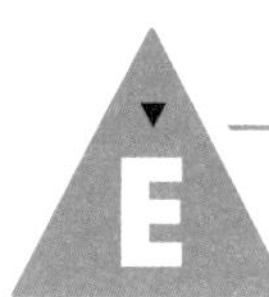

EXERCISE

Answers P.38

A

[ ] 안에서 알맞은 말을 고르시오.

1 If you [ate, eat] too much, you will get fat.

2 If she [is, were] here, she would tell us the correct answer.

3 If he [pours, poured] a little more water, the water will overflow.

4 If he [is, were] more polite, he would open the door for her.

5 If the meeting [is not, was not] canceled, I will meet you at 11:30.

6 If it [snows, snowed] tomorrow, let's go skiing together.

7 If we [have, had] more time, we could see the final scene of the movie.

8 If I [have, had] a plane of my own, I would fly around the world.

B

주어진 말을 이용하여 문장을 완성하시오.

1 If I ____________(be) not busy, I will call you later.

2 If he ____________(apologize) to the teacher, the teacher will not punish him.

3 If I ____________(know) her phone number, I would tell you.

4 If you ____________(not, understand), your teacher will explain it again.

5 If it ____________(not, be) far from here, we can go there on foot.

6 If he ____________(be) honest, my father would hire him.

7 If Ryan ____________(have) more money, he would buy an expensive car.

8 If you ____________(be) taller, you could be a model.

C

두 문장의 의미가 통하도록 문장을 완성하시오. (축약형으로 쓸 것)

1 If I were a millionaire, I could buy a castle for my family.
→ As I __________ a millionaire, I __________ a castle for my family.

2 If I had a lot of free time, I could write e-mails to my friends more often.
→ As I __________ a lot of free time, I __________ e-mails to my friends more often.

3 If he were good at math, he could help you solve the math problem.
→ As he __________ good at math, he __________ you solve the math problem.

4 If you were a university student, you could study the subjects you like.
→ As you __________ a university student, you __________ the subjects you like.

가정법 (과거완료, 기타 가정법)

가정법 과거완료	If I had left earlier, I could have caught the train.
I wish	I wish I were an eagle flying high up in the sky.
as if	He talks as if he knew everything.

1 가정법 과거완료

> If+주어+had p.p.~, 주어+would/could have p.p.~

If he had asked me, I would have told him the directions.
(= As he didn't ask me, I didn't tell him the directions.)

If we had had a laptop computer, it wouldn't have taken us a long time.
(= As we didn't have a laptop computer, it took us a long time.)

1
가정법 과거완료
: 과거 사실의 반대 (만약 ~했다면 …했을 텐데)

2 기타 가정법

(1) I wish+가정법
I wish I had a twin brother.
(→ I am sorry that I don't have a twin brother.)
I wish I had studied hard.
(→ I am sorry that I didn't study hard.)

(2) as if+가정법
He looks as if he were busy.
(= In fact, he is not busy.)
He is acting as if he had seen a ghost.
(= In fact, he didn't see a ghost.)

(3) If it were not for (~가 없다면)
If it were not for your help, I could not win the game.
(= Without your help, I could not win the game.)
(= But for your help, I could not win the game.)

2
(1) I wish+가정법 과거
: ~하면 좋을 텐데 (못해서 유감이다)
I wish+가정법 과거완료
: ~했다면 좋을 텐데 (못해서 유감이다)

(2) as if (= as though)
• as if+가정법 과거
: ~인 것처럼 …하다
• as if+가정법 과거완료
: ~였던 것처럼 …하다

(3) If it were not for
(지금) ~가 없다면
= Without
= But for

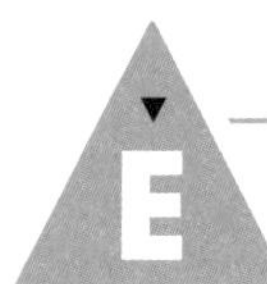

EXERCISE

Answers P.38

A [ ] 안에서 알맞은 말을 고르시오.

1 If they [had, had had] a good map, they would have found the hotel.

2 If Sally [told, had told] me immediately, I would not have been angry at her.

3 I wish my grades [are, were] better.

4 I wish I [saw, had seen] the play with you last night.

5 The girl talks as if she [is, were] ready to begin a presentation, but she isn't.

6 James talks as if it [were, had been] repaired, but it wasn't.

7 If it [were, had been] not for hope, we could not live.

8 [But, Without] my computer, I would be very bored.

B 주어진 말을 이용하여 문장을 완성하시오.

1 If we ________________(walk) quickly, we would get there earlier.

If we ________________(walk) quickly, we would have gotten there earlier.

2 If they had the tickets, they would ________________(see) the movie.

If they had had the tickets, they would ________________(see) the movie.

3 I wish I ________________(be) taught by that teacher. My friend is in his class now.

I wish I ________________(be) taught by that teacher last semester.

C 우리말과 같은 뜻이 되도록 주어진 말을 이용하여 문장을 완성하시오.

1 나에게 충분한 시간이 있었다면, 어제 TV를 봤을 텐데.

→ If I ________________(have) enough time, I would have watched TV yesterday.

2 선생님은 화나셨던 것처럼 말하신다.

→ The teacher talks as if he ________________(be) angry.

3 Amy는 오지 않았다. Amy가 올 수 있었다면 좋을 텐데.

→ Amy didn't come. I wish Amy ________________(come).

4 태양열이 없다면, 어느 것도 생존할 수 없다.

→ If it ________________(be, not) for the heat of the Sun, nothing could survive.

Unit 14 3 화법 / 부가의문문

직접화법 My mom said to me, "I want to help you."

주어 일치 시제 일치 목적어 일치

간접화법 My mom told me that she wanted to help me.

화법
직접화법: 인용부호(" ")를 직접 이용
간접화법: 내용을 풀어서 전달

직접화법 → 간접화법으로
(1) 주절의 동사: said to → told
(2) " "를 없애고 that으로 연결
(3) 주어, 시제, 목적어 일치

1 평서문의 화법

He said, "I need some vitamins now."
(→ He said that he needed some vitamins then.)

I said to her, "You can do it perfectly."
(→ I told her that she could do it perfectly.)

1
평서문 (직접화법 → 간접화법)

주절의 동사	say → say say to → tell
" "의 장소나 시간은 상황에 맞춘다.	here → there now → then today → that day last night → previous night 등

2 의문문의 화법

He asked her, "Where do you want to go?"
(→ He asked her where she wanted to go.)

Allan says to me, "Are you busy?"
(→ Allan asks me if I am busy.)

2
의문문 (직접화법 → 간접화법)
• 주절의 동사: say to → ask
• 의문사 있는 경우: 의문사를 접속사로
• 의문사 없는 경우: if, whether를 접속사로

3 명령문의 화법

My father says to me, "Do your homework."
(→ My father tells me to do my homework.)

He said to me, "Don't stay out too late."
(→ He ordered me not to stay out too late.)

3
명령문 (직접화법 → 간접화법)
• 주절의 동사 say to → tell, order
• 명령문 → to부정사로
• 부정명령문 → not to부정사로

■ 부가의문문

It is a beautiful day, isn't it?
He will say that again, won't he?
You know him well, don't you?

You aren't going with us, are you?
You cannot bring your comic books, can you?
She doesn't understand that, does she?

※ 부가의문문
be동사 → be동사로
조동사 → 조동사로
일반동사 → do(es)로

긍정 → 부정으로
부정 → 긍정으로

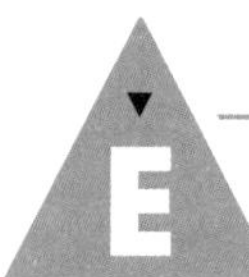

EXERCISE

Answers P.38

A

두 문장의 의미가 통하도록 [ ] 안에서 알맞은 말을 고르시오.

1 Jim said, "I want some orange juice with my breakfast."
→ Jim [said, told] that [he, I] wanted some orange juice with his breakfast.

2 They said to her, "You can find the book on the desk."
→ They [said, told] her that she [can, could] find the book on the desk.

3 She said to him, "Where are you going now?"
→ She [asked, said] him where he was going [now, then].

4 Mike says to me, "Will you climb the hill with me?"
→ Mike [asks, says] me [if, where] I will climb the hill with him.

5 Mom says to me, "Make your bed every morning."
→ Mom tells me [not to make, to make] my bed every morning.

B

빈칸에 알맞은 부가의문문을 써 넣으시오.

1 You are taking a vacation next month, ________________?

2 Your father cleans the house, ________________?

3 She is still training in the gym, ________________?

4 They must go there, ________________?

5 These books are not funny, ________________?

6 We can't eat at your place, ________________?

7 He doesn't understand the lecture, ________________?

C

두 문장의 의미가 통하도록 간접화법 문장을 완성하시오.

1 The officer said to him, "You seem very nervous today."
→ The officer told him that ________________________________.

2 Mom said to me, "Clean your room before leaving."
→ Mom told me ________________________________.

3 The guard said to her, "Don't go through these doors."
→ The guard ordered her ________________________________.

4 They said to me, "Where should we put the boxes?"
→ They asked me ________________________________.

REVIEW TEST

A

[ ] 안에서 알맞은 말을 고르시오.

1 The young nurse asked him [if, as if] he was feeling better.

2 Tom is a reliable person, [isn't he, is he]?

3 I wish he [is, were] on the list of people receiving awards.

4 If he [worked, had worked] harder, he would have completed the project on time.

5 She told me [didn't make, not to make] a loud noise.

6 You can bake your brother's birthday cake, [can you, can't you]?

7 [Without, Not] air, we could not hear anything.

8 If he [knew, had known] the whole story, he wouldn't have believed it.

B

빈칸에 들어갈 알맞은 말을 고르시오.

1 She talks ____________ she were pleased with the result.

ⓐ as ⓑ as if ⓒ if ⓓ without

2 Basketball players don't have small feet, ____________?

ⓐ is they ⓑ isn't they ⓒ do they ⓓ don't they

3 If they had e-mailed me, I would ____________ them immediately.

ⓐ answer ⓑ answered ⓒ will answer ⓓ have answered

4 If I ____________ Spiderman, I would climb the Empire State Building.

ⓐ am ⓑ were ⓒ will be ⓓ are

5 My lab partner asks me ____________ I am finished with my assignment.

ⓐ as if ⓑ as though ⓒ if ⓓ I wish

6 He ordered doctors ____________ the patients in a friendly way.

ⓐ to treat ⓑ treat ⓒ treating ⓓ treated

7 Sam ____________ us if we could do it without any difficulty.

ⓐ said ⓑ asked ⓒ tell ⓓ ordered

C [보기]에서 알맞은 말을 골라 문장을 완성하시오.

Word Bank	hasn't	were	had brought	as if	wish	went	if

1 He asked us __________ we were hungry after our long drive.

2 If I __________ a horse, I would gallop through the flowers in the fields.

3 He said that he __________ to bed at 11 last night.

4 The two young boys always pretend __________ they were brothers.

5 If they __________ the broken bike to him, he would have fixed it for them.

6 I __________ he were brave enough to express his idea in class.

7 Shelly has read hundreds of books, __________ she?

D 밑줄 친 부분을 바르게 고쳐, 문장을 다시 쓰시오.

1 If I had a new bike, I <u>would have let</u> you ride it.

→ __________

2 I don't speak French. I wish I <u>had spoken</u> French.

→ __________

3 Economics is very hard, <u>is</u> it?

→ __________

4 He speaks as though he <u>is</u> innocent of the charge, but he isn't.

→ __________

5 If she <u>attended</u> the seminar, she would have enjoyed hearing the professor.

→ __________

6 If June <u>were</u> not home, I will visit Liz in an hour.

→ __________

7 If Sue <u>didn't</u> go to school today, I will not let her watch TV.

→ __________

8 If I <u>am</u> a turtle, I would hide inside my shell.

→ __________

F FURTHER STUDY

Answers P.40

A 글을 읽고, 밑줄 친 부분을 바르게 고쳐 쓰시오.

It is time to buy a new digital camera. If I (1) <u>have</u> a new camera, I would take pictures of many things very easily. My old camera is difficult to use. It doesn't take good pictures indoors, either. When I bought it, the salesperson didn't tell me much about the camera. If he had asked, I (2) <u>told</u> him what kind of pictures I liked to take. I wish I had studied the camera choices before buying this one. If I (3) <u>am</u> able to go back in time, I wouldn't buy the same camera over again. I wish I had listened to my brother. He suggested that he choose a camera for me. But I didn't listen. My brother (4) <u>were</u> always busy, but if I ask, I'm sure he will go shopping with me for a new camera.

(1) ______________________

(2) ______________________

(3) ______________________

(4) ______________________

B 우리말과 같은 뜻이 되도록 주어진 말을 이용하여 문장을 완성하시오.

1 만약 내가 집에 있었다면, 그 쇼를 봤을 텐데. (watch, the show)
→ If I had been at home, ______________________.

2 그 운전사는 그에게 "그 트럭은 피아노를 쉽게 옮길 수 있어요."라고 말했다. (say to)
→ ______________________, "The truck can carry the piano easily."

3 그 꽃가게 주인은 내가 그녀의 작품에 만족하는지 안 하는지 물었다. (be satisfied with, her work)
→ The florist asked me ______________________.

4 만약 네 도움이 없다면, 나는 그 일을 끝낼 수 없을 거야. (if, your help)
→ ______________________, I couldn't finish the work.

5 내가 만약 새라면, 그들의 이야기를 들을 수 있을 텐데. (bird)
→ ______________________, I could hear their discussion.

MUST-KNOW

▶ 가정법

종류	의미	예문
가정법 과거	현재 사실의 반대	If I **were** a millionaire, I **could buy** an island. (내가 백만장자라면 섬을 하나 살 수 있을 텐데.)
가정법 과거완료	과거 사실의 반대	If I **had been** a millionaire, I **could have bought** an island. (내가 백만장자였다면 섬을 하나 살 수 있었을 텐데.)
I wish	희망, 바람	**I wish** I **were** a millionaire. (내가 백만장자라면 좋을 텐데.)
as if / as though	마치 ~처럼	He talks **as if** he **were** a millionaire. (그는 자신이 백만장자이기라도 한 것처럼 말한다.) He talks **as if** he **had been** a millionaire. (그는 자신이 백만장자이기라도 했던 것처럼 말한다.)

▶ 화법 전환 (직접화법 → 간접화법)

예문	직접 → 간접	변하는 어구
She **said**, "I am busy now." → She **said** that **she was** busy **then**. She **said to** me, "**I am** busy **today**." → She **told** me that **she was** busy **that day**.	※주절의 동사 : say → say said → said say to → tell said to → told	now → then / at that time ago → before yesterday → the day before, the previous day today → that day tonight → that night tomorrow → the next day the following day last night → the night before here → there this → that these → those 등
She **asked** me, "**Are you** busy **now**?" → She **asked** me **if/whether I was** busy **at that time**. She **said to** me, "**What is it**?" → She **asked** me **what it was**.	※주절의 동사 : ask → ask say to → ask ※의문사가 있는 경우 : 의문사를 접속사로 ※의문사가 없는 경우 : if, whether를 접속사로	
She **said to** me, "**Clean** here!" → She **ordered** me **to clean** there. She **said to** me, "**Do not run** here!" → She **told** me **not to run** there.	※주절의 동사 : say to → tell, order ※명령문 → to부정사로 ※부정명령문 → not to부정사로	

WRAP-UP TEST

Answers P.40

1 빈칸에 알맞은 말을 고르시오.

> You're going to Egypt this summer, ______?

ⓐ are you ⓑ aren't you
ⓒ were you ⓓ will you

2 빈칸에 알맞은 말을 고르시오.

> If I __________ you, I would take her advice.

ⓐ am ⓑ had been
ⓒ would ⓓ were

3 빈칸에 들어갈 말이 바르게 짝지어진 것을 고르시오.

> The policeman said to the old woman, "What are you looking for, ma'am?"
> →The policeman __________ the old woman what __________ looking for.

ⓐ told - you are ⓑ asked - she was
ⓒ asks - she is ⓓ said - is she

4 밑줄 친 부분의 쓰임이 어색한 것을 고르시오.

ⓐ The boy acts as if he were sick last night.
ⓑ If he is late again, the teacher will be angry.
ⓒ If he were a millionaire, he would buy his mother a big house.
ⓓ But for the book, I couldn't have completed the assignment.

5 어법상 어색한 문장을 고르시오.

ⓐ It's not a good day for a picnic, isn't it?
ⓑ If you take this medicine, you'll get better .
ⓒ He acts as if he inherited a large fortune.
ⓓ I wish I had taken the job offer then.

6 직접화법을 간접화법으로 바꾼 것이다. 어법상 어색한 것을 고르시오.

My friend said to me, "What are you doing now?"
→ My friend asked(ⓐ) me if(ⓑ) what I was(ⓒ) doing then(ⓓ).

7 주어진 문장과 의미가 통하는 문장을 고르시오.

> If I had taken a taxi then, I could have arrived at the airport in time.

ⓐ I took a taxi then, so I arrived at the airport in time.
ⓑ I took a taxi then, but I couldn't arrive at the airport in time.
ⓒ I didn't take a taxi then, so I didn't arrive at the airport in time.
ⓓ I took a taxi then, and I would have arrived at the airport in time.

8 두 문장이 같은 뜻이 되도록 문장을 완성하시오.

I didn't hand in my report, so I failed the course.
→ If I ______________________ my report,
I ______________________ the course.

[9-10] 글을 읽고 물음에 답하시오.

> (A) 만약 당신이 복권에 당첨된다면, 당신은 무엇을 하겠는가? You would buy an expensive house, ___(B)___? People buy lottery tickets, hoping to be the winner. They believe they'll be happy when they win. But it isn't always true. 80% of winners said they were unhappy. Only 20% were happy. For example, Philip Alcan, a lottery millionaire, was found dead on his sofa at his home.

9 (A)를 영어로 옮긴 것으로 가장 알맞은 것을 고르시오.

ⓐ What do you do, if you win the lottery?
ⓑ What will you do, if you won the lottery?
ⓒ What would you do, if you won the lottery?
ⓓ What do you do, if you will win the lottery?

10 (B)에 들어갈 알맞은 말을 쓰시오.

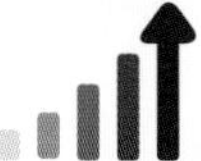

NEXUS Edu

LEVEL CHART

	초1	초2	초3	초4	초5	초6	중1	중2	중3	고1	고2	고3
VOCA	초등필수 영단어 1-2 · 3-4 · 5-6학년용											
VOCA					The VOCA + (플러스) 1~7							
VOCA			THIS IS VOCABULARY 입문 · 초급 · 중급					고급 · 어원 · 수능 완성 · 뉴텝스				
VOCA							WORD FOCUS 중등 종합 5000 · 고등 필수 5000 · 고등 종합 9500					
Grammar			초등필수 영문법 + 쓰기 1~2									
Grammar			OK Grammar 1~4									
Grammar			This Is Grammar Starter 1~3									
Grammar					This Is Grammar 초급~고급 (각 2권: 총 6권)							
Grammar						Grammar 공감 1~3						
Grammar						Grammar 101 1~3						
Grammar						Grammar Bridge 1~3						
Grammar						중학영문법 뽀개기 1~3						
Grammar						The Grammar Starter, 1~3						
Grammar								구사일생 (구문독해 Basic) 1~2				
Grammar									구문독해 204 1~2			
Grammar								그래머 캡처 1~2				
Grammar									[특급 단기 특강] 어법어휘 모의고사			

Concise and Core Grammar Points!

The Grammar

Nexus Contents Development Team

Workbook

NEXUS Edu

The Grammar

Nexus Contents Development Team

1
Level

Workbook

NEXUS Edu

be동사

A 네모 안에서 알맞은 말을 고르시오.

1 Pete and Cindy [am, are, is] the best students in my class.

2 The brown dog [am, are, is] with a pretty girl in the park.

3 [Am, Are, Is] we on the Number 12 bus to downtown?

4 The woman [am not, are not, is not] a secretary in our office.

5 He and I [was, were] in the same art class last year.

6 I [am, are, is] the owner of this cell phone.

7 Mr. Green [was, were] in the classroom with the students.

8 [Are, Were] Jim and his brother at the baseball game last night?

B be동사를 이용하여 대화를 완성하시오.

1 A ____________ they in the movie theater? B No, they aren't.

2 A ____________ the book on the desk yours? B No, it isn't.

3 A ____________ she on the train from New York yesterday? B No, she wasn't.

4 A Are you the new principal of our high school? B Yes, ____________.

5 A Were the two cheeseburgers for us? B No, ____________.

6 A Is the blue skirt for me? B Yes, ____________.

C 각각의 [보기]에서 알맞은 말을 골라 문장을 영작하시오.

They, The brown bear, Ben and I, My history book	was, are, were not, is	in the same music club, a new animal in our zoo, at the bus stop at that time, under the chair last night

1 그 갈색 곰은 우리 동물원에 새로운 동물이다.
→ ____________________

2 어젯밤에 내 역사책은 의자 밑에 있었다.
→ ____________________

3 Ben과 나는 같은 음악 클럽에 소속되어 있다.
→ ____________________

4 그들은 그 시간에 버스 정류장에 없었다.
→ ____________________

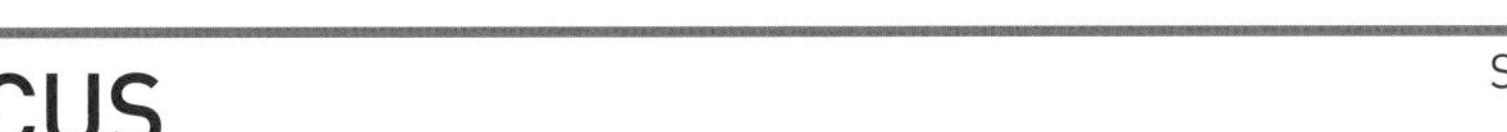

내신 FOCUS

SCORE:

A 주어와 be동사의 연결이 바르지 못한 것을 고르시오.

1 ⓐ you - are　ⓑ she - is　ⓒ I - am　ⓓ they - is

2 ⓐ it - was　ⓑ I - were　ⓒ you - were　ⓓ he - was

B 빈칸에 들어갈 알맞은 말을 고르시오.

1 Photos of the lizards ______________ on the living room table yesterday.

ⓐ was　ⓑ is　ⓒ were　ⓓ are

2 John ______________ the best player on our baseball team.

ⓐ is　ⓑ am　ⓒ are　ⓓ be

C 어법상 옳지 않은 문장을 고르시오.

1 ⓐ She is at the beach with my cousin a week ago.
ⓑ It was snowy this morning. It is very windy now.
ⓒ Mr. and Mrs. Benjamin are the parents of my best friend.
ⓓ They weren't teachers. They were engineers.

2 ⓐ You are not friendly to everyone.
ⓑ Sam and Nancy is at the cell phone store.
ⓒ He was on the train to Switzerland 5 hours ago.
ⓓ I am not a good guitar player.

D 우리말과 같은 뜻이 되도록 주어진 말을 이용하여 문장을 완성하시오.

1 빨간 장미는 내가 가장 좋아하는 꽃이다. (favorite)
The red rose ____.

2 Mac과 Mary는 이 학교의 학생이 아니다. (students)
Mac and Mary ____ in this school.

3 작년에 그는 뚱뚱했지만 지금은 날씬하다. (fat, thin)
He __________________________ last year, but he __________________________ now.

4 어제는 비가 오고 바람이 불었니? (rainy and windy)
______________ it ____ yesterday?

일반동사

A 네모 안에서 알맞은 말을 고르시오.

1 My brother [sleep, sleeps] with his teddy bear.

2 The gray cat [stay, stays] in her bed until morning.

3 The mail [come, comes] at 2 o'clock in the afternoon.

4 Larry and Karen [do, does] their best for every project.

5 Evan and Mark [drive, drives] the same cars.

6 My aunt [fly, flies] to Seattle on Friday afternoon.

7 Jane and her friends [hold, holds] the baby rabbits carefully.

8 Susan [have, has] a big apartment in downtown Manhattan.

B 주어진 말을 이용하여 현재시제 문장을 완성하시오.

1 My new kitten ______________(cry) a lot at night.

2 He ______________(buy) two bananas for his lunch.

3 A honeybee ______________(buzz) around beautiful flowers.

4 A horse ______________(eat) carrots on the farm.

5 Mike and Ginny ______________(dance) very well to many pop songs.

6 She ______________(go) to high school in Canada.

7 I ______________(wash) my school uniform every night.

8 My uncle ______________(drink) a glass of wine after dinner.

C 밑줄 친 부분을 바르게 고쳐 쓰시오. 틀리지 않았다면, O표 하시오.

1 My little brother goes to school. He <u>ride</u> his bike every morning. ______________

2 My husband and John <u>enjoys</u> the beautiful sunsets. ______________

3 Carol <u>copy</u> the words onto the blackboard for her teacher. ______________

4 The baker in that bakery <u>make</u> delicious bread and cakes. ______________

5 The repairman always <u>arrives</u> on time. ______________

6 My sister is a teacher in Boston. She <u>teach</u> science. ______________

내신 FOCUS

SCORE: 

A 동사의 변화가 <u>잘못된</u> 것을 고르시오.

1 ⓐ go - goes ⓑ study - studys ⓒ miss - misses ⓓ buy - buys

2 ⓐ have - haves ⓑ do - does ⓒ fly - flies ⓓ push - pushes

B 빈칸에 들어갈 알맞은 말을 고르시오.

1 Dad ______________ fishing on Sundays.

ⓐ goes ⓑ go ⓒ are going ⓓ go to

2 Mom ______________ chocolate chips into the flour.

ⓐ mix ⓑ mixes ⓒ is mixs ⓓ mixs

C 어법상 옳지 <u>않은</u> 문장을 고르시오.

1 ⓐ A wise person always plans for his future.
ⓑ Jeff watches too much television after school.
ⓒ Terry and I memorizes 30 English words every day.
ⓓ My cousin often buys books on the Internet.

2 ⓐ Tim often climbs the rock cliffs in Grand Ledge.
ⓑ Dad hide Mom's birthday gift every year.
ⓒ Kevin reads a book in the library every day.
ⓓ Wayne fixes cars in his father's shop.

D 우리말과 같은 뜻이 되도록 주어진 말을 이용하여 문장을 완성하시오.

1 Mike는 항상 일찍 일어난다. (get up early)
Mike always ____.

2 그녀는 항상 최선을 다한다. (try one's best)
She always ____.

3 농구 게임은 3시에 시작한다. (start, at 3 o'clock)
The basketball game ____.

4 우리 오빠는 방과 후에 아르바이트를 하러 간다. (go, to a part-time job)
My brother ____ after school.

일반동사의 부정문과 의문문

A 물음에 알맞은 응답을 연결하시오.

1 Does your sister like meat? • (a) No, he doesn't. Do you?

2 Do you buy books at Tom's bookstore? • (b) Yes, she does.

3 Do they have a plan for spring break? • (c) No, I don't. I prefer a black one.

4 Do you prefer a white dog for your pet? • (d) Yes, they do. They are going to China.

5 Does your brother know the way to the hospital? • (e) Yes, I do. I buy books there.

B 밑줄 친 부분을 바르게 고쳐 쓰시오. 틀리지 않았다면, O표 하시오.

1 Do she swim in the swimming pool? ____________

2 Mr. Kim don't put food or drinks on his desk. ____________

3 Does you call your mother every day? ____________

4 He doesn't rides his bike to school. ____________

5 Does Jason and Mandy want the movie tickets? ____________

6 My brother does not run fast after the bike accident. ____________

7 Do your cousins attends football games with you? ____________

C 괄호 안의 지시대로 문장을 완성하시오.

1 He saves $1 a week. (부정문)

→ ____________________ a week.

2 He has dinner at a Mexican restaurant on Mondays. (의문문)

→ ____________________ on Mondays?

3 She rides the Number 7 bus from Main Street to her home. (부정문)

→ ____________________ from Main Street to her home.

4 Does he visit his grandparents every weekend? (긍정문)

→ ____________________ every weekend.

5 The bakery sells wonderful pies. (의문문)

→ ____________________ wonderful pies?

6 She throws trash in the streets. (부정문)

→ ____________________ in the streets.

FOCUS

SCORE:

A 빈칸에 공통으로 들어갈 말을 써 넣으시오.

1 · She ______________ not read fashion magazines.
  · ______________ this bank open at 10 am?

2 · ______________ these shoes belong to you?
  · You ______________ not need to attend the meeting.

B 빈칸에 들어갈 알맞은 말을 고르시오.

1 They ______________ their mail until the end of the week.

ⓐ does not open ⓑ do not open ⓒ do opens ⓓ is open

2 ______________ your uncle make movies?

ⓐ Does ⓑ Are do ⓒ Do ⓓ are

C 어법상 옳지 않은 문장을 고르시오.

1 ⓐ Does she often work late in the office?
ⓑ Do your mother likes the operas at the new theater?
ⓒ My sister doesn't watch comedies.
ⓓ She usually orders a chicken salad in that restaurant.

2 ⓐ Does she take piano lessons after school?
ⓑ My new alarm goes off very late every morning.
ⓒ Don't your mom clean your room?
ⓓ The new repairman fixes problems quickly.

D 우리말과 같은 뜻이 되도록 주어진 말을 이용하여 문장을 완성하시오.

1 나의 삼촌은 한국에 살지 않는다. 그는 가족과 스페인에 산다. (not, live in, Korea, Spain, with his family)
My uncle ______________________________. He ______________________________.

2 그들은 선생님을 존경하니? (admire)
______________________________ their teacher?

3 이 기차는 New Jersey행입니까? (this train, go)
______________________________ to New Jersey?

4 우리 누나는 시끄러운 음악을 듣지 않는다. (my sister, not, listen to)
______________________________ loud music.

의문사 있는 의문문 / There is [are]

A 네모 안에서 알맞은 말을 고르시오.

1 Why [do, does] your dog bark all night every night?

2 There [is, are] five rules in our high school.

3 What [is, are] the price of the red sweater?

4 How [are, do] we find one report in all of these papers?

5 Who [was, were] the guest at your beach house last week?

6 [Was, Were] there much milk in the bottle?

7 When does your new computer [arrive, arrives]?

B 밑줄 친 부분을 바르게 고쳐 쓰시오. 틀리지 않았다면, O표 하시오.

1 Is there any good movies at the theater tonight? ____________

2 There are much money in my piggy bank. ____________

3 There is many students in my classroom. ____________

4 There was a department store here several years ago. ____________

5 Where are you want to put your textbooks? ____________

6 Why does she in the principal's office now? ____________

7 There are not a lot of space in the cabinet. ____________

C 괄호 안의 지시대로 문장을 완성하시오.

1 Lilly and Jerry walk the dog around the block. (When 의문문)

→ ______________________________ the dog around the block?

2 There are many fast cars on the country's new highway. (부정문)

→ ______________________________ on the country's new highway.

3 Steve and Linda practice baseball on the playground. (Why 의문문)

→ ______________________________ on the playground?

4 There are two books in your bag. (How many 의문문)

→ ______________________________ in your bag?

5 There was very little water in the swimming pool. (How much 의문문)

→ ______________________________ in the swimming pool?

내신 FOCUS

SCORE: 

A [ ] 안에서 알맞은 말을 고르시오.

1 · [What, Why] do Mike and Mary do after school?

· [What, Why] are you so angry?

2 · How many people [are, is] there in the backyard?

· There [were, was] a small cinema beside the bank 10 years ago.

B 빈칸에 들어갈 알맞은 말을 고르시오.

1 There ______ five DVDs in my book bag now.

ⓐ are ⓑ is ⓒ was ⓓ were

2 Why ______ you so late for the school bus yesterday?

ⓐ are ⓑ is ⓒ was ⓓ were

C 어법상 옳지 않은 문장을 고르시오.

1 ⓐ What does he like best about his cell phone?
ⓑ There is many players in the volleyball game.
ⓒ How much money do you have now?
ⓓ Where does she go skiing in the winter?

2 ⓐ How he goes to school?
ⓑ How many rooms does the hotel have free on Friday night?
ⓒ When does she leave for the cruise to the Caribbean islands?
ⓓ There was a lot of snow on the ground last night.

D 우리말과 같은 뜻이 되도록 주어진 말을 이용하여 문장을 완성하시오.

1 양동이에는 얼마나 많은 양의 물이 들어 있습니까? (water, there)
______________________ in the bucket?

2 너는 어제 누구와 공항에 있었니? (you)
______________________ with at the airport yesterday?

3 다락방에는 오래된 책들이 있다. (old books)
______________________ in the attic.

4 너의 오빠는 교회에 어떻게 가니? (your brother, go)
______________________ to church?

현재시제 / 현재진행형

A 네모 안에서 알맞은 말을 고르시오.

1 John [goes, is going] to church every Sunday.

2 Do you [like, liking] the cartoons in the newspaper?

3 The kittens [plays, are playing] with a ball right now.

4 Look! The young man [carries, is carrying] a huge bag.

5 Hundreds of e-mails [arrive, is arriving] every day.

6 Ellen usually [talks, is talking] to the manager about tickets.

B 주어진 말을 이용하여 문장을 완성하시오.

1 The pitcher ______________________(throw) a ball right now.

2 Tom ______________________(learn) fencing with his brother after school every day.

3 Bill is on a plane. He ______________________(fly) to New York.

4 My sister ______________________(catch) the train to work at 7 am every day.

5 Be quiet! I ______________________(talk) on the phone.

6 The doctor ______________________(come) to Jim's apartment now because he is so ill.

C 괄호 안의 지시대로 문장을 완성하시오.

1 He is counting the stars in the sky. (현재시제)

→ He ______________________ the stars in the sky before falling asleep.

2 The high school soccer team practices for the games. (현재진행형)

→ The high school soccer team ______________________ for tomorrow's game.

3 She is sending her mom a text message. (현재시제)

→ She ______________________ her mom text messages frequently.

4 My cousin has strawberries with cream for dessert very often. (현재진행형)

→ My cousin ______________________ strawberries with cream for dessert right now.

5 My puppy is getting all of his shots here today. (현재시제)

→ My puppy ______________________ his shots here regularly.

FOCUS

SCORE:

A 진행형을 만들 때 동사의 변화가 잘못된 것을 고르시오.

1 ⓐ speak - speaking ⓑ tie - tiing ⓒ cut - cutting ⓓ become - becoming

2 ⓐ swim - swimming ⓑ study - studying ⓒ lose - losing ⓓ get - geting

B 빈칸에 들어갈 알맞은 말을 고르시오.

1 Jim ____________ an ice cream cone with his girlfriend.

ⓐ is eating ⓑ is eat ⓒ is eatting ⓓ eat

2 The young girls ____________ because of the sad movie now.

ⓐ are cry ⓑ are crying ⓒ are crieing ⓓ cry

C 어법상 옳지 않은 문장을 고르시오.

1 ⓐ I am taking care of my younger sister after my homework every day.
ⓑ Sarah and Helen play tennis on Saturdays.
ⓒ The actors are practicing their parts now.
ⓓ The cat is scratching the back of the sofa now.

2 ⓐ She is resting for a short while in her room.
ⓑ David is bringing a potato salad to the picnic tomorrow.
ⓒ My sister is volunteer at a children's center these days.
ⓓ Martine is fat, and he daydreams about food all the time.

D 우리말과 같은 뜻이 되도록 주어진 말을 이용하여 문장을 완성하시오.

1 Schofield는 한 달에 한 번씩 도쿄에 간다. (go, to Tokyo)
Schofield ______________________________ once a month.

2 그들은 지금 모래성을 만들고 있다. (build, a sand castle)
They ______________________________ now.

3 마지막 기차는 이 역을 9시에 출발한다. (the last train, leave, at 9 o'clock)
______________________________ from this station.

4 그녀는 손을 컵 쪽으로 뻗고 있다. (reach)
She ______________________________ for the cup.

현재진행형 (부정문, 의문문, 불가동사)

A 네모 안에서 알맞은 말을 고르시오.

1 My husband [drive, is driving] his boss to the airport now.

2 Jennifer [talks, is talking] on the phone at this moment.

3 Liz [doesn't need, is not needing] your help.

4 Does she [have, is having] a membership in the Film Club?

5 My family [likes, is liking] the national parks of our country.

6 They [feel, are feeling] curious about the Rocky Mountains.

7 [Do you go, Are you going] to the chemistry lab now?

B 밑줄 친 부분을 바르게 고쳐 쓰시오. 틀리지 않았다면, O표 하시오.

1 What are the baby elephants <u>do</u> in the water now? ______________

2 She is <u>has</u> a snow cone with her little brother now. ______________

3 Jeff and Loy <u>train</u> the horses at the Honor Ranch every day. ______________

4 My uncle <u>is understanding</u> the research about the stars. ______________

5 Polly <u>doesn't</u> drinking tea with her professor now. ______________

6 <u>Are you wanting</u> another piece of pumpkin pie? ______________

C 괄호 안의 지시대로 문장을 완성하시오.

1 You are checking this book out from the city library. (의문문)

→ ______________ this book out from the city library?

2 The clerk wraps the present with the ribbon. (현재진행형 의문문)

→ ______________ the present with the ribbon?

3 My younger sister is going to bed soon. (현재시제 부정문)

→ My younger sister usually ______________ to bed very early.

4 Steve is not ordering the food for everyone now. (현재시제 긍정문)

→ Steve often ______________ the food for everyone.

5 The neighbor walks his big, brown dog in the park. (현재진행형 부정문)

→ The neighbor ______________ his big, brown dog in the park now.

6 James runs a souvenir shop downtown. (현재진행형)

→ James ______________ a souvenir shop downtown now.

FOCUS

SCORE: 

A 주어진 동사를 알맞게 바꿔 쓰시오.

1 · The Earth ______________(go) around the Sun.

· She ______________(go) shopping with her brother now.

2 · ______________ he ______________(stand) by the door now?

· The Statue of Liberty ______________(stand) in New York.

B 빈칸에 들어갈 알맞은 말을 고르시오.

1 ______________ to the basketball game at the university?

ⓐ Is going ⓑ Are go ⓒ Do you going ⓓ Are you going

2 I ______________ my friends in London very often.

ⓐ are not call ⓑ am calling not ⓒ am not call ⓓ do not call

C 어법상 옳지 않은 문장을 고르시오.

1 ⓐ Dave is spending a long time in the principal's office.
ⓑ The three men aren't moving the boxes into the warehouse.
ⓒ We are needing a report from you about the river.
ⓓ Is he sending the pictures from his trip to his cousins?

2 ⓐ Does she cutting that paper into the shape of a star?
ⓑ My mother does not like sea cruises in the winter.
ⓒ The choir is having a very successful concert in Europe.
ⓓ Sheila's sister and brother aren't flying to Ireland.

D 우리말과 같은 뜻이 되도록 주어진 말을 이용하여 문장을 완성하시오.

1 아이들은 밖에서 노는 것을 좋아한다. (like, playing outside)
Children ____.

2 그들은 지금 TV를 보고 있지 않다. (not, watch, TV)
They ____ now.

3 너는 지금 오렌지 껍질을 벗기고 있니? (peel, the oranges)
______________ you ______________________________________ now?

4 그녀는 우주에 대해 많은 것을 알고 있다. (know, a lot)
____ about space.

과거시제 / 과거진행형

A 네모 안에서 알맞은 말을 고르시오.

1 When [was, did] an American cook invent potato chips?

2 My uncle [graduates, graduated] from university in the mid-1990s.

3 He [go, went] to the auto show in Detroit with Fred a few weeks ago.

4 What [were they, did they] doing on the other side of the street?

5 My aunt [flies, flew] to my grandparents' house in California yesterday.

6 [Wasn't, Isn't] the Major League All-Star baseball game exciting last night?

7 John [was paddling, paddled] the canoe when he lost his glasses in the water.

B 주어진 말을 이용하여 문장을 완성하시오.

1 The man ______________(present) his speech last Friday.

2 We ______________(have) a surprise birthday party for him last week.

3 The workers ______________(build) a new office when I visited them.

4 The firefighter ______________(put out) the fire in the building one hour ago.

5 What did your mom ______________(find) on the table a few hours ago?

6 The student ______________(play) a new musical instrument in the marching band yesterday.

C [보기]에서 알맞은 말을 골라 어법에 맞게 바꿔 대화를 완성하시오.

Word Bank	call	clean up	rumble	eat

Paul: There is something on your lips. Is it peanut butter?

Karen: Really? Yes, it is peanut butter.

Paul: 1 ____________ you ____________ a peanut butter sandwich when I cleaned the garage?

Karen: 2 I'm so sorry, but I was really hungry. My stomach ______________ like thunder.

Paul: Aren't you going to have lunch with Nancy in the Italian restaurant?

Karen: 3 No. She ______________ this morning and canceled.

Paul: 4 All right, all right. Let's ______________ the kitchen together.

SCORE:

A 주어진 동사의 과거형을 쓰시오.

1 ⓐ read - ________ ⓑ make - ________ ⓒ think - ________ ⓓ meet - ________

2 ⓐ bite - ________ ⓑ drink - ________ ⓒ go - ________ ⓓ sing - ________

B 빈칸에 들어갈 알맞은 말을 고르시오.

1 The nurse ____________ the young doctor about the chart a minute ago.

ⓐ ask ⓑ asked ⓒ asks ⓓ is asking

2 The boy ____________ many plates on five long sticks when I came into the circus tent.

ⓐ balances ⓑ is balanced ⓒ was balancing ⓓ don't balance

C 어법상 옳지 않은 문장을 고르시오.

1 ⓐ The boss didn't fire the employee.
ⓑ What was the lion eat when you saw it at the zoo?
ⓒ My dad taught geometry at my school in 2013.
ⓓ What was Cindy doing with that package a few minutes ago?

2 ⓐ What were you thinking about for a new story title?
ⓑ She manages our department two years ago.
ⓒ Dylan stopped the car before it hit a squirrel on the road.
ⓓ Did the artist create a statue out of stone last year?

D 우리말과 같은 뜻이 되도록 주어진 말을 이용하여 문장을 완성하시오.

1 비가 내리기 시작했을 때 나는 숨바꼭질을 하고 있었다. (play, hide-and-seek)
I ________________________________ when it started raining.

2 나는 그들을 내 생일 파티에 초대하지 않았다. (invite, them, to my birthday party)
I ________________________________.

3 Rusty는 어제 10시간 동안 운전을 했다. (drive, for 10 hours)
Rusty ________________________________ yesterday.

4 어젯밤에 무엇을 먹었니? (have, for dinner)
________________________________ last night?

미래시제

A 네모 안에서 알맞은 말을 고르시오.

1 My family [will travel, will travels] to Cleveland, Ohio this weekend.

2 Ted [drove, is going to drive] to Texas for a convention next Friday.

3 She [will not, not will] be at the meeting in the morning.

4 Which city [will, are] you going to visit?

5 I'll remove the graffiti on the wall before my father [finds, will find] it.

6 If I [will have, have] time, I will stop by and see you.

B 밑줄 친 부분을 바르게 고쳐 쓰시오.

1 She will learns Spanish next year. __________

2 What day will you returned to Chicago? __________

3 It will snows in London tomorrow afternoon. __________

4 The waiter going to serve your main dish in a minute. __________

5 The professor not will cancel his class. __________

6 If I will be late for the meeting, I will take a taxi. __________

7 Will Tim ignores her phone calls and text messages? __________

C 괄호 안의 지시대로 문장을 완성하시오.

1 Chris leaves for Toronto, Canada tomorrow night. (be V-ing)

→ Chris __________ for Toronto, Canada tomorrow night.

2 The author is writing a book about the Southern U.S. (will)

→ The author __________ a book about the Southern U.S.

3 She goes to the dance studio on Monday. (be V-ing)

→ She __________ to the dance studio on the following Monday.

4 Peggy is spending her graduation day in bed with a cold. (will)

→ Peggy __________ her graduation day in bed with a cold.

5 My parents have their 40th wedding anniversary party. (be going to)

→ My parents __________ their 40th wedding anniversary party next month.

FOCUS

SCORE: 

A 밑줄 친 동사를 어법에 맞게 바꿔 쓰시오.

1 Carl get up early tomorrow morning.

2 He will takes off his thick coat when it is hot.

B 빈칸에 들어갈 알맞은 말을 고르시오.

1 The show ______________ in one hour.

ⓐ will starts ⓑ will start not ⓒ won't start ⓓ will does start

2 I ______________ a trip to the Bahamas for Christmas vacation this year.

ⓐ will takes ⓑ am going to take ⓒ am take ⓓ will taking

C 어법상 옳지 않은 문장을 고르시오.

1 ⓐ He's not going to repair my car until Friday.
ⓑ If he will change his mind again, I will break my promise.
ⓒ They will put off the meeting for another twenty minutes.
ⓓ Sam won't race in the Indianapolis 500 this year.

2 ⓐ Bill is not going to buy the books for the new class.
ⓑ Nancy bought nice dinner next weekend.
ⓒ The train for Chicago is arriving soon.
ⓓ The weather will be good for a while after it stops raining.

D 우리말과 같은 뜻이 되도록 주어진 말을 이용하여 문장을 완성하시오.

1 내가 나중에 다시 전화할게. (will, call, you back)
I ____ later.

2 8시 30분이야. 우리 수업에 늦을 거야. (be going to, late)
It's 8:30. We ____ for school.

3 너의 비밀을 누구에게도 말하지 않을게. (will, tell, your secret)
I ____ to anyone.

4 그는 이번 주말에 여행을 갈 것이다. (will, go on a trip)
He ____ this weekend.

현재완료 (계속)

A 네모 안에서 알맞은 말을 고르시오.

1 Sam [raise, has raised] three cats since he was 10.

2 She [graduated, has graduated] from Michigan State University in 2013.

3 How long [did, have] you worked in this department of the company?

4 Tammy [passed, has passed] her driver's test two years ago.

5 I [hear, have heard] about my grandfather's good fortune since I was a boy.

6 The team [prepare, has prepared] the important report for six weeks.

B 주어진 말을 이용하여 문장을 완성하시오.

1 The players ____________(win) the championship game last year.

2 The manager ____________ ____________(call) my father many times since yesterday.

3 The city ____________ ____________(celebrate) its birthday since 1940.

4 How long have Mr. and Mrs. Smith ____________(play) golf?

5 I ____________ ____________(take) pictures at weddings since I was twenty-five.

6 The class ____________(go) on a field trip to Washington, D.C. yesterday.

7 The students ____________ ____________(study) for their final exams for five hours.

C 두 문장이 같은 의미가 되도록 주어진 말을 이용하여 문장을 완성하시오.

1 Pete began working at the company two years ago, and he still works there.

→ He ____________ ____________(work) at the company for two years.

2 Debbie began piano lessons with my sister last year, and she still takes lessons with her.

→ Debbie ____________ ____________(take) piano lessons with my sister for one year.

3 It started snowing last Sunday, and it is still snowing.

→ It ____________ ____________(snow) since last Sunday.

4 I became a member of the golf team last year, and I am still a member of the team.

→ I ____________ ____________(be) a member of the golf team for 2 years.

5 My cousin started reading the book last week, and he is still reading it.

→ My cousin ____________ ____________(read) the book since last week.

FOCUS

SCORE:

A 빈칸에 알맞은 말을 써 넣으시오.

1 · The wind ____________ wildly last night. (blow)

· The wind ____________ ____________ wildly since yesterday. (blow)

2 · The television has broadcast the news ____________ five hours.

· Seoul has been famous ____________ the 1988 Olympics.

B 빈칸에 들어갈 알맞은 말을 고르시오.

1 The young men ____________ musical instruments for 10 years.

ⓐ has played　ⓑ was playing　ⓒ have played　ⓓ have play

2 The restaurant ____________ free meals to homeless people since 1999.

ⓐ have provided　ⓑ provides　ⓒ has provided　ⓓ provide

C 어법상 옳지 않은 문장을 고르시오.

1 ⓐ He repairs my laptop for two hours.
ⓑ Terry has fed my dog and cat for a month for me.
ⓒ The Andersons have been at the sailboat race since 2:30 pm.
ⓓ Bob hasn't heard any echoes since he started hiking in the mountain.

2 ⓐ The teacher plan the field trip since March.
ⓑ The dancers have rehearsed the ballet for almost three hours.
ⓒ They have displayed new CDs since Friday morning.
ⓓ She hasn't talked to her brother since he broke her cell phone.

D 우리말과 같은 뜻이 되도록 주어진 말을 이용하여 문장을 완성하시오.

1 그는 10년 동안 야구 경기를 했나요? (play, baseball)
____________ he ______________________________ for 10 years?

2 당신은 얼마나 오랫동안 안경을 꼈나요? (how long, wear)
____ glasses?

3 그 소녀는 5세 이후로 발레리나가 되는 꿈을 꾸고 있다. (dream)
The girl ______________________________ of being a ballerina since she was five.

4 Damon은 10년 동안 세계 역사에 관심을 가져왔다. (be interested in)
Damon ______________________________ world history for 10 years.

현재완료 (완료, 경험, 결과)

A 네모 안에서 알맞은 말을 고르시오.

1 The cat [has just caught, has just catch] a mouse in the garage.

2 Have you [ever bought, bought ever] a car before?

3 My aunt [has driven, has drove] to the market to buy some meat.

4 How many times [has he asked, he has asked] you to change the sign?

5 She [never has eaten, has never eaten] street snacks before today.

6 They [have already had, have already have] several interviews.

7 David [has left, leave] his wallet on the bus. So he doesn't have it now.

B 주어진 말을 이용하여 현재완료 문장을 완성하시오.

1 The students visited the science center two years ago.

→ The students ______________________(visit, not) the science center lately.

2 I made a clay pot on a potter's wheel for the first time last Sunday.

→ I ______________________(make) a clay pot on a potter's wheel once.

3 The chameleon changed colors a minute ago.

→ The chameleon ______________________(change, already) colors.

4 My brothers didn't finish cleaning their rooms this morning.

→ My brothers ______________________(finish, not) cleaning their rooms yet.

5 I took part in the half-marathon.

→ I ______________________(take, never) part in the half-marathon.

6 Jim read half of the novel yesterday, and he finished reading it a few minutes ago.

→ Jim ______________________(read, just) the novel.

C 밑줄 친 부분을 바르게 고쳐 쓰시오. 틀리지 않았다면, O표 하시오.

1 They have just reached the other side of the river. ______________

2 Your parents do not have called the school office yet. ______________

3 My father already has ordered a new seat for my bicycle. ______________

4 My friend hasn't saw any soccer matches these days. ______________

5 How many times have you readed *Gone with the Wind*? ______________

FOCUS

SCORE: 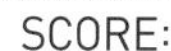

A 두 문장의 의미가 통하도록 주어진 동사를 알맞게 바꿔 쓰시오.

1 Jim went to Berlin last year, and he is still staying there.

→ He ____________ to Berlin. (go)

2 Jack and Jill went to Amsterdam two years ago, and they came back last year.

→ They ____________ to Amsterdam. (be)

B 빈칸에 들어갈 알맞은 말을 고르시오.

1 My boss has never flown to Jamaica ____________.

ⓐ already ⓑ yet ⓒ before ⓓ so

2 The children have ____________ done their homework for tomorrow.

ⓐ already ⓑ yet ⓒ ever ⓓ so

C 어법상 옳지 않은 문장을 고르시오.

1 ⓐ He has learns about it before.
ⓑ Have you ever been to Italy?
ⓒ We have begun our trip on the Canadian Snow Train.
ⓓ The nurse hasn't called my name.

2 ⓐ The concert has already begun in Fountain Square.
ⓑ He hasn't e-mailed the information yet.
ⓒ The program has already ended.
ⓓ I have never ate snails before.

D 우리말과 같은 뜻이 되도록 주어진 말을 이용하여 문장을 완성하시오.

1 한국은 몇 번이나 월드컵에 출전했나요? (how many times, play)

____________________________ in the World Cup?

2 그는 아직 숙제를 마치지 못했다. (finish one's homework)

He ____________________________ yet.

3 나는 롤러코스터를 한번 타본 적이 있다. (ride, a roller coaster)

I ____________________________ once.

과거완료와 미래완료

A 네모 안에서 알맞은 말을 고르시오.

1 Steve [had, will have] received his books by the time classes begin next week.

2 I talked to them after they [has been, had been] to the amusement park.

3 The crew [will have, have] stayed in the Space Station for one year by next June.

4 [Have, Had] the concert ended before they left?

5 The skunk saw me after I [have seen, had seen] it, and I got sprayed!

6 Mike [had already changed, have already changed] his mind when I asked him about it.

7 My secretary [will have, have] found all the accounting mistakes by tomorrow morning.

B 주어진 말을 이용하여 문장을 완성하시오.

1 She ______________(review) the case for a week by this time tomorrow.

2 The camera ______________(break, already) when I found it on the beach.

3 The movie ______________(start) by the time I get there.

4 The doctor ______________(look, not) at the patient's chart before the nurse told him.

5 Joe ______________(live) in Scotland before he attended university in London.

6 My sister ______________(finish, not) the book in time for tomorrow's test.

7 Next month, she ______________(teach) English for one year.

C 두 문장의 의미가 통하도록 문장을 완성하시오.

1 I bought a dog last year, and my sister received a cat last month.
→ I ______________ a dog before my sister received a cat.

2 I have driven a car for nine years, and I will continue to drive next year.
→ Next year, I ______________ a car for ten years.

3 Mark has sold china at the flea market for two years, and he will keep doing so next year.
→ Mark ______________ china for three years next year.

4 Tim graduated from high school four years ago, and Joe graduated from high school last August.
→ Tim ______________ from high school before Joe did.

FOCUS

SCORE:

A 두 문장의 의미가 통하도록 빈칸에 알맞은 말을 써 넣으시오.

1 He studied physics for years, and he became a science teacher.
→ He ____________ physics for years before he became a science teacher.

2 Mary arrived in Rome three weeks ago, and she will stay one more week.
→ Mary ____________ in Rome for almost one month by next week.

B 빈칸에 들어갈 알맞은 말을 고르시오.

1 The bus arrived late today. The class __________ by the time I get to school.
ⓐ will has ended ⓑ hadn't end ⓒ will have ended ⓓ didn't end

2 The car hit two students. They __________ both ways before they crossed the street.
ⓐ hasn't look ⓑ had not looked ⓒ has never looked ⓓ looked

C 어법상 옳지 않은 문장을 고르시오.

1 ⓐ She had never deleted the information from the computer file.
ⓑ The basketball game will have started by the time you get home.
ⓒ Cindy have already found the key before I told her where it was.
ⓓ In one month, she will have attended college for two years.

2 ⓐ He will have been in Switzerland for ten years next September.
ⓑ I was frightened. The bear looked at me after it has sniffed our food.
ⓒ Had you ever joined the Community Club before you joined this one?
ⓓ Will they have visited all major tourist attractions by the time they leave Italy?

D 우리말과 같은 뜻이 되도록 주어진 말을 이용하여 문장을 완성하시오.

1 Van Gogh는 죽기 전에 1,000장 이상의 그림을 그렸다. (paint)
Van Gogh ____________ over 1,000 paintings before he died.

2 다음 달쯤이면 그가 그 그림퍼즐 완성할 것이다. (complete)
He ____________ the jigsaw puzzle by next month.

3 그 글을 쓰기 전에 이 책을 몇 번 읽었나요? (how many times, read)
____________ this book before you wrote the paper?

4 내년이면 나는 3년 동안 영어 공부를 한 것이 된다. (study)
____________ for three years by next year.

Unit 04 1 조동사 (능력, 허가, 요청, 제안)

A 네모 안에서 알맞은 말을 고르시오.

1 Dora can [make, makes, made] different shapes of doughnuts.

2 Your cousin [will, do, is able to] play the trumpet very well now.

3 Where can my brother [catch, catches, caught] a bus to downtown?

4 [Could, Will can, Will be able to] we have soup with our sandwiches at lunch?

5 Barry couldn't [sing, sings, sang] because of a sore throat in the choir today.

6 Were you [shall, able to, can] find the book in the library?

7 [Could, Shall, May] you call a taxi for me?

B [보기]에서 알맞은 말을 골라 주어진 조동사를 이용하여 문장을 완성하시오.

Word Bank	play	send	go	count	leave

1 She looks tired. She ______________(may) in 10 minutes if she wants.

2 ________ we ________(shall) to the school dance together, Margie?

3 ________ you ________(will) me the check when you return to the office?

4 My friends ______________(cannot) numbers in English like I can.

5 He will ______________(be able to) the violin like Sara Jang in 10 years.

C 괄호 안에 지시대로 문장을 완성하시오.

1 Allen has just ordered a new car. He can drive his own car. (미래시제로)

→ Allen has just ordered a new car. So ______________.

2 Please come to my graduation on Thursday. (Can you ~? 형으로)

→ ______________?

3 My best friend can work for her father's company. (be able to 형으로)

→ My best friend ______________.

4 Let's introduce our speaker for this evening's event. (Shall ~? 형으로)

→ ______________?

5 Will you hold the door for me? (더 공손한 표현으로)

→ ______________?

FOCUS

SCORE: 

A 두 문장의 의미가 통하도록 빈칸에 알맞은 말을 써 넣으시오.

1 Bill can repair the broken copy machine.

= Bill ______________ the broken copy machine.

2 Please open the window for me.

= ______________ you open the window for me?

B 빈칸에 들어갈 알맞은 말을 고르시오.

1 My dad ______________ retire from his job next year.

ⓐ will can ⓑ able to ⓒ shall ⓓ will be able to

2 He couldn't ______________ the armchair alone.

ⓐ moves ⓑ move ⓒ moved ⓓ did move

C 어법상 옳지 않은 문장을 고르시오.

1 ⓐ Would you look for the book on the shelf again, please?
ⓑ Mary will does not order the photos for the team members tomorrow.
ⓒ Shall we open the package from your grandmother now?
ⓓ Jackie can paint a picture of a landscape with great skill.

2 ⓐ She may gets a small snack if she is hungry.
ⓑ Amanda will not be able to bring her turtle to class this week.
ⓒ Could you announce the changes to the group?
ⓓ Robert cannot reach the big jars on the top shelf.

D 우리말과 같은 뜻이 되도록 주어진 말을 이용하여 문장을 완성하시오.

1 그는 빨리 달릴 수 있으니까 경주에서 이길 거야. (run, fast, win)
He ______________ so, ______________ the race.

2 다시 한 번 말씀해 주시겠습니까? (say that again)
______________?

3 주말에는 늦게 일어나도 좋아요. (get up late)
You ______________ on weekends.

4 기차역에서 만나도 될까요? (shall, meet)
______________ we ______________ at the train station?

조동사 (의무, 금지, 충고, 과거의 습관)

A 네모 안에서 알맞은 말을 고르시오.

1 When the group was small, we [should, would] play card games.

2 You [must not, don't have to] walk on the grass. I planted it this morning.

3 They [had not better, had better not] be late for class today because of the test.

4 Eileen [had to, must] go to the doctor with her mother yesterday.

5 My cousins [would, used to] own a dairy farm two years ago, but they sold it.

6 You [don't have to, must not] do this homework if you don't want extra points.

7 Kerry [must have to, will have to] pay back the money to Ted.

B [보기]에서 알맞은 말을 골라 문장을 완성하시오.

Word Bank used to don't have to should not must had to

1 Jerry ____________________ open the jar for me because I hurt my hand yesterday.

2 Students ____________________ fill out the form before they talk to an advisor.

3 Brenda ____________________ wear a blue dress like this one.

4 They ____________________ bring their lunch. There is a cafe nearby.

5 He ____________________ make fun of people. It hurts their feelings.

C 괄호 안의 지시대로 문장을 완성하시오.

1 When the class was quiet, we would read our books. (should 긍정문)

→ When the class is quiet, we ______________________________ our books.

2 You called her late at night. (had better 부정문)

→ You ______________________________ her late at night.

3 He should not go to bed so late. (과거의 습관)

→ He ______________________________ to bed so late.

4 Devon must return my video game by Friday night. (미래시제 의무 표현으로)

→ Devon ______________________________ my video game by Friday night.

5 Visitors must enter the building through these doors. (부정문으로)

→ Visitors ______________________________ the building through these doors.

FOCUS

SCORE: 

A 두 문장의 의미가 통하도록 빈칸에 알맞은 말을 써 넣으시오.

1 Children must go to bed early.

= Children ____________ go to bed early.

2 I used to go fishing on the weekend when I was young.

= I ____________ go fishing on the weekend when I was young.

B 빈칸에 들어갈 알맞은 말을 고르시오.

1 You __________ follow the school rules.

ⓐ would ⓑ may ⓒ must ⓓ can

2 It __________ snow a lot in the winter when I was a young boy.

ⓐ used to ⓑ should ⓒ had better ⓓ will have to

C 어법상 옳지 않은 문장을 고르시오.

1 ⓐ All cars must stop when a traffic light turns red.
ⓑ They not should pay later.
ⓒ She will have to come back in the morning.
ⓓ I used to go hiking with my uncle on weekends.

2 ⓐ The coach will must change the game plan before tomorrow.
ⓑ When the game show was exciting, we would scream loudly.
ⓒ You had better not unpack your bag until I tell you.
ⓓ You must return your ID card when you go out.

D 우리말과 같은 뜻이 되도록 주어진 말을 이용하여 문장을 완성하시오.

1 감기에 걸렸구나. 집에 가서 쉬는 게 낫겠다. (go home)
You have a cold. You ______________________ and get some rest.

2 나는 어렸을 때 나무에 오르곤 했었다. (climb up, trees)
I ______________________ when I was young.

3 너는 부모님께 공손하게 말해야 한다. (speak, to your parents)
You ______________________ politely.

4 이 시험에 통과하면, 보고서를 쓸 필요가 없다. (write a report)
If you pass this test, you ______________________.

조동사 (추측, 가능성)

A 네모 안에서 알맞은 말을 고르시오.

1 The truck [could have, can have] run over the barking dog.

2 They [must, should have] left earlier to get tickets for the movie.

3 Sandy says that it [cannot be, may] Aaron. He wasn't here at that time.

4 Ray and Mandy [must, has to] be disappointed with the news.

5 Edward is sure he [could be, must be] the new president.

6 The technician [must changed, must have changed] the password on your computer yesterday.

7 I bought a computer, but I haven't used it for a long time. I [should, shouldn't] have bought it.

B [보기]에서 알맞은 말을 골라 문장을 완성하시오.

Word Bank	could be mowing	might have washed	can't be
	may not be	must have eaten	

1 Eugene ______________________ the last piece of cake. It is all gone.

2 Sally ______________________ your shirt already. Did you look in the laundry room?

3 Tommy ______________________ in the office now. He is not answering the phone.

4 What is Bob doing now? He ______________________ the grass for his dad.

5 The movie ______________________ over this quickly! It only lasted one hour.

C 우리말과 같은 뜻이 되도록 주어진 말을 이용하여 문장을 완성하시오.

1 너는 우유병을 떨어뜨려서 깨트렸을 수도 있었어. (could, drop)
→ You ______________________ the bottle of milk and broken it.

2 그들은 다른 방법을 택했어야 했어. (should, choose)
→ They ______________________ a different way.

3 미국 팀이 이번 게임을 위해 매우 열심히 연습했음이 틀림없어. (practice)
→ The American team ______________________ very hard for this game.

4 이사하는 사람들이 거실에 상자를 뒀을지도 몰라. (may, put)
→ The movers ______________________ the box in the living room.

내신 FOCUS

SCORE: 

A 우리말을 참고하여 빈칸에 알맞은 조동사를 써 넣으시오.

1 Tom went to school. It ______________ be him. (그일 리가 없어.)

2 I wonder where she is. She ______________ be in the mall. (그녀는 쇼핑몰에 있을지도 몰라.)

B 빈칸에 들어갈 알맞은 말을 고르시오.

1 They just came home after a long journey. They ______________ be very tired.

ⓐ will ⓑ must ⓒ can't ⓓ has to

2 Watch out! You ______________ broken the lamp on the table.

ⓐ could have ⓑ cannot have ⓒ must have ⓓ should have

C 어법상 옳지 않은 문장을 고르시오.

1 ⓐ She is scratching now. She might have gotten mosquito bites.
ⓑ The water is rising in the Colorado River. The dam must have broken.
ⓒ Look out! You must have hit the old man.
ⓓ Kent was in the car. He cannot have taken your notebook.

2 ⓐ Jack won first prize. He cannot be happy.
ⓑ Harold is not here now. He may be in the coach's office.
ⓒ It must be Carrie on the phone. I asked her to call me.
ⓓ She just went out for dinner. She can't be at home already.

D 우리말과 같은 뜻이 되도록 주어진 말을 이용하여 문장을 완성하시오.

1 그는 학교에 오지 않았어. 그는 아픈 것이 틀림없어. (be, sick)
He didn't come to school. He ____.

2 그 강의 정말 흥미로웠어. 네가 참석했어야만 했는데. (attend)
The lecture was really interesting. You ____.

3 내 치마를 찾을 수 없었어. 내 동생이 입었을지도 몰라. (wear)
I couldn't find my skirt. My sister ____ it.

4 그 공연은 취소 됐어요. 미리 말을 해 주었어야 했는데. (tell)
The concert was cancelled. I ____ you in advance.

to부정사의 역할

A 밑줄 친 to부정사를 쓰임에 따라 명사적 "N", 형용사적 "A", 부사적 "Ad"로 구분하시오.

1 The young women were excited to hear the stories. ____________

2 My life's goal is to find a cure for a terrible disease. ____________

3 My little brother wants something to eat. ____________

4 Henry doesn't spend a lot on snacks to save money. ____________

5 I have 50 birthday invitation cards to send out. ____________

6 It is good for dogs to walk outside every day. ____________

B [보기]에서 쓰임이 같은 to부정사를 고르시오.

(a) English grammar is hard to understand.
(b) To ask forgiveness is necessary for good human relationships.
(c) Becky's desire is to have her new car by Friday.
(d) Craig went to the market to get more juice.
(e) After the rain, the wet boys need something to change into.

1 His job is to assist travelers with their flight plans. ____________

2 Could you recommend a nice hotel to stay in? ____________

3 The package from my grandparents is easy to open. ____________

4 It is wise of you to get advice from your elders. ____________

5 My husband doesn't order French fries to avoid the fat. ____________

C [보기]에서 알맞은 말을 골라 어법에 맞게 문장을 완성하시오.

Word Bank be get on wear say become

1 My new teammates need soccer shoes ____________.

2 Katie was glad ____________ with her best friend in classes this year.

3 My cousin's hope is ____________ a lawyer.

4 ____________ the bus at 7:00, you should leave home at 6:00.

5 Your friends must be very angry ____________ so.

FOCUS

SCORE:

A 주어진 동사를 알맞게 바꿔 쓰시오.

1 ______________(learn) English is very interesting.

2 My dream is ______________(be) a pilot.

3 I need somebody ______________(help) me.

4 He called her ______________(invite) her to his birthday party.

B 빈칸에 들어갈 알맞은 말을 고르시오.

1 It is a good idea ______________ ahead in life.

ⓐ to plan ⓑ to plans ⓒ plan ⓓ plans

2 The middle school students need someplace ______________.

ⓐ go ⓑ went ⓒ to go ⓓ to goes

C 어법상 옳지 않은 문장을 고르시오.

1 ⓐ Tina didn't draw many pictures to display in exhibitions.
ⓑ This is my piggy bank. I have seven quarters put.
ⓒ My cousin is training to be a jet engine mechanic.
ⓓ To register for this class, you should pay $10.

2 ⓐ His mother was happy to get his letter.
ⓑ My primary aim in life is to help other people.
ⓒ It is a pleasure to met you and your wife.
ⓓ The man in the office wants something to write on.

D 우리말과 같은 뜻이 되도록 주어진 말을 이용하여 문장을 완성하시오.

1 그는 올림픽에서 금메달을 따기 위해 열심히 연습했다. (practice, hard, get)
He ______________________________ the gold medal in the Olympics.

2 Jerry는 그 제안을 받아들이기로 했다. (decide, accept, the offer)
Jerry ______________________________.

3 앉을 의자가 필요해. (sit on)
I need ______________________________.

4 그녀는 마실 것을 주문했다. (something, drink)
She ordered ______________________________.

to부정사의 의미상 주어 / 부정

A 네모 안에서 알맞은 말을 고르시오.

1 Her friend wants [her, she] to move to Boston to attend college.

2 It is foolish [for them, of them] to leave their coats here.

3 Jimmy's brother asked [him to not, him not to] drive the car last night.

4 It was very kind [with him, of him] to call back about the problem.

5 It is a great honor [to her, for her] to meet the president.

6 Cathy told [his, him] to find the important file.

7 His plan is [not to, to not] eat fast food for his health.

B 주어진 말을 to부정사의 의미상 주어로 하여 문장을 완성하시오.

1 Dad needs to take the garden plants home today. (he)

→ Dad needs ____________ to take the garden plants home today.

2 It is difficult to write an essay in a short time. (they)

→ It is difficult ____________ to write an essay in a short time.

3 My father doesn't want to forget the manual for the cell phone. (you)

→ My father doesn't want ____________ to forget the manual for the cell phone.

4 It is unusual to leave a voice message. (she)

→ It is unusual ____________ to leave a voice message.

5 She doesn't want to hang a modern art work in her home. (her son)

→ She doesn't want ____________ to hang a modern art work in her home.

C 밑줄 친 부분을 바르게 고쳐 쓰시오.

1 Our boss told <u>I</u> to contact our customer. ____________

2 It was rude <u>to</u> him to speak to the woman like that. ____________

3 It is helpful <u>with</u> him to listen to the explanation again. ____________

4 The doctor wants <u>he</u> to take these pills for his illness. ____________

5 It is unwise of them <u>to not prepare</u> for bad weather. ____________

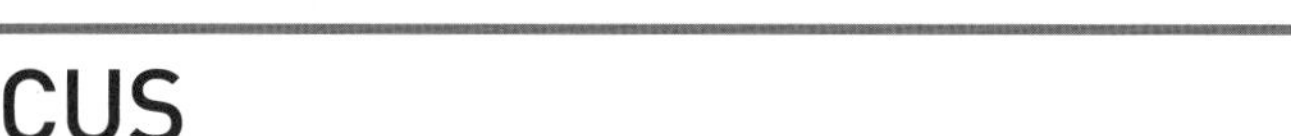

내신 FOCUS

SCORE:

A 주어진 단어를 to부정사의 의미상 주어로 바꿔 문장을 다시 쓰시오.

1 My uncle wants to be honest. (his son)

→ ______________________________

2 It is smart to hand in the paper in advance. (he)

→ ______________________________

B 빈칸에 들어갈 알맞은 말을 고르시오.

1 He told them __________ the desserts until the guests arrive.

ⓐ not to make ⓑ to not make ⓒ do not make ⓓ to make not

2 Does Leslie want __________ the pizzas to the party?

ⓐ his to bring ⓑ him to bring ⓒ for him bring ⓓ him to brought

C 어법상 옳지 않은 문장을 고르시오.

1 ⓐ His son asked her not to join the club without him.
ⓑ It is dangerous for us to play with a ball in the street.
ⓒ It's very difficult for my to speak in another language.
ⓓ Is it unusual for the cat to wander away from home?

2 ⓐ The doctor told her to not stay up all night.
ⓑ It is very urgent for him to contact us at this phone number.
ⓒ Was it sad for them to move to another city?
ⓓ It was bold of him to make such a difficult decision.

D 우리말과 같은 뜻이 되도록 주어진 말을 이용하여 문장을 완성하시오.

1 Mike는 그녀에게 문을 닫아 달라고 부탁했다. (ask, close the door)
Mike ______________________________.

2 아이들이 친구들과 어울려 노는 것은 중요하다. (children, play with)
It is important ______________________________ their friends.

3 무거운 가방을 들어주시다니 당신은 정말 친절하군요. (very kind, you, carry)
It is ______________________________ the heavy bag.

4 그는 딸에게 전화를 너무 오래 사용하지 말라고 말했다. (tell, his daughter, use, the phone)
He ______________________________ for too long.

부정사의 기타 쓰임

A 네모 안에서 알맞은 말을 고르시오.

1 The rope is [to, too] short to tie to the pole.

2 He flies planes well [so, enough] to be a pilot.

3 The police saw the thief [run, to run] into the movie theater.

4 Could you tell me [how to get, where to get] to the Vancouver Art Gallery?

5 Please send me instructions for [where to catch, what to catch] the bus.

6 The school can't decide when [to open, open] the new physics course.

7 The singer is [good enough, enough good] to appear on "American Idol."

B 밑줄 친 부분을 바르게 고쳐 쓰시오.

1 The company let me to take my vacation in the summer. __________

2 The boxes are to heavy for the movers to lift. __________

3 On the beach, I felt the sun to burn my skin. __________

4 The model didn't understand how wear the unusual outfit. __________

5 The mouse was enough cautious to avoid the mousetrap. __________

6 Jeff had his little sister to plan the birthday party. __________

7 The man couldn't figure out where put the tree. __________

C 두 문장의 의미가 통하도록 문장을 완성하시오.

1 The company is big enough to hire more workers.
= The company is ______ ______ that it ______ ______ more workers.

2 The students are too slow to compete against the faster children.
= The students are ______ ______ that they ______ ______ against the faster children.

3 The storm is so strong that it can damage many homes.
= The storm is ______ ______ ______ ______ many homes.

4 The man is so weak that he can't win the arm-wrestling contest.
= The man is ______ ______ ______ ______ the arm-wrestling contest.

FOCUS

SCORE:

A 두 문장의 의미가 통하도록 주어진 단어를 이용하여 문장을 완성하시오.

1 He'll tell me where to put the broken vase. (should)

= He'll tell me ____.

2 The movie is interesting enough to attract over 10 million people. (so, that)

= The movie is ____.

B 빈칸에 들어갈 알맞은 말을 고르시오.

1 The teacher let the student ____________ asking him questions.

ⓐ to continue ⓑ continue ⓒ continuing ⓓ continued

2 Unfortunately, he doesn't know ____________ the machine.

ⓐ to fixes ⓑ how fix ⓒ to fix how ⓓ how to fix

C 어법상 옳지 않은 문장을 고르시오.

1 ⓐ His brother helped him do his science project for school.
ⓑ The new curtains are enough wide to cover the window.
ⓒ My brother is too big to ride on the children's roller coaster.
ⓓ The new secretary doesn't know how to make plans for business trips.

2 ⓐ The officer let him make a phone call from the police station.
ⓑ The children saw the rabbits hop out of their cages.
ⓒ The tutors showed me how to study for the test.
ⓓ He got up so late to catch the early train.

D 우리말과 같은 뜻이 되도록 주어진 말을 이용하여 문장을 완성하시오.

1 그녀는 너무 어려서 회전목마를 탈 수 없었다. (young, ride)
She was ______________________________ a merry-go-round.

2 그 소년은 내가 울타리에 페인트칠하는 것을 도와주었다. (help, paint, the fence)
The boy ______________________________.

3 어떻게 이 자판기를 사용하는지 가르쳐 주시겠어요? (use, this vending machine)
Could you tell me ______________________________?

4 그 주전자는 그의 손가락을 델 만큼 뜨거웠다. (hot, burn)
The kettle was ______________________________ his finger.

동명사의 역할

A 네모 안에서 알맞은 말을 고르시오.

1 Talking on a cell phone [is, are] one of my sister's favorite things to do.

2 The man's plan [were beginning, was beginning] a new business.

3 His boss considered [send, sending] another request to the supplier.

4 Emma makes plenty of friends by [pay, paying] for their movie tickets.

5 [Be, Being] a good teacher is very important to Mr. Anderson.

6 Their passion is [climb, climbing] the great mountains of the world.

7 Jeff doesn't care about [acquire, acquiring] great honors for himself.

8 The mover's plan is [transferring, to transferring] the old furniture to the garage.

B 밑줄 친 –ing를 쓰임에 따라 동명사 "G", 현재분사 "P"로 구분하시오.

1 The basketball player is <u>discussing</u> a new play with his teammates. ____________

2 The coach's goal is <u>discussing</u> the new season with his team. ____________

3 Our bush is <u>dying</u> of a disease from another country. ____________

4 <u>Dying</u> of a disease from another country is the fate of our bush. ____________

5 The girl's favorite memory is <u>knitting</u> with her grandmother. ____________

6 The child is <u>knitting</u> a sweater for her grandfather. ____________

C 밑줄 친 부분을 괄호 안의 지시대로 바꿔 문장을 완성하시오.

1 I <u>jumped into the pool</u>. It was a great feeling. (주어 역할)

→ ________________________________ was a great feeling.

2 She avoids her old boyfriend. She doesn't <u>see her old boyfriend</u> these days. (목적어 역할)

→ She avoids ________________________________.

3 He <u>calls his mother on weekends</u>. He enjoys it. (목적어 역할)

→ He enjoys ________________________________.

4 My son is a policeman. He <u>prevents crime and keeps order</u>. (보어 역할)

→ My son's job as a policeman is ________________________________.

5 The teens <u>clean up the city</u>. It helps them develop good character. (주어 역할)

→ ________________________ helps the teens develop good character.

FOCUS

SCORE: 

A 주어진 단어를 동명사로 바꿔 문장을 완성하시오.

1 ______________ a pet is good for your health. (have)

2 His dream was ______________ to the top of Mt. Everest. (go)

3 The kid is good at ______________ poems. (memorize)

4 Did you finish ______________ the newspaper? (read)

B 빈칸에 들어갈 알맞은 말을 고르시오.

1 Is the school known for ______________ women from poor families?

ⓐ educate ⓑ educating ⓒ to educate ⓓ educates

2 ______________ a hat in the bright sunshine is a wise practice.

ⓐ Wears ⓑ Wear ⓒ Wearing ⓓ To wearing

C 어법상 옳지 않은 문장을 고르시오.

1 ⓐ My child has a sweet tooth. He really likes eat chocolate.
ⓑ Making lists of things to do helps me manage time.
ⓒ Thank you for sending me pretty flowers and a nice gift.
ⓓ Did they enjoy listening to the presentations?

2 ⓐ This kind of book is great for developing kids' imagination.
ⓑ Do you mind opening the door for me?
ⓒ This part's function is to spinning the gears in the motor.
ⓓ The concern of freshmen is deciding what to study.

D 우리말과 같은 뜻이 되도록 주어진 말과 동명사를 이용하여 문장을 완성하시오.

1 Bill의 꿈은 큰 병원을 짓는 것이다. (build, a big hospital)
Bill's dream is ______________________________________.

2 매일 일기를 쓰는 것은 나에게는 힘든 일이다. (keep a diary every day, difficult)
______________________________________ for me.

3 그는 정말 숨이 찼지만, 계속해서 강아지를 뒤쫓았다. (continue, run after, his dog)
He was out of breath, but he ______________________________________.

동명사의 의미상 주어 / 부정

A 네모 안에서 알맞은 말을 고르시오.

1 His mother will prevent [he, his] calling on her cell phone.

2 I look forward to [make, making] a fresh start in life.

3 He went [hike, hiking] last weekend.

4 She can't understand his [not answering, answering not] her calls.

5 Is your child busy [to do, doing] his homework?

6 I am so sorry for [not coming, not to come] on time.

7 Her good fortune [was finding, was find] a $5 bill on the ground.

B 밑줄 친 동사를 동명사로 바꿔 문장을 완성하시오.

1 She likes to listen to classical music.
→ Does she enjoy ____________ to classical music?

2 I fish in the Florida Keys with my dad every summer.
→ Do you go ____________ in the Florida Keys with your dad every summer?

3 She sends letters to soldiers until they return home.
→ Will she keep ____________ letters to soldiers until they return home?

4 The doctor told him to eat healthy food.
→ Did the doctor recommend him ____________ healthy food?

5 Tom has an allergy for dogs. He never touches them.
→ Does Tom avoid ____________ dogs?

C 밑줄 친 부분을 바르게 고쳐 쓰시오. 틀리지 않았다면, O표 하시오.

1 She dislikes her son playing violent computer games. ____________

2 Linda is interested in he making DIY furniture. ____________

3 The woman hates keeping not promises. ____________

4 I didn't feel like go home and taking care of my sister. ____________

5 Do you mind I asking some questions? ____________

6 His teacher hates his doing not homework and being late. ____________

FOCUS

SCORE: 

A 빈칸에 알맞은 말을 써 넣으시오.

1 She loves + She sings old songs.

→ She loves ________________ old songs.

2 She loves + Her mother sings lullabies.

→ She loves her mother's ________________ lullabies.

B 빈칸에 들어갈 알맞은 말을 고르시오.

1 This program prevents viruses from ____________ my computer.

ⓐ attacking ⓑ attacked ⓒ attack ⓓ to attack

2 He was angry about ____________ putting off his birthday party.

ⓐ they ⓑ I ⓒ her ⓓ he

C 어법상 옳지 않은 문장을 고르시오.

1 ⓐ Tony and James go fishing almost every Saturday.
ⓑ His early arrival is not helping anyone in the office.
ⓒ My joy is watching my children grow.
ⓓ My husband likes doing not anything except for sleeping on weekends.

2 ⓐ Does she hate I changing plans for our trip?
ⓑ His education is not costing him a lot of money.
ⓒ The boy is very busy packing his bag for camp.
ⓓ I don't feel like making eye contact with you.

D 우리말과 같은 뜻이 되도록 주어진 말을 이용하여 문장을 완성하시오.

1 그는 그녀의 편지를 받길 학수고대하고 있다. (look forward to, receive)
He ____ her letter.

2 내가 당신의 휴대 전화를 써도 괜찮겠습니까? (mind, use)
Do you ________________________________ your cell phone?

3 날씨가 좋으면, 이번 주말에 나는 수영을 하러 갈 것이다. (will, go, swim)
If the weather is fine, ________________________________ this weekend.

4 그들은 파티에 가지 않는 것에 대해 얘기하고 있다. (talk about, go to the party)
They ____.

동명사/to부정사를 쓰는 동사

A 네모 안에서 알맞은 말을 고르시오.

1 The principal postponed [going, to go] on a field trip because of strong winds.

2 After he heard the bad news, he stopped [to talk, talking] for a while.

3 She didn't pretend [knowing, to know] the strange man at the table.

4 The teacher will consider [changing, to change] the test.

5 Please don't forget [to pick up, pick up] the items from the grocery store.

6 Did she promise [paying, to pay] the rent by the due date?

7 Will the doctor begin [explain, to explain] the procedure to me later?

B 주어진 말을 어법에 맞게 바꿔 문장을 완성하시오.

1 I remember ______________(meet) my boyfriend for the very first time.

2 I remember ______________(meet) him at 7 pm. I'm on the way now.

3 I stopped ______________(watch) TV to help Mom prepare dinner.

4 I was lost. So I stopped ______________(ask) the way to Central Station.

5 I wondered if a dog can eat something cold. So I tried ______________(give) my dog a bowl of ice cream.

6 It was very hot today. I tried ______________(find) something cold, but there was nothing in the refrigerator.

C 주어진 말을 이용하여 문장을 완성하시오.

1 I kept ______________(read) my book and tried not ______________(listen) to their conversation, but I couldn't.

2 Did Frank quit ______________(eat) junk food and start ______________(choose) healthy snacks?

3 He wanted ______________(come), but he missed ______________(catch) his flight.

4 The man pretended ______________(be) a worker and tried ______________(break) into the office.

5 Kenny gave up ______________(smoke) for his health and began ______________(run) on the high school track.

내신 FOCUS

SCORE: 

A 밑줄 친 부분을 어법에 맞게 고쳐 쓰시오.

1 She avoided talk about her test scores.

2 She promised not talk about his test scores.

3 Once she starts crying, she never stops cry.

4 She is such a bad liar. He has to try not believe her.

B 빈칸에 들어갈 알맞은 말을 모두 고르시오.

1 My family likes __________ shopping at the flea market.

ⓐ to go ⓑ go ⓒ to going ⓓ going

2 My brother started __________ my sister and me to school.

ⓐ to drive ⓑ drive ⓒ driving ⓓ to driving

C 어법상 옳지 않은 문장을 고르시오.

1 ⓐ They hope to donate a couch to the church youth center.
ⓑ Would you mind helping me move these boxes?
ⓒ The chubby girl failed to lose weight.
ⓓ Dustin will never forget to go sky diving in Australia. It was really awesome.

2 ⓐ She didn't mean to spill my coffee on you.
ⓑ Don't pretend being asleep when you are awake.
ⓒ His car began making a terrible noise, and the engine began smoking.
ⓓ The students liked writing about the field trip to Iron Mountain.

D 우리말과 같은 뜻이 되도록 주어진 말을 이용하여 문장을 완성하시오.

1 Mary와 Mike는 Washington으로 이사하는 것을 고려 중이다. (consider, move to)
Mary and Mike ______________________________ Washington.

2 그는 우유를 사야 한다는 것은 기억했지만, 지갑을 가지고 오는 것을 깜박했다. (remember, buy, forget, bring)
He ____________________ milk, but he ____________________ his wallet.

3 폭우 때문에, 우리는 테니스를 연기했다. (put off, play tennis)
Because of heavy rain, we ______________________________.

4 우리는 그가 올 것이라고 예상했으나 그는 오지 않았다. (expect, come)
We ______________________________, but he didn't.

분사의 종류 및 의미

A 네모 안에서 알맞은 말을 고르시오.

1 She wants to see an [amazed, amazing] magic show.

2 The [confused, confusing] man got on the wrong train.

3 The response of the sales department was not [satisfying, satisfied].

4 The potatoes will help your [burnt, burning] skin get better.

5 Her [stolen, stealing] money was found in a bag in the thief's car.

6 The [spotted, spotting] dog came to the kitchen and ate my pancakes.

7 The last scene of *Cinema Paradiso* was very [touching, touched].

B 밑줄 친 부분을 참고하여 문장을 완성하시오.

1 I read a boring book in class yesterday. I was so ______________!

2 My mom lit the candle. The ______________ candle smelled very good.

3 Some fruit was spoiling in a basket. My mom threw out the ______________ fruit.

4 Harry broke the mirror in the bedroom this morning. The mirror is ______________ now.

5 They had to choose a room for the meeting. They are meeting in the ______________ room.

6 The boy did something embarrassing with his friends. He felt really ______________.

7 The reports surprised the scientists. The damage from the earthquake was ______________.

C 밑줄 친 –ing를 쓰임에 따라 동명사 "G", 현재분사 "P"로 구분하시오.

1 Mom asked me to take care of my crying sister. ______________

2 The police study new techniques for catching criminals. ______________

3 Do you know the name of the smiling girl by the door? ______________

4 She wrote a very interesting paper on honey bees last night. ______________

5 The goal is finding a safe place to build a campfire for dinner. ______________

6 My grandparents bought my brother a sleeping bag for camping. ______________

7 The students went on a fascinating field trip to the science museum. ______________

내신 FOCUS

SCORE:

A 밑줄 친 부분을 어법에 맞게 고쳐 쓰시오.

1 Look at the sing bird in the tree.

2 This article was about lose children.

3 She was shock by the news.

4 This book contains many interest stories.

B 빈칸에 들어갈 알맞은 말을 고르시오.

1 My grandparents were ______________ by the clowns at the circus.

ⓐ amuse ⓑ amused ⓒ amuses ⓓ amusing

2 Kathy likes playing the flute in the ______________ band.

ⓐ march ⓑ marches ⓒ marched ⓓ marching

C 어법상 옳지 않은 문장을 고르시오.

1 ⓐ The slept cat looks like Garfield.
ⓑ The upsetting news is so sad to all of us here.
ⓒ It is a very tiring time in our country these days.
ⓓ My brother was taking the injured people to the hospital.

2 ⓐ The boss was disappointed by the sales report.
ⓑ The thief broke into my house from the opened window.
ⓒ She saw a writing report about the fight in the police station.
ⓓ My teacher was impressed with my knowledge of the literature.

D 우리말과 같은 뜻이 되도록 주어진 말을 이용하여 문장을 완성하시오.

1 그 소문은 정말로 놀라웠다. (really, surprise)
The rumor ____.

2 그는 삶은 두부를 먹지 않는다. (boil)
He doesn't eat ______________ tofu.

3 지도를 가지고 민속촌에 가는 길을 찾는 것은 정말 헷갈렸다. (very, confuse)
To find the way to the folk village with the map ____________________________.

4 영화 "13일의 금요일 밤"을 볼 때 나는 무서워 죽는 줄 알았다. (scare to death)
I was ____________________________ when I saw the movie *Friday the 13th*.

분사의 쓰임

A 네모 안에서 알맞은 말을 고르시오.

1 The young boy [dived, diving] into the cold water is my brother.

2 Please take the [coughing, coughed] child into the examination room.

3 The boy [talked, talking] with the old woman is wearing his shirt backward.

4 I like to see dragonflies [flying, flown] in the clear sky.

5 Do you think this advertisement will help me find my [missing, missed] dog?

6 We heard someone [screaming, screamed] in the forest.

B 주어진 말을 이용하여 문장을 완성하시오.

1 The beautiful stone ______________(take) from the cave was a jewel.

2 The people ______________(stand) near the door are my new relatives.

3 The book ______________(tear) by the boy is very old.

4 The ______________(slice) cheese on the table is very salty.

5 The small package ______________(pick up) by Jane is my sister's.

6 The field trip to the zoo was very ______________(interest).

7 The ______________(encourage) team practiced hard and won the game.

C 밑줄 친 부분을 바르게 고쳐 쓰시오.

1 I spent one hour washing the dirty dishes <u>piling</u> up in the sink. ______________

2 The bottle <u>filling</u> with international coins is my father's. ______________

3 Who is the boy <u>play</u> in the sandbox? ______________

4 I think a <u>using</u> car won't work well. ______________

5 Watch out for a <u>dance</u> bear in the back row. ______________

6 The <u>break</u> laptop computer is my grandfather's. ______________

FOCUS

SCORE:

A 주어진 말을 이용하여 문장을 완성하시오.

1 나무 밑에서 졸고 있는 강아지를 봐. (the puppy, doze off)

Look at ______________________________ under the tree.

2 "So Far From the Bamboo Grove"라는 제목의 책을 찾고 있어요. (the book, title)

I'm looking for ________________ *So Far From the Bamboo Grove*.

B 빈칸에 들어갈 알맞은 말을 고르시오.

1 I think __________ are the best in the world.

ⓐ cars made in Germany ⓑ made in Germany cars
ⓒ Germany cars making ⓓ cars make in Germany

2 You should be careful when you open a __________ soda can.

ⓐ shaking ⓑ shake ⓒ shook ⓓ shaken

C 어법상 옳지 않은 문장을 고르시오.

1 ⓐ I want to know the name of the song played during *Phantom of the Opera*.
ⓑ The boy wore a hat is my best friend at school.
ⓒ We should clean all the fallen leaves in the yard.
ⓓ The repairman came and fixed the blocked sink.

2 ⓐ I ate delicious cookies baked by my grandmother.
ⓑ My son found a meowing cat in the box.
ⓒ The tiny bugs made my niece to scare of all bugs.
ⓓ My children saw a panda sleeping on its back.

D 우리말과 같은 뜻이 되도록 주어진 말을 이용하여 문장을 완성하시오.

1 나는 짖는 개가 무서웠다. (bark)

I was afraid of the __________ dog.

2 Edward는 침대 옆에 놓여 있는 안경을 거의 밟을 뻔 했다. (the glasses, lie, by the bed)

Edward almost stepped on ______________________________.

3 Mary는 누군가가 그녀의 셔츠를 당기는 것을 느꼈다. (pull, her shirt)

Mary felt someone ______________________________.

4 너의 잃어버린 가방을 찾았니? (lose, bag)

Did you find your ______________________________?

수동태의 개념과 형태

A 네모 안에서 알맞은 말을 고르시오.

1 The koala [fed, was fed] eucalyptus leaves by the zookeeper.

2 The ice skaters [helped, were helped] by the hockey coach after practice.

3 The actress [complains, is complained] to the movie director about the script.

4 The report will [make, be made] by the committee on Monday.

5 The window in the living room [broke, was broken] by the baseball.

6 [Was, Did] this book borrowed by Jennifer from the library?

7 The train to Chicago [delay, was delayed] because of a broken rail.

B 밑줄 친 부분을 바르게 고쳐 쓰시오. 틀리지 않았다면 O표 하시오.

1 The new student exchange program <u>started</u> by my old teacher. ____________

2 The German and French languages <u>understand</u> in Switzerland. ____________

3 Was your order <u>receive</u> by the staff politely? ____________

4 The deer <u>startled</u> by the campers in the national forest. ____________

5 The dinner plates should be <u>clean</u> up by the busboys. ____________

6 He <u>brings</u> ice cream for everyone once a month. ____________

C 주어진 문장을 수동태 문장으로 바꿔 쓰시오.

1 Sam orders a large pepperoni pizza once a month.
→ A large pepperoni pizza ____________ by Sam once a month.

2 The coffee shop workers developed a new drink.
→ A new drink ____________ by the coffee shop workers.

3 The farmers welcomed the rain because of the terrible drought.
→ The rain ____________ by the farmers because of the terrible drought.

4 Those parents didn't hold the meeting for the new semester.
→ The meeting for the new semester ____________ by those parents.

FOCUS

SCORE: 

A 주어진 문장을 참고하여 빈칸에 알맞은 말을 써 넣으시오.

1 My uncle built this church 20 years ago.

→ This church ______________ by my uncle 20 years ago.

2 Alexander Graham Bell invented the telephone.

→ __________ the telephone __________ by Alexander Graham Bell?

B 빈칸에 들어갈 알맞은 말을 고르시오.

1 A picture was hung __________ the artist in the store.

ⓐ to ⓑ from ⓒ at ⓓ by

2 The horse __________ by my sister along the Grand Canyon.

ⓐ was ridden ⓑ rode ⓒ did ride ⓓ was rode

C 어법상 옳지 않은 문장을 고르시오.

1 ⓐ The computer was repaired by my friend for free.
ⓑ His new camera takes great photos in the daylight.
ⓒ Was the salad ate by him before he got sick?
ⓓ The path is taken by many hikers in these woods.

2 ⓐ The workers were paid not on time by their employer.
ⓑ The building was designed by the architect in 2001.
ⓒ The test was taken by the class in a different room.
ⓓ Was the delicious food prepared by your mother?

D 우리말과 같은 뜻이 되도록 주어진 말을 이용하여 문장을 완성하시오.

1 그 웨딩 케이크는 유명한 요리사에 의해 장식되었다. (decorate, a famous chef)
The wedding cake ____.

2 매년 많은 숲이 홍수와 산불에 의해 피해를 입는다. (damage, floods and fires)
Many forests ____ every year.

3 그 문제는 내 남동생에 의해 해결되었다. (solve, my brother)
The problem ____.

4 그 영화는 언제 처음 상연되었니? (the movie, first, show)
When ____?

여러 가지 수동태

A 네모 안에서 알맞은 말을 고르시오.

1 The children were scared [of, to] the big dog near the house.

2 The sweet doughnut was filled [with, in] delicious white cream.

3 Edward was worried [at, about] the next social studies test.

4 The vase was made [of, on] yellow glass, silver, and copper.

5 I am amazed [at, for] the progress of this class.

6 The audience was satisfied [to, with] the opening show.

7 The woman was pleased [from, with] the manager's decision to refund all her money.

B 밑줄 친 부분을 바르게 고쳐 쓰시오. 틀리지 않았다면, O표 하시오.

1 A huge turkey was cooked <u>of</u> many relatives. ____________

2 My little sister is amazed <u>at</u> the size of Disneyland. ____________

3 She is interested <u>with</u> making documentaries about artists. ____________

4 The greeting card was made <u>of</u> me by my grandson this morning. ____________

5 Was the assignment sent <u>with</u> the students in an e-mail yesterday? ____________

C 주어진 문장을 수동태 문장을 바꿔 쓰시오.

1 The little grasshoppers from the fields cover the road.

→ The road ________________________________ from the fields.

2 The new teacher asked me a question about the stars.

→ A question about the stars ________________________ by the new teacher.

3 Daniel showed me the map after we had been lost.

→ The map ________________________ by Daniel after we had been lost.

4 My friend gave me a sandwich on my lunch break.

→ A sandwich ________________________ by my friend on my lunch break.

5 The boy wrote postcards to his grandparents.

→ Postcards ________________________________ by the boy.

내신 FOCUS

SCORE: 

A 빈칸에 알맞은 전치사를 써 넣으시오.

1 My secret was told ______________ everyone by my best friend, Jim.

2 Dinner was made ______________ all the family by my aunt.

3 The square is filled ______________ a lot of tourists to see the fireworks.

4 We are worried ______________ being late for school.

B 빈칸에 들어갈 알맞은 말을 고르시오.

1 The doctor was pleased ______________ my lab results this time.

ⓐ to　ⓑ with　ⓒ of　ⓓ for

2 The crowd was amazed ______________ the performance of the circus stars.

ⓐ at　ⓑ from　ⓒ to　ⓓ in

C 어법상 옳지 않은 문장을 고르시오.

1 ⓐ The gifts were bought for guests and carefully wrapped.
ⓑ The cat is belonged by the family in the next door.
ⓒ Much of his work has been done for the poor.
ⓓ The brownies cannot be made from butter and chocolate syrup.

2 ⓐ You might be surprised at the answer to your question.
ⓑ The new information was told for him in a week.
ⓒ Was the newspaper article written by a friend of yours?
ⓓ A message was whispered to me by my best friend.

D 우리말과 같은 뜻이 되도록 주어진 말을 이용하여 문장을 완성하시오.

1 Brenda는 선생님에게 상을 받았다. (give, an award, her teacher)
Brenda ____.

2 그 편지는 Billy가 쓴 것이었다. (write, Billy)
The letter ____.

3 그녀는 자신의 수학 점수에 만족했다. (be satisfied with, her math score)
She ____.

4 많은 아이들이 주사를 무서워한다. (be scared of, injections)
Many children ____.

명사 (I)

A 네모 안에서 알맞은 말을 고르시오.

1 The little boy found two [coin, coins] in the park.

2 His [class, classes] works on a new English grammar unit today.

3 Their study group is reading about [a Korean history, Korean history].

4 Terry asked [a Grace, Grace] to go to a dance with him.

5 My sister's twin [babys, babies] were wrapped in pretty pink blankets.

6 The physics class [was, were] very challenging for me, so I have to retake it.

7 The [sheep, sheeps] were blocking the road to my grandparents' house.

B 주어진 말을 어법에 맞게 바꿔 문장을 완성하시오.

1 He seems to have good ______________(luck) on his jobs.

2 My stolen ______________(car) was found in a deserted area.

3 Have you heard any ______________(news) about the earthquake in California?

4 The ______________(pant) are too short for me to wear.

5 Lots of ______________(person) gathered at City Hall.

6 My ______________(key) were in the drawer, but they have disappeared.

7 Who are the ______________(man) in this photo?

8 I saw two ______________(mouse) running into a hole in the wall.

C 밑줄 친 부분을 바르게 고쳐 쓰시오. 틀리지 않았다면, O표 하시오.

1 Please trim the <u>bushs</u> in the yard for me. ______________

2 The <u>moneys</u> for your field trip is on the table. ______________

3 Did you wash my new <u>jeans</u> with my white shirt? ______________

4 My uncle bought two <u>piano</u> for his family in Canada. ______________

5 The recipe says to add two <u>egg</u> to the mixture. ______________

6 Please buy <u>a milk</u> at the grocery store for our dinner tonight. ______________

7 Would you like <u>creams and sugars</u> with your coffee? ______________

FOCUS

SCORE:

A 명사의 복수형이 잘못 연결된 것을 고르시오.

1 ⓐ star - stars ⓑ potato - potatoes ⓒ bus - buses ⓓ city - citys

2 ⓐ wolf - wolfs ⓑ monkey - monkeys ⓒ box - boxes ⓓ piano - pianos

B 빈칸에 들어갈 알맞은 말을 고르시오.

1 My friends enjoy eating these ______________ from the market.

ⓐ steak ⓑ grapes ⓒ food ⓓ mango

2 There is not much ______________ left before we close.

ⓐ works ⓑ chores ⓒ time ⓓ assignments

C 어법상 옳지 않은 문장을 고르시오.

1 ⓐ There is a big apple on the table for you.
ⓑ The water in the fishes tank is clean now.
ⓒ There are four buses to the zoo every day.
ⓓ I talked to my father about my homework.

2 ⓐ My little brother is 4 feet tall now.
ⓑ Jane can't find her new scissor in the cabinet.
ⓒ His reports must be rewritten by Wednesday morning.
ⓓ As they get older, I am concerned about my parents' happiness.

D 우리말과 같은 뜻이 되도록 주어진 말을 이용하여 문장을 완성하시오.

1 아이들은 미래를 위한 우리의 희망이다. (hope, for, the future)
Children are ______________________________.

2 살아 있는 모든 것은 공기를 들이마신다. (breathe in, air)
All living things ______________________________.

3 그녀는 오렌지 하나와 토마토 여덟 개를 샀다. (orange, tomato)
She bought ______________________________.

4 그 동물원에는 늑대 두 마리와 사슴 다섯 마리가 있다. (wolf, deer)
There are ______________________________ in the zoo.

명사 (Ⅱ)

A 네모 안에서 알맞은 말을 고르시오.

1 We have [many, much] snacks left for my friends.

2 I want [a slice of, a spoon of] cheese on my hamburger.

3 Please get some [juice, juices] from the grocery store on your way home.

4 I don't have [Ben, Ben's] watch in my pocket anymore.

5 Does your son know the name [of, at] this song?

6 A lot of [dancer, dancers] are performing on the stage in the theater.

7 Do we have [any, many] string to make a tail for the kite?

8 My Christmas gift to him was [a pair of, a piece of] jeans.

B [보기]에서 알맞은 말을 골라 문장을 완성하시오.

Word Bank a carton of　a piece of　many loaves of　three boxes of　a spoonful of

1 My mother ordered ____________ chocolate for the party.

2 Would you like ____________ apple pie for your dessert?

3 She put ____________ sugar into the cookies this time.

4 We have ____________ milk for lunch at school every day.

5 We have ____________ bread to eat.

C 밑줄 친 부분을 바르게 고쳐 쓰시오.

1 My mom made pizza and cut it into six piece. ____________

2 I like a lot black pepper on my fried chicken. ____________

3 Do you want to have a glass of wines? ____________

4 There are many slice of cake for the wedding. ____________

5 I didn't hear yesterdays news about the accident. ____________

6 My mother gave me seven jar of fruit. ____________

7 I don't have many space to put the chair in my office. ____________

내신 FOCUS

SCORE:

A 셀 수 없는 명사를 세는 단위가 옳지 않은 것을 고르시오.

1 ⓐ a cup of tea ⓑ two glasses of juice ⓒ a slice of cheese ⓓ a pound of paper

2 ⓐ a piece of cake ⓑ two spoonfuls of olive oil ⓒ a bottle of bread ⓓ three cartons of milk

B 빈칸에 들어갈 알맞은 말을 고르시오.

1 I have had ______ baseball glove for almost a week.

ⓐ Bobby ⓑ Bobby' ⓒ Bobbies ⓓ Bobby's

2 Please gather ______ rubber bands for my school project next week.

ⓐ a slice of ⓑ much ⓒ many ⓓ some pieces of

C 어법상 옳지 않은 문장을 고르시오.

1 ⓐ We ate three slices of sausage pizza at the restaurant.
ⓑ My father socks are in a basket.
ⓒ I have looked in the parking lot. Where is Jerry's car?
ⓓ My cousin showed me a picture of his girlfriend.

2 ⓐ My aunt picked some vegetables from her garden.
ⓑ I think the bean soup needs some salt and pepper.
ⓒ My sister didn't drink even one pound of wine because she had to drive.
ⓓ She put a piece of strawberry cake in his lunchbox.

D 우리말과 같은 뜻이 되도록 주어진 말을 이용하여 문장을 완성하시오.

1 Bill의 방은 항상 지저분하다. (Bill, room)
______ always dirty.

2 그는 목이 매우 말라서 물 두 병을 마셨다. (water)
He was very thirsty, so he drank ______.

3 밀가루 일 파운드와 계란 세 개를 그릇에 넣으세요. (flour, egg)
Put ______ into the bowl.

4 냉장고에 과일이 없어. (no)
There is ______ in the refrigerator.

관사

A 네모 안에서 알맞은 말을 고르시오.

1 I have [a, an, the] package of crackers to go with my soup.

2 Would you move [a, an, the] desk to the other side of the room?

3 My father always told me that you should be [a, an, the] honest man.

4 Look! [A, An, The] zookeeper is feeding some bananas to the monkeys.

5 My mother says [a, an, the] apple every day keeps the doctor away.

6 His friend is [a, an, the] lawyer in New York City.

7 Jennifer asked a librarian for help. [A, An, The] librarian helped her find a book.

B a, an, the, ø 중 알맞은 것을 골라 문장을 완성하시오.

1 Our assignment is writing ______________ essay on former President Ronald Reagan.

2 Sara plays ______________ cello in an orchestra.

3 Andy heard ______________ new song on the radio last night.

4 My dad went to get our ______________ luggage out of the car.

5 Mary is ______________ smartest member of our science club.

6 They traveled Western Europe by ______________ train.

C [보기]에서 밑줄 친 관사의 쓰임이 같은 것을 고르시오.

Example

(a) See <u>the</u> manual on the table for your technical questions.
(b) She received <u>a</u> package from her son in Oregon.
(c) My nephew sent me a postcard. I put <u>the</u> postcard on my living room table.
(d) That motorcycle's maximum speed is over 100 miles <u>an</u> hour.

1 The office has <u>a</u> phone on the desk for you to use. ______________

2 Watch out for <u>the</u> boy in the green shirt. He is mean. ______________

3 The crew changes flight schedules only two times <u>a</u> month. ______________

4 I borrowed a book from the library. <u>The</u> book is about jazz. ______________

SCORE:

A 빈칸에 a, an, the, Ø 중 알맞은 것을 써 넣으시오.

1 The gift doesn't need to cost ______________ arm and a leg.

2 Look at ______________ smiling girl. She is very cute.

3 We go to ______________ church on Sundays.

4 ______________ penguin is a bird.

B 빈칸에 들어갈 알맞은 말을 고르시오.

1 I have ______________ wonderful story to tell you.

ⓐ an ⓑ a ⓒ the ⓓ Ø

2 My sister goes ______________ middle school.

ⓐ an ⓑ a ⓒ the ⓓ Ø

C 어법상 옳지 않은 문장을 고르시오.

1 ⓐ Jim went to the church to find his son.
ⓑ I always skip the dinner to lose weight.
ⓒ Would you open the windows in the kitchen?
ⓓ A snail is a very slow creature.

2 ⓐ Would you recommend a interesting book?
ⓑ I usually play basketball with my roommate on weekends.
ⓒ Listen to some English dialogues in the language lab.
ⓓ My sister is the kindest person in the world.

D 우리말과 같은 뜻이 되도록 주어진 말을 이용하여 문장을 완성하시오.

1 하늘에는 별이 정말 많다. (lots of, star, in the sky)
There are ______________________________.

2 그는 보통 방과 후에 친구들과 축구를 한다. (usually, play, soccer)
He ______________________________ after school with his friends.

3 나는 그 검은 상자 안에서 오래된 책을 발견했다. (old, book, in, black, box)
I found ______________________________.

4 나는 식당에서 한 남자를 만났다. 그 남자는 치과의사였다. (man)
I met a man in the restaurant. ______________________________ a dentist.

인칭/지시/의문대명사

A 네모 안에서 알맞은 말을 고르시오.

1 The students are coming to [I, me, my] house for a party.

2 [We, Our, Us] asked a policeman for directions to the theater.

3 The small package on the desk is for [he, his, him].

4 He forgot to send the information to [we, our, us].

5 [Who, Whose, Whom] backpack is lying on the table in the kitchen?

6 I want to have [this, those] picture for my scrapbook.

7 I received an engagement ring from my fiancé. [It is, They are] really beautiful.

8 He visited a 600-year-old castle. [Its, They, There] windows are all stained glass.

9 The stewardess welcomed [they, their, them] aboard the flight to Washington.

10 Do you know [who, which, what] is going with us to the national park?

B 밑줄 친 부분을 대명사로 바꿔 문장을 완성하시오.p

1 The woman near the taxi wears a pretty hat. → __________ has a colorful dress, too.

2 I have a very old computer in my office. → __________ computer should be replaced.

3 I love my grandparents. → __________ called me last night.

4 He needs a good friend these days. → __________ best friend has moved.

5 My dad is a very strong man. → __________ works out at a gym.

6 She took the bus to school this morning. → __________ bus left ten minutes ago.

7 Our school is preparing a science fair. → __________ will be held in November.

C 의문사를 이용하여 대화를 완성하시오.

1 A __________ flower do you like better? B I like the red one better.

2 A __________ do the children want for Christmas? B They want some toys and clothes.

3 A __________ car is parked in the driveway? B It is your uncle's car.

4 A __________ cake will you buy? B I'll buy the one with chocolate.

5 A __________ is the title of this story? B It's called "An Easter Surprise."

6 A __________ hid my shoes? B Jack did.

SCORE:

A 빈칸에 알맞은 말을 써 넣으시오.

주격	소유격	목적격
you	your	ⓐ ______
it	ⓑ ______	it
they	their	ⓒ ______
who	ⓓ ______	ⓔ ______

B 빈칸에 들어갈 알맞은 말을 고르시오.

1 Please give the baseball back to ____________.

ⓐ us ⓑ we ⓒ our ⓓ ours

2 ____________ way does the map say we should go?

ⓐ What ⓑ Who ⓒ Which ⓓ Whose

C 어법상 옳지 않은 문장을 고르시오.

1 ⓐ These are four plates, and those are four cups.
ⓑ We are meeting them at the mall at 5 o'clock.
ⓒ These is the best kind of chocolate in the U.S.
ⓓ Please tell me about your recent trip to Switzerland.

2 ⓐ Who video game is on the computer?
ⓑ What did the teacher say about the next test?
ⓒ Which building is your dad's company?
ⓓ Whom do you prefer to study with at school?

D 우리말과 같은 뜻이 되도록 주어진 말을 이용하여 문장을 완성하시오.

1 Julie가 우리를 위해 점심을 준비할 거야. (will, prepare, lunch)
Julie ____________________________________.

2 이 그림들은 내가 그렸고 저 그림들은 내 동생이 그렸어. (this, picture, that, picture)
I painted ____________________, and my sister painted ____________________.

3 여름에 장마 기간이 있어. 이 시기에는 비가 많이 내려. (rain, a lot)
We have a rainy season in summer. ______________________________ during that time.

4 누구와 함께 놀이 공원에 갔었니? (go)
____________________________________ to the amusement park with?

소유/재귀대명사

A 네모 안에서 알맞은 말을 고르시오.

1 I ordered a T-bone steak. [Mine, Him, Their] was served last.

2 You really like taking pictures. Are they all [you, your, yours]?

3 I'll show you our seats. [Ours, Us, Mine] are in the middle of the front row.

4 Sara told me that you wanted to borrow her book. Here is [her, hers, your].

5 My father enjoys collecting antiques. This old lamp is [hers, his, ours] as well.

6 I think it is your computer, right? Could I use [yours, you, our] for a moment?

7 My sisters and I have different flavors of cakes. I want to try [theirs, they, her].

B [보기]에서 알맞은 말을 골라 문장을 완성하시오.

Word Bank	myself	yourself	himself	herself	ourselves	themselves

1 Has she hurt ____________ in a minor accident recently?

2 He made all these cookies in the kitchen ____________.

3 My children moved their heavy beds and desks ____________.

4 Please don't talk to me. Just keep your thoughts to ____________.

5 We ____________ would like to meet the man from Russia.

6 I will take care of the complicated problem ____________.

C 우리말을 참고하여 문장을 완성하시오.

1 I have to wash the pile of dishes ____________ ____________. (홀로)

2 It didn't happen ____________ ____________. Someone broke the vase. (저절로)

3 One should make every effort to stay healthy ____________ ____________. (스스로를 위해서)

4 After he broke up with his girlfriend, he was ____________ ____________ for a while. (제정신이 아닌)

5 Let's keep this unfortunate event ____________ ____________. (우리끼리의 얘기로, 비밀로)

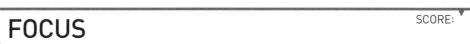

내신 FOCUS

SCORE:

A 두 단어의 연결이 잘못된 것을 고르시오.

1 ⓐ my - mine ⓑ his - his's ⓒ her - hers ⓓ your - yours

2 ⓐ I - myself ⓑ them - themself ⓒ we - ourselves ⓓ it - itself

B 빈칸에 들어갈 알맞은 말을 고르시오.

1 I wore my sister's skirt, and I tore it. I should haven't worn ________.

ⓐ theirs ⓑ his ⓒ her ⓓ hers

2 Welcome to our house. Please make ________ at home.

ⓐ yourself ⓑ himself ⓒ herself ⓓ itself

C 어법상 옳지 않은 문장을 고르시오.

1 ⓐ Please stop talking to yourself.
ⓑ I just want to be by mineself right now.
ⓒ One book is mine, and two books are hers.
ⓓ You won't understand the story before you read it yourself.

2 ⓐ What a nice car it is! Is this your?
ⓑ He sent a letter to himself as a reminder.
ⓒ I hope you enjoy yourself at the baseball game tonight.
ⓓ Make a place for yourself to sit on the floor. We will start the movie soon.

D 우리말과 같은 뜻이 되도록 주어진 말을 이용하여 문장을 완성하시오.

1 내 어린 남동생이 이 사진들을 직접 찍었어. (this, picture, oneself)
My little brother took ________________________.

2 이 재미있는 책은 그녀의 것이니, 아니면 그의 것이니?(she, he)
Is this interesting book ________________________?

3 너는 너 자신을 사랑해야 해. (should, love oneself)
You ________________________.

4 그는 혼자 힘으로 자신의 자동차를 고쳤다. (fix, one's car, by oneself)
He ________________________.

부정대명사 (I)

A 네모 안에서 알맞은 말을 고르시오.

1 The visitor had gifts from China for [all, every] student.

2 [Both, Either] are coming to the meeting this afternoon.

3 My oldest cousin resembles [either, neither] of the siblings in her family.

4 [Some, Any] of the cars have bigger trunks than the others.

5 He removed [all, every] of the paint from the desk.

6 Does your family know [any, each] famous singers?

7 She doesn't have [neither, either] of the books from the library now.

B [보기]에서 알맞은 말을 골라 문장을 완성하시오.

Word Bank all every both some any either neither

1 My family goes to church ____________ Sunday.

2 You can take ____________ of the shirts. Which color do you prefer?

3 Her project sounds like ____________ of her co-workers'. It's unique.

4 Would you like ____________ potato soup with your dinner tonight?

5 I don't have ____________ worries about my own health.

6 ____________ the social studies books are ready for the students.

7 I have two children. My husband took ____________ to the county fair.

C 밑줄 친 부분을 바르게 고쳐 쓰시오. 틀리지 않았다면, O표 하시오.

1 Each fruit has a different taste. ____________

2 I need any air in my bicycle tires again. ____________

3 I don't have some interesting magazines to read. ____________

4 They don't need to clean neither of the rooms. ____________

5 All of his friend graduated from the same school with him. ____________

6 Every classes starts at 9:30 and lasts one hour. ____________

FOCUS

SCORE: 

A [ ] 안에서 알맞은 말을 고르시오.

1 Would you like to have [some, any] coffee?

There aren't [some, any] zebras in the zoo.

2 [All, Every] children feel happy on Children's Day.

[Both, Either] are fine with me.

B 빈칸에 들어갈 알맞은 말을 고르시오.

1 ______________ of the pictures were placed into a photo album.

ⓐ Any ⓑ Either ⓒ Much ⓓ All

2 ______________ of cats were in the barn.

ⓐ Every ⓑ Each ⓒ Either ⓓ Both

C 어법상 옳지 않은 문장을 고르시오.

1 ⓐ I have each of the files from last month.
ⓑ Every patient is cared for by a registered nurse.
ⓒ Do you have either problems with planning so far?
ⓓ All of the girls went swimming at the beach.

2 ⓐ Every things depend on your attitude.
ⓑ My mom ordered some milk for my sister's baby.
ⓒ All shoes are on sale at the department store.
ⓓ Neither of the pictures is an example of great Renaissance art.

D 우리말과 같은 뜻이 되도록 주어진 말을 이용하여 문장을 완성하시오.

1 나는 수학과 영어 중 한 과목은 낙제할지 모른다. (fail, math, English)
I might ____.

2 Sally는 열 그루의 나무를 기르는데 각각의 나무들은 다른 이름을 가지고 있다. (have, different, name)
Sally has raised ten trees, and ____________________________________.

3 그에 대한 모든 신문 기사는 스크랩이 되어 있었다. (article, about him, be scrapped)
All of the ____.

4 두 소년 모두 부정행위에 대한 벌을 받지 않았다. (neither, the two boys, was punished)
____ for cheating on the exam.

부정대명사 (Ⅱ)

A 네모 안에서 알맞은 말을 고르시오.

1 [One, Most] should wait in a line to use a public toilet.

2 He always tells a lie. It is [no, most] wonder people don't believe him.

3 Some parents attended the school carnival, and [the others, another] didn't.

4 The bird usually sings in the tree, but [one, it] is gone today.

5 I had seven cards. I kept only one, and I threw out [other, the others].

6 The suitcase is too small for my travel plans. Please show me [another, each another].

B [보기]에서 알맞은 말을 골라 문장을 완성하시오.

Word Bank one another the others each other most no

1 The flight was long, but ______________ people enjoyed it.

2 ______________ shouldn't smoke in a public place.

3 Her bus is empty. She has ______________ passengers now.

4 I don't like that kind. I would like to try ______________ flavor of ice cream.

5 Stop fighting. You must learn to be kind to ______________.

6 He is the best player in the NBA. He plays better than ______________.

C 우리말과 같은 뜻이 되도록 문장을 완성하시오.

1 우리 팀 대부분의 선수들은 경기를 할 준비가 되어 있었지만, 일부는 아니었다.
→ ________________ of our team was ready for the game, but ________________ were not.

2 내가 좋아하는 노래 중 한 곡은 인기가 없지만, 다른 나머지 곡은 잘 알려져 있다.
→ ________________ of my favorite songs is not popular, but ________________ are well-known.

3 몇몇 선수들은 부상을 입었고, 다른 몇몇 선수들은 건강했다.
→ ________________ of the players were hurt, but ________________ were healthy.

4 어떤 사람도 그 파란 방에 들어가는 것은 허락되어 있지 않다.
→ ________________ one is allowed to enter the blue room.

내신 FOCUS

SCORE:

A 빈칸에 알맞은 말을 써 넣으시오.

1 I have two puppies. ____________ is a Maltese, and ____________ is a Dalmatian.

2 There are three rooms in my house. One is a bedroom, ____________ is a bathroom, and ____________ is a living room.

B 빈칸에 들어갈 알맞은 말을 고르시오.

1 This list shows ____________ books about history.

ⓐ another ⓑ others ⓒ one ⓓ most

2 I have ____________ energy left to go hiking. I need to rest.

ⓐ another ⓑ no ⓒ one ⓓ most

C 어법상 옳지 않은 문장을 고르시오.

1 ⓐ Some patients in the room take the new medication, but the others don't.
ⓑ These shoes are too tight. Do you have another size that is bigger?
ⓒ Every is always responsible for his own actions in life.
ⓓ Some people respect, and others are respected.

2 ⓐ Most of his paintings costs over $2,000.
ⓑ This snack is very delicious. Please bring me another.
ⓒ No cats are permitted in the apartment.
ⓓ One of my friends passed the test, but the others failed.

D 우리말과 같은 뜻이 되도록 주어진 말을 이용하여 문장을 완성하시오.

1 내 배낭이 너무 낡아서 엄마가 새것을 사 주셨어. (buy, new)
My backpack was too worn, so my mom ______________________________.

2 누구도 그 지루한 영화에 대해 불평하지 않았다. (no, complain about)
______________________________ the boring movie.

3 그 사고로 몇몇 사람은 죽었고, 다른 몇몇은 심하게 다쳤다. (people, die, be severely injured)
____________________, and ____________________ because of the accident.

4 대부분의 내 책은 추리 소설이다. (my books)
______________________________ mystery books.

형용사

A 네모 안에서 알맞은 말을 고르시오.

1 She bought [a lot of, much] potatoes for the soup.

2 Jane put three kittens in a [pretty, prettily] basket.

3 We thought the World Cup games were very [excited, exciting].

4 My brother wants to buy [fun something, something fun] to play with.

5 The [plastic, plastically] parts broke easily when she dropped the radio.

6 Does he want [a little, a few] syrup on his pancakes?

7 She resembles her [grandmother favorite, favorite grandmother] a lot.

8 The [careless, carelessly] child didn't look both ways before crossing the street.

B 밑줄 친 부분을 바르게 고쳐 쓰시오.

1 It is <u>lot of</u> work to clean up after a parade. ______________

2 There are <u>any</u> hamburgers for you on the grill. ______________

3 My first science class was <u>bored</u>. ______________

4 They bought a <u>little</u> bats for the baseball game. ______________

5 The <u>boy young</u> was very courteous to the King and Queen. ______________

6 There are not <u>much</u> players on the basketball court. ______________

7 Did you discover <u>new anything</u> about the disaster last week? ______________

C 우리말과 같은 뜻이 되도록 주어진 말을 알맞게 배열하시오.

1 there / in the pond / much water / not / is (그 연못에는 물이 많지 않다.)

→ ______________________________

2 from this book / interesting / were / stories / a few (이 책의 몇몇 이야기는 재미있었다.)

→ ______________________________

3 to her mother / the / child / good / flowers / gave (그 착한 아이는 엄마에게 꽃을 드렸다.)

→ ______________________________

4 something / want to buy / in Paris / memorable / I (나는 파리에서 기억에 남는 무언가를 사고 싶다.)

→ ______________________________

내신 FOCUS

SCORE: 

A 우리말을 참고하여 빈칸에 알맞은 말을 써 넣으시오.

1 My sister is ____________________. (사랑스러운 소녀)

The lake near my house is ____________________. (아름다운)

2 Is there ______________________________ to see? (흥미로운 것)

There is ______________________________ in the bottle. (많은 물이)

B 빈칸에 들어갈 알맞은 말을 고르시오.

1 My father used to be a very _______________ and stern man.

ⓐ strong　　ⓑ strongly
ⓒ strength　　ⓓ strengthen

2 Can you pour _______________ milk on my cereal?

ⓐ many　　ⓑ one　　ⓒ a few　　ⓓ a little

C 어법상 옳지 않은 문장을 고르시오.

1 ⓐ I like Fargo. It's a friendly city.
ⓑ I need many cream cheese to make cheesecake.
ⓒ He told me that the lecture was boring today.
ⓓ Do you have any small brown luggage?

2 ⓐ He chased his barking dog for almost a mile.
ⓑ Don't say bad anything about other people.
ⓒ There were few people left to agree with the man.
ⓓ Mr. Johnson is an outgoing and talkative man.

D 우리말과 같은 뜻이 되도록 주어진 말을 이용하여 문장을 완성하시오.

1 부엌에서 무언가 달콤한 냄새가 나. (smell, sweet, something)
I can ____ in the kitchen.

2 우리 부모님은 이웃들에게 다정하다. (my parents, friendly)
____ to their neighbors.

3 내 돼지 저금통에는 동전이 거의 없었다. (coin, in my piggy bank)
There were ____.

Unit 10 2 부사

A 네모 안에서 알맞은 말을 고르시오.

1 The man [was always, always was] nice to me in the store.

2 All of the city's firefighters are [very brave, brave very] men.

3 My wife [rare, rarely] comes into my office.

4 The ballerina performed *Swan Lake* [good, well] on the stage.

5 The woman wasn't injured [severe, severely] in the auto accident.

6 He has studied [hardly, hard] to get a good score on the final exams.

7 [Thankful, Thankfully], she has prepared all paperwork for the meeting.

8 She [plays usually, usually plays] soccer with her friends on Thursday.

B [보기]에서 알맞은 말을 골라 문장을 완성하시오.

Word Bank slowly patiently early finally weakly frequently

1 The train arrived ______________ at the station this morning.

2 The injured man called out ______________ to the rescue crew.

3 Tom is here. ______________, we can start the meeting.

4 The older students waited ______________ for their friend.

5 The bus driver drove ______________ with children nearby.

6 He ______________ wrote to us about his classes at university.

C 주어진 부사를 적절한 위치에 넣어 문장을 다시 쓰시오.

1 His mother is worried about his grades. (never)

→ ______________________________

2 She talks to her family about her boyfriend. (always)

→ ______________________________

3 My sister drives very fast everywhere she goes. (usually)

→ ______________________________

4 The young man makes mistakes often. (too)

→ ______________________________

내신 FOCUS

SCORE:

A 의미가 같은 형용사와 부사의 연결이 잘못된 것을 고르시오.

1 ⓐ late - lately ⓑ sweet - sweetly ⓒ polite - politely ⓓ high - high

2 ⓐ early - early ⓑ lucky - luckily ⓒ clear - clearly ⓓ hard - hardly

B 빈칸에 들어갈 알맞은 말을 고르시오.

1 She wrote the essay very ______________ according to her teacher.

ⓐ poorly ⓑ poor ⓒ never ⓓ easy

2 He talked ______________ on the phone for a long time.

ⓐ rare ⓑ quiet ⓒ happily ⓓ happy

C 어법상 옳지 않은 문장을 고르시오.

1 ⓐ My grown son has moved to another city lately.
ⓑ The nurses at this hospital are always very good.
ⓒ The hockey players practice hardly to win the next game.
ⓓ She spoke cheerfully about her life after attending university.

2 ⓐ The street has rarely flooded since we moved here.
ⓑ My husband never hears the telephone ring at night.
ⓒ The team members in this group work very diligently.
ⓓ Lucky, the dress came a day later.

D 우리말과 같은 뜻이 되도록 주어진 말을 이용하여 문장을 완성하시오.

1 왜 이렇게 일찍 일어났니? (get up, so)
Why ____?

2 이상하게도, 그의 메시지는 삭제되어 있었다. (be deleted)
______________, his message __________________________________.

3 그는 친절하게 우리를 콘서트홀로 안내했다. (guide, us, to the concert hall)
He ____.

4 Cindy는 항상 신중하게 미래의 일을 계획한다. (plan, future work)
Cindy ____.

비교급과 최상급 (규칙, 불규칙)

A 네모 안에서 알맞은 말을 고르시오.

1 My mom likes this ice cream [many, more, most].

2 I think Mary is the [busy, busier, busiest] worker in her office.

3 The new camera is not [bad, worse, worst] than my old one.

4 His dad felt [well, better, best] than before after taking medicine.

5 Vickie is the [old, older, oldest] daughter of her family.

6 George Washington was one of the [great, great, greatest] presidents in U.S. history.

7 The policeman looked at the criminals [very, more, most] carefully than before.

B 밑줄 친 부분을 바르게 고쳐 쓰시오. 틀리지 않았다면, O표 하시오.

1 This novel was the worse one on my bookshelf. ______________

2 My brother plays music quietly than I do. ______________

3 This wooden bench is the longer one in the park. ______________

4 Would you please explain the rules clearlier? ______________

5 This street will be less busier than the one you had chosen. ______________

6 She bought a nicest cell phone than the one she had before. ______________

7 My daughter smiles most happily among four girls in this picture. ______________

C 주어진 말을 이용하여 문장을 완성하시오.

1 What is the ______________(small) animal in the world?

2 It is ______________(cold) in the restaurant now than it was before.

3 This plane arrived ______________(late) of all of the planes.

4 His new suitcase is ______________(big) than the one he used to have.

5 She is the ______________(fast) runner on the track team.

6 I wake up ______________(early) every morning to walk my dog.

7 She makes cookies ______________(well) than her mother does.

FOCUS

SCORE: 

A 괄호 안의 지시대로 바꿔 문장을 완성하시오.

1 Jack is a very curious boy. (최상급)

→ Jack is the ________________ boy in his class.

2 Jinni is thin. (비교급)

→ Jinni ________________ than Cathy.

B 빈칸에 들어갈 알맞은 말을 고르시오.

1 The blue jeans look ____________ on you than the white jeans.

ⓐ good ⓑ well ⓒ best ⓓ better

2 Her second knee surgery was ____________ among four surgeries.

ⓐ the most successful ⓑ more successful

ⓒ success ⓓ the more successful

C 어법상 옳지 않은 문장을 고르시오.

1 ⓐ The new photographer is the best in the business.
ⓑ It is going to be the hotest day of the year.
ⓒ Fewer students entered the program than in 2005.
ⓓ This fabric is softer than the one you had before.

2 ⓐ An e-mail is the quicker way to keep in touch with my sister in Japan.
ⓑ The painter purchased less paint than before.
ⓒ Her train left later than the city bus did.
ⓓ The water level in the dam is higher than 20 meters.

D 우리말과 같은 뜻이 되도록 주어진 말을 이용하여 문장을 완성하시오.

1 좀 더 크게 말씀해 주시겠어요? (speak, loudly)
Could ____?

2 손톱을 물어뜯는 것이 나의 가장 나쁜 습관이다. (bad, habit)
Biting my nails is ____.

3 난 그가 그녀보다 더 재능이 있다고 생각해. (talented)
I think he ____ her.

4 2월은 12달 중 가장 추운 달이다. (cold, month)
February ____ of the year.

비교급과 최상급 (기타)

A 네모 안에서 알맞은 말을 고르시오.

1 Your bag is [twice as big as, twice as big so] mine.

2 There are [very, much] better cell phones than mine.

3 The temperature in the house is getting hotter and [hottest, hotter].

4 The performance was not [as good as, as best as] people said it would be.

5 She is the [friendlier, friendliest] person I have ever seen.

6 The more I talk to him, [the more, the most] I agree with his opinions.

B 밑줄 친 부분을 바르게 고쳐 쓰시오. 틀리지 않았다면, O표 하시오.

1 Skydiving is more frightening <u>that</u> you thought. ______________

2 Look at the clouds! The storm is getting <u>close</u> and closer. ______________

3 The young man recycles as <u>many</u> bottles as possible. ______________

4 The more exercise you do, <u>many</u> calories you will burn. ______________

5 He is not one of the <u>richer</u> men in the world. ______________

6 The project is <u>very</u> more difficult than I expected. ______________

C 주어진 말을 이용하여 문장을 완성하시오.

1 그 콘서트는 내가 생각했던 것만큼 나쁘지는 않았다. (bad, not)
→ The concert was ______________________ I had thought.

2 가능한 한 빨리 저에게 전화해 주세요. (soon, you can)
→ Please call me ______________________.

3 이 오페라는 내가 봤던 오페라 중 가장 재미있었다. (entertaining)
→ This is the ______________________ I have ever seen.

4 네 고양이는 내 고양이보다 세 배만큼 크다. (large)
→ Your cat is ______________________ mine.

5 우리가 더 오랫동안 같이 일하면 일할수록 더 많은 것을 성취하게 될 것이다. (long, many)
→ ______________ we work together, ______________ we will accomplish.

FOCUS

SCORE:

A 두 문장의 의미가 통하도록 문장을 완성하시오.

1 My history score is not as good as Mike's.
= Mike's history score ______________________________ mine.

2 She has to write as many letters as she can.
= She has to write ______________________________.

B 빈칸에 들어갈 알맞은 말을 고르시오.

1 This squirrel is twice __________ that bird.
ⓐ the hunger of　ⓑ hunger　ⓒ as hungry so　ⓓ as hungry as

2 The artist is __________ more famous than I thought.
ⓐ very　ⓑ much　ⓒ many　ⓓ so

C 어법상 옳지 않은 문장을 고르시오.

1 ⓐ Talking to you is less stressful than talking to my teacher.
ⓑ The rain is not as heavy as it has been recently.
ⓒ The more I hear this music, the more I like it.
ⓓ It is the shorter race I've ever entered.

2 ⓐ My organic chemistry class is getting harder and harder.
ⓑ Your cake is twice as bigger as mine.
ⓒ He is the smartest student in the whole school.
ⓓ Some country roads are as rough as these city roads.

D 우리말과 같은 뜻이 되도록 주어진 말을 이용하여 문장을 완성하시오.

1 지구는 점점 더 따뜻해지고 있다. (get, warm)
The Earth ______________________________.

2 Jim은 Robby 만큼이나 성공했다. (successful)
Jim is ______________________________ Robby.

3 내 침낭은 그녀의 것보다 두 배 비싸다. (twice, expensive)
My sleeping bag ______________________________ hers.

4 네 일을 빨리 끝내면 끝낼수록, 너는 집에 일찍 갈 수 있을 것이다. (fast, you, finish, early, you)
______________________ your work, ______________________ go.

장소, 방향 전치사

A 네모 안에서 알맞은 말을 고르시오.

1 My best friend sat [behind, between] me in my science class.

2 Please put your backpack [at, on] the desk.

3 The new children's museum is [on, near] the old library.

4 My sister put the card games [into, toward] a box.

5 The bus travels [from, out of] Juniper Street to Mason Avenue.

6 My mother put the large flower pot [among, in front of] the bookcase.

B in, on, at 중 알맞은 것을 넣어 대화를 완성하시오.

1 A Did you meet Jenny ____________ the bus stop? B Yes, I did.

2 A My brother looked at the bike ____________ the store. B Did he like it?

3 A Are your photos ____________ a nice photo album? B No, they aren't.

4 A You can find the newspapers ____________ the living room floor. B Thank you.

5 A Mom, are the keys to the car ____________ your purse? B Yes, they are.

6 A Is he writing the word list ____________ the blackboard? B Yes, he is.

C 우리말을 참고하여 알맞은 전치사를 써 넣으시오.

1 Please take the clean glasses ____________ the kitchen to the table. (부엌에서)

2 The baby crawled up the stairs and back ____________ again. (아래로)

3 There is a church ____________ tall buildings. (큰 건물들 사이에)

4 The lamp is ____________ the sofa and the chair. (소파와 의자 사이에)

5 Bobby walked ____________ the man with the heavy bags. (남자를 향해서)

6 The kids are hiding ____________ the table in the kitchen. (탁자 아래)

7 Our office is across ____________ the meeting room. (회의실 반대편에)

FOCUS

SCORE:

A 우리말을 참고하여 빈칸에 알맞은 전치사를 써 넣으시오.

1 The black cat jumped ______________ the fence and ran away. (울타리 위로)

2 She hid ______________ the door. (문 뒤에)

3 The bees are coming ______________ the beehive. (벌집 밖으로)

4 There are lots of old books ______________ the box. (상자 안에)

B 빈칸에 들어갈 알맞은 말을 고르시오.

1 The photographer asked the little girl to stand ______________ the tree.

ⓐ between ⓑ out ⓒ from ⓓ next to

2 The department store is ______________ the old City Hall.

ⓐ into ⓑ on ⓒ across from ⓓ away

C 어법상 옳지 않은 문장을 고르시오.

1 ⓐ The students waited in line quietly below the teacher.
ⓑ I like the red tulips among all the other flowers.
ⓒ The lecturer flew from Oklahoma to Florida last night.
ⓓ The accident victims in the hospital are getting better now.

2 ⓐ Can you find a pencil in the drawer for me?
ⓑ Could you put these leftovers at a doggy bag?
ⓒ My family went to the amusement park by the seashore.
ⓓ The parade route is between Market Street and Fifth Avenue.

D 우리말과 같은 뜻이 되도록 주어진 말을 이용하여 문장을 완성하시오.

1 주차장은 우체국과 경찰서 사이에 있다. (the post office, the police station)
There is a parking lot ____.

2 내 여동생은 가장 좋아하는 인형을 침대 밑에 놓아두곤 했다. (the bed)
My sister used to put her favorite doll ____________________________.

3 시청 앞에 큰 분수대가 있다. (City Hall)
There is a big fountain ____________________________________.

4 이 버스는 Queens 몰에서 Meyer 백화점까지 운행한다. (Queens Mall, Meyer's Department Store)
This bus goes ____.

시간 전치사

A 네모 안에서 알맞은 말을 고르시오.

1 His family will leave for the party [in, on, at] 2 o'clock.

2 Jerry took his first vacation to Rome [in, on, at] May.

3 I have an appointment with the doctor [in, on, at] Thursday.

4 They have saved money for a rainy day [in, on, at] the future.

5 Children dress up like ghosts and witches [in, on, at] Halloween night.

6 My sister will take my grandmother to the market [in, on, at] a few minutes.

7 The delivery truck with the furniture shouldn't arrive [in, on, at] night.

B [보기]에서 알맞은 말을 골라 문장을 완성하시오.

Word Bank	until	during	since	around	by	in

1 He will graduate from university ______________ 2034. (2034년에)

2 I will arrive at your home ______________ dinnertime. (저녁식사 시간 즈음에)

3 He was at his desk in the classroom ______________ 10. (10시까지 – 계속)

4 You should hand in your paper ______________ 4 pm. (4시까지 – 완료)

5 The guests have stayed in our home ______________ last Monday. (지난 월요일 이후로)

6 The meeting took place ______________ the large conference. (큰 회의 동안)

C 우리말을 참고하여 문장을 완성하시오.

1 The first train leaves ______________________. (정각 6시에)

2 The bus for Boston will leave ______________________. (몇 분 후에)

3 The white cat slept on the chair ______________________. (30분 동안)

4 I ordered the book for you ______________________. (화요일 아침에)

5 Let's go to the park downtown ______________________. (콘서트 전에)

6 She will have to check in the hotel ______________________. (내일 1시 정각까지)

7 Does the movie last ______________________? (7시부터 10시까지)

FOCUS

SCORE: 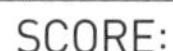

A 우리말을 참고하여 빈칸에 알맞은 전치사를 써 넣으시오.

1 · I couldn't sleep ______________ 4 am. (4시까지)
  · You had better arrive ______________ 9 o'clock. (정각 9시까지)

2 · She has been outside ______________ three hours. (3시간 동안)
  · We will travel to Eastern Europe ______________ summer vacation. (여름 방학 동안)

B 빈칸에 들어갈 알맞은 말을 고르시오.

1 My sister takes a walk with her dog ______________ the morning.

ⓐ in　ⓑ on　ⓒ at　ⓓ for

2 My grandparents will arrive by train ______________ 10 o'clock.

ⓐ from　ⓑ during　ⓒ before　ⓓ for

C 어법상 옳지 않은 문장을 고르시오.

1 ⓐ The cake will not be done in an hour.
ⓑ You must finish your homework before dinner.
ⓒ My cousins haven't visited our home since last fall.
ⓓ The baseball game starts in 1 o'clock in the afternoon.

2 ⓐ The writing assignment isn't due until late November.
ⓑ Let's meet each other in front of the library at about 7.
ⓒ He practices the violin for 2 to 4 in the afternoon.
ⓓ Did you and your friend eat breakfast together before school on Friday?

D 우리말과 같은 뜻이 되도록 주어진 말을 이용하여 문장을 완성하시오.

1 서울 올림픽은 1988년에 열렸다. (be held, 1988)
The Seoul Olympics ______________________________________.

2 Kim은 매일 아침 6시부터 7시까지 수영을 한다. (swim, 6, 7)
Kim ______________________________________ every morning.

3 우리 삼촌은 2000년 이래로 우리와 함께 살고 있다. (live with, 2000)
My uncle ______________________________________.

4 7시 정도에 전화해 주실 수 있나요? (call, me, 7)
Could you please ______________________________________?

기타 전치사

A 네모 안에서 알맞은 말을 고르시오.

1 He didn't build a new doghouse [with, by] bricks.

2 The girl put on a pretty dress [for, about] the party.

3 She kept surfing the Internet until she found out [along, about] the movie.

4 The trains ran [about, through] the tunnel and into the station.

5 Happy birthday [to, on] you! This is for you.

6 The boy walked [opposite, along] the street to the ice cream shop.

7 Trains leave [for, by] Amsterdam Central Station about five times per hour.

B [보기]에서 알맞은 말을 골라 문장을 완성하시오.

Word Bank	by	on	around	with	through	along

1 I would prefer to go to the theater ______________ you. (너와 함께)

2 Did you hear the noises made ______________ the cat? (고양이에 의한)

3 The Han River flows ______________ the center of Seoul. (서울의 중심부를 통과하여)

4 The family tied a yellow ribbon ______________ the tree. (나무 주위에)

5 I have been fishing ______________ the Missouri River near my home. (Missouri강을 따라)

6 It takes 30 minutes to get to the botanical garden ______________ foot. (걸어서)

C 우리말을 참고하고 문장을 완성하시오.

1 Can you make a nice bookshelf ______________________? (나무로)

2 I have to walk ______________________ to get to my car. (그 연못 주위를)

3 The woman talked ______________________ about their school. (그 학생들에게)

4 Can they reach the British Museum of Natural History ______________________? (버스로)

5 She bought a silver necklace ______________________ at the duty-free shop. (30달러의 가격에)

6 This TV program is ______________________ in the world. (가장 높은 빌딩들에 대한)

FOCUS

SCORE: 

A 빈칸에 공통으로 들어갈 전치사를 써 넣으시오.

1 · Tina and Bill swept the floor ______________ a broom.

· They are very busy ______________ their exams.

2 · How long does it take to get to London ______________ plane?

· These pictures were taken ______________ my mom.

B 빈칸에 들어갈 알맞은 말을 고르시오.

1 The cat chased the mouse ______________ the house.

ⓐ around ⓑ with ⓒ for ⓓ about

2 Larry has studied ______________ the causes of the greenhouse effect.

ⓐ by ⓑ with ⓒ about ⓓ along

C 어법상 옳지 않은 문장을 고르시오.

1 ⓐ They used to walk along the beach around sunset.
ⓑ The lesson is to a new volcano discovered in Indonesia.
ⓒ Is the boss taking his wife to New Jersey for a vacation?
ⓓ He wiped the sweat off his brow with a handkerchief.

2 ⓐ Are your grandparents going to the park about a walk?
ⓑ I asked the clerk about the sign in the store's window.
ⓒ The church will serve a dinner for its members.
ⓓ We walked around the stage at the carnival.

D 우리말과 같은 뜻이 되도록 주어진 말을 이용하여 문장을 완성하시오.

1 사람들은 도심지를 통과해 행진했다. (march, downtown)
People ____.

2 그는 자신의 수학 점수 때문에 기뻤다. (be pleased with, math score)
He ____.

3 엄마는 계속해서 내 자전거 사고에 대해서 물으셨다. (ask about, bike accident)
Mom kept ____.

4 아침을 거르는 것은 너의 건강에 좋지 않아. (bad, health)
Skipping breakfast ____.

등위접속사

A 네모 안에서 알맞은 말을 고르시오.

1 She can take a taxi, [but, or] I can give her a ride.

2 She went to the zoo, [but, so] she didn't see the monkeys.

3 He bought the book, [so, but] he could study English.

4 The cake wasn't ready, [or, so] I bought some cookies.

5 His bike was repaired, [but, or] the tire quickly became flat.

6 Run, [and, or] you will miss her because she is leaving.

7 She bought the birthday card, [or, and] I bought the gift.

B 두 문장의 의미가 통하도록 'and' 또는 'or'를 써 넣으시오.

1 If you arrive in time, we will visit a palace.

→ Arrive in time, ______________ we will visit a palace.

2 If you don't return very soon, you will miss the movie.

→ Return very soon, ______________ you will miss the movie.

3 If you make a reservation now, you can get a table.

→ Make a reservation now, ______________ you can get a table.

4 If you don't bake a cake, I will bring cookies.

→ Bake a cake, ______________ I will bring cookies.

C 우리말을 참고하여 문장을 완성하시오.

1 My sister is ______________ kind, but also pretty. (친절할 뿐 아니라)

2 You can reach Madrid either by bus ______________ by train. (버스 또는 기차를 타고)

3 I like both blue ______________ white candles. (파란색과 흰색 양초 모두)

4 ______________ Jim and Ken are my cousins in Oklahoma. (Jim과 Ken 모두)

5 He has traveled ______________ only in the Middle East, but also in Africa. (중동뿐 아니라)

6 ______________ the doctor nor the nurse has seen the rash before. (의사나 간호사 모두 ~ 없다)

7 He is not my father, ______________ my brother. (우리 아버지가 아니라, 형이다)

내신 FOCUS

SCORE: 

A 빈칸에 and, but, so, or 중 알맞은 접속사를 써 넣으시오.

1 I washed the dishes ______________ did the laundry.

2 We are going to play a game. Are you in ______________ out?

3 She has had five pieces of pizza, ______________ she still feels hungry.

4 The milk had gone bad ______________ he didn't drink it.

B 빈칸에 들어갈 알맞은 말을 고르시오.

1 He got very good grades, ______________ he won a college scholarship.

ⓐ but also ⓑ so ⓒ but ⓓ or

2 ______________ China nor Japan beat the Korean soccer team.

ⓐ Both ⓑ Either ⓒ Neither ⓓ But

C 어법상 옳지 <u>않은</u> 문장을 고르시오.

1 ⓐ You can have either coffee or tea.
ⓑ He is my brother, and she is my best friend.
ⓒ Wait and you might hurt yourself by falling off the ladder.
ⓓ I lost a tooth in an accident, so I had to rush to the dentist.

2 ⓐ They are not tigers or ligers.
ⓑ To be or not to be, that is the problem.
ⓒ Both my aunt and my uncle are here now.
ⓓ She is not only clever but also creative.

D 우리말과 같은 뜻이 되도록 주어진 말을 이용하여 문장을 완성하시오.

1 그는 잘생긴 게 아니라, 귀여운 거야. (handsome, cute)
He is ____.

2 Kevin도 Cathy도 내 자전거를 고치지 못했다. (neither, repair)
____ my bike.

3 지금 영화 티켓을 사, 그것들은 매진 될 거야. (the movie tickets, be sold out)
Buy ____.

4 태양은 우리에게 빛을 줄 뿐만 아니라 에너지도 준다. (give, not only, light, energy)
The sun ____.

명사절을 이끄는 종속접속사

A 네모 안에서 알맞은 말을 고르시오.

1 I don't know [that, if] she can help me.

2 I saw on the weather report [that, if] it was going to rain.

3 I wonder [that, if] my new computer will come today.

4 My little brother imagines [that, if] he is like Spiderman.

5 [That, Whether] we go to the mountains or not is the choice.

6 The problem is [that, whether] we don't have the tickets with us.

7 I wonder [that, whether] he will look for a new job or not.

B "It~that" 구문을 이용하여 문장을 완성하시오.

1 Karen helped us. It was very thoughtful.

→ It was very thoughtful ______________________________.

2 Vickie didn't call us again. It is curious.

→ It is curious ______________________________.

3 You are going to college next year. It is wonderful.

→ It is wonderful ______________________________.

C 간접의문문을 완성하시오.

1 I can't see. What is he doing in the yard?

→ I can't see ______________________________.

2 How did she find the name of the store? I don't know.

→ I don't know ______________________________.

3 Who are the people by the door? I don't know.

→ I don't know ______________________________.

4 Where is she going? She won't tell.

→ She won't tell ______________________________.

5 Why did my parents ground me for a week? I wonder.

→ I wonder ______________________________.

FOCUS

SCORE: 

A 빈칸에 공통으로 들어갈 접속사를 써 넣으시오.

1 · I believe ______________ there is a ghost.
 · It is disappointing ______________ I can't see you for a month.

2 · My parents don't know ______________ I passed the exam.
 · She wonders ______________ he will come to the party.

B 빈칸에 들어갈 알맞은 말을 고르시오.

1 They have to choose ______________ they will drive their car or not.

ⓐ what ⓑ that ⓒ how ⓓ whether

2 The issue is ______________ we all must leave now.

ⓐ what ⓑ that ⓒ if ⓓ whether

C 어법상 옳지 않은 문장을 고르시오.

1 ⓐ It is great that they are on the plane now.
ⓑ She made the discovery that her tire had been cut.
ⓒ Where do you think the conference will be held next year?
ⓓ I don't know if will the teacher give us homework tonight.

2 ⓐ Do you know what does she do for a living?
ⓑ No one is sure if the train will arrive on time.
ⓒ She shared the news that he has Alzheimer's disease.
ⓓ The concern is whether the students will learn the information or not.

D 우리말과 같은 뜻이 되도록 주어진 말을 이용하여 문장을 완성하시오.

1 그것이 사실인지 아닌지 너는 알고 있니? (know, true)
Do you ____ or not?

2 나는 그녀에게 그가 그녀의 제안을 거절했는지 물어보았다. (ask, he, refuse, her offer)
I ____.

3 경찰은 Mandy가 지갑을 훔쳤다는 사실을 알고 있다. (the fact, steal, the wallet)
The police know ____.

4 그 작은 소년이 그 큰 바위를 옮겼다는 것은 놀라운 일이다. (the little boy, move, the big rock)
It is surprising ____.

부사절을 이끄는 종속접속사

A 네모 안에서 알맞은 말을 고르시오.

1 [Unless, If] you study hard, you won't do well in school this year.

2 I went to work, [unless, even though] I didn't have to.

3 The team arrived late [because, though] the storm was very bad.

4 My father has taken medicine [until, since] he started coughing last night.

5 He couldn't call you [because of, until] a dead cell phone battery.

6 [If, As] the group wants a discount, everyone must come to the theater together.

7 He fed the dog [before, if] he went to school this morning.

8 [When, Until] Dan picks her up, she will wait for him here.

B 주어진 접속사를 이용하여 문장을 완성하시오.

1 I had breakfast, and I read the newspaper. (after)

→ ______________________________, I read the newspaper.

2 They practiced hard yesterday, but they lost the game today. (though)

→ ______________________________, they lost the game today.

3 If they don't finish work quickly, they can't go to the party. (unless)

→ ______________________________, they can't go to the party.

C 우리말을 참고하여 문장을 완성하시오.

1 ____________ it was dark outside, we went into the building. (어두웠기 때문에)

2 He was so mad ____________ his girlfriend was lying to him. (거짓말을 했기 때문에)

3 The cat scratched the sofa ____________ I was in the kitchen. (부엌에 있는 동안)

4 ____________ the camera was old, it took very good pictures. (오래됐음에도)

5 I called you ____________ I got home. (도착했을 때)

6 I took my father to the station ____________ his train left. (기차가 떠나기 전에)

내신 FOCUS

SCORE:

A 빈칸에 though, because, until 중 알맞은 접속사를 써 넣으시오.

1 Tim broke his leg ______________ he fell off the ladder.

2 ______________ he had a cold, he went swimming.

3 My son read a book loudly ______________ I told him to stop.

B 빈칸에 들어갈 알맞은 말을 고르시오.

1 ______________ the team wins tonight, they will go to the playoffs.

ⓐ While ⓑ Since ⓒ If ⓓ Even though

2 ______________ he allowed me to go, I couldn't leave.

ⓐ Since ⓑ Although ⓒ If ⓓ Because

C 의미상 접속사의 쓰임이 어색한 문장을 고르시오.

1 ⓐ She will travel with you if she gets paid.
ⓑ He will make some cakes before the party starts.
ⓒ Though he disagreed, he voted to approve the project.
ⓓ While you call the man, he will not make an appointment with you.

2 ⓐ As the speaker had already arrived, the conference began.
ⓑ Tom worked on his homework while I was playing a video game.
ⓒ They are on their way to the airport because they are going on vacation today.
ⓓ If he has an important test tomorrow, he will spend the whole evening in front of the TV.

D 우리말과 같은 뜻이 되도록 주어진 말을 이용하여 문장을 완성하시오.

1 숙제를 하지 않으면, 엄마가 벌을 주실 거야. (unless, do one's homework)
______________________________________, Mom will punish you.

2 우리는 밥을 먹은 후에 양치질을 해야 한다. (have, a meal)
We should brush our teeth ______________________________________.

3 나는 어제 아팠지만 학교에 갔다. (sick)
______________________________________ yesterday, I went to school.

4 그는 돈이 충분하지 않아서 겨우 햄버거 하나를 주문했다. (not, have, enough, money)
______________________________________, he just ordered a hamburger.

부사절의 축약 (분사구문)

A 네모 안에서 알맞은 말을 고르시오.

1 [Hearing, Heard] the dog, we found it in a box.

2 [Focus, Focusing] on the dot, I saw the optical illusion.

3 [Being sad, Been sad], he began to cry in front of her.

4 [Leave, Leaving] the army, he began a new life in Seoul.

5 If you [turn, turning] right at the corner, you will see the bank.

6 [Not saying, Saying not] anything to him, she still didn't show up for the appointment.

B [ ] 안에서 알맞은 말을 고르시오.

1 Knowing the license plate of the thief's car, he called the police.
= [Though, As] he knew the license plate of the thief's car, he called the police.

2 Being damaged slightly, the computer still worked.
= [Although, As] the computer was damaged slightly, it still worked.

3 Arriving at the hotel, he saw a large party.
= [If, When] he arrived at the hotel, he saw a large party.

4 Losing our photos, we still had a wonderful trip.
= [Even though, While] we lost our photos, we still had a wonderful trip.

5 The tent being too small, someone had to sleep outside.
= [Because, After] the tent was too small, someone had to sleep outside.

C 부사절을 분사구문으로 바꿔 쓰시오.

1 After she broke the vase, she called for her mother.
→ ______________________________, she called for her mother.

2 Because he didn't work hard, he was fired.
→ ______________________________, he was fired.

3 While he walked his dog, he met many people in the park.
→ ______________________________, he met many people in the park.

4 If you look into the microscope, you can see the bacteria.
→ ______________________________, you can see the bacteria.

SCORE:

A 부사절을 분사구문으로 바꿔 쓰시오.

1 When she cleaned her room, she listened to classical music.

→ ______________________, she listened to classical music.

2 Because I watch the weather forecast, I took an umbrella.

→ ______________________, I took an umbrella.

B 빈칸에 들어갈 알맞은 말을 고르시오.

1 __________ the cat, the mouse grabbed the cheese.

ⓐ No seeing ⓑ Not seeing ⓒ Don't seeing ⓓ Seeing not

2 __________ the cake, she added some candy flowers.

ⓐ Make ⓑ What making ⓒ Making ⓓ Made

C 어법상 옳지 않은 문장을 고르시오.

1 ⓐ Because the soup was too salty, he put some water in it.
ⓑ If you turn over the pancakes, they will look nicer.
ⓒ Having a headache, she took some aspirin.
ⓓ Move to New York, he made some new friends.

2 ⓐ Turning on the light, he saw the broken window.
ⓑ Since the rock was heavy, he needed a friend to help.
ⓒ Taking not the right bus, Kyle found himself in Insadong.
ⓓ Opening your book, you can read the instructions.

D 우리말과 같은 뜻이 되도록 주어진 말을 이용하여 문장을 완성하시오.

1 나는 이유도 모른 채, 그 상을 받았다. (not, know, the reason)

______________________________________, I received the award.

2 내 강아지는 그를 보자 짖기 시작했다. (see, him, dog, start)

______________________, ______________________ barking.

3 나는 회의에 늦었기 때문에 택시를 탔다. (be, late, take a taxi)

______________________ for the meeting, ______________________.

4 당신이 창문을 열면, 파란 바다가 보일 거예요. (open, the window, see)

______________________, ______________________ the blue sea.

관계대명사

A 네모 안에서 알맞은 말을 고르시오.

1 He has a car [who, which] has a radio in it.

2 Trina bought a purse [who, that] has many pockets.

3 The man was the fortune teller [who, which] read her palm.

4 The fence [that, who] you painted looks very nice now.

5 I saw my neighbor and his dog [who, that] took a walk in the park.

6 The policeman talked to the people [which, who] had seen the accident.

B 밑줄 친 부분을 바르게 고쳐 쓰시오.

1 I am replacing the old TV who broke yesterday. ______________

2 She called the store who sells the comfortable shoes. ______________

3 Talk to the man which is sitting in the waiting room. ______________

4 The guest signed the book who the hostess showed him. ______________

5 The repairman which I called has no time to fix my bike. ______________

6 Did you see the man who he was wearing pink pants? ______________

C 밑줄 친 단어를 선행사로 하여 관계대명사를 이용한 문장으로 바꿔 쓰시오.

1 Mary will buy something. We can eat it.

→ ______________________________

2 I waved at Frank. He is my best friend at school.

→ ______________________________

3 I don't know the woman. She is standing by the cash register.

→ ______________________________

4 The ring has a big stone. It sparkles in the sunlight.

→ ______________________________

5 I lost my phone. I bought it last week.

→ ______________________________

내신 FOCUS

SCORE: 

A 두 문장을 한 문장으로 만들 때 빈칸에 알맞은 말을 써 넣으시오.

1 I'll take care of my niece. + She is only 4 years old.

→ I'll take care of my niece ______________ is only 4 years old.

2 She can't find her car. + It was parked next to the fire station.

→ She can't find her car ______________ was parked next to the fire station.

B 빈칸에 들어갈 알맞은 말을 고르시오.

1 Can you hear the strange sounds ______________ are coming from the radio?

ⓐ who ⓑ which ⓒ whose ⓓ what

2 This is the cat ______________ caught the two mice.

ⓐ that ⓑ who ⓒ whose ⓓ what

C 어법상 옳지 않은 문장을 고르시오.

1 ⓐ I have a cousin which is coming to visit us.
ⓑ The truck hit the car that was turning left.
ⓒ My brother told the man who was mowing his lawn.
ⓓ The amusement park built a roller coaster that runs very fast.

2 ⓐ My friends took a trip which was very tiring.
ⓑ Her mother went to the meeting that was held at school.
ⓒ His girlfriend went to the store that sold him the necklace.
ⓓ The game who was scheduled for 1 o'clock has been postponed.

D 우리말과 같은 뜻이 되도록 주어진 말을 이용하여 문장을 완성하시오.

1 Tom은 자신의 어머니가 준 가방을 잃어버렸다. (the bag, give)
Tom lost ____ to him.

2 해바라기는 이제까지 내가 본 것 중에 가장 큰 꽃이다. (the biggest flower, ever, see)
A sunflower ____.

3 그들은 5월에 파라오 무덤인 피라미드를 여행할 것이다. (the Pyramids, tombs for Pharaohs)
They will travel to ____ in May.

4 너는 가난한 사람을 도울 수 있는 것을 가지고 와야 한다. (bring, something, help, poor people)
You should ____.

관계대명사의 쓰임

A 네모 안에서 알맞은 말을 고르시오.

1 I don't like the table and chairs [that, whom] he bought.

2 He is the boy [whose, whom] I chose for the team.

3 Jim gave me the DVD [that, whose] was just released.

4 Harold sent him the report [whose, which] wasn't finished.

5 This is the ring [for which, for whom] I have looked.

6 The path was long for the child [whose, who] is only five.

7 Do you know the young man [whose, which] bike is green?

8 That woman isn't the waitress [who, whom] works at the coffee shop.

B 밑줄 친 부분을 바르게 고쳐 쓰시오. 틀리지 않았다면, O표 하시오.

1 Do you see the cat <u>who</u> ate the bird? ____________

2 They own a house <u>which</u> yard is very big. ____________

3 They are the people <u>which</u> I have been searching for. ____________

4 She has a brother <u>who</u> friends enjoy playing Scrabble. ____________

5 I sent a Christmas card <u>that</u> I purchased last week. ____________

6 The kids are wearing the hats <u>whose their</u> color is red. ____________

C 밑줄 친 단어를 선행사로 하여 관계대명사를 이용한 문장으로 바꿔 쓰시오.

1 I talked to <u>his cousin</u>. She has a new car.

→ ____

2 She tries to move <u>the desk</u>. The desk is very heavy.

→ ____

3 The man orders <u>a sandwich</u>. The sandwich is healthy.

→ ____

4 Mike is <u>the only one</u>. I can count on him.

→ ____

FOCUS

SCORE: 

A 빈칸에 알맞은 관계대명사를 써 넣으시오.

1 The boy ______________ sits next to me is crying a lot.

2 I know the woman ______________ garden is very beautiful.

3 She has to buy some toys ______________ his son will play with.

4 Randy Johnson is the baseball player ______________ I like most.

B 빈칸에 들어갈 알맞은 말을 고르시오.

1 He isn't the man ______________ paid for our bill.

ⓐ whose　　ⓑ who　　ⓒ whom　　ⓓ what

2 I have a brother ______________ job is to make bread in a bakery.

ⓐ whose　　ⓑ that　　ⓒ whom　　ⓓ what

C 어법상 옳지 않은 문장을 고르시오.

1 ⓐ My father took a class which was on weekends.
ⓑ The road is filled with holes whom need to be repaired.
ⓒ She wondered about the dog whose picture she had seen.
ⓓ The nuts that are left over from the party are very good.

2 ⓐ It is the biggest church that I've ever visited.
ⓑ I found the girl whom you like most among the people.
ⓒ Do you want to drink something whose contains lemons?
ⓓ This machine makes ice which is used for snow cones.

D 우리말과 같은 뜻이 되도록 주어진 말을 이용하여 문장을 완성하시오.

1 우리 오빠는 자신의 친구가 자신에게 준 강아지를 기른다. (raise, the puppy, that)
My brother ____ to him.

2 그가 저와 함께 발표를 한 사람이에요. (the person, who, make a presentation with me)
He is ____.

3 너는 내가 파티에서 소개해 줬던 소녀를 기억하니? (the girl, who, introduce, to you)
Do you remember ____ at the party?

4 나는 다리가 부러진 의자를 고쳤다. (fix, the chair, was broken)
I ____.

관계대명사의 특별 용법

A 선행사를 찾아 밑줄 그으시오.

1 He made two wedding cakes that he has to deliver.

2 She bought a Korean mask, which was a good buy.

3 This is the picture that she painted yesterday.

4 He ate some ice cream that he had bought from a vendor.

5 She lost her sister's sweater, which was a Christmas gift from their aunt.

6 This is my sister's friend, who has just arrived from Busan.

7 I drank milk whose expiration date had passed.

8 I traveled across the country by motorcycle, which made my mom worried.

B 우리말과 같은 뜻이 되도록 빈칸에 알맞은 관계사를 써 넣으시오.

1 부두 근처에 있는 생선 시장에 갈 것이다.
I will go to the fish market ______________ is near the port.

2 그 회의는 금요일이었는데, 금요일은 휴일이었다.
The meeting was on Friday, ______________ was a holiday.

3 나는 Sara와 역할극을 했는데, 그녀는 전학생이었다.
I did role-playing with Sara, ______________ was new in our class.

4 그는 네가 겪었던 것과 같은 것을 경험하고 있는 중이다.
He is experiencing the very same thing ______________ you did.

C 밑줄 친 that을 접속사 'C', 관계대명사 'R'로 구분하시오.

1 My cousin liked the book <u>that</u> you gave to him. ______________

2 It is amazing <u>that</u> the dog rides a skateboard. ______________

3 He wrote the letter <u>that</u> you asked him about. ______________

4 The fact is <u>that</u> the work is not difficult. ______________

5 I worried <u>that</u> the car would need expensive repairs. ______________

6 He knows the student <u>that</u> is graduating this year. ______________

FOCUS

SCORE:

A 주어진 문장을 관계대명사의 용법에 주의하여 해석하시오.

1 I gave her advice, which made her angry.

→ ______________________

2 Last Sunday I met James, who is very handsome and cute.

→ ______________________

B 빈칸에 들어갈 알맞은 말을 고르시오.

1 English summer camp, __________ is a busy place, has just opened.

ⓐ what ⓑ who ⓒ which ⓓ whose

2 This shirt was washed three times, __________ made it fade very quickly.

ⓐ that ⓑ which ⓒ who ⓓ what

C 어법상 옳지 않은 문장을 고르시오.

1 ⓐ Two cars are parked in front of the house that I own.
ⓑ Do you know which the class will begin late today?
ⓒ The ladder belongs to my dad, who is a construction worker.
ⓓ The horse race is at ABC Sports Complex, which is near the baseball stadium.

2 ⓐ This is the song that the woman sang for us.
ⓑ He has a dog that plays with him all the time.
ⓒ This apartment has three windows, that look out onto the river.
ⓓ My mom called someone who could help her with the problem.

D 우리말과 같은 뜻이 되도록 주어진 말을 이용하여 문장을 완성하시오.

1 나는 어제 시계를 샀는데, 그것은 100달러였다. (buy, which, cost, $100)
Yesterday ______________________.

2 Mary가 Jake를 소개해 줬는데, 그는 대머리였다. (introduce, who, bald)
Mary ______________________.

3 그녀는 이기적인 남자와 결혼을 했고, 그것이 그녀의 인생을 망쳤다. (marry, a selfish man, which, ruin, her life)
She ______________________.

4 라이트 형제는 비행기를 발명했고, 그들은 미국의 오하이오 주에서 태어났다. (who, invent, the airplane, be born)
The Wright Brothers, ______________________ in Ohio in the U.S.

관계부사

A 네모 안에서 알맞은 말을 고르시오.

1 Tell me [how, why] he was late tonight.

2 Do you understand [the way, for which] the game is played?

3 I asked him the time [when, where] he would arrive in the city.

4 She told him about the park [where, how] the fireworks would be held.

5 I don't know [how, where] I can open a checking account at a bank.

6 I will tell him of the reasons [why, where] he has to retake the test.

7 I don't know the place [where, when] I can buy French magazines.

8 She found out the day [how, when] you returned the borrowed books to the library.

B 빈칸에 where, when, why, how 중 알맞은 것을 써 넣으시오.

1 Your bill is ______________ I am calling you now.

2 The home ______________ I lived is on First Street.

3 1995 was the year ______________ the team was formed.

4 She bought the unusual fruit from the market ______________ I shop.

5 He will show us ______________ we can use this program.

6 The reporter pointed out ______________ the accident occurred here last night.

C [보기]와 같이 관계부사를 이용한 문장으로 바꿔 쓰시오.

Example	The hotel wasn't very clean. We stayed there. → The hotel where we stayed wasn't very clean.

1 This is the coffee shop. I can have the best coffee there.

→ ____

2 This map tells me the way. I can find the airport in the way.

→ ____

3 The manual explains the reason. It made a noise for the reason.

→ ____

내신 FOCUS

SCORE:

A 빈칸에 알맞은 관계부사를 써 넣으시오.

1 This is the house ______________ I was born.

2 It was last winter ______________ he had a car accident.

3 Now, I know ______________ Kevin calls you a genius.

4 Adam wants to learn ______________ Korean can use chopsticks.

B 빈칸에 들어갈 알맞은 말을 고르시오.

1 Buckingham Palace is the place ______________ Queen Elizabeth lives.

ⓐ which ⓑ where ⓒ what ⓓ that

2 1547 was the year ______________ King VIII died.

ⓐ where ⓑ which ⓒ in which ⓓ who

C 어법상 옳지 않은 문장을 고르시오.

1 ⓐ My dad went to a meeting where politics was discussed.
ⓑ The 14th is the day where I will take the exam.
ⓒ I don't know how I can go to the party.
ⓓ She told me why she hadn't come home.

2 ⓐ I don't know the way how I am supposed to fill out this form.
ⓑ The train left the station where the accident had happened.
ⓒ Can you remind him why we do things in this way?
ⓓ January 22nd was the date when I graduated from high school.

D 우리말과 같은 뜻이 되도록 주어진 말과 관계사를 이용하여 문장을 완성하시오.

1 나는 내가 처음으로 자동차를 운전한 날을 기억한다. (drive, a car)
______________________________________ for the first time.

2 내가 그 파일을 열 수 있는 방법을 얘기해 줄 수 있니? (tell, can, open. the file)
Can you ______________________________________?

3 이 나무 집이 내가 어릴 적에 놀던 곳이야. (used to, play)
The tree house ______________________________________ when I was young.

4 나는 내가 왜 학교에 늦었는지 그에게 이야기했다. (tell, be)
______________________________________ late for school.

가정법

A 네모 안에서 알맞은 말을 고르시오.

1 If she [tells, told] me that she is sorry, I will forgive her.

2 If I [am, were] an astronaut, I could step on the moon.

3 If she [is not, was not] in class today, she will miss the test.

4 If I [invent, invented] a time machine, I would travel back to 1500.

5 If he [stops, stopped] complaining, he will think more positively.

6 If you [drive, drove] me home, I can spend a little more time with my daughter.

7 If I [have, had] a longer arm, I could reach the cupboard and take out the honey jar.

B 주어진 말을 이용하여 문장을 완성하시오.

1 If I ____________________(know) the answer, I would be a winner.

2 If you ____________________(lend) me some money, I will buy new sneakers.

3 If our team ____________________(be) better, we would beat these teams.

4 If you ____________________(be) Superman, what would you do?

5 If you ____________________(not, fix) the mirror, the mirror will drop and break.

6 If the desk ____________________(not, be) in this room, we would have more space to work.

7 If I ____________________(be) in the marching band, I could participate in the parade.

C 두 문장의 의미가 통하도록 문장을 완성하시오. (축약형으로 쓸 것)

1 If I were a cartoon character, I could do impossible things.
→ As I ______________ a cartoon character, I ______________ impossible things.

2 If the car were more powerful, it could drive up this mountain easily.
→ As the car ______________ more powerful, it ______________ up this mountain easily.

3 If she were a movie star, she could get a table in this busy restaurant.
→ As she ______________ a movie star, she ______________ a table in this busy restaurant.

4 If he had a better job, he could afford a new car.
→ As he ______________ a better job, he ______________ a new car.

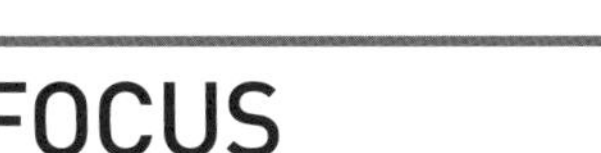

SCORE:

A 두 문장의 의미가 통하도록 빈칸에 알맞은 말을 써 넣으시오.

1 I don't find her report, so I don't call her.
→ If I found her report, I __________ her.

2 He doesn't ask me about the rule, so I don't tell him.
→ If he __________ me about the rule, I would tell him.

B 빈칸에 들어갈 알맞은 말을 고르시오.

1 If he __________ a wealthy man, he could buy the diamond ring.
ⓐ be ⓑ were ⓒ is ⓓ has been

2 If she __________ at home tomorrow, she will help us with the project.
ⓐ is ⓑ are ⓒ was ⓓ were

C 어법상 옳지 않은 문장을 고르시오.

1 ⓐ If I were a bird, I will fly away to Sydney.
ⓑ If my boss were here, he would know what to do.
ⓒ If they had a new car, they could save a lot of money on repair costs.
ⓓ If we work together, the work will be finished much faster.

2 ⓐ If you look for the best in people, you will find it.
ⓑ If he were a friend, I would lend him my notes.
ⓒ If you don't offer him the job, you will regret your decision.
ⓓ If he fails to persuade her, he would give her another choice.

D 우리말과 같은 뜻이 되도록 주어진 말을 이용하여 문장을 완성하시오.

1 나는 내일 날씨가 좋으면 공원에 소풍을 갈 거야. (fine, go on a picnic)
If it __________ tomorrow, I __________ in the park.

2 내가 큰 집을 소유하고 있다면 친구를 모두 초대할 수 있을 텐데. (a big house, invite)
If I __________, I __________ all of my friends.

3 Sara가 일찍 떠난다면 나는 무척 슬플 것이다. (leave, very sad)
If Sara __________, I __________.

4 그녀가 진실을 안다면 그에게 말할 텐데. (know the truth, tell)
If she __________, she __________.

가정법 (과거완료, 기타 가정법)

A 네모 안에서 알맞은 말을 고르시오.

1 She acts as if she [is, were] very ill today, but she isn't.

2 Kylie wishes she [has, had] a little dog for this Christmas.

3 If they [had seen, seen] the cat first, they wouldn't have given it away.

4 She acts as if she [were, had been] in the situation before, but she hasn't.

5 [But, Without] the team's hard work, I couldn't have won this award.

6 If she [had, had had] a good dictionary, she would have done better in the class.

7 If it [is, were] not for your assistance, I couldn't complete the project.

B 주어진 말을 이용하여 문장을 완성하시오.

1 He wishes he ______________(have) an English tutor this year.

He wishes he ______________(have) an English tutor last year.

2 They look as if they ______________(be) happy in their jobs, but they aren't.

They look as if they ______________(be) happy in their jobs, but they weren't.

3 If I ______________(save) more money, I could buy a better computer.

If I ______________(save) more money, I could have bought a better computer.

4 If she ______________(talk) slowly, I would understand her better.

If she ______________(talk) slowly, I would have understood her better.

C 우리말과 같은 뜻이 되도록 주어진 말을 이용하여 문장을 완성하시오.

1 그 소녀는 마치 모든 것을 다 아는 것처럼 행동하지만, 아니다.
→ The girl acts as if she ______________________(know) everything, but she doesn't.

2 그들의 친절이 없다면, 지금 우리는 여기에 있지 못할 텐데.
→ If it ______________________(be, not) for their kindness, we could not be here now.

3 그가 깜짝 파티에 대해서 몰랐었다면 좋을 텐데.
→ I wish he ______________________(know, not) about the surprise party.

4 그 학생들이 일찍 시험을 봤다면, 그들은 시험에 통과했을 텐데.
→ If the students ______________________(take) the test earlier, they would have passed it.

FOCUS

SCORE: 

A 빈칸에 들어갈 수 없는 말을 고르시오.

1 I wish he ______________________.

ⓐ entered college ⓑ took the first train
ⓒ can buy the white house ⓓ was the winner of the race

2 ______________________, I couldn't go there.

ⓐ Without her permission ⓑ Because of her permission
ⓒ But for her permission ⓓ If it were not for her permission

B 빈칸에 들어갈 알맞은 말을 고르시오.

1 If I ____________ my kitten to the vet, my kitten couldn't have survived.

ⓐ haven't taken ⓑ hadn't taken ⓒ didn't take ⓓ don't take

2 She acts as if she ____________ him before, but she didn't.

ⓐ had met ⓑ could meet ⓒ have met ⓓ didn't meet

C 어법상 옳지 않은 것을 고르시오.

1 ⓐ The teacher looks as if she helped someone.
ⓑ If the company had requested it, I would had done it.
ⓒ I wish I had borrowed a costume for Halloween from her.
ⓓ Without the school's support, the team couldn't do well.

2 ⓐ If it not were for the scholarship, I couldn't attend university.
ⓑ My friend speaks as if he had visited all of the countries in the Middle East.
ⓒ Jerry wishes he had eaten a doughnut from the new bakery.
ⓓ If we had had the proper tools, we would have repaired it quickly.

D 우리말과 같은 뜻이 되도록 주어진 말을 이용하여 문장을 완성하시오.

1 나에게 쌍둥이 형제가 있으면 좋을 텐데. (have, a twin brother)
I wish ______________________________________.

2 그는 마치 유령이라도 봤던 것처럼 행동하지만, 아니었다. (see, ghost)
He acts ______________________________________, but he didn't.

3 네 도움이 없으면 우리는 그 경기에서 우승할 수 없을 것이다. (can, win the game)
If it ____________________ your help, we ____________________.

화법/부가의문문

A 네모 안에서 알맞은 말을 고르시오.

1 Tina said to him, "You can use my cell phone."

→ Tina [said, told] him that he [could, can] use her cell phone.

2 She said to me, "Wait by the Fisher Building."

→ She told me [to wait, wait] by the Fisher Building.

3 My uncle said to me, "Did you make your bed before you went to school?"

→ My uncle [asked, spoke] me if I [make, had made] my bed before I went to school.

4 The hotel clerk said to me, "How many days will you stay?"

→ The hotel clerk [told, asked] me how many days I [will, would] stay.

5 The man said, "I want a newspaper to read with my coffee."

→ The man [said, spoke] that [him, he] wanted a newspaper to read with his coffee.

B 빈칸에 알맞은 부가의문문을 써 넣으시오.

1 They aren't having ice cream with us, ____________________?

2 He will have a brownie for dessert, ____________________?

3 The busy convention is all over now, ____________________?

4 Mike doesn't remember that event, ____________________?

5 She cannot buy that book from the same store, ____________________?

6 They can reach the finals of the soccer championship, ____________________?

7 The doctors wonder how often they can repeat the procedure, ____________________?

C 간접화법 문장을 완성하시오.

1 My cousin says to her, "Eat all of your soup."

→ My cousin tells her ____.

2 Jenny says to me, "Are you going to school now?"

→ Jenny asks me ____.

3 Kim said to me, "Don't behave so poorly around your parents."

→ Kim ordered me ____.

4 The pilot said to them, "You are flying at 10,000 feet."

→ The pilot told them that ____.

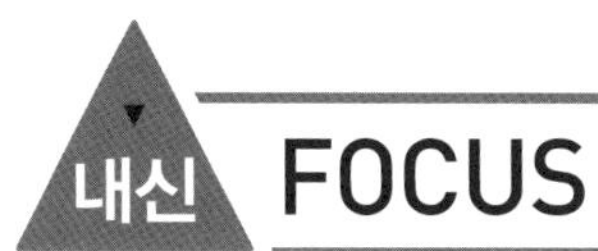

FOCUS

SCORE:

A 간접화법 문장으로 바꿀 때 빈칸에 알맞은 말을 써 넣으시오.

1 He said, “I am innocent.”

→ He __________ that ________________ innocent.

2 The boy said to me, “Do you want some oranges?”

→ The boy __________ me ________________ some oranges.

B 빈칸에 들어갈 알맞은 말을 고르시오.

1 The customer needs some more green grapes, __________ she?

ⓐ does ⓑ need ⓒ doesn't ⓓ didn't

2 They don't have to work overtime, __________ they?

ⓐ do ⓑ don't ⓒ aren't ⓓ are

C 어법상 옳지 않은 문장을 고르시오.

1 ⓐ She isn't going with us to the party, is she?
ⓑ He will order that bike part again, won't he?
ⓒ Chris asked me that I had time to help him with something.
ⓓ Mom told me to water the flowers in the garden.

2 ⓐ I told him that he could have another one.
ⓑ Tim said to me, “Are you going to the dance?”
ⓒ My teacher tells us to write our English papers now.
ⓓ They don't usually bring their books with them, do you?

D 우리말과 같은 뜻이 되도록 주어진 말을 이용하여 문장을 완성하시오.

1 그는 “나는 지금 비타민이 좀 필요해.”라고 말했다. (some vitamins)
He said, “____.”

2 그는 그녀에게 어디에 가고 싶으냐고 물었다. (want, go)
He asked her ____.

3 아빠는 내게 숙제를 하라고 말씀하신다. (do one's homework)
My father tells me ____.

4 Mary는 그걸 이해할 수 없지, 그렇지? (she)
Mary can't understand that, ____________________?

The Grammar

Concise & Core Grammar

불필요하고 잘 사용하지 않는 문법은 배제하고 핵심적인 부분만을 간결하고 정확하게 예문 중심으로 이해할 수 있도록 구성

Sentence Expansion

기초 문법을 기반으로 문장을 완성, 확장해 가는 학습 방법 적용

A Variety of Question Types

문법 포인트 확인 · 기초 문법 문제 · 응용 문제 · 리뷰 테스트 · 문법 확장 문제 · 종합 문제

Preparation for School Tests

다양한 문제 유형을 통해 내신 대비는 물론 말하기 및 쓰기 실력 향상

Grammar Summary

배운 학습 내용을 차트 및 표로 정리하여 쉽게 암기할 수 있도록 구성

Workbook

내신 대비 및 서술형 평가 대비를 위한 충분한 분량의 문제가 수록된 워크북 제공

www.nexusEDU.kr
넥서스 초 · 중 · 고등 사이트

www.nexusbook.com
넥서스 홈페이지

NEXUS makes your next day
www.nexusEDU.kr | 책에 대해 궁금한 사항은 넥서스에듀 홈페이지 1:1 **고객상담 게시판**을 이용하세요.

	교재	초1	초2	초3	초4	초5	초6	중1	중2	중3	고1	고2	고3
Writing	공감 영문법+쓰기 1~2				●	●	●	●					
Writing	도전만점 중등내신 서술형 1~4						●	●	●	●			
Writing	영어일기 영작패턴 1-A, B · 2-A, B				●	●	●	●	●				
Writing	Smart Writing 1~2				●	●	●	●	●	●			
Reading	Reading 101 1~3					●	●	●	●	●			
Reading	Reading 공감 1~3					●	●	●	●	●			
Reading	This Is Reading Starter 1~3					●	●	●	●	●			
Reading	This Is Reading 전면 개정판 1~4						●	●	●	●	●		
Reading	This Is Reading 1-1 ~ 3-2 (각 2권; 총 6권)					●	●	●	●	●	●		
Reading	원서 술술 읽는 Smart Reading Basic 1~2						●	●	●	●			
Reading	원서 술술 읽는 Smart Reading 1~2									●	●	●	
Reading	[특급 단기 특강] 구문독해 · 독해유형									●	●	●	●
Listening	Listening 공감 1~3						●	●	●				
Listening	The Listening 1~4					●	●	●	●				
Listening	After School Listening 1~3						●	●	●				
Listening	도전! 만점 중학 영어듣기 모의고사 1~3						●	●	●				
Listening	만점 적중 수능 듣기 모의고사 20회 · 35회									●	●	●	
TEPS	NEW TEPS 입문편 실전 250⁺ 청해 · 문법 · 독해					●	●	●	●	●			
TEPS	NEW TEPS 기본편 실전 300⁺ 청해 · 문법 · 독해						●	●	●	●	●		
TEPS	NEW TEPS 실력편 실전 400⁺ 청해 · 문법 · 독해							●	●	●	●	●	
TEPS	NEW TEPS 마스터편 실전 500⁺ 청해 · 문법 · 독해								●	●	●	●	●

The Grammar

Nexus Contents Development Team

Answers

NEXUS Edu

Answers ▸▸

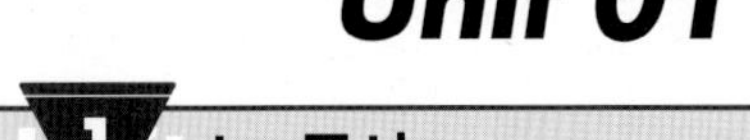

Unit 01

Unit 1 be동사

EXERCISE

P.9

A
1 is 2 is 3 are
4 are 5 are 6 was not
7 Is 8 Were

B
1 Is
2 Was
3 you are
4 I'm not[I am not]
5 wasn't[was not]
6 Were

C
1 Jenny isn't an English teacher.
2 My English book is under the table.
3 Mike and Sam are nice and handsome.
4 Jane was in the library yesterday.
5 Harry and I were classmates last year.

Unit 2 일반동사

EXERCISE

P.11

A
1 drinks 2 flies 3 speak
4 catches 5 enjoys 6 have
7 practices 8 fixes

B
1 wears 2 takes 3 buys
4 has 5 washes 6 worries
7 teaches 8 plays

C
1 reaches 2 pays 3 bite
4 know 5 tells 6 collects

C
1 3인칭 단수 주어, 현재시제: -ch로 끝나는 동사+es
2 3인칭 단수 주어, 현재시제: 〈모음+y〉 동사+-s
3 복수 주어: 동사원형
4 복수 주어: 동사원형
5 3인칭 단수 주어, 현재시제: 대부분의 동사+-s
6 3인칭 단수 주어, 현재시제: 대부분의 동사+-s

Unit 3 일반동사의 부정문과 의문문

EXERCISE

P.13

A
1 (b) 2 (e) 3 (d)
4 (c) 5 (a)

B
1 Does 2 like 3 Do
4 send 5 doesn't 6 don't
7 cook

C
1 Do you have lunch
2 He doesn't[does not] brush his teeth
3 This store sells
4 Does his uncle arrive
5 My brother and I don't[do not]

B
1 주어가 3인칭 단수(he)이므로 Does가 적절
2 〈Does+주어+동사원형〉이므로 like가 적절
3 주어가 복수(Jane and Bob)이므로 Do가 적절
4 〈Does+주어+동사원형〉이므로 send가 적절
5 주어가 3인칭 단수(Henry)이므로 doesn't가 적절
6 복수 주어(Nancy and her boyfriend)이므로 don't가 적절
7 does not 다음에 오는 동사는 동사원형이 적절

Unit 4 의문사 있는 의문문 / There is [are]

EXERCISE

P.15

A
1 come 2 do 3 is
4 is 5 are 6 was
7 was not

B
1 go 2 are 3 are
4 O 5 Were 6 Was
7 do

C
1 When do Kate and Bill feed
2 Where does your brother take
3 There isn't[is not] a polar bear
4 How many students are there
5 How much juice is there

B
1 의문사가 있는 의문문: 〈의문사+do동사+주어+동사원형 ~?〉
2 주어가 복수(many tourists)이므로 are가 돼야 함

3 "교실이 어디에 있니?"라고 묻는 질문으로 are가 돼야 함
5 과거를 나타내는 말(last week)이 있으므로 과거시제가 돼야 함
6 주어가 단수(a good restaurant)이므로 Was가 돼야 함
7 일반동사 의문문이므로 do가 돼야 함

REVIEW TEST

P.16

A 1 are 2 wasn't 3 There are
4 don't lend 5 lie 6 draw
7 climbs 8 doesn't have

B 1 ⓒ 2 ⓐ 3 ⓓ
4 ⓐ 5 ⓑ 6 ⓒ 7 ⓑ

C 1 looks 2 do, commute
3 writes 4 want
5 order 6 doesn't wait
7 don't take

D 1 Who is your favorite actor?
2 My friends and I go to a concert today.
3 Danny studies a lot of subjects.
4 Wasn't Sarah at her grandmother's thirty minutes ago?
5 He prefers cookies for snacks, but I prefer chocolate.
6 When does his flight arrive?
7 My father and I do not wash our car when it rains or snows.

A 1 Jack과 나는 같은 반이다.
▶ 복수 주어(Jack and I)이므로 are가 적절
2 어제는 화요일이 아니었다. 월요일이었다.
▶ yesterday가 과거를 나타내므로 wasn't가 적절
3 옷장 안에 담요들이 있다.
▶ blankets가 복수이므로 There are가 적절
4 Pete와 Tony는 어느 누구에게도 돈을 빌려주지 않는다.
▶ 복수 주어(Pete and Tony)이므로 don't lend가 적절
5 그들은 왜 그렇게 거짓말을 많이 하니?
▶ 〈의문사+do+주어+동사원형〉
6 Kris와 Kerry는 날씨가 좋은 날에는 해변에서 그림을 그린다.
▶ 복수 주어(Kris and Kerry)이므로 draw가 적절
7 Andy는 일요일마다 등산을 한다.
▶ 3인칭 단수 주어(Andy)이므로 climbs가 적절
8 Brenda는 저녁에 커피를 마시지 않는다.
▶ 3인칭 단수 주어(Brenda)이므로 doesn't have가 적절

B 1 그녀는 학교 연극의 감독이다.
▶ '이다'란 의미의 be동사가 와야 하고 주어가 3인칭(She) 단수이므로 is가 적절
2 찬장에 참치 캔이 몇 개 있니?
▶ '얼마나 많은 참치 캔'이라는 의미: 〈How many+셀 수 있는 명사의 복수형〉
3 Cathy가 미국에서 온 네 사촌이니?
▶ '이다'란 의미의 be동사가 와야 하고 주어가 3인칭 단수이므로 Is가 적절
4 그녀는 한 달에 한 번 출장을 간다.
▶ '가다'란 의미의 go가 와야 하고 주어가 3인칭 단수이므로 goes가 적절
5 그들은 인터넷에서 새로운 노래를 찾는다.
▶ 주어가 복수(They)이므로 find가 적절
6 Helen은 왜 그렇게 자주 거울을 보니?
▶ do동사 다음에는 동사원형이 와야 하므로 look이 적절
7 Kelly는 이번 주말에 하와이로 떠나니?
▶ do동사 다음에는 동사원형이 와야 하므로 leave가 적절

C 1 네 티셔츠 정말 멋지다. 너에게 잘 어울려.
▶ 주어가 3인칭 단수(It)이므로 looks가 적절
2 너는 어떻게 출근하니, 지하철로 아니면 버스로 출근하니?
▶ 〈의문사+do+주어(you)+동사원형〉
3 Glen은 추리소설을 쓴다.
▶ 주어가 3인칭 단수(Glen)이므로 writes가 적절
4 Lisa는 물 한 잔을 원하니?
▶ 〈Does+3인칭 단수 주어+동사원형〉
5 우리는 대개 콤비네이션 피자를 주문한다.
▶ 복수 주어(we)이므로 order가 적절
6 Jenny는 친구들을 참을성 있게 기다려 주지 않는다.
▶ 〈3인칭 단수 주어+doesn't+동사원형〉
7 Jones 부부는 오후에 낮잠을 자지 않는다.
▶ 〈복수 주어(Mr. and Mrs. Jones)+don't+동사원형〉

D 1 네가 가장 좋아하는 배우는 누구니?
▶ your favorite actor는 단수이므로 is가 적절
2 내 친구들과 나는 오늘 콘서트에 간다.
▶ My friends and I는 복수이므로 go가 적절
3 Danny는 많은 과목을 공부한다.
▶ 3인칭 단수 현재형 변화: studies가 적절
4 Sarah는 삼십 분 전에 할머니 댁에 있지 않았니?
▶ thirty minutes ago는 과거이므로 Wasn't가 적절
5 그는 간식으로 쿠키를 선호하지만, 나는 초콜릿을 더 좋아한다.
▶ 3인칭 단수 현재형 변화: prefers가 적절
6 그의 비행기가 언제 도착하니?
▶ 〈의문사+do(es)+주어+동사원형〉이므로 arrive가 적절
7 아버지와 나는 비가 오거나 눈이 오면 세차를 하지 않는다.
▶ 주어가 복수(My father and I)이므로 wash가 적절

FURTHER STUDY

P.18

A (1) is (2) approaches
(3) buys (4) goes

B 1 eat breakfast 2 begins
3 teach English 4 6 o'clock
5 finish, have 6 starts, ends

A

Tony는 택시를 타고 공항에 도착한다. 그는 지금 해외에 가기 위해 공항에 있다. 그는 오늘 스페인으로 가는 비행기 표를 사기를 원한다. 그는 지갑을 찾으려 하는데, 지갑이 없다. 곧 한 여성이 그의 지갑을 가지고 그에게 다가온다. 그는 그녀에게 감사를 전한다. 그는 가방을 열어 여권을 꺼낸다. 그는 현금으로 표 값을 지불한다. 그는 카운터에서 티켓을 사고 탑승 수속을 밟는다. 그는 보안 검색을 받고 게이트를 찾는다. 곧 그는 스페인으로 떠난다.

(1) 현재 상황을 설명하므로 is가 적절
(2) 3인칭 단수 주어, 현재시제: -ch로 끝나는 동사+es
(3) 3인칭 단수 주어, 현재시제: 〈모음+y〉로 끝나는 동사+s
(4) 3인칭 단수 주어, 현재시제: -o로 끝나는 동사+es

B 1 학생들은 8시부터 9시까지 아침을 먹는다.
2 아침 운동은 6시 30분에 시작한다.
3 원어민 선생님들은 9시부터 10시 30분까지 영어를 가르친다.
4 선생님들은 6시 정각에 학생들을 깨운다.
5 학생들은 영어 수업이 끝난 후에 간식을 먹는다.
6 퀴즈와 간식 시간은 10시 30분에 시작해서 11시에 끝난다.

MUST-KNOW

P.19

▶ be동사 변화표
① was ② isn't ③ Is it ④ were

▶ 일반동사의 문장 형태
① Do you ② runs ③ do not

WRAP-UP TEST

P.20

1 ⓒ 2 ⓐ is 3 ⓑ
4 ⓑ 5 ⓓ
6 ⓐ many ⓑ much
7 ⓒ 8 ⓑ
9 Are, are, Are, aren't, are, am, is, is
10 (1) There aren't[are not] many old paintings in the shop
(2) Does it happen very often?

1 ⓐ 그는 말이 많지 않다.
ⓑ 그들은 나의 조카들이다.
ⓒ 나는 가장 친한 친구와 같은 반이 아니다.
ⓓ 중학교 때 내 성적은 그렇게 나쁘지 않았다.
▶ ⓒ am not은 줄여 쓸 수 없음

2 병에는 우유가 많지 않다.
▶ ⓐ milk는 셀 수 없는 명사이므로 단수 취급: are → is

3 · A 문구점에서 무엇을 사니?
B 나는 연필과 공책을 사
· A 저녁 식사 후에 누가 설거지를 하니?
B 내 여동생이 해.
· A 생일이 언제니?
B 11월 29일이야.
▶ 각각 What, Who, When이 들어감

4 ⓐ 그는 왜 아이처럼 행동하니?
ⓑ 그는 자주 약속을 어긴다.
ⓒ 그녀는 여름에는 야외에서 많은 시간을 보내지 않는다.
ⓓ 우리 부모님은 자주 친척들에게 편지를 받는다.
▶ ⓑ 3인칭 단수 주어(He)이므로 break는 breaks가 돼야 함

5 A 그것이 그의 감정을 상하게 하니?
B 응, 그래.
▶ 〈Does+3인칭 단수 주어+동사원형 ~?〉

6 · 가족이 몇 명이니?
· 돈이 얼마나 있니?
▶ 〈many+셀 수 있는 명사의 복수형(people)〉, 〈much+셀 수 없는 명사(money)〉

7 ⓐ 그 영화의 제목을 모르니?
ⓑ Mary는 사고 후로 자전거를 타지 않는다.
ⓒ 그는 항상 방과 후에 숙제를 한다.
ⓓ Harry Potter 책을 어떻게 생각하니?
▶ ⓐ 의문문을 만드는 조동사 ⓑ 부정문을 만드는 조동사
ⓒ do one's homework '숙제를 하다'라는 뜻의 일반동사
ⓓ 의문문을 만드는 조동사

8 ⓐ Bill은 항상 나의 점심 값을 낸다.
ⓑ Mary는 겨울에 심한 감기에 걸린다.
ⓒ 내 동생은 내 뒤에 숨는다.
ⓓ 우리 반 친구가 계속해서 내 책상을 민다.
▶ ⓑ have의 3인칭 단수형은 has

9 Jina 안녕, 나 Jina야.
Paul 안녕, Jina. 나 Paul이야. Josh와 Kerry가 거기 있니?
Jina 응, 있어. 잠깐 기다려.
Josh 안녕, Paul. 나 Josh야.
Paul 안녕, Josh. 너희들 바쁘니?
Josh 아니, 안 바빠. 너 어디니?
Paul 나 극장이야. 와서 나랑 같이 영화 볼래?
Josh 좋은 생각이야! 영화가 몇 시에 시작하니?
Paul 영화 시작하기 전에 시간이 많이 있어.
Josh 알겠어! 출발할게!

10 (1) 가게에는 오래된 그림이 많이 있다.

▶ 〈be동사+not〉

(2) 그것은 아주 자주 발생해요.

▶ 〈Does+3인칭 단수 주어+동사원형 ~?〉

Unit 02

1 현재시제/현재진행형

EXERCISE

P.23

A 1 boils 2 go 3 likes
4 am traveling 5 carries 6 brush
7 is taking

B 1 runs 2 is making
3 flows 4 calls
5 is leaving/leaves 6 tastes
7 sets

C 1 sings 2 goes
3 is tying 4 is writing

2 현재진행형(부정문, 의문문, 불가동사)

EXERCISE

P.25

A 1 take 2 doesn't want
3 Are 4 hates
5 following 6 is not
7 are having

B 1 belongs to 2 cooking
3 isn't cutting 4 know
5 O 6 is having

C 1 Are, working
2 feeds
3 doesn't (does not) drive
4 is asking
5 am not watering

B 1 belong은 진행형을 쓸 수 없음
2 〈be동사+주어+V-ing ~?〉
3 〈be동사+not+V-ing〉
4 know는 진행형으로 쓸 수 없음
6 has는 '먹다'의 의미이므로 진행형 사용

3 과거시제/과거진행형

EXERCISE

P.27

A 1 dropped 2 become 3 didn't
4 Did you 5 met 6 lived
7 did not come 8 grew

B 1 destroyed 2 bought 3 cried
4 teach 5 invented 6 built
7 gave

C (1) told (2) liked
(3) know (4) milked

4 미래시제

EXERCISE

P.29

A 1 will buy 2 be 3 am not
4 stay 5 won't move 6 is
7 will

B 1 will 2 build 3 will not see
4 rent 5 are 6 win

C 1 are going to go 2 is arriving
3 will be 4 am not going to quit
5 Will, pick

B 1 미래를 나타내므로 will이 적절
2 〈Will+주어+동사원형 ~?〉
3 〈will+not+동사원형〉
4 〈will+주어+동사원형〉
5 〈의문사+are+they+going to〉
6 조건을 나타내는 if절에서는 현재시제가 미래를 대신

REVIEW TEST

P.30

A 1 ate 2 departs 3 eat
4 has 5 am taking 6 am going
7 studied

B 1 ⓒ 2 ⓑ 3 ⓓ
4 ⓓ 5 ⓐ 6 ⓓ 7 ⓑ

C 1 is making 2 will reply 3 closes
4 saves 5 know 6 left
7 will [are going to] watch

D 1 My father and I will drive to Chicago tomorrow for a motor show.
2 After he repaired my bike, I treated him to dinner downtown.
3 Who is going to the grocery store this weekend?
4 I told my mother about the accident last night.
5 We were talking about the science project when the teacher came in.
6 She will be very disappointed if you don't come to the party tonight.
7 We really need desks and chairs in the computer lab.

A 1 나는 어제 점심으로 치킨 샐러드와 양파 수프를 먹었다.
▶ 어제의 일이므로 ate가 적절
2 우리 비행기는 내일 아침 7시에 떠날 것이다.
▶ 출발, 도착의 의미를 가진 동사가 가까운 미래를 나타내는 표현과 함께 쓰일 때는 현재시제로 미래를 나타내기도 함
3 미국인들은 행운을 비는 의미에서 새해 첫날 black-eyed peas(까만 점이 박힌 콩)를 먹는다.
▶ 반복적인 일이므로 현재시제인 eat가 적절
4 그녀는 파란 눈과 길고 곱슬곱슬한 금발머리를 지니고 있다.
▶ have동사가 소유의 뜻으로 쓰였으므로 진행형이 될 수 없음
5 나는 전화를 받을 수 없다. 나는 지금 샤워 중이다.
▶ 현재 샤워를 하고 있는 중이므로 am taking이 적절
6 나는 정원에서 몇 가지 식물을 기를 예정이다.
▶ 뒤에 to grow가 있으므로 be going to가 될 수 있는 am going이 적절
7 Philip은 대학생 때 물리학을 공부했다.
▶ 과거 사실을 나타내므로 과거형 studied가 적절

B 1 네가 책상 위에 있는 내 CD를 옮겼니?
▶ 〈Did+주어+동사원형 ~?〉
2 Kathy는 화산의 역사에 대해 알지 못한다.
▶ 〈do/does+not+동사원형〉
3 너는 대학을 졸업한 후에 무엇을 할 거니?
▶ 〈의문사+will+주어+동사원형 ~?〉
4 아무도 수업을 듣지 않고 있었기 때문에 우리 선생님은 화가 나셨다.
▶ got angry로 보아 시제가 과거임을 알 수 있으므로 과거진행형인 was listening이 적절
5 내가 방에 들어갔을 때 너는 무엇을 하고 있었니?
▶ were you doing으로 보아 시제가 과거임을 알 수 있으므로 과거시제인 entered가 적절
6 Nancy는 우리가 숙제를 끝낸 후에 우리를 우주박물관으로 데리고 갈 것이다.
▶ 시간 부사절에서는 현재시제가 미래를 대신함
7 나의 학급 친구들은 지금 해변에서 즐거운 시간을 보내고 있다.
▶ have 동사가 '~을 보내다'라는 뜻으로 쓰였을 때는 진행형이 가능

C 1 Peter는 지금 남동생을 위해 모형 비행기를 만들고 있다.
▶ 현재 진행되고 있는 일이므로 현재진행형이 적절
2 그녀가 출장에서 돌아오면 당신의 이메일에 답장을 할 거예요.
▶ 답장을 할 거라는 뜻이므로 미래시제인 will reply가 적절
3 그 가게는 평일 아침에는 9시에 문을 열고 밤 10시에 문을 닫는다.
▶ 일상적인 일, 반복적으로 행해지는 일이므로 현재시제가 적절
4 Alicia는 항상 돈을 저축한다.
▶ all the time으로 보아 일상적인 일이므로 현재시제가 적절
5 이제 나는 이 수학 문제의 올바른 답을 안다.
▶ know는 현재진행형으로 쓰지 않는 동사이므로 현재형이 적절
6 내 친구들이 블로그를 방문해서 새해 인사를 남겼다.
▶ 과거에 방문해서 메시지를 남긴 것이므로 과거가 적절
7 내 친구와 나는 내일 결승전을 볼 것이다.
▶ tomorrow는 미래를 나타내므로 미래시제가 적절

D 1 아버지와 나는 모터쇼를 보기 위해 내일 시카고로 차를 운전해 갈 것이다.
▶ 〈will+동사원형〉
2 그가 내 자전거를 고친 후에 나는 시내에서 그에게 저녁을 사주었다.
▶ treated로 보아 과거시제이므로 과거형이 적절
3 누가 이번 주말에 식료품 가게에 갈 거니?
▶ 〈be V-ing〉
4 나는 지난밤에 사고에 대하여 어머니께 말씀 드렸다.
▶ last night이 과거를 나타내므로 과거형이 적절
5 우리는 선생님이 들어오셨을 때, 과학 프로젝트에 대하여 말하고 있었다.
▶ 선생님이 들어오셨을 때 진행되던 일이므로 과거진행형이 적절
6 네가 오늘 밤 파티에 오지 않는다면 그녀는 매우 실망할 것이다.
▶ 오늘 밤에 일어날 일이므로 미래시제가 적절
7 우리는 컴퓨터실에 책상과 의자가 필요하다.
▶ need(~를 필요로 하다)는 진행형으로 쓸 수 없으므로 현재형이 적절

FURTHER STUDY

P.32

A (1) will take off (2) will fly
(3) is (4) are going to/will

B 1 traveled, ten, went
2 went, had
3 is going to, five
4 visit, take
5 two, stay

A

신사 숙녀 여러분, 저는 기장입니다. 파리로 가는 293편에 탑승하신 것을 환영합니다. 우리는 약 15분 후면 이륙할 것입니다. 안전벨트를 매주시고, 자리에 앉아 편안히 계십시오. 우리는 3만 5천 피트 높이로 비행할 것이며, 한 시간 반 후에 착륙할 예정입니다. 일기 예보에 따르면, 목적지의 날씨는 좋습니다. 따라서 우리는 평온하고 순조로운 비행을 할 것입니다. 휴대 전화를 끄는 것을 잊지 말아 주십시오. 즐거운 비행하시기를 바랍니다. 감사합니다.

(1) 〈will+동사원형〉
(2) be와 fly가 나란히 쓰일 수 없으므로 will fly가 적절
(3) 목적지의 현재 날씨에 대해 말하고 있으므로 is가 적절
(4) 미래를 나타내는 내용이므로 are going to 또는 will이 적절

B
1 작년에 Cathy는 열흘 동안 알래스카를 여행했다. 첫째 날, 그녀는 바다 카약을 하러 갔다.
2 알래스카에서의 마지막 날, 그녀는 빙하 여행을 가서 즐거운 시간을 보냈다.
3 올해에 그녀는 라스베이거스를 방문할 예정이며 그곳에서 5일을 보낼 것이다.
4 8월 3일, 그녀는 후버 댐을 방문하여 사진을 찍을 것이다.
5 또한 그녀는 이틀 동안 그랜드 캐니언을 방문하고 멋진 호텔에서 묵을 것이다.

MUST-KNOW

P.33

▶ 동사변화표

① became ② broke ③ caught
④ cried ⑤ destroyed ⑥ drank
⑦ ate ⑧ fell ⑨ felt
⑩ gave ⑪ heard ⑫ knew
⑬ lied ⑭ lost ⑮ paid
⑯ read ⑰ sang ⑱ stopped
⑲ took ⑳ wrote

WRAP-UP TEST

P.34

1 ⓓ 2 ⓑ 3 ⓒ will tell
4 ⓒ 5 ⓑ 6 ⓒ 7 ⓓ
8 ⓓ 9 will share 10 will get

1 ⓐ 그녀는 토마토와 양파를 자르고 있다.
ⓑ 그녀는 토마토와 양파를 섞고 있다.
ⓒ 그녀는 부엌에서 빵을 굽고 있다.
ⓓ 그녀는 감자를 튀기고 있다.
▶ ⓓ friing → frying

2 그녀는 어제 Carrie에게 약간의 돈을 빌렸다.
▶ 과거를 의미하는 부사(yesterday)가 왔으므로 과거형이 적절

3 Cathy가 내 비밀을 퍼뜨린다면, 나는 모든 사람에게 그녀의 수학 점수를 말할 거야.
▶ ⓒ 미래를 의미하므로 will tell이 적절

4 ⓐ ~에 두다 ⓑ 시작하다 ⓒ 날다 ⓓ 떠나다
▶ ⓒ fly - flew

5 그들은 어제 그 파란색 셔츠를 샀다.
→ 그들은 어제 그 파란색 셔츠를 사지 않았다.
▶ 〈did+not+동사원형〉

6 ⓐ 정직이 최선의 방책이다.
ⓑ 너는 금요일에 회의에 참석할 것이다.
ⓒ Kent는 자신의 누나를 도와주지 않을 것이다.
ⓓ 한국 전쟁이 언제 시작됐니?
▶ ⓒ 〈is not going to+동사원형〉: will → is

7 ⓐ 이 큰 집은 Donald의 소유이다.
ⓑ 나는 손목이 부러졌을 때 붕대가 필요했다.
ⓒ John은 누나를 많이 좋아한다.
ⓓ 그는 지금 고급 식당에서 저녁을 먹고 있다.
▶ ⓐ 소유의 의미를 지닌 belong to는 진행형으로 쓰지 않으므로 belongs to가 적절 ⓑ '필요하다'라는 의미의 need는 진행형으로 쓰지 않으므로 needed가 적절 ⓒ '좋아하다'라는 의미의 like는 진행형으로 쓰지 않으므로 likes가 적절

8 A 너는 지난 주말에 ⓐ 조부모님을 방문했니 ⓑ 집안일을 했니 ⓒ 나에게 편지를 썼니?
B 응, 그랬어.
▶ 〈Did+주어+동사원형〉

9-10 Youtube.com은 인기 있는 웹사이트이다. 사람들은 이 사이트에서 음악, TV쇼, 다른 미디어를 공유한다. 곧, 이 사이트는 회원들과 이익을 공유할 것이다. 나도 회원이므로 YouTube로부터 약간의 돈을 받게 될 것이다.

9 ▶ 〈will+동사원형〉 ~할 것이다
10 ▶ 〈will+동사원형〉 ~할 것이다

Unit 03

1 현재완료 (계속)

EXERCISE

P.37

A
1 have lived 2 met
3 visited 4 has studied
5 has listened 6 since
7 have

B
1 read 2 designed
3 collected 4 known
5 completed 6 eaten
7 been

C 1 has studied　2 have been
3 have read　4 has used

현재완료 (완료, 경험, 결과)

EXERCISE

P.39

A 1 have met　2 has interviewed
3 has gone　4 never seen
5 ever been　6 has lost
7 have you read

B 1 have ridden　2 has moved
3 have never studied　4 have lost
5 has made　6 has gone

C 1 has never lost　2 has
3 met　4 have not
5 asked

C 1 현재완료의 계속적 용법으로 has never lost가 적절
2 the last bus는 단수이므로 has가 적절
3 when은 과거의 한 시점을 나타내므로 met이 적절
4 〈have(has) not p.p.〉: have not이 적절
5 〈의문사 + have(has) + 주어 + p.p. ~?〉: asked가 적절

과거완료와 미래완료

EXERCISE

P.41

A 1 had　2 had　3 will have
4 had　5 will have　6 will have

B 1 had burned/burnt　2 had already cooked
3 had taught　4 will have memorized
5 will have passed　6 will have been

C 1 had quit　2 had, heard
3 had finished　4 will have read
5 will have sold

R REVIEW TEST

P.42

A 1 have　2 will have visited
3 had already eaten　4 have not seen
5 has been　6 hadn't finished
7 have you been

B 1 ⓑ　2 ⓒ　3 ⓑ
4 ⓓ　5 ⓑ　6 ⓓ　7 ⓐ

C 1 had lost　2 heard
3 had won　4 hasn't given
5 have had　6 will have stayed
7 have slept

D 1 She has lost her key so she is waiting for her mom outside.
2 Martin is sleeping now. He has slept on the sofa since 3 o'clock.
3 How many times have you ridden a horse so far?
4 I had practiced writing essays for almost three years before I took the entrance test.
5 We will have studied all the verb tenses by the end of next week.
6 I don't know Mark at all. I have never met him before.
7 By the end of this class, he will have made great progress in English grammar.

A 1 너는 얼마나 오랫동안 Bill Gates와 아는 사이였니?
▶ 〈how long+have+주어+p.p.〉 얼마나 오랫동안 ~해 왔니?
2 내일 독일에 다시 가면 나는 독일에 네 번 방문하게 되는 것이다.
▶ 미래시제를 나타내는 when절이 있으므로 주절에서는 미래완료형인 will have visited가 적절
3 내가 집에 왔을 때는 Jinny가 이미 모든 쿠키를 다 먹어버렸다.
▶ 내가 집에 온 시점보다 Jinny가 쿠키를 먹은 것이 더 이전에 일어난 일이므로 과거완료형인 had already eaten이 적절
4 너는 내 지갑을 본 적이 있니? 금요일 이후로 나는 그것을 보지 못했어.
▶ 〈have not p.p.〉: have not seen이 적절
5 Scott은 7년 동안 음악가로 지내고 있다.
▶ 과거부터 현재까지 계속되는 일이므로 현재완료형인 has been이 적절
6 Susan이 숙제를 끝내지 못해서 우리가 그녀를 도와주었다.
▶ Susan이 숙제를 끝내지 못한 것이 우리가 그녀를 도와준 것보다 이전의 일이므로 과거완료형인 hadn't finished가 적절
7 너는 오후에 어디에 있었니?
▶ 과거부터 현재까지 어디 있었는지를 물어보는 것이므로 현재완료형인 have you been이 적절

B 1 나는 며칠 전에 가장 좋아하는 CD를 잃어버렸다.
▶ 과거시제를 나타내는 a few days ago가 있으므로 과거형 lost가 적절

2 영어는 수년 동안 다른 언어로부터 많은 단어를 빌려왔다.
▶ 과거부터 현재까지 계속되는 일이므로 현재완료형인 has borrowed가 적절

3 나는 요전 날 밤 파티에 중국인 친구들을 초대했다.
▶ 과거를 나타내는 the other night가 있으므로 과거형인 invited가 적절

4 그들은 내년까지 집 없는 사람들을 위해 집 백 채를 더 지을 것이다.
▶ by next year로 보아 미래완료임을 알 수 있으므로 will have built가 적절

5 내 친구들은 내가 교실에 들어갔을 때 나를 위해 깜짝 파티를 준비하고 있었다.
▶ 내가 교실에 들어간 것보다 친구들이 준비하고 있었던 것이 먼저이므로 과거완료인 had prepared가 적절

6 다음 주 일요일까지 나는 모두에게 초대장을 보낼 것이다.
▶ By next Sunday로 보아 미래완료임을 알 수 있으므로 will have sent가 적절

7 Ellie는 오늘 아침 아버지가 일어나시기 전에 아버지의 차를 세차했다.
▶ Ellie의 아버지가 일어난 것보다 Ellie가 차를 세차한 것이 먼저 일어난 일이므로 과거완료인 had washed가 적절

C 1 그 사고로 두 명이 목숨을 잃었다고 보도되었다.
▶ 보도된 것(was reported)보다 목숨을 잃은 것이 더 과거의 일이므로 had lost가 적절

2 너는 그의 새 영화에 관해 들어본 적 있니?
▶ 현재완료의 경험적 쓰임으로 heard가 적절

3 그의 축구팀은 지난주 경기에서 지기 전까지 모든 경기에서 이겨왔었다.
▶ 지난주 경기에 지기 전까지 일어난 일을 말하고 있으므로 과거완료인 had won이 적절

4 나의 여동생은 나를 위해 선물을 샀지만 아직 내게 그것을 주지는 않았다.
▶ 선물을 산 과거부터 현재까지의 이야기를 하고 있으므로 현재완료인 have p.p.가 적절. 내용상 선물을 아직(yet) 주지 않은 것이므로 hasn't given가 적절

5 나는 여행에서 돌아온 후로 계속 이 끔찍한 두통을 앓아오고 있다.
▶ 현재완료의 계속적 쓰임으로 have had가 적절

6 오늘은 일요일이다. 다음 주 토요일이면 우리는 일주일 동안 여기에 머무르는 것이 될 것이다.
▶ by next Saturday로 보아 미래완료인 will have stayed가 적절

7 어서 일어나! 너는 16시간 이상을 잤어.
▶ 현재완료의 계속적 쓰임으로 have slept가 적절

D 1 그녀는 집 열쇠를 잃어버려서 밖에서 엄마를 기다리고 있다.
▶ 현재완료의 결과적 쓰임으로 has lost가 적절

2 Martin은 지금 자고 있다. 그는 3시부터 소파에서 자고 있다.
▶ 3 o'clock이 특정한 시점을 나타내고 있으므로 since가 적절

3 너는 지금까지 몇 번이나 말을 타 봤니?
▶ 현재완료의 경험을 나타내는 문장이므로 ridden이 적절

4 나는 입학시험을 보기 전 거의 3년 동안 논술을 연습해 왔다.
▶ 입학시험을 본 과거 시점까지의 계속을 나타내므로 had practiced가 적절

5 우리는 다음 주 말까지 동사의 모든 시제에 대해 공부할 것이다.
▶ by the end of next week는 미래시제를 나타내므로 will have studied가 적절

6 나는 Mark를 전혀 모른다. 나는 전에 그를 만난 적이 없다.
▶ 현재완료의 경험을 나타내는 문장으로 내용상 부정어구가 필요하다. 따라서 ever는 never나 not이 되어야 적절

7 이 수업이 끝날 때쯤 그는 영어 문법 실력이 크게 향상될 것이다.
▶ 〈will have p.p.〉: made가 적절

F FURTHER STUDY

P.44

A (1) have found (2) invented
(3) created (4) have enjoyed

B 1 have lived, for
2 live
3 studied
4 will [am going to] study
5 will have dated
6 will [am going to] marry

A

> 나는 크리스마스트리 전구에 관한 흥미로운 이야기를 알게 되었다. Edison이 전구를 발명하기 전에, 사람들은 크리스마스트리를 장식하기 위해 초를 사용했다. Edison의 조수인 Edward Johnson이 1882년에 나무에 장식하는 전구를 생각해 냈고, Edison은 첫 크리스마스트리 전구를 개발했다. Edison은 80개의 전구를 발명하여 그 전구로 크리스마스트리를 장식했다. 전 세계적으로 많은 사람들이 그때 이후로 크리스마스트리 전구를 즐기고 있다.

(1) 과거부터 현재 사이에 크리스마스트리 전구에 관한 흥미로운 이야기를 알게 된 것이므로 현재완료가 적절
(2) Edison이 과거에 전구를 발명한 것이므로 과거가 적절
(3) in 1882이 과거를 나타내므로 과거가 적절
(4) since then으로 보아 과거부터 현재까지의 계속을 나타내므로 현재완료가 적절

B 1 나는 3년 동안 중국에서 살고 있다.
▶ 〈have+p.p.+for+기간〉: 현재완료의 계속

2 나는 지금 중국에서 살고 있다.
▶ 현재의 상태를 설명

3 나는 3년 전에 중국어를 공부했다.
▶ three years ago가 과거 시점을 나타내므로 과거형이 적절

4 나는 한 달 후에 프랑스어를 배울 것이다.
▶ one month later는 미래를 나타내므로 미래형이 적절

5 나는 내년 말이면 거의 4년 동안 남자친구와 데이트를 하게 될 것이다.
▶ by the end of next year가 미래시제를 나타내므로 미래완료 will have dated가 적절

6 나는 다음 달에 남자친구와 결혼할 것이다.
▶ next month는 미래를 나타내므로 미래형이 적절

MUST-KNOW

P.45

▶ 시제에 따른 동사 형태
① given
② was(were) giving
③ will have given

WRAP-UP TEST

P.46

1 ⓒ　　2 ⓐ for ⓑ since
3 ⓒ　　4 ⓑ
5 has forgotten
6 (1) has stolen (2) had hidden
(3) have worn (4) have raised
7 ⓓ ridden　　8 have been　　9 ⓑ
10 has attracted many tourists

1 ⓐ 이 작은 소년은 네 살 이후로 백 개의 그림을 그렸다.
ⓑ 나는 신문을 막 다 읽었다.
ⓒ 그들은 뒷마당에서 채소를 길러 왔다.
ⓓ Kate가 그 소문을 퍼뜨리고 있다.
▶ ⓒ grew → grown

2 · Mike는 차고에서 세 시간 동안 차를 수리하고 있다.
· 나는 2000년 이후로 영업 부장으로 일해 왔다.
▶ 〈for+기간〉, 〈since+시점〉

3 ⓐ 터키 아이스크림을 먹어 본 적이 있니?
ⓑ 나는 콩코드를 타고 아테네에 한 번 가 본 적이 있다.
ⓒ 그는 아들과 방금 10그루의 사과나무를 심었다.
ⓓ 나는 한 번도 길거리에 쓰레기를 버려본 적이 없다.
▶ ⓐ 경험 ⓑ 경험 ⓒ 완료 ⓓ 경험

4 · 내가 파티에 도착했을 때 Jane은 그곳에 없었다. 그녀는 이미 떠나버렸다.
· 내가 파티에 도착했을 때 Jane은 그곳에 없었다. 그녀는 한 시간 전에 떠났다.
▶ 내가 도착한 과거 시점보다 그녀가 먼저 떠난 것이므로 과거완료가 적절. an hour ago라는 과거 시점을 나타내는 부사구가 있으므로 과거형이 적절

5 Sue는 그의 이름을 잊어버렸고, 아직도 기억을 할 수가 없다.
→ Sue는 그의 이름을 잊어버렸다.
▶ 〈has+p.p.〉: 과거에 발생한 일이 현재에도 영향을 미치므로 현재완료가 적절

6 (1) 그 도둑은 도서관에서 지금까지 열 권을 훔쳤다.
(2) 그는 도둑이 떠나기 전 3시간 동안 침대 아래 숨어 있었다.
(3) 나는 기모노를 한 번 입어 본 적이 있다. 그것은 불편했다.
(4) 그녀는 다음 달이면 1년 동안 야생화를 기르게 될 것이다.
▶ (1) 과거부터 지금까지 일어난 일이므로 현재완료가 적절
(2) 도둑이 떠난 과거시점 이전에 일어난 일이므로 과거완료가 적절
(3) 현재까지의 경험을 나타내므로 현재완료가 적절
(4) 다음 달까지를 나타내므로 미래완료가 적절

7 지금까지 말을 몇 번 타 봤니?
▶ 과거부터 지금까지의 경험을 묻는 것이므로 현재완료가 적절: 〈have+주어+p.p.〉

8-10 나는 오하이오에 있는 클리블랜드에 여러 번 가 본 적이 있어. 그곳은 흥미로운 박물관이 많이 있는 놀라운 도시야. 나는 클리블랜드에 있을 때 이리 호에 있는 특별한 박물관을 방문했어. 그것은 박물관이 되기 전, 제 이차 세계 대전 동안 잠수함으로 쓰였어. 그래서 그것은 물 위에 자리하고 있어. 그 박물관은 많은 관광객을 끌어들이고 있어.

8 ▶ 내가 방문해 본 적이 있는 것이므로 have been
9 ▶ 박물관이 된 과거 시점 이전에 일어난 일이므로 과거완료가 적절
10 ▶ 현재까지의 일을 나타내는 것이므로 현재완료가 적절

Unit 04

조동사 (능력, 허가, 요청, 제안)

EXERCISE

P.49

A 1 take　　2 Will　　3 do
4 won't　　5 Could　　6 able to

B 1 can play　　2 be able to treat
3 may go　　4 cannot read
5 were able to experience

C 1 he will be able to cook for himself
2 Can you turn up the volume a little bit?
3 Would(Could) you say your name once more, please?
4 Shall we start our meeting now?
5 Is he able to rent DVDs on the Internet?

조동사 (의무, 금지, 충고, 과거의 습관)

EXERCISE

P.51

A 1 must　　2 don't have to
3 had better　　4 should
5 had to　　6 would
7 used to

B 1 must 2 would
3 don't have to 4 must not

C 1 had to pay 2 used to be
3 had better not make 4 don't have to bring
5 sleeps

Unit 3 조동사 (추측, 가능성)

EXERCISE

P.53

A 1 must 2 may 3 can't
4 might 5 must 6 could
7 should

B 1 must have hurt 2 may snow
3 should have made 4 must be
5 may have left

C 1 might(may) have put back
2 cannot have sold 3 must have spent
4 could have missed 5 should have asked

REVIEW TEST

P.54

A 1 don't have to 2 can 3 must not
4 may 5 had better
6 would 7 should

B 1 ⓒ 2 ⓒ 3 ⓓ
4 ⓓ 5 ⓐ 6 ⓑ 7 ⓐ

C 1 would 2 had better
3 is able to 4 don't have to
5 must 6 might

D 1 He won't be able to move into his uncle's apartment.
2 You don't have to worry about the fruit. I can pick up some from the market.
3 I don't have the book right now, but you might be able to borrow it from Angie.
4 Be careful! You might fall down. You have to hold the handrail.
5 Joe looked upset. He must have heard the gossip.
6 Will you take my dog for a walk? I don't have enough time now.
7 He failed the test. He should have studied harder for the exam.

A 1 당신은 지금 돈을 낼 필요가 없어요. 나중에 수표를 보내주실 수 있어요.
▶ don't have to '~할 필요가 없다',
2 나는 그것을 나 스스로 할 수 있다. 그것은 매우 쉬워 보인다.
▶ can '~할 수 있다'
3 너는 다시는 수업에 늦어서는 안 된다.
▶ must not '~해서는 안 된다'
4 수업이 끝났다. 너희들은 이제 가도 좋다.
▶ may '~해도 된다'
5 그녀는 매우 피곤해 보인다. 그녀는 집에 가서 휴식을 취하는 편이 좋겠다.
▶ had better '~하는 편이 좋겠다'
6 날씨가 좋을 때마다 Sandra는 윈드서핑을 가곤 했다.
▶ would '~하곤 했다'
7 나는 아버지의 골동품 꽃병을 깼다. 좀 더 조심했어야 했는데.
▶ should have p.p. '~했어야 했는데 (그렇게 하지 못했다)'

B 1 그녀는 시험에 통과한 후에 취직을 할 수 있었다.
▶ 과거 시제이고, 3인칭 단수 주어(She)이므로 was able to가 적절
2 그들은 여기에서 살았지만, 다른 도시로 이사를 갔다.
▶ 과거의 상태를 나타내는 used to가 적절
3 너는 거기 혼자 가지 않는 게 좋겠어. 누군가를 데려가야 해.
▶ '~하지 않는 게 좋다'라는 의미인 〈had better not〉이 적절
4 우리 부모님은 뉴질랜드로 여행을 다녀오신 뒤라서 매우 피곤하신 게 분명하다.
▶ 강한 추측을 나타내는 must가 적절
5 네가 원한다면 오늘 밤 여기에 머물러도 좋지만, 내일은 떠나야 해.
▶ 허락을 나타내는 may가 적절
6 너는 식사를 걸러서는 안 된다. 그것은 건강에 나쁘다.
▶ 조언을 나타내는 should not이 적절
7 나는 다음 주 금요일에 다른 약속이 있어서 너를 만날 수 없을 거야.
▶ 미래 부사구(next Friday)가 나오므로 will not이 적절

C 1 내 여동생이 잠들지 못할 때, 나는 그녀에게 자장가를 불러주곤 했다.
2 너는 우산을 가져가는 것이 좋겠어. 오후에 비가 올 거야.
3 John은 오 개 국어로 말할 수 있다.
4 나는 오늘 교복을 입을 필요가 없다. 나는 캐주얼한 옷을 입을 수 있다.
5 그녀는 매우 아픈 것이 틀림없다. 그녀는 전에는 수업을 한 번도 빠진 적이 없다.
6 그녀는 전화를 받지 않았다. 그녀는 회의 중이었을지도 모른다.

D 1 그는 삼촌의 아파트로 이사 갈 수 없을 것이다.
▶ 〈조동사 + be able to〉
2 과일에 대해 걱정할 필요 없어. 내가 시장에서 좀 사다 줄 수 있어.
▶ 〈조동사 + 동사원형〉

3 나는 지금 당장은 그 책을 가지고 있지 않지만, 너는 그 책을 Angie에게서 빌릴 수 있을지도 몰라.

▶ 조동사는 두 개를 같이 쓸 수 없으므로 〈might be able to〉가 적절

4 조심해! 넘어질 뻔 했잖아. 난간을 꼭 잡아야 해.

▶ 현재시제이므로 have to가 적절

5 Joe는 화가 나 보였어. 험담을 들은 것이 분명해.

▶ 과거 일의 추측을 표현할 때는 〈must have p.p.〉가 적절

6 내 개를 좀 산책시켜 주겠니? 난 지금 충분한 시간이 없어.

▶ 〈조동사+주어+동사원형 ~?〉이므로 take가 적절

7 그는 시험에 떨어졌다. 그는 그 시험을 위해 좀 더 열심히 공부했어야 했다.

▶ 하지 않은 일에 대한 유감을 나타내는 〈should have p.p.〉 '~했어야 한다'가 적절

FURTHER STUDY

P.56

A (1) had to (2) couldn't
(3) must (4) make

B 1 must not speed
2 can find the entrance
3 will get a ticket
4 cannot park here
5 have to slow down

A

> 오늘은 3월 7일이다. 우리 어머니의 생신이 다가오고 있다. 작년 어머니의 생신날에, 아버지는 대만으로 출장을 가셔야 했기 때문에 집에 안 계셨다. 남동생과 나도 그 주 내내 현장학습 여행을 가서 어머니의 생일 파티에 참여할 수 없었다. 어머니는 틀림없이 무척 슬프셨을 것이다. 올해에도 아버지는 어머니 생신날 우리와 함께 보내시지 못할지도 모른다. 아버지는 어딘가로 출장을 가실지도 모른다. 그래서 남동생과 나는 올해 어머니를 위해 특별한 선물을 사려고 한다. 그리고 우리는 어머니를 위해 미역국을 끓이고 쿠키를 구울 것이다.

(1) 작년의 일이므로 과거시제인 had to가 적절
(2) 작년의 일이므로 과거시제인 couldn't가 적절
(3) 확실한 추측인 '~임이 틀림없다'라는 의미이므로 must가 적절
(4) 〈조동사 + 동사원형〉이므로 make가 적절

B 1 길이 매우 미끄러우므로 속도를 내지 말아야 한다.
2 이 길을 따라가면 입구를 찾을 수 있다.
3 시속 40마일의 제한속도 이상으로 운전한다면, 교통 위반 딱지를 뗄 것이다.
4 여기에 주차할 수 없다.
5 이 교통표지판을 보면, 속도를 줄이고 아이들이 있는지 살펴야 한다.

WRAP-UP TEST

P.58

1 ⓓ 2 ⓑ escape
3 ⓒ 4 ⓓ 5 ⓐ
6 ⓐ must ⓑ can't[cannot]
7 (1) used to (2) must have
(3) don't have to (4) should
8 (1) I should have kept the promise with him.
(2) He can't[cannot] have done such a thing.
9 will be able to 10 ⓐ

1 A 당신의 전화를 써도 될까요?
B 물론이죠, 하지만, 너무 오래 사용하시면 안 돼요.
▶ 허락을 구하는 조동사가 필요하므로 Can이 적절

2 일곱 명의 수감자는 감옥에서 탈출해서 도망칠 수 있었다.
▶ 〈could+동사원형〉: escape가 적절

3 ⓐ 너는 이 빨간색 버튼을 누르면 안 된다.
ⓑ 그들은 경찰에게 진실을 말해야 한다.
ⓒ 많은 학생들이 역사 시험에서 떨어졌다. 매우 어려웠음이 틀림없다.
ⓓ 차가 당신을 칠 수도 있어요. 횡단보도로 건너야 해요.
▶ ⓐ 의무, 금지 ⓑ 의무, 금지 ⓒ 추측 ⓓ 의무, 금지

4 ⓐ 그는 에너지를 절약하기 위해 전구를 발명할 수 있다.
ⓑ Jack은 매일 운동하는 것을 그만두지 않는 것이 좋겠다.
ⓒ 그 비행기는 정시에 이륙해야 할 것이다.
ⓓ 그 어린 소년은 길을 잃었을지도 모른다.
▶ ⓐ 〈can+동사원형〉: can invent가 적절 ⓑ had better not ⓒ will have to

5 ① 그 쥐는 미로를 매우 빠르게 통과할 수 있다.
② 도서관에서 그 책을 빌릴 수 있나요?
③ 일찍 일어날 수 있는 비결을 좀 알려 줄래요?
④ 그가 그 반지를 찾을 수 있을 것이라고 생각하나요?
⑤ 우체국에 가는 길을 알려 줄래요?
⑥ 10개 중에서 2개의 컵을 고를 수 있어요.
▶ ① 능력 ② 허가 ③ 요청 ④ 능력 ⑤ 요청 ⑥ 허가

6 · 내 전화에 문제가 있음이 틀림없어. 네 소리를 들을 수가 없어.
· 그것이 거짓말일 리가 없어. 그는 결코 거짓말을 하지 않아.
▶ ⓐ must: 강한 추측 ⓑ can't[cannot]: 강한 부정의 추측

7 (1) 시청 근처에 고급 식당이 있었다.
(2) 그가 이 무거운 상자를 옮겼음이 틀림없다. 그는 매우 친절하다.
(3) 너는 파티에 가기 위해 정장을 입을 필요가 없어. 평상복을 입어도 돼.
(4) 자기 전에 이를 닦아야 해.
▶ (1) 과거의 상태: 〈used to+동사원형〉 '하곤 했다'
(2) 과거 사실에 대한 추측: 〈must have p.p.〉 '~했음이 틀림없다'
(3) 불필요 〈don't have to+동사원형〉 '~할 필요가 없다'
(4) 의무: 〈should+동사원형〉 '~해야 한다'

8 ▶ (1) 〈should have p.p.〉 '~했어야 했는데 (~하지 않았다)'
▶ (2) 〈can't[cannot] have p.p.〉 '~했을 리가 없다'

9-10 우리 부모님은 다음 달에 새 차를 살 수 있을 것이다. 그들은 그것을 위해 2년 동안 저축해 왔다. 그들은 좋은 차를 소유했었지만, 5년 전에 자동차 사고가 있은 후로 폐차를 해야 했다. 아빠는 파란색을 가장 좋아하기 때문에 파란색 차를 살지도 모른다.

9 ▶ 조동사는 두 개를 나란히 쓸 수 없으므로 will be able to가 적절

10 ▶ 과거의 일이므로 had to가 적절

2 나는 이 학용품을 넣을 상자가 필요하다.
▶ 명사(box) 뒤에서 명사를 수식하는 형용사적 쓰임

3 그는 선생님께 칭찬을 받아서 무척 기뻤다.
▶ '~해서'라는 뜻으로 감정의 원인을 나타내는 부사적 쓰임

4 나는 기술자가 되기를 원한다.
▶ 문장의 목적어로 명사적 쓰임

5 그들은 식사할 좌석을 예약하기 위해 식당에 전화했다.
▶ '~하기 위해서'란 뜻으로 목적을 나타내는 부사적 쓰임

Unit 05

1 to부정사의 역할

EXERCISE P.61

A 1 Ad 2 N 3 A
4 N 5 A 6 Ad

B 1 (b) 2 (d) 3 (e)
4 (c) 5 (a)

C 1 to watch 2 To become 3 to buy
4 to eat 5 to pass

A 1 나는 사촌을 방문하기 위해 캘리포니아에 갔다.
▶ '~하기 위해서'라는 뜻으로 목적을 나타내는 부사적 쓰임

2 그의 꿈은 자기 자신의 집을 짓는 것이다.
▶ 문장의 보어로 명사적 쓰임

3 그녀는 기차를 타는 동안 읽을 무언가를 원한다.
▶ 명사(something) 뒤에서 수식하는 형용사적 쓰임

4 내 방을 청소하는 것은 나의 의무이다.
▶ 문장의 주어로 명사적 쓰임

5 그녀의 어머니가 그녀에게 가지고 놀 장난감을 주었다.
▶ 명사(toys) 뒤에서 수식하는 형용사적 쓰임

6 너를 보게 되어서 기뻤어.
▶ '~해서'라는 뜻으로 감정의 원인을 나타내는 부사적 쓰임

B (a) 그는 의사가 되기 위해 열심히 공부했다.
▶ '~하기 위해서'란 뜻으로 목적을 나타내는 부사적 쓰임

(b) 산을 오르는 것은 힘들다.
▶ 문장의 주어로 명사적 쓰임

(c) 나는 현장학습을 위한 시간표를 짜는 것을 계획하고 있다.
▶ 문장의 목적어로 명사적 쓰임

(d) 그녀는 해야 할 일이 아무것도 없었다.
▶ 명사(anything) 뒤에서 수식하는 형용사적 쓰임

(e) 그는 그녀를 다시 만나게 되어서 기뻤다.
▶ '~해서'라는 뜻으로 감정의 원인을 나타내는 부사적 쓰임

1 유성을 보는 것은 흔치 않은 일이다.
▶ 문장의 주어로 명사적 쓰임

2 to부정사의 의미상 주어/부정

EXERCISE P.63

A 1 him 2 for her
3 not to use 4 me
5 of you 6 not to close

B 1 them 2 her little sister
3 for you 4 of him
5 her

C 1 of you 2 for me
3 him 4 not to think

C 1 칭찬하는 의미의 형용사 nice가 있으므로 of you가 적절

2 <It ~ to부정사> 구문에서 의미상 주어이므로 for me가 적절

3 <told+목적어>이므로 him이 적절

4 to부정사의 부정은 <not+to부정사>이므로 not to think가 적절

3 부정사의 기타 쓰임

EXERCISE P.65

A 1 where to meet 2 find
3 how to solve 4 fix
5 put 6 old enough
7 to concentrate

B 1 how to contact
2 too difficult to find
3 scream
4 where to sit〔where I should sit〕
5 warm enough to
6 wash
7 introduce

C 1 so old, can't walk
2 so smart, can find

3 too sick to go
4 wise enough to encourage

B 1 〈의문사+to부정사〉
2 〈too+형용사+to+동사원형〉
3 〈지각동사(hear)+목적어+동사원형〉
4 〈의문사+to부정사〉 = 〈의문사+주어+should+동사원형〉
5 〈형용사+enough+to+동사원형〉
6 〈사역동사(make)+목적어+동사원형〉
7 〈사역동사(let)+목적어+동사원형〉

R REVIEW TEST

P.66

A 1 walk 2 too 3 run
4 to play 5 not to be
6 how to talk 7 for her

B 1 ⓐ 2 ⓑ 3 ⓒ
4 ⓐ 5 ⓐ 6 ⓒ 7 ⓓ

C 1 tell 2 to give 3 to make
4 to live 5 run 6 to eat
7 to wear

D 1 He is strong enough to move these boxes.
2 She gave me a red pen to write with.
3 I want to have some chocolate to help (to) relieve my stress.
4 The coach made all the players run around the stadium track.
5 David is brave enough to bungee jump.
6 He decided to be a soccer player when he was seven.
7 It was unwise of you to criticize your friend like that.

A 1 우리는 많은 사람들이 거리에서 빨리 걸어가는 것을 보았다.
▶ 〈지각동사(see)+목적어+동사원형〉
2 이 시계는 내가 사기에는 너무 비싸다.
▶ 〈too+형용사+to+동사원형〉 '너무 ~해서 …할 수 없다'
3 그는 아들에게 가게로 달려가 우유를 사오도록 시켰다.
▶ 〈사역동사(have)+목적어+동사원형〉
4 그는 함께 놀 친구가 필요하다.
▶ to부정사의 형용사적 쓰임으로 명사(friend)를 꾸미는 to play가 적절
5 그녀는 다시는 내게 화를 내지 않겠다고 약속했다.
▶ 〈not+to부정사〉
6 Jake는 소녀들에게 어떻게 말을 해야 하는지 알기를 원한다.
▶ 〈의문사+to부정사〉
7 그녀는 대화의 주제를 따라가는 것이 어려웠다.
▶ 〈difficult+for+목적격+to부정사〉

B 1 그들은 이 경기에서 이길 수 있도록 열심히 연습했다.
▶ 〈형/부+enough+to부정사〉
2 그들은 그녀의 생일에 그녀에게 무엇을 줘야 할지 결정할 수 없었다.
▶ 〈의문사 + to부정사〉
3 제게 기차역까지 가는 길을 알려 주시다니 친절하시네요.
▶ 사람을 칭찬하는 형용사(kind)는 의미상 주어로 〈of+목적격〉을 취하므로 of you가 적절
4 우리 선생님은 내게 학교 연극을 위한 의상을 디자인하게 하셨다.
▶ 〈사역동사(let)+목적어+동사원형〉
5 요즘 나는 기타 치는 법을 배우고 있다.
▶ 〈how+to부정사〉 '~하는 법'
6 네 성적에 대해 너와 의논할 것이 있다.
▶ to부정사의 형용사적 쓰임으로 something을 꾸미는 to discuss가 적절
7 의사는 나에게 정기적으로 운동을 하라고 충고했다.
▶ 〈advise+목적어+to부정사〉

C 1 나의 학교생활에 대해 네게 좀 말해 줄게.
▶ 〈사역동사(let)+목적어+동사원형〉
2 나는 크리스마스에 남동생에게 무엇을 주어야 할지 몰랐다.
▶ 〈의문사+to부정사〉
3 나는 절대 너를 화나게 만들 의도는 아니었다.
▶ 〈intend+to부정사〉: intend의 목적어로 명사적 쓰임
4 너는 살 곳을 찾고 있니?
▶ '살 곳'이라는 뜻으로 place를 수식하는 to부정사의 형용사적 쓰임
5 나는 큰 트럭이 교차로에서 빨간 불에 (멈추지 않고) 가는 것을 보았다.
▶ 〈지각동사(see)+목적어+동사원형〉
6 이 치즈는 내가 먹기에는 냄새가 너무 강하다.
▶ 〈too+형용사+for+목적격+to+동사원형〉 '너무 ~해서 …할 수 없다'
7 학생들이 교복을 입는 것은 우리 학교의 규칙이다.
▶ to부정사의 명사적 쓰임으로 진주어 역할을 하는 to wear가 적절

D 1 그는 이 상자들을 나를 수 있을 만큼 충분히 힘이 세다.
▶ 〈형용사+enough+to부정사〉
2 그녀는 내게 (가지고) 쓸 빨간 펜을 주었다.
▶ 펜을 가지고 쓰는 것이므로 수단을 나타내는 with가 적절
3 나는 스트레스를 푸는 것을 돕기 위해 초콜릿을 조금 먹고 싶다.
▶ 〈help(+to)+동사원형〉
4 그 코치는 모든 선수들에게 경기장 트랙을 뛰도록 시켰다.

▶ 〈사역동사(make)+목적어+동사원형〉

5 David는 번지점프를 할 정도로 충분히 용감하다.

▶ 〈형용사+enough+to부정사〉

6 그는 일곱 살 때 축구 선수가 되기로 결심했다.

▶ 〈decide+to부정사〉

7 네 친구를 그런 식으로 비난하다니 너는 현명하지 않았다.

▶ unwise는 비판하는 의미를 담고 있는 형용사로, 의미상 주어로 〈of+목적격〉이 와야 함

FURTHER STUDY

P.68

A (1) to make (2) enough time
(3) buy (4) set

B 1 not easy for Koreans to learn
2 too small to ride
3 wants a puppy to play with
4 large enough to accommodate about 100 people
5 when to hand in the report

A

요리는 내가 가장 좋아하는 취미 중 하나이다. 그리고 나는 일요일마다 가족을 위해 점심을 만든다. 지난주 일요일, 우리 부모님은 내가 토마토소스 스파게티를 만들기를 원하셨다. 우리 아버지는 마늘빵도 드시고 싶어 하셨다. 그런데, 집에는 마늘빵이 없었고 나는 집 근처의 빵집에서 마늘빵을 살 수 있는 충분한 시간도 없었다. 그래서 나는 스파게티 면을 삶는 동안 남동생에게 마늘빵을 사오도록 시켰다. 우리 부모님은 내가 점심을 준비하는 것과 뒤뜰에 야외용 테이블을 설치하는 것을 도와주셨다. 가족 모두와 함께 점심을 먹어서 매우 기뻤다.

(1) 〈want+to부정사〉

(2) 〈enough+명사+to부정사〉

(3) 〈사역동사(have)+목적어+동사원형〉

(4) 〈help(+to)+동사원형〉이지만, prepare가 왔으므로 병렬 구조를 위해 set이 적절

MUST-KNOW

P.69

▶ to부정사를 목적어로 취하는 동사들
① to return
② to put off
③ to comment

WRAP-UP TEST

P.70

1 ⓓ 2 ⓓ to have
3 ⓐ of ⓑ for 4 ⓒ 5 ⓓ
6 ⓒ 7 to find
8 (1) huge enough to hold 1,000 people
(2) so, that he can't concentrate on this work
(3) is very important for me, exercise regularly
9 ⓐ 10 to be

1 내 희망은 전 세계를 여행하는 것이다.

▶ 보어로 쓰인 to부정사의 명사적 쓰임

2 A 우리 엄마의 생일이 내일이야. 엄마를 위해 무엇을 사야 할지 모르겠어.

B 엄마가 무엇을 가지고 싶어 하셔?

▶ ⓓ 〈want+to부정사〉

3 · 내가 이 탁자를 옮기는 것을 도와주다니 당신은 정말 친절하군요.

· 나는 이 지도로 길을 찾는 것이 어려워요.

▶ ⓐ 칭찬의 의미가 담긴 형용사 kind가 왔으므로 of가 적절
ⓑ 칭찬이나 비판의 의미가 담긴 형용사가 아닌 일반적인 형용사 hard가 왔으므로 for가 적절

4 ⓐ 백화점은 쇼핑하기에 좋은 장소이다.

ⓑ 이 복사기 사용법을 나에게 말해 줄래요?

ⓒ 그는 회의에 참석하지 않는 것에 동의했다.

ⓓ 식사를 거르는 것은 건강에 나쁘다.

▶ ⓒ 〈not+to부정사〉

5 그는 의사가 되기 위해 열심히 공부했다.

ⓐ 내 꿈은 유명한 배우가 되는 것이다.

ⓑ 나는 어머니날을 위한 카네이션을 사지 않기로 결심했다.

ⓒ 나는 생일 파티에 초대할 많은 사람이 있다.

ⓓ 그는 우유를 좀 사러 가게에 갔다.

▶ 부사(목적) ⓐ 명사(보어) ⓑ 명사(목적) ⓒ 형용사(명사 수식) ⓓ 부사(목적)

6 ⓐ 그는 나로 하여금 거짓된 소문을 퍼뜨리게 했다.

ⓑ 우리는 고양이가 발톱으로 문을 긁는 소리를 들었다.

ⓒ 그 소년은 엄마가 집을 청소하는 것을 돕기 위해 일찍 집에 갔다.

ⓓ 그는 침대 아래에서 무엇인가 움직이는 것을 느꼈다.

▶ ⓐ 〈사역동사(have)+목적어+동사원형〉 ⓑ 〈지각동사(hear)+목적어+동사원형〉 ⓒ 〈help+목적어(+to)+동사원형〉 ⓓ 〈지각동사(feel)+목적어+동사원형〉

7 ▶ '~하기 위해'라는 뜻의 목적을 나타내는 to부정사의 부사적 쓰임

8 (1) 그 콘서트홀은 매우 커서 천 명을 수용할 수 있다.

▶ 〈so+형용사+that+주어+can+동사원형〉
= 〈형용사+enough+to+동사원형〉

(2) 그는 너무 피곤해서 이 일에 집중을 할 수가 없다.

▶ 〈too+형용사+to+동사원형〉
= 〈so+형용사+that+주어+can't〉

(3) 규칙적으로 운동을 하는 것은 나에게 있어서 매우 중요하다.
▶ to부정사가 주어로 쓰인 경우 〈it ~ to부정사〉구문으로 바꿔 쓸 수 있음

9-10 Henry 8세는 16세기 영국의 왕이었다. 그는 6명의 부인을 둔 것으로 유명하다. 사람들은 왕의 부인이 매우 짧고 불행한 삶을 살았기 때문에 왕이 자신의 딸을 아내로 선택하는 것을 원하지 않았다. 하지만, 그들은 선택권이 없었다. 왕이 그들의 딸을 선택했다면, 그들은 그녀가 왕의 부인이 되는 것을 허락 해야 했다.

9 ▶ (A) 〈want+목적어+to부정사〉 (B) 〈명사+to부정사〉

10 ▶ 〈allow+목적어+to부정사〉

Unit 06

1 동명사의 역할

EXERCISE P.73

A 1 is 2 being 3 disturbing
4 makes 5 talking 6 wearing
7 winning 8 decorating

B 1 G 2 P 3 P
4 G 5 G 6 P

C 1 Walking by a bakery
2 listening to pop music
3 Becoming a detective
4 helping me clean the classroom
5 teaching history

B 1 '손톱을 물어뜯는 것'이라는 의미의 보어 = 동명사
2 '물어뜯고 있다'라는 뜻의 현재진행형 = 현재분사
3 '연주하고 있다'라는 뜻의 현재진행형 = 현재분사
4 '장난감 병정들을 가지고 노는 것'이라는 의미의 보어 = 동명사
5 '세탁을 하는 것'이라는 의미의 보어 = 동명사
6 '숙제를 하고 있다'라는 뜻의 현재 진행형 = 현재분사

2 동명사의 의미상 주어/부정

EXERCISE P.75

A 1 camping 2 not helping
3 my 4 from adding
5 her 6 arranging
7 to going

B 1 visiting 2 climbing 3 cleaning
4 going 5 eating

C 1 his 2 hearing
3 not eating 4 taking
5 preparing

C 1 동명사의 의미상 주어는 소유격, 구어체에서는 목적격도 쓸 수 있음
2 〈look forward to+-ing〉 '~하기를 고대하다'
3 〈not+동명사〉
4 〈feel like -ing〉 '~하고 싶다'
5 〈be busy -ing〉 '~하느라 바쁘다'

3 동명사/to부정사를 쓰는 동사

EXERCISE P.77

A 1 finding 2 to hurt
3 to increase 4 answering
5 complaining 6 to bring

B 1 to play 2 playing 3 studying
4 not to think 5 buying 6 to buy

C 1 riding, hitting 2 to be, to be
3 writing, to watch 4 to help, to bring
5 to paint(painting), to finish

R REVIEW TEST P.78

A 1 going 2 not to make
3 applying 4 giving
5 is 6 not keeping
7 selecting

B 1 ⓒ 2 ⓓ 3 ⓑ
4 ⓒ 5 ⓑ 6 ⓒ 7 ⓒ

C 1 to forgive 2 To graduate/Graduating
3 looking 4 watching 5 going
6 to close 7 to sleep

D 1 They wish to organize a schedule for the club's activities.
2 His staying in Seoul makes me happy.
3 My sister continued taking[to take] care of the children in the orphanage for a year.
4 This town is very famous for making noodles with rice.

5 My hobby is to collect news articles in my scrapbook.
6 They finished presenting the report at 2 pm.
7 Eating[To eat] protein is necessary for muscle growth.

A 1 Nancy는 겨울에 스키 타러 가는 것을 즐긴다.
▶ 〈enjoy+동명사〉
2 Jack은 Jim을 야구팀 단원으로 만들지 않기로 결심했다.
▶ 〈not+to부정사〉
3 나는 사립대학에 지원하는 것을 고려한 적이 없다.
▶ 〈consider+동명사〉
4 그녀는 실수를 하지 않기 위해 대답을 빨리하는 것을 피해야 한다.
▶ 〈avoid+동명사〉
5 사람들의 이름을 기억하는 것은 어렵다.
▶ 동명사 주어는 단수 취급
6 약속을 지키지 않아서 미안해.
▶ 〈for+not+동명사〉
7 Susan은 패션쇼를 위한 노래를 선별하느라 바쁘다.
▶ 〈be busy -ing〉 '~하느라 바쁘다'

B 1 그 영화가 너무 슬퍼서 나는 울고 싶었다.
▶ 〈feel like -ing〉 '~하고 싶다'
2 Albert는 이번 주 일요일 Nepal에 트레킹을 가서 한 달 후에 돌아올 것이다.
▶ 〈go -ing〉 '~하러 가다'
3 패스트푸드를 너무 많이 먹는 것은 건강에 해롭다.
▶ 주어로 동명사나 to부정사가 나와야 하므로 Eating이 적절
4 그들은 다음 주까지 숙제를 끝내야 하는 것을 명심해야 한다.
▶ 다음 주까지 숙제를 끝내야 하는 것을 기억하는 것이므로 to부정사가 적절
5 시민들은 시장이 새 시청을 짓는 것을 막으려 애쓰고 있다.
▶ 〈prevent A from -ing〉 'A가 ~하는 것을 막다'
6 우리 선생님은 우리의 시험이 끝날 때까지 우리에게 과제물을 내 주는 것을 연기했다.
▶ 〈postpone+동명사〉
7 Jordan은 Egypt로 여행을 가기 위해 지금 짐을 싸고 있다.
▶ 현재 진행되고 있는 일이므로 is packing이 적절

C 1 나는 그녀에게 화가 났지만, 실수를 용서하기로 결심했다.
▶ 〈decide+to부정사〉
2 반에서 일등으로 졸업하는 것이 올해 나의 목표이다.
▶ to부정사나 동명사가 주어로 올 수 있으므로 Graduating 또는 To graduate가 적절
3 우리는 좋은 식당을 찾는 데 많은 시간을 보냈다.
▶ 〈spend+시간/돈+-ing〉 '~하는 데 시간/돈을 사용하다'
4 나는 어젯밤에 본 아름다운 불꽃놀이를 결코 잊지 못할 것이다.
▶ '~한 일을 잊지 않을 것이다'라는 뜻이므로 watching이 적절
5 나는 오늘 밤에 영화관에 가고 싶다.
▶ 〈feel like+동명사〉
6 외출하기 전에 창문 닫는 것을 기억해라.
▶ 앞으로 해야 할 일을 의미하므로 to close가 적절
7 그녀는 수업 중에 잠들지 않으려고 노력했지만, 선생님이 수업을 시작하자마자 졸기 시작했다.
▶ 〈try+to부정사〉 '~하려고 노력하다'

D 1 그들은 그 클럽 활동을 위한 계획표를 짜고 싶어 한다.
▶ 〈wish+to부정사〉
2 그가 서울에 머무르는 것이 나를 행복하게 한다.
▶ 동명사 주어는 단수 취급
3 내 여동생은 1년 동안 고아원에서 아이들을 돌봐주는 일을 계속해 오고 있다.
▶ 〈continue+to부정사/동명사〉
4 이 도시는 쌀국수를 만드는 것으로 아주 유명하다.
▶ 〈for+동명사〉
5 나의 취미는 내 스크랩북에 뉴스 기사들을 모으는 것이다.
▶ 보어 자리이므로 to collect나 collecting이 되어야 하는데 앞에 to가 있으므로 collect가 적절
6 그들은 2시에 보고서 발표를 끝마쳤다.
▶ 〈finish+동명사〉
7 단백질 섭취는 근육 성장에 필수적이다.
▶ 동명사나 to부정사가 주어 자리에 와야 하므로 Eating이나 To eat이 적절

FURTHER STUDY

P.80

A (1) want to live (2) stop eating
(3) forget to drink (4) give up eating

B 1 Laughing a lot is
2 Reading this magazine
3 studying English grammar is boring
4 getting up early in the morning

A

우리 모두는 오래 살고 건강하게 살기를 원합니다. 우리는 건강을 위해 많은 일을 할 수 있습니다. 건강을 유지하는 데 도움이 되는 다섯 가지 비결을 알려 드리겠습니다. 첫째, 너무 많은 지방 섭취를 하지 마십시오. 둘째, 매일 더 많은 과일과 채소를 섭취하려고 노력하십시오. 셋째, 매일 충분한 양의 물을 섭취하는 것을 잊지 마십시오. 물은 우리 몸 속 모든 기관에 중요합니다! 넷째, 정기적으로 운동해야 함을 명심하십시오. 심지어 일주일에 세 번 십 분씩 걷는 것도 기분이 나아지게 해 줄 것입니다. 마지막으로, 밤에 너무 늦게 먹지 마십시오. 이러한 것을 명심한다면, 당신은 그렇게 자주 병원에 갈 필요가 없을 것입니다.

(1) 〈want+to부정사〉

(2) 지방을 많이 섭취하는 것을 중단하라는 내용이므로 〈stop+-ing〉가 적절

(3) 마셔야 할 것을 잊지 않는 것이므로 〈forget+to부정사〉가 적절

(4) 〈give up+동명사〉

MUST KNOW

P.81

▶ 동명사를 목적어로 취하는 동사

① delivering ② delivering
③ changing ④ holding

WRAP-UP TEST

P.82

1 ⓐ 2 sleep → sleeping
3 ⓐ 4 ⓓ 5 ⓑ
6 ⓓ
7 (1) sliding (2) going
(3) to discover (4) sending
8 looking forward to reading
9 my changing 10 ⓐ

1 · 불꽃놀이를 보는 것은 매우 신 나는 일이다.
· 그 집이 갑자기 불타기 시작했다.
▶ 주어 자리에는 to부정사나 동명사가 적절: Seeing/To see, 〈start+to부정사/동명사〉: burning/to burn

2 Mary는 큰 집에서 혼자 자는 것이 무섭다.
▶ 〈be afraid of+동명사〉 '~하는 것을 무서워하다'

3 ⓐ 우리는 초상화를 그리고 있다.
ⓑ Matt의 취미는 아이스하키를 하는 것이다.
ⓒ 내가 가장 좋아하는 활동은 쿠키를 만드는 것이다.
ⓓ 그의 꿈은 Michael Jordan 같은 유명한 농구 선수가 되는 것이다.
▶ ⓐ 현재분사(현재진행) ⓑ 동명사(보어) ⓒ 동명사(보어) ⓓ 동명사(보어)

4 ⓐ 선생님은 소풍 가는 것을 연기했다.
ⓑ Kate는 동유럽으로 여행했던 것을 항상 그리워한다.
ⓒ Jim은 살을 빼기 위해 밤에 스낵을 먹는 것을 그만뒀다.
ⓓ 그들은 길을 잃었다. 그들은 방향을 묻기 위해 운전을 멈췄다.
▶ 〈stop+동명사〉 '~하던 것을 멈추다', 〈stop+to부정사〉 '~하기 위해 멈추다'

5 ⓐ 그는 도서관에서 책을 빌리는 것을 그만뒀다.
≠ 그는 도서관에서 책을 빌리기 위해 멈췄다.
ⓑ 그녀는 크리스마스 캐럴에 맞춰 계속 춤을 췄다.
ⓒ Tom은 불을 꺼야 한다는 것을 기억하지 못했다.
≠ Tom은 불을 껐다는 것을 기억하지 못했다.
ⓓ Jim은 대나무 막대기로 낚시를 하려고 애썼다.
≠ Jim은 대나무 막대기로 낚시를 해 보았다.
▶ ⓐ 〈stop+동명사〉 '~하던 것을 멈추다', 〈stop+to부정사〉 '~하기 위해 멈추다' ⓑ 〈continue+동명사/to부정사〉 '~을 계속하다' ⓒ 〈remember+to부정사〉 '~할 것을 기억하다', 〈remember+동명사〉 '~했던 것을 기억하다' ⓓ 〈try+to부정사〉 '~하려고 노력하다', 〈try+동명사〉 '(시험 삼아 한번) ~해 보다'

6 ⓐ Mike는 입학시험에 통과하지 못했다.
ⓑ 그녀는 너를 무섭게 하려는 의도는 아니었어.
ⓒ 나는 꽃을 준비하는 데 관심이 있어.
ⓓ 아버지는 내 남동생을 밖에 나가지 못하게 한다.
▶ ⓐ 〈fail+to부정사〉 ⓑ 〈mean+to부정사〉 ⓒ 〈in+동명사〉 ⓓ 〈prevent+목적어+from+동명사〉

7 (1) 그 길은 매우 미끄러웠다. 내 친구와 나는 길에서 계속 미끄러졌다.
▶ 〈keep+-ing〉 '계속 ~하다'
(2) 미안해. 나는 너랑 영화 보러 가고 싶지 않아.
▶ 〈feel like -ing〉 '~하고 싶다'
(3) 그녀는 멸종된 동물에 대한 새로운 사실을 알아내기 위해 노력했지만, 발견할 수 없었다.
▶ 〈try+to+동사원형〉 '~하려고 노력하다'.
(4) 나는 그에게서 같은 메시지를 두 번 받았다. 아마 그는 나에게 그 메시지를 보낸 것을 잊었을 것이다.
▶ 〈forget+-ing〉 '~했던 것을 잊다'

8 ▶ 〈look forward to+-ing〉 '~할 것을 기대하다'

9-10 내가 우리 휴가 계획을 바꿔도 괜찮겠니? 나는 워싱턴에 있는 성 헬렌스 산을 방문하고 싶어. 그 산은 1980년에 폭발했어. 나는 그 이후의 놀라운 풍경의 변화를 보고 싶어. 그것은 많은 사람을 매혹하는 것 같아.

9 ▶ 〈mind+의미상 주어(my)+-ing〉

10 ▶ 〈hope+to+동사원형〉, 〈seem+to+동사원형〉

Unit 07

분사의 종류 및 의미

EXERCISE

P.85

A 1 tiring 2 boiled
3 thrilling, exciting 4 laughing
5 satisfied 6 broken
7 carrying

B 1 swimming 2 opened
3 dancing 4 interesting
5 exciting 6 broken

C 1 P 2 P 3 G
4 G 5 P 6 G

Unit 2 분사의 쓰임

EXERCISE
P.87

A 1 barking 2 folded 3 running
4 sitting 5 stolen 6 confusing
7 pulling

B 1 parked 2 amused 3 sitting
4 worried 5 lost 6 fixing/fix

C 1 rolling stone 2 excited
3 bored 4 jacket found
5 frightened 6 taken

C 1 분사가 단독으로 명사를 꾸밀 때 분사는 명사 앞에서 수식
2 우리가 신 나는 감정을 느끼는 것이므로 과거분사가 적절
3 Dana가 지루함을 느끼는 것이므로 과거분사가 적절
4 수식어(in the library)가 붙은 분사가 명사를 꾸밀 때는 명사 뒤에서 수식
5 내 작은 남동생이 무서움을 느끼는 것이므로 과거분사가 적절
6 다이아몬드가 빼앗는 것이 아니라 다이아몬드를 빼앗기는 것이므로 과거분사가 적절

Unit 3 수동태의 개념과 형태

EXERCISE
P.89

A 1 were served 2 was cleaned
3 was solved 4 orders
5 taken 6 be reported
7 was damaged

B 1 were shocked 2 be delivered
3 was repaired 4 be done
5 was cut 6 are brought

C 1 are painted 2 was stolen
3 will be developed 4 will be held
5 was, presented

B 1 많은 사람이 그 소식에 의해 충격을 받는 것이므로 수동태가 적절
2 피자가 배달되는 것이므로 수동태가 적절, 〈will be+p.p.〉
3 과거시제를 나타내는 부사(yesterday)가 있으므로 was repaired가 적절
4 〈should be+p.p.〉
5 머리카락이 자르는 것이 아니라 잘리는 것이므로 수동태가 적절
6 〈be+p.p.〉이므로 are brought이 적절

Unit 4 여러 가지 수동태

EXERCISE
P.91

A 1 of 2 from 3 at
4 with 5 at 6 with

B 1 belongs to 2 for
3 from 4 for me
5 in 6 were shown

C 1 was told a strange story
2 is taught to us
3 was made for me
4 was cooked for us
5 was given to his son

B 1 belong to(~에 속하다)는 수동태로 쓰지 않음
2 동사가 make일 때 사람 목적어 앞에 전치사 for가 적절
3 성질이 변하는 재료 앞에는 전치사 from이 적절
4 '~를 위해 사주다'라는 동사 buy가 수동태 문장으로 쓰였으므로 for me가 적절
5 〈be interested in〉 '~에 흥미가 있다'
6 용의자의 사진이 보는 것이 아니라 나에게 보여지는 것이므로 수동태가 적절

REVIEW TEST
P.92

A 1 fascinating 2 read
3 broken 4 with
5 was canceled 6 moving
7 be planted 8 given

B 1 ⓑ 2 ⓑ 3 ⓐ
4 ⓓ 5 ⓑ 6 ⓒ 7 ⓑ

C 1 made 2 satisfied
3 touching 4 exhausted
5 be presented 6 annoying

D 1 He was very excited to see his friend in Korea.
2 She was not satisfied with my explanation for being late.
3 Mike resembles his father.
4 The patient will be scheduled for surgery in the morning by the doctor.
5 We were all surprised and horrified when we saw the horror movie.

6 Here is a list of the top ten most embarrassing fashion trends.
7 The news was shocking. We were interested in the news.

A 1 Lisa는 아주 재미있는 소설을 읽고 있다.
▶ 소설이 재미있게 만들어 주는 것이므로 현재분사가 적절
2 그 책은 수백만 명의 사람들이 읽었다.
▶ 책이 사람들에 의해 읽히는 것이므로 과거분사가 적절
3 그 마녀는 깨진 거울을 가지고 있다.
▶ 거울이 깨는 것이 아니라 깨지는 것이므로 과거분사가 적절
4 그의 노트는 강의 내용이 아니라 작은 스케치로 가득 차 있다.
▶ 〈be filled with〉 '~로 가득 차 있다'
5 학교 축제는 비 때문에 취소되었다.
▶ 축제가 취소하는 것이 아니라 취소되는 것이므로 수동태가 적절
6 어제 아침 우리 교장 선생님의 연설은 감동적이었다.
▶ 연설이 감동을 느끼게 만드는 것이므로 현재분사가 적절
7 사과나무는 John에 의해서 심어질 것이다.
▶ 사과나무가 심는 것이 아니라 심어지는 것이므로 수동태가 적절
8 방과 후 학교에 남는 벌을 받은 학생은 그 다음날 더 예의바르게 행동한다.
▶ 학생이 벌을 주는 것이 아니라 벌을 받는 것이므로 과거분사가 적절

B 1 David의 이야기는 유쾌하고 재미있었다.
▶ 이야기가 재미있게 느끼게 만드는 것이므로 현재분사가 적절
2 그들은 아무 음식도 준비하지 않았다. 나는 그것에 실망했다.
▶ 〈be disappointed with〉 '~에 실망하다'
3 그 소년들은 소녀들 앞에 서 있다.
▶ '~하고 있다'라는 뜻으로 현재진행형이 적절
4 그 컴퓨터는 Max가 고치지 않았다.
▶ 수동태의 부정 〈be+not+p.p.〉
5 프랑스 어로 쓰인 그 소설은 내가 읽기에 너무 어려웠다.
▶ 소설이 프랑스 어로 쓰는 것이 아니라 쓰인 것이므로 과거분사가 적절
6 회의에서 나는 너무 많은 질문을 받았다.
▶ ask를 수동태로 만들 때 사람 목적어 앞에 of를 사용
7 나는 전 세계에서 가장 멋진 호텔 200개에 관한 책을 가지고 있다.
▶ 호텔이 매력을 느끼는 것이 아니라 매력을 느끼게 만드는 것이므로 현재분사가 적절

C 1 이집트 피라미드는 돌로 만들어졌다.
▶ 피라미드가 돌로 만들어진 것이므로 수동태가 적절
2 너는 그 시험 결과에 만족하니?
▶ 〈be satisfied with〉 '~에 만족하다'
3 어제 내가 본 영화는 매우 감동적이었다.
▶ 영화가 감동을 느끼게 만드는 것이므로 현재분사가 적절
4 그는 4킬로미터를 뛰었지만, 전혀 지쳐 보이지 않았다.
▶ 그가 기진맥진함을 느끼는 것이므로 과거분사가 적절
5 그 연구는 내일 회의에서 Sally에 의해 발표될 것이다.
▶ 연구가 발표되는 것이므로 수동태가 적절, 〈will be+p.p.〉
6 봐! Fred가 또 다리를 떨고 있어. 정말 신경 쓰여.
▶ 다리를 떠는 것이 신경 쓰이게 만드는 것이므로 현재분사가 적절

D 1 그는 한국에서 친구를 만나게 되어 매우 흥분되었다.
▶ 그가 흥분을 느끼는 것이므로 과거분사가 적절
2 그녀는 왜 늦었는지에 대한 나의 설명에 만족하지 않았다.
▶ 〈be satisfied with〉 '~에 만족하다'
3 Mike는 아버지를 닮았다.
▶ resemble은 수동태로 쓰지 않으므로 resembles가 적절
4 의사가 아침에 환자의 수술 일정을 잡을 것이다.
▶ 환자가 수술 일정을 잡는 것이 아니라 수술 일정이 정해지는 것이므로 수동태가 적절 〈will+be+p.p.〉
5 우리는 모두 그 공포 영화를 보고 놀랐고 공포에 떨었다.
▶ 우리가 놀라운 감정을 느낀 것이므로 과거분사가 적절
6 여기 가장 당혹스러운 패션 경향 상위 10개의 목록이 있다.
▶ 패션 경향이 사람을 당혹스럽게 만드는 것이므로 현재분사가 적절
7 그 뉴스는 깜짝 놀랄만한 것이었다. 우리는 그 뉴스에 흥미가 있었다.
▶ 〈be interested in〉 '~에 흥미가 있다'

F FURTHER STUDY

P.94

A (1) say/saying (2) worried
(3) invented (4) opened

B 1 was invented by Alexander Graham Bell
2 was written by Dan Brown
3 was sung by The Beatles
4 invented the television
5 was directed by Chris Columbus

A 당신은 사람들이 만약 실내에서 우산을 편다면 불행을 가져올 것이라고 말하는 것을 들을지도 모른다. 나는 실수로 집안에서 우산을 펼 때마다 걱정한다. 그것이 정말 불행을 가져올까? 아니면 단지 의미 없는 미신일까? 실제로, 그것은 가장 흔한 미신 중의 하나이고, 다른 많은 미신처럼 배경이 되는 이야기가 있다. 우산이 처음 발명되었을 때, 우산은 매우 컸다. 그래서 거대한 우산이 실내에서 펼쳐지면, 가족을 다치게 하거나 집안에 있는 무엇인가를 깰 수도 있었다. 당신은 이제 왜 사람들이 그러한 미신을 만들어내야 했는지 이해할 수 있을 것이다.

(1) 사람들이 말하는 것이므로 say 또는 saying이 적절 〈지각동사(hear)+목적어+동사원형/-ing〉
(2) 내가 걱정스러운 감정을 느끼는 것이므로 과거분사가 적절

(3) 우산이 발명하는 것이 아니라 발명되는 것이므로 수동태가 적절

(4) 우산이 펴는 것이 아니라 펼쳐지는 것이므로 수동태가 적절

B 1 전화는 1876년 Alexander Graham Bell에 의해 발명되었다.

2 '다빈치 코드'는 2003년 Dan Brown에 의해 쓰였다.

3 'Yesterday'는 1960년대에 비틀즈에 의해 불려졌다.

4 John Logie는 1926년에 텔레비전을 발명했다.

5 '해리포터와 마법사의 돌'은 2001년에 Chris Columbus에 의해서 (영화로) 연출되었다.

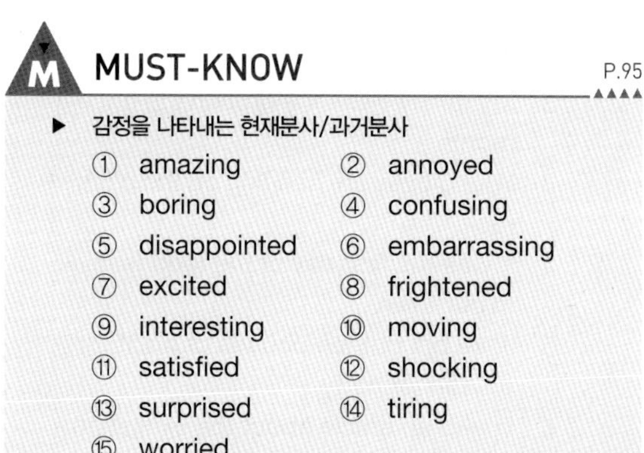

MUST-KNOW

P.95

▶ 감정을 나타내는 현재분사/과거분사

① amazing	② annoyed
③ boring	④ confusing
⑤ disappointed	⑥ embarrassing
⑦ excited	⑧ frightened
⑨ interesting	⑩ moving
⑪ satisfied	⑫ shocking
⑬ surprised	⑭ tiring
⑮ worried	

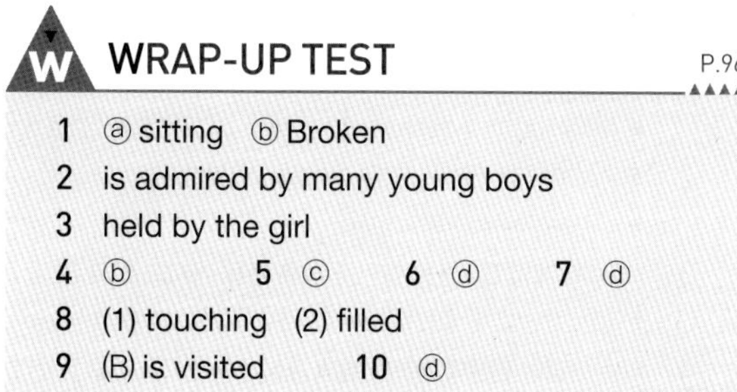

WRAP-UP TEST

P.96

1 ⓐ sitting ⓑ Broken

2 is admired by many young boys

3 held by the girl

4 ⓑ 5 ⓒ 6 ⓓ 7 ⓓ

8 (1) touching (2) filled

9 (B) is visited 10 ⓓ

1 · 벤치에 앉아 있는 소년은 책을 읽고 있다.
· 깨진 유리는 매우 위험할 수 있다.
▶ ⓐ 소년이 앉아 있는 것이므로 현재분사가 적절 ⓑ 유리가 깨진 것이므로 과거분사가 적절

2 많은 어린 소년들이 그 아름다운 여배우를 숭배한다.
→ 그 아름다운 여배우는 많은 어린 소년들의 숭배를 받는다.
▶ 〈be p.p. by+행위자〉

3 그 강아지는 매우 귀엽다. 그 강아지는 소녀에게 안겨 있다.
= 소녀에게 안겨 있는 그 강아지는 매우 귀엽다.
▶ 수식어구를 동반한 분사는 명사의 뒤에서 명사를 수식

4 ⓐ 달리고 있던 차가 갑자기 멈췄다.
ⓑ 우표를 수집하는 것이 그녀의 취미이다.
ⓒ 그의 지루한 수업은 학생들을 하품하게 만들었다.
ⓓ 우리 선생님은 우리에게 당혹스러운 문제를 낸다.
▶ ⓐ 현재분사(명사 수식) ⓑ 동명사(주어) ⓒ 현재분사(명사 수식) ⓓ 현재분사(명사 수식)

5 ⓐ 내 동생은 자신의 생일 선물에 실망했다.
ⓑ 이 떡갈나무는 할아버지가 심었다.
ⓒ 이 그림들은 모네의 그림과 닮았다.
ⓓ 그 도둑들은 체포되었다.
▶ ⓒ resemble은 수동태로 쓰지 않으므로 are resembled with가 아니라 resemble이 적절

6 ⓐ 과일 바구니가 탁자 위에 놓여 있다.
ⓑ 학생들은 현장학습에 신이 났다.
ⓒ 영리한 학생이 그 문제를 해결했다.
ⓓ 연필은 삼나무와 탄소로 만들어진다.
▶ ⓓ 〈be made of〉 '~으로 만들어지다'

7 A 그 영화 어땠어? 지루했니?
B 전혀. 나는 정말 흥미 있게 봤어.
▶ 영화가 지루함을 느끼게 만드는 것이므로 boring이 적절, 내가 흥미를 느끼는 것이므로 interested가 적절

8 (1) 그리스도에 대한 그 영화는 정말 감동적이었다.
▶ 영화가 감동을 느끼게 하는 것이므로 현재분사가 적절
(2) 그녀의 눈은 눈물로 가득 찼다.
▶ 〈be filled with〉 '~로 가득 차다'

9-10 큐피드 상은 정말 흥미로운 것이다. 이 유명한 동상은 많은 사람들의 방문을 받는다. 큐피드는 사랑의 신으로 알려져 있다. 내 동생은 작년에 그곳을 방문했다. 그는 큐피드처럼 화살을 쏘는 척했다. 그는 큐피드의 사진을 많이 찍었다. 그는 아직도 그때 그 조각상과 같이 찍은 사진들을 가지고 있다. 그 사진들은 볼 때마다 그를 미소 짓게 만든다.

9 ▶ (B) 조각상이 방문하는 것이 아니라 방문을 받는 것이므로 is visited가 되어야 함

10 ▶ 사진은 찍히는 것이므로 taken이 되어야 하고, 수식어구를 동반한 분사는 명사 뒤에서 명사를 수식하므로 the photos taken with the statue가 적절

Unit 08

1 명사 (I)

EXERCISE

P.99

A 1 tomatoes 2 Vancouver 3 salt
4 pianos 5 memories 6 teeth
7 are

B 1 glasses 2 wives 3 boxes
4 puppies 5 boys 6 deer
7 geese, oxen 8 feet

C 1 snow 2 Mathematics
3 cars 4 dishes
5 time 6 O
7 women

C 1 snow는 셀 수 없는 명사
2 Mathematics는 -s가 항상 붙는 학과명(수학)
3 〈two+복수 명사〉
4 〈There are+복수 명사〉, 〈a lot of(많은)+셀 수 있는 명사의 복수형〉
5 time(시간), times(~배)
7 〈all+셀 수 있는 명사의 복수형〉

Unit 2 명사 (Ⅱ)

EXERCISE

P.101

A 1 wine 2 bread
3 sugar 4 many
5 much 6 sheet
7 pieces 8 Karen's

B 1 a glass of 2 three bottles of
3 a piece of 4 four cups of
5 three cartons of

C 1 much 2 beef
3 sisters' 4 O
5 stories 6 pair
7 O

C 1 〈many+셀 수 있는 명사의 복수형〉, 〈much+셀 수 없는 명사〉
2 beef는 셀 수 없는 명사
3 복수형이 -s로 끝나는 명사의 소유격: sisters'
5 〈two+셀 수 있는 명사의 복수형〉
6 〈a+단수 명사〉

Unit 3 관사

EXERCISE

P.103

A 1 The 2 an 3 an
4 the 5 an 6 a
7 the

B 1 ø 2 ø 3 the
4 the 5 a 6 an

C 1 (c) 2 (d) 3 (a)
4 (b)

R REVIEW TEST

P.104

A 1 the 2 children 3 much
4 the 5 The 6 ø
7 is 8 Jacob's

B 1 ⓓ 2 ⓒ 3 ⓑ
4 ⓐ 5 ⓓ 6 ⓒ 7 ⓐ

C 1 ø 2 the 3 The
4 ø 5 ø 6 a

D 1 The President lives in the White House.
2 My family visits the orphanage once a month.
3 Your gloves are hanging on the clothes rack.
4 It was the first day of the food festival in our town.
5 Jake bought ten pounds of meat for the dinner party.
6 I need an article about the exhibition in Hong Kong.
7 My brother and I don't usually have breakfast.

A 1 책상 위에 있는 가위를 내게 건네줄래?
▶ 수식어(on the desk)의 꾸밈을 받아 의미가 한정된 경우
2 작년에 이 유치원에는 많은 아이들이 있었다.
▶ 〈There were+복수 명사〉
3 나는 저 게임 CD들을 살만큼 많은 돈을 가지고 있지 않다.
▶ 〈much+셀 수 없는 명사〉
4 나는 건강이 인생의 행복을 위해 가장 중요한 요소라고 믿는다.
▶ 〈the+형용사의 최상급〉
5 지구는 태양계에서 태양으로부터 세 번째 있는 행성이다.
▶ 세상에서 단 하나뿐인 지구 앞에 붙는 The가 적절
6 Ellie는 학교 운동장에서 배드민턴 치는 것을 좋아한다.
▶ 운동경기 앞에는 관사를 붙이지 않음
7 정치학은 내게 흥미로운 과목이 아니다.
▶ economics(경제학), mathematics(수학), politics(정치학) 등의 학과명은 단수 취급
8 Jacob의 바지는 그에게 너무 꽉 낀다.
▶ '~의'란 소유를 표현하는 소유격 Jacob's가 적절

B 1 디저트로 케이크 한 조각 어때?
▶ a piece of cake 케이크 한 조각
2 큰 바구니 안에 우산 하나가 있다.
▶ 〈There is+단수 명사〉, 〈an+umbrella(모음으로 시작하는 단어)〉

3 나는 부엌 조리대를 가로질러 달려가는 두 마리의 쥐를 보았다.
▶ mouse의 복수형은 mice

4 경제학은 그가 대학생이었을 때 그의 전공과목이었다.
▶ 과목명은 단수 취급, 대학 때는 과거

5 너는 대개 몇 시에 일하러 가니?
▶ 〈go to work〉 '일하러 가다'

6 나는 지금까지 15개 이상의 도시를 방문해 왔다.
▶ 〈자음+y〉로 끝나면 -y를 -i로 고치고 -es

7 그녀는 매일 두 병의 포도 주스를 산다.
▶ bottle로 셀 수 있는 것은 보기 중에서 juice와 water인데 water 자체는 셀 수 없으므로 grape juice가 적절

C 1 나는 우유 대신에 키위 주스를 원한다.
▶ 주스는 셀 수 없으므로 부정관사를 쓰지 않음

2 나의 사촌은 학교 관현악단에서 바이올린을 연주한다.
▶ 〈play+the+악기〉 '~을 연주하다'

3 그 가게 진열창에 있는 빨간 모자는 멋져 보인다.
▶ 수식어(in the shop window)의 꾸밈을 받아 한정된 단어 앞에는 the를 사용

4 점심 먹으러 나갈까요?
▶ 식사 앞에는 관사가 쓰이지 않음

5 미술관에 가는 데 버스로 얼마나 걸릴까요?
▶ 〈by + 탈 것〉 '~로'
eg) by bus (버스로), by car (자동차로) 등

6 너는 하루에 몇 시간 자니?
▶ a day '하루에'

D 1 대통령은 백악관에 산다
▶ 백악관은 미국에 하나뿐인 건물이므로 the가 적절

2 우리 가족은 한 달에 한 번씩 고아원에 방문한다.
▶ 〈once a month〉 '한 달에 한 번', per(~마다) = a

3 너의 장갑은 옷걸이에 걸려 있어.
▶ gloves(장갑)는 복수이므로 are가 적절

4 우리 마을 음식 축제의 첫날이었다.
▶ 서수 앞에는 정관사 the가 적절

5 Jake는 저녁 파티를 위해서 10파운드의 고기를 샀다.
▶ 셀 수 없는 명사는 pound, kilogram, gram 등의 단위를 사용해서 세므로 pounds가 적절

6 나는 홍콩에 있는 전시회에 대한 기사가 필요하다.
▶ article은 첫소리가 모음으로 발음되므로 an이 적절

7 남동생과 나는 보통 아침을 먹지 않는다.
▶ breakfast, lunch, dinner 등의 식사 이름 앞에는 관사를 붙이지 않음

FURTHER STUDY

P.106

A (1) Italy (2) Italians
(3) juice (4) were

B 1 six bottles of water
2 Beijing, China, by plane
3 two loaves of bread
4 on foot

A

나는 이탈리아를 방문할 때마다 노천카페에 매료된다. 많은 이탈리아인들은 그곳에서 친구들과 이야기하는 것을 즐긴다. 그들은 문화, 예술, 영화, 음식 그리고 스포츠와 같은 생활의 다양한 것들에 대하여 이야기한다. 나는 그들과 함께 디저트를 먹고 주스를 마시고 싶다. 또 다른 볼거리는 역사적인 사건(특히 중세 시대)을 기념하는 민속의상을 입고 하는 퍼레이드일 것이다. 대부분의 이탈리아 도시들은 수세기 전에 만들어졌고, 그래서 이탈리아 곳곳에는 기념해야 할 전투나 역사적 사건이 있다.

(1) 나라 이름 앞에는 대부분 관사를 붙이지 않음. 단, the USA나 the Philippines처럼 여러 주가 하나의 나라, 또는 여러 군도가 하나의 나라가 된 경우 the를 붙임

(2) 〈Many+복수 명사(Italians)〉

(3) juice는 셀 수 없는 명사이므로 a를 삭제

(4) Most Italian towns는 복수이므로 were가 적절

B 1 Angela는 물 여섯 병을 사려고 자동차로 슈퍼마켓에 갈 것이다.

2 이번 주 일요일, Ben은 회의에 참석하려고 중국의 베이징에 갈 것이다. 그는 비행기로 거기에 갈 것이다.

3 Donald는 자전거를 타고 빵집에 가서 빵 두 덩어리를 살 것이다.

4 Edward는 Christine을 만나러 시청에 갈 것이다. 그는 시청이 집과 가깝기 때문에 걸어서 갈 것이다.

MUST-KNOW

P.107

▶ 셀 수 있는 명사의 복수형 변화
① colors ② boxes ③ buses
④ flies ⑤ keys ⑥ wives
⑦ children ⑧ men ⑨ sheep
⑩ safes

▶ 셀 수 없는 물질명사를 세는 단위
① three loaves of
② ten bottles of
③ three pounds of

WRAP-UP TEST

P.108

1	ⓒ	2	ⓑ
3	ⓓ seven men and six women		
4	ⓓ	5	ⓑ
6	money, peace, bread, Jones		
7	not mine		
8	(1) a loaf		(2) five slices
	(3) three pounds		(4) a bottle
9	ⓓ	10	ⓒ

1 ▶ ⓒ tomato - tomatoes

2 · 너는 여기 처음 도착한 사람이다.
· 콩코드는 한 시간에 약 2,400킬로미터를 날아갔다.
▶ 〈the+서수〉, 〈an hour〉 '한 시간에'

3 A 너의 반에는 몇 명이 있니?
B 남자 일곱 명과 여자 여섯 명이 있어.
▶ ⓓ seven men and six women이 적절

4 ⓐ 지구는 태양 주변을 돈다.
ⓑ 나는 프랑스의 파리에서 칠 일 동안 머물 것이다.
ⓒ 나는 오늘 학교에 일찍 가야 했다.
ⓓ 나는 책을 한 권 빌렸다. 그 책은 "바람과 함께 사라지다"이다.
▶ ⓓ 앞에 나온 책을 받는 것이므로 A book이 아니라 The book이 돼야 함

5 ⓐ Susan은 슈퍼마켓에서 많은 주스를 샀다.
ⓑ 내 커피에 설탕을 조금도 넣지 말아 주세요.
ⓒ 나는 수필을 쓸 종이 두 장이 필요하다.
ⓓ Ben은 고기를 채소와 같이 먹는 것을 좋아한다.
▶ ⓐ much juices → much juice ⓒ two piece → two pieces ⓓ meats → meat

6 ▶ money(물질명사), peace(추상명사), bread(물질명사), Jones(고유명사)

7 A 네 가방이 멋지구나.
B 고마워, 하지만 내 것이 아니야.
▶ my bag = mine

8 (1) 빵 한 덩어리를 여덟 조각으로 자르시오.
▶ a loaf of bread 빵 한 덩어리
(2) 각각의 접시 위에 치즈 다섯 장을 놓으시오.
▶ five slices of cheese 치즈 다섯 장
(3) 3인분의 스테이크를 만들기 위해, 우선 3파운드의 쇠고기를 준비하시오.
▶ three pounds of beef 3파운드의 쇠고기
(4) 상을 차리고 와인 한 병을 따세요.
▶ a bottle of wine 와인 한 병

9-10 고래는 바다에 살며 물고기처럼 헤엄친다. 하지만, 고래는 물고기가 아니다. 고래는 왜 포유동물일까? 첫째, 다른 모든 포유동물처럼 고래는 온혈동물이다. 둘째, 고래는 폐를 통해서 공기를 들이마신다. 하지만 물고기는 아가미를 통해 물을 들이마시면서 호흡한다. 마지막으로 고래는 모유를 먹는 새끼를 낳는다. 물고기는 알을 낳고, 어미는 새끼에게 먹이를 주지 않는다.

9 ▶ (A) 일반적인 고래들을 지칭하는 것이므로 Whales가 적절

10 ▶ (B) air는 셀 수 없는 명사이므로 air가 적절 (C) egg는 셀 수 있는 명사이며, 알을 여러 개 낳으므로 eggs가 적절

Unit 09

Unit 1 인칭/지시/의문대명사

EXERCISE

P.111

A 1 your 2 them 3 us
4 her 5 My 6 his
7 It is 8 Those 9 It
10 it

B 1 He 2 She 3 them
4 They 5 Its 6 They
7 We

C 1 What 2 Who 3 Which
4 Who 5 What 6 Whose

Unit 2 소유/재귀대명사

EXERCISE

P.113

A 1 Ours 2 yours 3 hers
4 yours 5 mine 6 his
7 theirs

B 1 yourself 2 myself 3 ourselves
4 himself 5 herself 6 yourselves

C 1 beside myself 2 by yourself
3 of itself 4 between ourselves

Unit 3 부정대명사 (I)

EXERCISE

P.115

A 1 Every 2 some 3 All
4 Every 5 any 6 Each
7 either

B 1 Both 2 Every 3 All
4 either 5 some 6 any
7 neither

C 1 word　2 O　3 Some
4 were　5 O　6 bags

C 1 〈every+단수 명사〉
3 긍정문에서는 some이 적절, 「〈some+복수 동사〉 '어떤 사람들은'+〈others+복수 동사〉 '다른 사람들은'」, some이 사람을 의미할 때는 복수임
4 All 뒤에 나오는 명사에 동사의 수를 일치시킴, 사람을 의미할 때는 복수 취급
6 〈All+셀 수 있는 명사의 복수형〉

Unit 4 부정대명사 (Ⅱ)

EXERCISE

P.117

A 1 it　2 One　3 the other
4 each other　5 the others

B 1 no　2 the other　3 Most
4 one another　5 One　6 another

C 1 One, the others　2 Some, the others
3 No

R REVIEW TEST

P.118

A 1 both　2 of itself　3 us
4 mine　5 child　6 it
7 some

B 1 ⓒ　2 ⓓ　3 ⓑ
4 ⓓ　5 ⓒ　6 ⓑ　7 ⓒ

C 1 herself　2 any　3 All
4 the others　5 another　6 his
7 It

D 1 My father and I go to watch a baseball game every weekend.
2 Do it yourself. I don't have enough time to help you.
3 There are three balls. One is for me, another is for Daniel, and the other is for Jake.
4 Every girl in my school is expected to wear a skirt.
5 Some birds sat on eggs in their nests.
6 I found these cool links about cartoons on my friend's blog.
7 Who left the door open?

A 1 Ben은 여름방학에 독일과 이탈리아에 갔다.
▶ 〈both A and B〉 '둘 다'
2 한밤중에 문이 저절로 열렸다.
▶ 〈of itself〉 '저절로'
3 그 문제는 우리 스스로 해결하기에는 너무 어렵다.
▶ 〈for+목적격〉
4 이 양말은 내 것일 리가 없어. 냄새가 너무 지독해.
▶ '나의 것'= 소유대명사(mine)
5 모든 아이들은 테이프를 들을 준비가 되었다.
▶ 〈every+단수 명사〉
6 Jim은 멋진 스카프를 샀다. 그는 그것을 내일 Julie에게 줄 것이다.
▶ 앞에서 언급한 스카프를 지칭하므로 it이 적절
7 너는 아르바이트를 하면 돈을 벌 것이다.
▶ 긍정문이므로 some이 적절

B 1 그곳에 가는 데 약 5시간 걸린다.
▶ 거리를 나타내는 비인칭주어 it이 적절
2 서랍에 초가 있니? 불이 나갔어.
▶ '약간의'라는 뜻의 수량형용사, 의문문이므로 any가 적절
3 사고와 관련한 너의 설명은 그녀의 설명과 일치하지 않는다.
▶ '그녀의 것'이란 의미의 소유대명사 hers가 적절
4 디저트를 마음껏 드세요.
▶ 명령문의 주어는 you이므로 재귀대명사는 yourself가 적절
5 그는 딸이 둘 있다. 한 명은 간호사이고, 한 명은 선생님이다.
▶ 두 명 중 나머지 한 명은 the other
6 사람은 다른 사람을 탓하기 전에 자신의 실수를 먼저 생각해야 한다.
▶ 불특정한 일반인은 One
7 어떤 사람들은 다른 사람들을 존경하고, 또 어떤 사람들은 존경을 받는다.
▶ 일부 중 나머지는 others

C 1 Shelly는 혼자서 간신히 모든 책을 집으로 가져갔다.
▶ 〈by oneself〉 '혼자서'
2 나는 학교에 대한 어떤 불만도 없다.
▶ 〈not ~ any〉
3 우리가 도착했을 때는 모든 표가 매진되었다.
▶ '모두'란 의미가 되어야 하므로 All이 적절
4 나의 반 친구 중 몇몇은 공부를 하고 있었고, 나머지 전부는 얘기를 하고 있었다.
▶ 한정된 범위에서 일부는 some, 나머지 전부는 the others
5 이 스커트는 너무 작아요. 다른 것을 보여주시겠어요?
▶ '또 다른 하나'란 의미의 another
6 Kenny는 항상 내가 자신의 밥값을 내기를 원한다.
▶ 명사 앞에서 '그의'라는 의미의 소유격 his가 적절
7 가장 가까운 우체국까지 4마일이다.
▶ 시간, 거리를 나타낼 때는 비인칭주어 it이 적절

D 1 우리 아버지와 나는 주말마다 야구를 보러 간다.
▶ 〈every+단수 명사〉

2 너 스스로 그 일을 해라. 나는 너를 도울 충분한 시간이 없다.
▶ 명령문의 주어 you와 목적어가 같으므로 재귀대명사 yourself가 적절

3 세 개의 공이 있다. 하나는 나를 위한 것이고, 또 다른 하나는 Daniel을 위한 것이고 나머지 하나는 Jake를 위한 것이다.
▶ 요소가 셋일 때 하나는 one, 또 다른 하나는 another, 나머지 하나는 the other

4 학교에 있는 모든 소녀는 치마를 입을 것으로 예상된다.
▶ 〈every+단수 명사+단수 동사〉

5 어떤 새들은 자신들의 둥지에서 알을 품었다.
▶ 명사 앞에서 소유를 나타낼 때는 소유격 their가 와야 함

6 나는 친구의 블로그에서 만화에 관한 좋은 링크를 찾았다.
▶ 복수 명사(links)가 왔으므로 this는 these가 되어야 함

7 누가 문을 열었니?
▶ 의문사가 주어이므로 주격 Who가 적절

FURTHER STUDY

P.120

A (1) One (2) themselves
(3) they are (4) some

B 1 He is weak for his age.
2 Children play among themselves.
3 Is there any life on Jupiter?
4 How long does it take to get to the airport?
5 I have two brothers. One is tall, and the other is short.

A

아일랜드 방문객 사이에서 가장 인기 있는 기념품 중 하나는 곤봉이다. 곤봉은 지팡이이고, 19세기에 사람들은 지역 장터에서 싸움을 하고 자신을 보호하는 데 그것을 이용했다. 그것은 길고, 단단한 나무로 만들어졌다. 곤봉은 참나무로 만들어지곤 했지만, 요즘 그것들은 참나무 대신에 서양호랑가시나무나 서양물푸레나무, 산사나무로 만들어진다. 여러분이 아일랜드에 갔을 때, 어떤 가게에서는 짧은 가짜 곤봉을 팔기 때문에 곤봉을 주의해서 사야 한다.

(1) 〈one of the 최상급+복수 명사+단수 동사〉 '가장 ~한 것 중 하나'
(2) 주어가 people이므로 themselves가 되어야 함
(3) Shillelaghs인 복수를 지칭하므로 they are가 되어야 함
(4) 긍정문에서는 막연한 수량 중 약간을 지칭하는 some이 와야 함

B 1 주격 대명사 He와 소유격 his를 이용
2 주어와 목적어가 같으므로 재귀대명사를 이용
3 의문문에는 some이 아닌 any를 이용
4 시간, 거리를 나타내는 문장에는 비인칭주어 it을 이용
5 둘 중 하나는 one, 나머지 하나는 the other를 이용

MUST-KNOW

P.121

▶ 인칭대명사 정리
① mine ② yours
③ his ④ itself
⑤ us ⑥ yourselves

▶ 부정대명사 정리
① knows ② is
③ is ④ the other
⑤ another ⑥ the others

WRAP-UP TEST

P.122

1 It 2 ⓑ 3 ⓒ yours
4 ⓓ 5 ⓓ 6 ⓑ, ⓒ
7 Neither of them gave me any advice.
8 (1) Which (2) Whom
(3) Whose (4) Who
9 Their 10 ⓑ

1 · 점점 어두워지고 있다.
· 7시 10분 전이다.
· 어제는 날씨가 험악했다.
▶ 명암, 시간, 날씨를 나타내는 비인칭주어 it

2 ⓐ 사람은 노인을 존중해야 한다.
ⓑ 나는 가방이 단 하나 있는데, 그것을 잃어버렸다.
ⓒ 누구에게도 이 문을 여는 것은 허락되지 않는다.
ⓓ 너는 파란색 차를 선호하지만, 나는 검은색 차를 좋아한다.
▶ ⓐ 부정대명사 ⓑ 수량형용사(하나의) ⓒ 부정대명사 ⓓ 부정대명사

3 A 엄마, 장갑을 찾을 수가 없어요. 장갑을 본 적이 있나요?
B 이것들은 너의 것이니 아니면 네 형의 것이니?
▶ ⓒ '너의 것'이라는 의미의 소유대명사(yours)가 적절

4 ⓐ 그녀는 스스로 자동차를 수리했다.
ⓑ 너는 너 자신을 믿어야 한다.
ⓒ 그는 회의에 오지 않았다. 그는 제정신이 아니었다.
ⓓ 그들은 이번 주말에 우리를 방문할 것이다. 나는 그들을 위해 호텔방을 예약할 것이다.
▶ ⓓ 내가 그들을 위해 방을 예약하는 것이므로 themselves가 아니라 them이 되어야 함

5 ⓐ 산의 모든 나무가 불탔다.
ⓑ 저 케이크와 차를 좀 드실래요?
ⓒ 몇몇 페이지는 찢겨나갔고, 다른 페이지에는 낙서가 되어 있었다.
ⓓ 그는 두 권의 책을 썼다. 한 권은 자신의 삶에 대한 것이고 나머지 한 권은 자신의 업적에 대한 것이다.

▶ ⓓ 두 개 중 하나는 one 나머지 하나는 the other이므로 other 가 아니라 the other가 돼야 함

6 각각의/모든 학생은 기숙사에서 자신의 방을 갖게 될 것이다.

▶ 〈each, every+단수 명사〉

7 Jane은 나에게 어떤 충고도 해주지 않았다. James는 나에게 어떤 충고도 해주지 않았다.

→ 그들 둘 다 나에게 어떤 충고도 해주지 않았다.

▶ 〈neither of them〉 '둘 다 ~ 아니다'

8 (1) 나는 초콜릿 케이크와 딸기 케이크를 만들었어. 어떤 것을 먹을래?

▶ which 어떤 것

(2) 나는 미술관에서 너를 보았어. 누구랑 갔었니?

▶ 〈go with+whom〉 누구와 함께 가다, 전치사 with의 목적어

(3) 뒤뜰에 새 자전거가 있어. 누구의 자전거니?

▶ 〈whose+명사(bicycle)〉 누구의 자전거

(4) 누가 이 담장을 페인트칠했니?

▶ who 누가(의문사가 주어)

9-10 뾰족뒤쥐는 겨우 3인치까지 자라는 매우 작은 포유류이다. 그들은 갈색이나 회색 털을 가지고 있다. 그들의 털은 여름에는 흐려지고, 겨울에는 진해진다. 그들은 작은 곤충이나 적은 양의 씨앗, 과일을 먹는다. 그들을 보는 것은 매우 어렵다. 운 좋게도 내 친구와 나는 지난밤 거실에서 뾰족뒤쥐를 하나 보았다. 내 친구는 그것을 잡고 싶어 했다. 하지만 뾰족뒤쥐는 해롭지 않기 때문에 그가 그렇게 하기 전에 내가 그를 막았다.

9 ▶ (A) '그들의 털'이라는 뜻이므로 Their가 적절

10 ▶ (B) 거실에서 본 그 뾰족뒤쥐를 지칭하므로 it이 적절

Unit 10

1 형용사

EXERCISE

P.125

A 1 loud 2 A lot of
3 much 4 heavy
5 few 6 something new
7 any 8 a few

B 1 any 2 anything wrong
3 O 4 O
5 many 6 exciting
7 few

C 1 Tina is a cute and fun girl.
2 There were a few students in the classroom.
3 The girl is looking for something delicious.

B 1 부정문이므로 any가 적절
2 -thing으로 끝나는 단어는 형용사가 뒤에서 수식
5 〈many+셀 수 있는 명사의 복수형〉
6 온라인 게임이 신 나게 만드는 것이므로 exciting이 적절
7 books가 왔으므로 few가 적절

2 부사

EXERCISE

P.127

A 1 enviously 2 hard
3 late 4 well
5 quietly 6 sometimes eat
7 usually have 8 is often

B 1 easily 2 loudly
3 highly 4 dangerously
5 carefully

C 1 Swimming is often called the perfect exercise.
2 Do you usually have a lot of homework?
3 I have never been to Scotland.
4 The woman drove her car too fast.

3 비교급과 최상급 (규칙, 불규칙)

EXERCISE

P.129

A 1 better 2 warmer
3 dirtier 4 the prettiest
5 worse 6 the biggest
7 the most

B 1 the smallest 2 later
3 less expensive 4 the tallest
5 O 6 the thinnest
7 quicker

C 1 more educational 2 better
3 the coldest 4 longer
5 more easily 6 the funniest
7 busier

B 1 small의 최상급은 smallest
2 '더 늦게'라는 의미이므로 later가 적절
3 than 앞에는 비교급이 쓰여야 하므로 less expensive가 적절
4 셋 이상의 대상 중에서 가장 큰 것이므로 tallest가 적절
6 〈단모음 + 단자음〉으로 끝나는 단어는 자음을 하나 더 붙이고 -est를 붙이므로 the thinnest가 적절
7 quick의 비교급은 quicker

비교급과 최상급 (기타)

EXERCISE

P.131

A 1 darker 2 the better
3 as smart as 4 not as
5 much 6 twice as fast as
7 the best

B 1 possible 2 the more
3 as much as 4 as easy as
5 less 6 the laziest

C 1 The longer, the happier
2 shorter and shorter
3 not older than
4 the hardest class (that) I have ever taken
5 twice as large as

B 1 〈as+원급+as possible〉
2 〈the+비교급 ~, the+비교급 ...〉
3 〈배수사+as+원급+as〉
4 〈as+원급+as〉
5 〈비교급+than+절〉
6 〈최상급+(that)+주어+have ever p.p.〉

REVIEW TEST

P.132

A 1 well 2 terrible
3 longer than 4 a lot more
5 certainly informative
6 as 7 long

B 1 ⓐ 2 ⓑ 3 ⓓ
4 ⓓ 5 ⓒ 6 ⓒ 7 ⓑ

C 1 the worst 2 the more
3 calmer 4 the cleanest
5 fewer 6 cheaper, cheaper
7 farther

D 1 Bella is the nicest girl I've ever known.
2 We are terribly sorry for this inconvenience.
3 The red shirt looks better on you than the white one.
4 Riding a motorcycle is not as easy as riding a bike.
5 Teresa and I can often see these plays on Broadway.
6 The dentist was twice as busy as usual, so I couldn't make an appointment.
7 Drinking too much Coke is bad for your health.

A 1 그 어린 소년은 영어를 매우 잘한다.
▶ speak를 수식하는 부사 well이 적절
2 그는 이기적이다. 그래서 친구들과의 관계가 형편없다.
▶ 주어를 보충 설명해 주는 형용사 terrible이 적절
3 여성이 남성보다 더 오래 산다.
▶ 여성과 남성이라는 두 대상을 비교하므로 longer than이 적절
4 이번 일이 지난번 일보다 훨씬 더 어렵다.
▶ 이번 일과 지난번 일이라는 두 대상을 비교하므로 a lot more가 적절
5 그의 강의는 확실히 유익하다.
▶ 부사가 형용사를 수식할 때는 보통 형용사 앞에 오므로 certainly informative가 적절
6 가르치는 것은 배우는 것만큼 많은 노력이 필요하다.
▶ 〈as+원급+as〉
7 가능한 한 오래 수업에 집중하려고 노력해라.
▶ 〈as+원급+as possible〉

B 1 그들은 부지런한 노동자가 아니다.
▶ 명사를 수식하는 형용사 diligent가 적절
2 그는 우리가 생각했던 것보다 더 나쁜 점수를 받았다.
▶ than 앞에는 비교급이 와야 하므로 worse가 적절
3 Millet는 다른 예술가들보다 훨씬 더 평화로운 방법으로 자연을 표현했다.
▶ 뒤에 than이 왔으므로 앞에 비교급이 와야 함. much는 비교급을 강조
4 그는 우리 팀에서 가장 유능한 사람이다.
▶ 3음절 단어의 최상급은 most를 붙이며 뒤에 guy가 있으므로 the most intelligent가 적절
5 그 문제는 어렵지 않았기 때문에 나는 전보다 쉽게 질문에 답할 수 있었다.
▶ 동사를 꾸며주는 부사가 필요하므로 more easily가 적절
6 네가 생각한 것의 3배 많은 돈이 들 것이다.
▶ 〈as+원급+as〉, 셀 수 없는 명사 앞에는 much가 적절
7 그녀는 지난밤보다 덜 우울해 보인다.
▶ than이 있으므로 비교급 less가 적절

C 1 그 책은 형편없다. 그것은 내가 읽은 것 중 최악의 책이다.
▶ 〈최상급+(that)+주어+have ever p.p.〉
2 네가 빨리 운전할수록 너는 더 많은 연료를 사용할 것이다.
▶ 〈the 비교급 ~, the 비교급 …〉
3 폭풍 후, 오늘의 바다는 어제의 바다보다 훨씬 더 고요하다.
▶ than 앞에는 비교급 calmer가 적절
4 태양에너지는 난방용으로 가장 깨끗한 연료 중 하나이다.

▶ 〈one of the+최상급+복수 명사〉

5 다행히 우리는 생각했던 것보다 더 적은 실수를 했다.
▶ than이 왔으므로 비교급 fewer가 적절

6 컴퓨터는 새로운 기술의 발명 덕분에 점점 더 싸지고 있다.
▶ 〈비교급+and+비교급〉

7 사무실에서 공장까지의 거리는 내가 생각한 것보다 더 멀다.
▶ 〈비교급+than+절〉

D 1 Bella는 지금까지 내가 알아온 소녀 중 가장 멋진 소녀이다.
▶ 〈최상급+단수 명사+주어+have ever p.p.〉 지금까지 ~한 중 가장 …한

2 불편하게 해드려서 대단히 죄송합니다.
▶ 형용사를 수식하는 것은 부사이므로 terribly가 적절

3 빨간색 셔츠가 하얀색 셔츠보다 너에게 더 잘 어울린다.
▶ 두 개의 대상을 비교하고, than이 있으므로 better가 적절

4 오토바이를 타는 것은 자전거를 타는 것만큼 쉽지 않다.
▶ 〈A is not so(as) 원급 as B〉

5 Teresa와 나는 자주 브로드웨이에서 이 연극들을 볼 수 있다.
▶ 〈조동사+빈도부사〉

6 그 치과의사는 평소보다 두 배나 바빠서 나는 예약을 할 수 없었다.
▶ 〈배수사+as+원급+as〉

7 콜라를 너무 많이 마시는 것은 당신의 건강에 나쁘다.
▶ 〈much+셀 수 없는 명사〉

FURTHER STUDY

P.134

A (1) better (2) strongly
(3) usually choose (4) can often

B 1 less expensive 2 the cheapest
3 as expensive as 4 cheaper

A

> 연구에 따르면, 만약 학생들이 악기 연주를 배우면 그들은 다른 학생들보다 더 나은 시험 점수를 받는 경향이 있다고 한다. 그래서 많은 미국의 부모들은 자녀들이 악기를 배우도록 강하게 부추긴다. 그들은 보통 밴드 악기, 현악기, 피아노 중에서 선택한다. 만약 학생들이 밴드 악기를 연주할 수 있게 되면 종종 학교의 행진 악대에 참여할 수 있고, 축구 경기나 퍼레이드에서 연주할 수 있다. 만약 그들이 바이올린이나 첼로 같은 현악기를 배우면 그들은 학교와 지역사회 오케스트라 프로그램에 참여할 수 있다.

(1) 두 개의 대상을 비교, than이 있으므로 better가 적절
(2) 동사를 수식하는 부사 strongly가 적절
(3) 〈빈도부사+일반동사〉
(4) 〈조동사+빈도부사〉

B 1 Camry는 소나타보다 덜 비싸다.
2 Explorer는 목록에서 가장 싼 차이다.
3 S40은 Camry만큼 비싸다.
4 소나타는 Z3보다 싸다.

MUST-KNOW

P.135

▶ 형용사를 만드는 접미사

① responsible ② believable
③ useful ④ useless
⑤ dangerous ⑥ various
⑦ curious ⑧ healthy
⑨ historic ⑩ creative
⑪ cultural ⑫ global
⑬ typical ⑭ western
⑮ southern ⑯ lovely

▶ 비교급과 최상급 정리

① shorter ② shortest
③ larger ④ largest
⑤ nicer ⑥ nicest
⑦ bigger ⑧ biggest
⑨ hotter ⑩ hottest
⑪ busier ⑫ busiest
⑬ happier ⑭ happiest
⑮ more famous ⑯ most famous
⑰ more interesting ⑱ most interesting
⑲ worse ⑳ worst
㉑ less ㉒ least
㉓ older ㉔ elder

W WRAP-UP TEST

P.136

1 ⓓ
2 cold something → something cold
3 ⓑ 4 ⓒ 5 ⓑ
6 more crowded, the most crowded
7 ⓐ
8 (1) Noah always skips breakfast.
(2) What do you usually do on weekends?
(3) Your advice is sometimes really helpful
9 the longest word 10 ⓐ

1 ▶ ⓓ busy – busier – busiest

2 A 엄마, 나 정말 목말라요. 시원한 마실 것이 필요해요.
B 냉장고 안을 보렴.
▶ -thing으로 끝나는 명사는 형용사가 뒤에서 수식: cold something → something cold

3 ⓐ 내 수학 성적이 점점 좋아지고 있다.

ⓑ 너의 책은 그녀의 것보다 두 배만큼 두껍다.
ⓒ 더 많이 가질수록 더 많이 나눠 줘야 한다.
ⓓ Tina는 지금까지 내가 본 소녀 중 가장 아름다운 소녀이다.
▶ ⓑ 〈as+원급+as〉: as thicker as → as thick as

4 ⓐ 그들은 좀처럼 경기에서 이겨본 적이 없다.
ⓑ 그를 최근에 만난 적이 있니?
ⓒ 독수리는 높이 난다.
ⓓ 그 기차는 일찍 도착했다.
▶ highly '매우', high '높이'

5 · 나는 해야 할 일이 많다.
· 소금이 거의 남아 있지 않다.
· 나는 우리 가족 중 가장 적은 선물을 받았다.
▶ 〈many+셀 수 있는 명사의 복수형〉, 〈little+셀 수 없는 명사〉, 〈fewest+셀 수 있는 명사의 복수형〉

6 Times Square에는 사람이 많았다.
(1) Times Square에는 Central Park보다 더 사람이 많았다.
(2) Times Square에는 가장 사람이 많았다.

7 ⓐ Daniel은 Robin만큼 빠르지 않다.
≠ Daniel은 Robin보다 빠르다.
ⓑ 가능한 한 빨리 수영해라.
ⓒ 그녀는 발레를 잘 한다.
ⓓ Danny는 Tony보다 영리하지 않다.

8 ▶ 〈빈도부사+be동사〉, 〈일반동사+빈도부사〉

9-10 영어에서 가장 긴 단어를 들어 본 적이 있나요? 그 단어는 폐의 질병인데, 45개의 알파벳으로 되어 있어요. 이것은 "pneumonoultamicroscopicsilicovolcanoconiosis"라고 불려요. 하지만 우리는 이 단어를 사용하지 않아요.
가장 짧은 단어는 "I"와 "a"라고 여겨져요. 이 두 단어는 우리의 일상생활에서 항상 사용돼요.

9 ▶ (A) 가장 긴 단어 〈the longest word〉, long의 최상급

10 ▶ (B) 가장 짧은 단어들 〈the shortest words〉, short의 최상급

Unit 11

Unit 1 장소, 방향 전치사

EXERCISE P.139

A 1 up 2 between 3 out of
4 into 5 near 6 above
7 below

B 1 at 2 on 3 in
4 in 5 at 6 on

C 1 behind 2 next to/beside/by
3 from 4 under 5 in front of
6 across 7 into

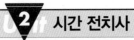

Unit 2 시간 전치사

EXERCISE P.141

A 1 in 2 on 3 at
4 on 5 at 6 on
7 at

B 1 around 2 until 3 since
4 during 5 by 6 for

C 1 on Easter Day 2 by 6 (o'clock)
3 in the afternoon 4 before Christmas
5 for 5 days 6 from 9 am

Unit 3 기타 전치사

EXERCISE P.143

A 1 around 2 with 3 for
4 for 5 through 6 with

B 1 around 2 about 3 for
4 by 5 with 6 through

C 1 by card 2 by train
3 for your health 4 to them
5 along this line
6 on(about) my summer vacation

R REVIEW TEST P.144

A 1 about 2 during 3 until 4 under
5 for 6 among 7 with

B 1 ⓓ 2 ⓐ 3 ⓑ
4 ⓓ 5 ⓓ 6 ⓑ 7 ⓒ

C 1 for 2 about 3 at 4 on
5 near 6 into 7 with

D 1 What should I pack for my backpacking trip to India?
2 Almost every day from June to August, I went to the gym to work out.
3 You should give your paper to me before class.
4 He took off his coat and laid it down on the sofa.
5 I saw a cat playing with a small ball near the door.

6 I want you to buy some snacks at the store across from the school entrance.
7 Kelly visited New York during the winter vacation. She went there by train.

A 1 나의 남동생은 외계인에 관한 영화 보는 것을 좋아한다.
▶ '~에 관한'이라는 의미의 about
2 나는 휴일 동안에 중간고사를 대비하기 위해 공부해야 한다.
▶ 기간을 나타내는 명사 앞이므로 during이 적절
3 그들은 이번 10월까지 우리와 함께 있을 것이다.
▶ 10월까지 계속됨을 의미하므로 until이 적절
4 미신에 따르면 사다리 아래를 걷는 것은 불운을 가져온다.
▶ '~아래'란 의미의 under가 적절
5 나는 8년 동안 영어 공부를 하고 있다.
▶ 지속된 기간 앞에는 for가 적절
6 Jordan은 자신의 반 학생들 사이에서 매우 인기 있다.
▶ 셋 이상 사이이므로 among이 적절
7 나는 지난주에 여자 친구와 함께 축제에 갔다.
▶ '~와 함께'란 의미의 with가 적절

B 1 그는 2주 후에 서울로 돌아올 것이다.
▶ '~후에'란 의미의 in이 적절
2 나는 당신의 할머니를 위해서 꽃 몇 송이를 샀다.
▶ '~를 위한'이란 의미의 for가 적절
3 당신은 Tolstoy가 쓴 책을 읽은 적이 있어요?
▶ '~ 의해'란 의미의 by가 적절
4 내 남동생과 나는 1월에 태어났다.
▶ 월 앞이므로 in이 적절
5 그 남자는 테이블 옆에 있는 의자에 조용히 앉아 있었다.
▶ '~옆에'라는 의미의 beside가 적절
6 5시쯤에 저의 사무실에 들려 주시겠습니까?
▶ 대략적인 시간을 나타내는 around가 적절
7 어린 소녀들이 커다란 거울 앞에서 발레를 연습하고 있다.
▶ '~앞에서'란 의미의 in front of가 적절

C 1 여러분의 미래를 위해서 열심히 공부하세요!
▶ '~을 위해'란 의미의 for가 적절
2 나는 약 1년 전에 영어 공부를 시작했다.
▶ '약'이란 의미를 대략적인 시간을 나타내는 about이 적절
3 모퉁이에서 오른쪽으로 도세요.
▶ '~에서'란 의미로 장소의 한 지점을 나타내는 at이 적절
4 우리 가족은 일요일마다 교회에 간다.
▶ 요일 앞에서는 전치사 on이 적절
5 개가 뭔가를 먹고 있을 때 개 근처에 가지 마라.
▶ '가까이에'란 의미로 near가 적절
6 John은 필통에 연필을 도로 넣었다.
▶ '~안으로'란 의미로 into가 적절
7 교실에 있는 새로 온 소녀는 자신의 머리카락을 가지고 장난을 쳤다.
▶ '~을 가지고'란 의미로 수단을 나타내는 with가 적절

D 1 인도로 가는 배낭여행을 위해서 무엇을 싸야 할까?
▶ '~로'라는 의미의 방향을 나타내는 to가 적절
2 나는 6월부터 8월까지 거의 매일 운동하러 체육관에 갔다.
▶ 〈from A to B〉 'A부터 B까지'
3 여러분은 수업 전에 저에게 보고서를 제출해야 합니다.
▶ '~에게'란 의미의 전치사가 와야 하므로 to가 적절
4 그는 자신의 코트를 벗어서 소파 위에 놓았다.
▶ 접촉해서 위를 의미하므로 on이 적절
5 나는 문 근처에서 작은 공을 가지고 노는 고양이를 보았다.
▶ '~를 가지고'란 의미로 수단을 나타내는 전치사인 with가 적절
6 나는 네가 학교 정문 맞은편 가게에서 과자를 사 오기를 원한다.
▶ 〈across from〉 '맞은편'
7 Kelly는 겨울 방학 동안 뉴욕을 방문했다. 그녀는 기차를 타고 그곳에 갔다.
▶ 〈by+교통수단〉 '~을 타고'

FURTHER STUDY

P.146

A (1) in (2) in
(3) to (4) with

B 1 brush your teeth after every meal
2 in the library for two hours
3 hand in your homework before noon
4 at a Chinese restaurant in the evening
5 you come down the stairs

A

일요일마다 나는 아침에 일찍 일어나서 개와 함께 한 시간 동안 마을 주변을 조깅을 한다. 조깅 후에 나는 마을에 있는 강 근처의 아름다운 공원에 가서 사람들이 축구하는 것을 구경한다. 집으로 돌아오는 길에 나는 공원 맞은편에 있는 작은 커피숍에 들러서 커피를 마신다. 오후에 나는 대개 휴식을 취하거나 TV를 보면서 시간을 보낸다. 때때로 나는 친구와 함께 영화를 보러 가기도 한다.

(1) 〈in the morning〉 '아침에'
(2) '마을 안에'라는 의미가 되어야 하므로 in이 적절
(3) 〈on one's way back to somewhere〉 '~로 돌아오는 중에'
(4) '~와 함께'라는 의미가 되어야 하므로 with가 적절

MUST-KNOW

P.147

▶ 전치사별 쓰임과 예시

① 연도 ② 후에
③ 위에 ④ 요일
⑤ ~에게 ⑥ ~까지
⑦ ~동안 ⑧ ~를 위해

WRAP-UP TEST

P.148

1 ⓑ 2 on → in 3 ⓒ
4 ⓐ 5 ⓒ 6 ⓓ
7 by/beside 8 (1) by (2) for
9 ⓐ 10 with

1 · 나는 여섯 시간 동안 작은 차 안에 있었다.
· 비행기는 오 분 후에 이륙할 예정입니다.
▶ 〈in+장소〉 '~안에', 〈in+시간〉 '~후에'

2 많은 사람 사이에서 그녀는 나를 쉽게 찾을 수 있었다. 나는 빨간 색 바지를 입고 개와 함께 길을 따라 걷고 있었다.
▶ 〈in+옷〉 '~을 입은': on red pants → in red pants

3 ⓐ 비행기가 구름 위에 있다.
ⓑ 바다 밑에는 많은 생명체가 있다.
ⓒ 그들은 독립기념일에 큰 퍼레이드를 했다.
ⓓ 너는 점심 전에 가방을 싸야 한다.
▶ ⓒ 〈on+특정한 날〉: in Independence Day → on Independence Day

4 ⓐ 그녀는 배를 타고 일본에 갔다.
ⓑ 너는 방과 후에 주로 무엇을 하니?
ⓒ 그는 오염에 관한 연구를 했다.
ⓓ 그들은 정원을 손보느라 바쁘다.
▶ ⓐ 〈by+교통수단〉 '~을 타고' : with → by

5 · 우리 집은 우리 할아버지에 의해 지어졌다.
· 그 소년은 어머니를 위해 멋진 카드를 만들었다.
· 우리는 오전 7시 이후로 도서관에서 공부를 하고 있다.
▶ 〈be built by+행위자〉 '~에 의해 지어지다', 〈for+목적격〉 '~을 위해', 〈현재완료+since+시간〉 '~이후로 …하다'

6 ⓐ 제발 나에게 그것을 주세요.
ⓑ 너에게 무슨 일이 있었니?
ⓒ 그들은 매일 아침 공원에 간다.
ⓓ 약국에 가는 법을 알려 주실래요?
▶ ⓐ 전치사 ⓑ 전치사 ⓒ 전치사 ⓓ to부정사의 to

7 우리는 떡갈나무 옆에 텐트를 쳤다.
▶ next to = beside = by '~옆에'

8 (1) ▶ 〈by+시간〉 '~까지'
(2) ▶ 〈for a long time〉 오랫동안

9-10 나는 네덜란드에 있는 동안 반 고흐 박물관에 갔다. 그는 일생동안 약 천 점의 그림을 그렸다. 나는 박물관에서 "Sun Flowers"와 "Starry Night" 같은 유명한 그림을 볼 수 있었다. 나는 그가 아를에서 고갱과 함께 살았다는 것을 알게 되었다. 고갱이 그를 떠난 후에 그는 자신의 귀를 잘라버렸다.

9 ▶ about 약

10 ▶ 〈with+사람〉: with Gauguin '고갱과 함께'

Unit 12

1 등위접속사

EXERCISE

P.151

A 1 and 2 but 3 or
4 but 5 so 6 so
7 and 8 or

B 1 and 2 or 3 or
4 and

C 1 and 2 but (also) 3 or
4 but 5 nor 6 and

2 명사절을 이끄는 종속접속사

EXERCISE

P.153

A 1 that 2 whether
3 if 4 that
5 whether 6 that
7 if

B 1 that she keeps asking questions
2 that we exercise regularly
3 that Karen always wins first prize

C 1 who he is
2 where Harry was going
3 how you solved the math problem
4 why you left early
5 whether/if he can finish the work by 10 (or not)

3 부사절을 이끄는 종속접속사

EXERCISE

P.155

A 1 If 2 As
3 Unless 4 even though

5 because 6 before
7 until 8 When

B 1 finishes 2 O
3 while/when 4 O
5 unless 6 because of

C 1 because I woke up late
2 If he doesn't leave early
3 Though I made some mistakes

B 1 시간부사절에서는 미래시제 대신에 현재시제를 사용
3 의미상 until(~할 때까지는)보다는 while(동안)이나 when(때)이 적절
5 '모든 사람이 먹을 충분한 간식을 가져오지 못한다면'이라는 뜻이므로 unless가 적절
6 명사구 앞에는 because of가 적절

Unit 4 부사절의 축약 (분사구문)

EXERCISE

P.157

A 1 was 2 Being
3 Finding 4 reads
5 finish 6 Not winning

B 1 As 2 Since
3 Even though 4 When
5 If

C 1 Standing in front of the house
2 Being very scared
3 Buying two of them
4 Finishing my homework

R REVIEW TEST

P.158

A 1 that 2 when 3 since
4 unless 5 until 6 but
7 while

B 1 ⓒ 2 ⓐ 3 ⓑ
4 ⓒ 5 ⓑ 6 ⓒ
7 ⓓ

C 1 if 2 because 3 unless
4 where 5 or 6 after
7 Though

D 1 He won't believe me unless I give him the evidence.
2 Although it was a sudden request, they didn't complain at all.
3 Kelly doesn't remember what she did yesterday.
4 Waking up early, we weren't late for school.
5 You will not pass the exam, unless you study hard.
6 As/When/Before you enter the concert hall, you should check your seat number.
7 Although/Though/Even though it's new, this lap top computer doesn't function properly.

A 1 나는 그가 무죄라고 생각했지만 그는 아니었다.
▶ think의 목적어절을 이끄는 접속사 that이 적절
2 우리는 그들이 언제 올지 모른다.
▶ '언제'라는 의미의 의문사 when이 적절
3 Ryan은 서울에 온 이후로 많은 궁을 방문했다.
▶ '서울에 도착한 이후로'라는 의미이므로 since가 적절
4 방을 청소하지 않는다면 너는 TV를 볼 수 없다.
▶ '방을 청소하지 않는다면'이라는 뜻이므로 unless가 적절
5 날씨가 맑아질 때까지 난 할 수 있는 게 없다.
▶ '~할 때까지'라는 의미가 적절하므로 until이 적절
6 Wanda는 목요일에 발레 수업에 가지만 나는 금요일에 간다.
▶ 전후 문장의 내용이 대조를 이루므로 but이 적절
7 무엇인가를 먹고 있을 때는 말을 해서는 안 된다.
▶ '먹는 동안'이라는 뜻이므로 while이 적절

B 1 지난밤에 눈이 많이 내려서 나는 스키 타러 간다.
▶ 인과관계를 나타내는 접속사 so가 적절
2 오늘, 아침에는 비가 내렸지만 오후에는 맑았다.
▶ 전후 문장의 내용이 대조를 이루므로 but이 적절
3 기차가 조금 후에 떠나기 때문에 나는 서두르고 있다.
▶ 원인을 나타내는 절을 이끄는 접속사는 because가 적절
4 우리는 극장에 들어가기 전에 휴대 전화를 꺼야 한다.
▶ '들어가기 전에'라는 뜻이므로 before가 적절
5 너는 이 컴퓨터와 저 컴퓨터 중 어느 쪽을 원하니?
▶ 선택의문문에는 선택의 접속사 or가 적절
6 Eric의 어린 남동생은 장난감 자동차와 로봇 둘 다 갖고 싶어 한다.
▶ 'A와 B 둘 다'라는 의미의 〈both A and B〉 구문
7 그는 난로 앞에 앉아 있지만 매우 추웠다.
▶ '~임에도 불구하고'라는 뜻의 Although가 적절

C 1 네가 싫어하지 않는다면 너와 함께 가고 싶다.
▶ '만약 ~라면'이라는 뜻이므로 if가 적절

2 그 연극은 모든 연령을 위한 것이어서 Mary는 여동생을 연극에 데려갔다.
▶ 이유를 표현하는 절을 이끄는 접속사 because가 적절

3 너는 병원에 가지 않으면 점점 더 아플 것이다.
▶ '~하지 않는다면'이라는 뜻이므로 unless가 적절

4 Patrick은 개를 잃어버렸고 개가 어디 있는지 모른다.
▶ '어디'라는 뜻의 의문사 where이 적절

5 가능한 한 빨리 저에게 전화를 주시거나 메시지를 남겨주세요.
▶ '또는'에 해당되는 등위접속사 or가 적절

6 베토벤은 귀머거리가 된 후에도 여전히 음악을 작곡했다.
▶ '~후에'라는 뜻이므로 after가 적절

7 그는 매우 어리지만 영어를 유창하게 한다.
▶ '비록 ~이지만'이라는 뜻이므로 Though가 적절

D 1 그는 내가 그에게 증거를 주지 않는 한 나를 믿지 않을 것이다.
▶ 조건을 의미하는 부사절에서는 현재형으로 미래를 나타내므로 give가 적절

2 그것은 갑작스러운 요구였지만 그들은 전혀 불평하지 않았다.
▶ 과거의 일이므로 was가 적절

3 Kelly는 어제 그녀가 한 일을 기억하지 못한다.
▶ 간접의문문은 〈의문사+주어+동사〉 어순임

4 우리는 일찍 일어났기 때문에 학교에 늦지 않았다.
▶ Because we woke ~를 분사구문으로 만드는 것이므로 Waking이 적절

5 열심히 공부하지 않는다면 너는 시험에 통과하지 못할 것이다.
▶ '~하지 않는다면'이라는 뜻이므로 unless가 적절

6 콘서트 장에 들어가기 전에 좌석번호를 확인해야 한다.
▶ '~하기 전에, ~할 때'라는 뜻이므로 Before나 When이 적절

7 이 노트북 컴퓨터는 새것이지만 제대로 작동하지 않는다.
▶ '비록 ~이지만'이라는 뜻이므로 Even though나 Although, Though가 적절

FURTHER STUDY

P.160

A (1) that (2) Hearing
(3) As/When/After (4) what

B 1 When you called me
2 Although it is raining heavily
3 that Mike quit the school
4 until we moved here
5 unless you finish your homework

A

집에 돌아왔을 때 나는 현관문이 열려 있는 것을 알았다. 나는 나갈 때 문을 잠근 것을 확실히 기억했기 때문에 집에 도둑이 들었을까 봐 무서웠다. 나는 굳은 채로 귀를 기울였다. 어떤 소리도 들리지 않아서 나는 들어가서 어떻게 된 일인지 알아보기로 결심했다. 내가 집 안으로 들어섰을 때 나는 어떤 것도 없어지거나 깨지지 않았음을 알았다. 나는 기분이 나아지기 시작했다. 그때 화장실에서 소리가 났다. 누군가 그곳에 있었다. 나는 그곳에서 무슨 일이 벌어지고 있는지 궁금했다. 몇 초 후에 문이 열렸고 나는 낯익은 얼굴인 나의 남동생을 보았다. 그는 나를 보러 들른 것이었다. 그는 화장실에 급히 가려고 서둘러서 현관문을 제대로 닫지 못했던 것이었다.

(1) remember의 목적어절을 이끄는 접속사가 필요
(2) 분사구문이므로 Hearing이 적절
(3) '~했을 때, ~한 후에'란 뜻으로 As나 When, After 등이 적절
(4) '무슨'이라는 뜻이므로 의문사이면서 wonder의 목적어절을 이끄는 접속사가 되는 what이 적절

MUST-KNOW

P.161

▶ 접속사의 종류
① when ② because ③ if

WRAP-UP TEST

P.162

1 ⓐ
2 because → because of
3 ⓑ
4 (1) and (2) or
5 that
6 ⓓ
7 Not studying hard
8 (1) both (2) nor
9 Being young
10 ⓒ

1 · 나는 그녀에게 전화를 걸었지만, 그녀는 받지 않았다.
· 나는 엄마가 집에 오실 때까지 밖에 나갈 수 없다.
· 그들은 매우 피곤했지만, 계속 연습을 했다.
▶ '~했지만'이라는 뜻이므로 but이 적절, '~할 때까지'라는 뜻이므로 until이 적절, '~했음에도 불구하고'라는 뜻이므로 Although가 적절

2 야구 경기는 강한 폭우와 바람 때문에 연기되었다.
▶ 〈because+절〉이므로 because of가 적절

3 ⓐ 나는 늦게 일어났기 때문에 택시를 탔다.
ⓑ 나는 그녀가 나에게 왜 화가 났는지 아주 궁금했다.
ⓒ 우리는 식사를 하기 전에 물 한 잔을 마신다.
ⓓ 의사가 그에게 운동을 하라고 충고했음에도 그는 하지 않았다.
▶ ⓑ 간접의문문 〈의문사+주어+동사〉: was she → she was

4 (1) 네가 이 약을 먹으면 기분이 나아질 것이다.
▶ 〈If ~, 주어+동사〉 = 〈명령문 and 주어+동사〉 '~해라, 그러면 ~할 것이다'
(2) 우산을 가져가지 않는다면, 너는 젖게 될 것이다.

▶ 〈Unless, 주어+동사〉 = 〈명령문 or 주어+동사〉 '~해라. 그렇지 않으면 ~할 것이다'

5 · 엄마가 나를 용서할 가망이 없다.
· 그녀가 같은 실수를 하다니 믿을 수가 없다.
· 우리 계획은 각 과목을 서로 가르쳐 주는 것이다.
▶ hope와 동격을 이끄는 접속사 that, 〈It ~that〉 가주어, 진주어 구문, 보어절을 이끄는 접속사 that

6 ⓐ 내 도움이 필요할 때 나에게 전화해.
ⓑ 내가 버스 정류장에 도착했을 때, 그 버스는 이미 떠나고 없었다.
ⓒ 나는 어렸을 때 달리기를 잘했었다.
ⓓ 우리는 그 영화가 언제 시작하는지 매표소에 물었다.
▶ ⓐⓑⓒ '~할 때'라는 의미의 시간부사절 접속사
ⓓ '언제'라는 의미의 의문사

7 그는 열심히 공부하지 않아서, 기말고사에서 잘하지 못했다.
▶ 분사구문의 부정: 〈not+-ing〉 '

8 (1) 에디슨은 라디오와 축음기를 발명했다.
▶ 〈both A and B〉 'A와 B 둘 다'
(2) 남편과 나 둘 다 호텔을 예약하지 않았다.
▶ 〈neither A nor B〉 'A와 B 둘 다 ~ 아니다'

9-10 많은 사람들이 성 패트릭의 날에 대해서는 들어보았지만, 성 패트릭에 대해서는 들어본 적이 한 번도 없다. 그는 어렸을 때 아일랜드 군사들에게 잡혀 노예가 되었다. 후에 젊은 영국인들은 탈출을 했다. 그는 기독교의 성직자가 된 후에 아일랜드로 돌아와서 그곳에 있는 사람들에게 기독교를 전했다.

9 ▶ 접속사와 주어를 생략하고, 동사를 -ing으로 바꿔 분사구문을 만듦

10 ▶ '~ 후에'라는 뜻으로 After가 적절

Unit 13

1 관계대명사

EXERCISE

P.165

A 1 who 2 who 3 which
4 that 5 who 6 that

B 1 who/that 2 which/that
3 O 4 which/that
5 that 6 which/that

C 1 I always ask my friend who/that is good at math.
2 Korea has many cities which/that are modern.
3 He rescued a little girl who/that was drowning.
4 You are the only person that can help me.
5 She will bring something that will make you surprised.

B 1 선행사가 사람(a guy)이므로 who 또는 that이 적절
2 선행사가 사물(the school bus)이므로 which 또는 that이 적절
4 선행사가 동물(the dog)이므로 which 또는 that이 적절
5 -thing으로 끝나는 명사가 선행사로 올 때는 주로 that을 씀
6 선행사가 사물(the car)이므로 which 또는 that이 적절

2 관계대명사의 쓰임

EXERCISE

P.167

A 1 which 2 who 3 whose
4 that 5 whom 6 that
7 for which 8 whom

B 1 that 2 who/that
3 that 4 whose
5 which/that 6 who/that
7 who(m)/that

C 1 I have a friend whose sister goes to Harvard University.
2 There is a book which/that is very similar to mine.
3 Every Sunday, he visits his grandmother who/that really enjoys cooking.
4 This is the first event that Charles has planned.
5 This is a brand-new TV which/that we bought yesterday.

B 1 선행사가 anything이므로 that이 적절, -thing류의 선행사에는 주로 that을 씀
2 선행사가 사람(the boy)이므로 who 또는 that이 적절
3 선행사가 the only member이므로 that이 적절, the only가 선행사에 포함되면 주로 that을 사용
4 명사 eyes를 꾸미는 소유격 관계대명사가 whose가 적절
5 선행사가 calendars이므로 which 또는 that이 적절
6 선행사가 boyfriend이므로 who 또는 that이 적절
7 likes의 목적어가 되면서 teacher를 선행사로 받는 who(m) 또는 that이 적절

3 관계대명사의 특별 용법

EXERCISE

P.169

A 1 two sisters 2 a brother
3 sneakers 4 a skirt
5 Yesterday I broke some windows

6 some windows
7 The salesperson visited a house
8 a house

B 1 which/that 2 that
3 which 4 who

C 1 R 2 C 3 R
4 C 5 C 6 R

Unit 4 관계부사

EXERCISE

P.171

A 1 where 2 when 3 the way
4 why 5 where 6 when
7 why 8 how

B 1 where 2 when 3 how
4 how 5 when 6 where

C 1 The circus where we saw some clowns was closed down.
2 2013 was the year when my team won the championship.
3 Tell me how you made the cake.
4 I can tell (the reason) why Matt painted his house red.

R REVIEW TEST

P.172

A 1 who 2 whose 3 where
4 whom 5 how 6 which
7 that

B 1 ⓑ 2 ⓑ 3 ⓓ
4 ⓒ 5 ⓓ 6 ⓓ 7 ⓒ

C 1 who 2 that 3 , who
4 which 5 why 6 whose
7 , which

D 1 This is the first time that I have won a prize.
2 He loves that girl who/that is wearing glasses.
3 Somebody hit my brother, which made me mad.
4 My mom bought a computer whose color is black.
5 Those colored pencils, which are blue, are my sister's.
6 I'll never forget the day when I first met you.
7 My grandmother lent me a book which / that has the recipe.

A 1 나는 미국의 오리곤에 사는 친구에게 편지를 썼다.
▶ lives의 주어가 되면서 friend를 선행사로 받는 who가 적절
2 나는 차가 고장 난 그 사람을 도와야 했다.
▶ car를 수식하는 소유격 관계대명사 whose가 적절
3 나는 아버지가 태어난 마을을 방문했다.
▶ 장소를 선행사로 취하는 관계부사인 where가 적절
4 그는 내가 얘기했던 사람이다.
▶ about의 목적어가 되면서 person을 선행사로 받는 whom이 적절
5 그 과목에서 A를 받은 방법을 알려줄 수 있니?
▶ the way와 how는 함께 쓰일 수 없으므로 how가 적절
6 그녀는 그들이 도착하는 날짜를 쓰지 않았다.
▶ on의 목적어가 되면서 date를 선행사로 받는 which가 적절
7 Tina는 나를 행복하게 해 주는 유일한 사람이다.
▶ 선행사가 사람이고, the only를 포함하고 있으므로 that이 적절

B 1 그의 누이는 한 달 된 개를 샀다.
▶ 선행사가 a dog이므로 which가 적절
2 우리에게는 고향이 London인 영어 선생님이 있다.
▶ 명사 hometown을 꾸미는 소유격 관계대명사 whose가 적절
3 나는 Jessy가 사는 도시를 안다.
▶ the city가 선행사이고, live 뒤에 in이 없으므로 전치사를 포함한 관계부사 where가 적절
4 그는 가장 좋아하는 여동생에게 전화했다.
▶ likes의 목적어가 되면서 sister를 선행사로 받는 whom이 적절
5 Amy는 Susie가 기르는 것과 같은 고양이를 기르고 싶어 한다.
▶ the same cat을 선행사로 받는 that이 적절
6 Jake는 지붕이 파란색인 집을 샀다.
▶ 명사 roof를 꾸미는 소유격 관계대명사 whose가 적절
7 Kenny는 길을 잃은 소녀와 강아지를 도와주었다.
▶ 사람과 사물이 모두 선행사이므로 that이 적절

C 1 해변에 앉아 있는 소녀는 내 여동생이다.
▶ 선행사가 The girl이고 주어가 필요하므로 who가 적절
2 그는 내가 예상한 1등은 아니었다.
▶ 선행사에 the first가 있으므로 that이 적절
3 나의 친구 Amy는 옆집에 살고 있는데, 어제 나를 위해 케이크를 만들어 주었다.
▶ 선행사가 Amy이고 선행사를 보충 설명하고 있으므로 계속적 용법의 , who가 적절
4 그녀는 백금으로 만든 목걸이를 샀다.
▶ 선행사가 a necklace이고 주격이 필요하므로 which가 적절

5 무슨 일로 전화하셨는지 알려 주시겠습니까?
▶ 선행사가 the reason이므로 why가 적절

6 우리는 지느러미가 나비의 날개처럼 생긴 커다란 물고기를 보았다.
▶ fins를 꾸미는 소유격 관계대명사 whose가 적절

7 스웨덴의 수도인 스톡홀름은 세계에서 박물관이 가장 많이 밀집된 도시 중 하나이다.
▶ 선행사가 Stockholm이고 선행사를 보충 설명하고 있으므로 계속적 용법의, which가 적절

D 1 이번이 내가 처음 상을 탄 것이다.
▶ 선행사에 the first가 있으므로 that이 적절

2 그는 안경을 낀 저 소녀를 사랑한다.
▶ is의 주어가 필요하므로 who/that이 적절

3 누군가가 나의 형을 때렸고 그것으로 인해 나는 화가 났다.
▶ 선행사가 절 전체이므로 which가 적절

4 엄마는 검은색인 컴퓨터를 샀다.
▶ computer를 꾸미는 소유격 관계대명사가 whose가 적절

5 이 파란색 색연필들은 나의 여동생의 것이다.
▶ 선행사가 pencils로 복수이므로 are가 적절

6 나는 너를 처음 만난 날을 결코 잊지 못할 것이다.
▶ 선행사가 the day이므로 when이 적절

7 나의 할머니는 요리법이 들어 있는 책을 나에게 빌려 주셨다.
▶ a book이 선행사이고 has의 주어가 되는 which/that이 적절

FURTHER STUDY

P.174

A (1) which/that (2) that
(3) which/that (4) who

B 1 who/that is wearing blue jeans
2 which/that has a big garden
3 which came early
4 why the test was postponed
5 when the next bus will arrive

A

내가 여섯 살이 되었을 때 곱슬거리는 흰 털과 긴 귀를 가진 애완동물을 길렀다. 그것은 나의 생일 선물이었고, 2개월 된 강아지였다. 나는 Harry라는 이름을 지어 주었다. 나는 Harry를 갖게 되어 매우 행복했지만, 곧 애완동물을 기르는 것이 힘든 일이라는 것을 깨닫게 되었다. 엄마는 Harry가 나의 애완동물이지 엄마의 애완동물이 아니라고 말씀하셨다. 그래서 엄마는 Harry에게 먹이를 주거나 씻기지 않으셨다. 나는 책임감을 배우게 되었다. 엄마는 내가 해야 할 일의 목록을 써 주셨다. Harry에게 먹이를 주고 씻기는 일 외에도, 주말마다 Harry를 산책을 시켜야 했다. 그리고 Harry가 아플 때는 아픈 동물을 치료해 주는 수의사에게 그를 데려갔다.

(1) had의 주어가 되고, a pet을 선행사로 받는 which/that이 적절

(2) realized의 목적어절을 이끄는 접속사 that이 적절

(3) 선행사가 사물이고 -things가 왔으므로 that이 적절

(4) take의 주어가 되고 vet을 선행사로 받는 who가 적절

B 1 his brother가 선행사이므로 who/that이 적절

2 a house가 선행사이므로 which/that이 적절

3 My school bus가 선행사이고, 계속적 용법이므로 which가 적절

4 the reason이 선행사이므로 why가 적절

5 the time이 선행사이므로 when이 적절

MUST-KNOW

P.175

▶ 관계대명사
① that ② which
③ whom ④ whose

▶ 관계부사
① where ② when
③ why ④ how

WRAP-UP TEST

P.176

1 ⓒ 2 ⓓ 3 ⓒ
4 ⓐ 5 (that/which) I enjoy
6 ⓐ 7 which/that
8 which 9 ⓑ
10 who(m)/that

1 내 자전거 어디 있어? 그것은 네 자동차 옆에 있었어.
= 네 자동차 옆에 있던 내 자전거 어디 있어?
▶ bike를 선행사로 받으면서 used의 주어가 되는 주격 관계대명사 which가 적절

2 · 내가 만나기를 원했던 의사는 휴가 중이었다.
· 나는 기사를 쓰는 것이 직업인 한 남자를 안다.
· 그들은 아들이 태어난 날을 잊을 수가 없었다.
▶ doctor를 선행사로 받으면서 meet의 목적어가 되는 whom이 적절, a man을 선행사로 받으면서 job을 수식하는 소유격 관계대명사 whose가 적절, the day를 선행사로 받으면서 전치사 in을 포함한 관계부사 when이 적절

3 ⓐ 나는 회의가 개최되는 방을 찾을 수가 없었다.
ⓑ Amy는 내 친구인데, 일등을 했다.
ⓒ 당신이 카푸치노 한 잔을 만든 방법을 나에게 알려주세요.
ⓓ 오늘 나는 내가 지금까지 본 여자 중에서 가장 아름다운 여자를 보았다.
▶ ⓒ the way와 how는 같이 쓸 수 없음

4 그는 네가 가지고 싶은 것은 어느 것이든 사 줄 수 있다.
ⓐ 네가 찾고 있던 그 책은 다락에서 발견되었다.

ⓑ 그녀는 우리에게 여섯 명의 수감자가 감옥에서 탈출했다는 소식을 전했다.
ⓒ 내가 와인 한 잔을 마시고 있는 저 남자를 소개해 줄게.
ⓓ 그녀는 그가 법대를 졸업했다는 것을 믿지 않는다.
▶ 목적격 관계대명사 ⓐ 목적격 관계대명사 ⓑ 동격절을 이끄는 접속사 ⓒ 지시형용사 ⓓ 목적어절을 이끄는 접속사

5 ▶ the sport를 선행사로 받으면서, enjoy의 목적어가 되는 목적격 관계대명사 that이나 which를 사용, 목적격 관계대명사는 생략 가능

6 ⓐ 나는 그녀가 왜 불평을 하는지 이해하지 못한다.
ⓑ 그녀는 내가 만나기를 원했던 소녀이다.
ⓒ 그는 여기 처음으로 도착한 사람이었다.
ⓓ 8월 23일은 그녀가 태어난 날이다.
▶ ⓐ '~한 이유, 왜 ~했는지'라는 의미: which → why

7 작년에 불에 탄 그 집은 1년 후에 다시 지어질 것이다.
▶ house를 선행사로 받으면서 burned의 주어가 되는 주격 관계대명사가 필요: where → which/that

8 · 그는 아내에게 완벽하게 맞는 빨간색 드레스를 샀다.
· 파란색 바지와 검은색 바지 중 어떤 것을 입어보고 싶니?
▶ dress를 선행사로 받으면서 fits의 주어가 되는 주격 관계대명사, '어느 것'이라는 뜻의 의문사 which가 적절

9-10 당신은 왜 1990년대 미국에서 Will Rogers가 그렇게 유명했는지 아는가? 여기 그 이유가 있다. 그는 "나는 좋아하지 않는 사람은 만나지 절대로 만나지 않았다."라는 신조를 가진 인디언이자 카우보이였다. 그는 50편 이상의 영화에 출연한 영화배우였다. 일생 동안 그는 세 번 세계여행을 했다. 그는 또한 여섯 권의 책을 썼다. 그는 아내인 Betty와 네 명의 아이와 아주 가깝게 지내는 가정적인 남자였다.

9 ▶ '~이유, 왜'라는 뜻이므로 why가 적절

10 ▶ man을 선행사로 받으며 like의 목적어가 되는 관계대명사 who(m)이나 that이 적절

Unit 14

Unit 1 가정법

EXERCISE

P.179

A 1 eat 2 were 3 pours
4 were 5 is not 6 snows
7 had 8 had

B 1 am 2 apologizes
3 knew 4 don't understand
5 is not 6 were
7 had 8 were

C 1 am not, can't buy
2 don't have, can't write
3 isn't, can't help
4 aren't, can't study

Unit 2 가정법 (과거완료/기타 가정법)

EXERCISE

P.181

A 1 had had 2 had told
3 were 4 had seen
5 were 6 had been
7 were 8 Without

B 1 walked, had walked 2 see, have seen
3 were, had been

C 1 had had 2 had been
3 could have come 4 were not

Unit 3 화법/부가의문문

EXERCISE

P.183

A 1 said, he 2 told, could
3 asked, then 4 asks, if
5 to make

B 1 aren't you 2 doesn't he
3 isn't she 4 mustn't they
5 are they 6 can we
7 does he

C 1 he seemed very nervous that day
2 to clean my room before leaving
3 not to go through those doors
4 where they should put the boxes

R REVIEW TEST

P.184

A 1 if 2 isn't he
3 were 4 had worked
5 not to make 6 can't you
7 Without 8 had known

B 1 ⓑ 2 ⓒ 3 ⓓ
4 ⓑ 5 ⓒ 6 ⓐ 7 ⓑ

C 1 if 2 were 3 went
4 as if 5 had brought
6 wish 7 hasn't

D 1 If I had a new bike, I would let you ride it.
2 I don't speak French. I wish I spoke French.
3 Economics is very hard, isn't it?
4 He speaks as though he were innocent of the charge, but he isn't.
5 If she had attended the seminar, she would have enjoyed hearing the professor.
6 If June is not home, I will visit Liz in an hour.
7 If Sue doesn't go to school today, I will not let her watch TV.
8 If I were a turtle, I would hide inside my shell.

A 1 그 어린 간호사는 그에게 더 나아졌는지 물었다.
▶ 의문사가 없는 의문문의 간접화법에 해당하므로 if가 적절
2 Tom은 신뢰할 만한 사람이야, 그렇지 않니?
▶ 주절이 긍정이면 부가의문문은 부정
3 나는 그가 상을 받는 사람들의 명단에 있기를 바란다.
▶ 현재 사실에 대한 바람이므로 were가 적절
4 만약 그가 더 열심히 일을 했다면 그 프로젝트를 제 시간에 끝냈을 텐데.
▶ 과거 사실에 대한 반대이므로 가정법 과거완료가 적절
5 그녀는 내게 큰 소리를 내지 말라고 했다.
▶ 명령문의 간접화법: 부정형은 〈not to부정사〉
6 너는 동생의 생일 케이크를 구울 수 있지, 그렇지?
▶ 주절이 긍정이면 부가의문문은 부정
7 공기가 없다면 우리는 어떤 것도 들을 수 없을 것이다.
▶ '~이 없다면'이란 의미의 Without이 적절
8 그가 전반적인 내용을 알았다면 그것을 믿지 않았을 텐데.
▶ 과거 사실에 대한 반대이므로 가정법 과거완료가 적절

B 1 그녀는 결과에 대해 기쁜 것처럼 말한다.
▶ '~한 것처럼'이란 뜻의 as if가 적절
2 농구 선수들은 발이 작지 않아, 그렇지?
▶ 주절이 부정이면 부가의문문은 긍정
3 그들이 내게 이메일을 보냈다면 나는 즉시 답변을 했을 텐데.
▶ 과거 사실에 대한 반대이므로 가정법 과거완료가 적절
4 내가 스파이더맨이라면 엠파이어 스테이트 빌딩을 오를 텐데.
▶ 현재 사실에 대한 반대이므로 가정법 과거가 적절
5 나의 실험 파트너가 내게 과제를 끝마쳤는지 물어 본다.
▶ '~인지(아닌지)를'라는 뜻이므로 if가 적절
6 그는 환자에게 친절하게 대하라고 의사들에게 지시했다.
▶ 명령문의 간접화법으로 to treat가 적절
7 Sam은 우리가 어려움 없이 그것을 할 수 있는지를 물었다.
▶ '~를 물었다'라는 의미이므로 asked가 적절

C 1 그는 우리에게 오랫동안 운전한 후라 배가 고픈지를 물었다.
▶ '~인지(아닌지)를'이라는 뜻이므로 if가 적절
2 내가 말이라면 나는 들판에서 꽃들 사이를 질주할 텐데.
▶ 현재 사실에 대한 반대이므로 가정법 과거가 적절
3 그는 지난밤 11시에 잠자리에 들었다고 말했다.
▶ 과거의 사실을 얘기할 때는 과거시제 went가 적절
4 두 명의 어린 소년은 항상 형제인척 한다.
▶ '마치 ~인 것처럼'이라는 뜻이므로 as if가 적절
5 그들이 부서진 자전거를 그에게 가져왔더라면, 그는 그것을 고쳐주었을 텐데.
▶ 과거 사실에 대한 반대이므로 가정법 과거완료가 적절
6 나는 그가 수업 시간에 자신의 의견을 표현할 정도로 용감하기를 바란다.
▶ '~하기를 바라다'라는 뜻으로 가정법 주절에는 wish가 적절
7 Shelly는 수백 권의 책을 읽었어, 그렇지 않니?
▶ 주절이 긍정일 때 부가의문문은 부정, 현재완료이므로 hasn't가 적절

D 1 내게 새 자전거가 있다면, 네가 그것을 타도록 할 텐데.
▶ 현재 사실의 반대이므로 가정법 과거가 적절
2 나는 불어를 못한다. 불어를 잘하면 좋을 텐데.
▶ 현재 사실에 대한 가정이므로 가정법 과거가 적절
3 경제학은 매우 어려워, 그렇지 않니?
▶ 주절이 긍정이면 부가의문문은 부정이 적절
4 그는 마치 그 혐의에 대해 무죄인 것처럼 말하지만, 그는 무죄가 아니다.
▶ 현재 사실에 대한 반대이므로 가정법 과거가 적절. 가정법에서 be동사는 주어에 상관없이 were를 사용
5 그녀가 세미나에 참가했다면 그녀는 교수님의 말씀을 듣는 것을 즐겼을 텐데.
▶ 과거 사실에 대한 반대이므로 가정법 과거완료가 적절
6 June이 집에 없으면 나는 한 시간 후에 Liz에게 갈 것이다.
▶ 실제로 일어날 수 있는 일을 말하는 것이므로, 가정법이 아니라 조건문을 사용해야 함
7 Sue가 오늘 학교에 가지 않으면, 나는 그녀가 텔레비전을 시청하도록 놔두지 않을 것이다.
▶ 실제로 일어날 수 있는 일을 말하는 것이므로, 가정법이 아니라 조건문을 사용해야 함
8 내가 거북이라면 나는 등딱지 안에 숨을 텐데.
▶ 현재 사실에 대한 반대를 가정하므로 가정법 과거가 적절

FURTHER STUDY

P.186

A (1) had (2) would have told
(3) were (4) is

B 1 I would have watched the show
2 The driver said to him
3 if/whether I was satisfied with her work
4 If it were not for your help
5 If I were a bird

A

새 디지털 카메라를 살 때이다. 내게 새 디지털 카메라가 있다면 많은 사진을 쉽게 찍을 수 있을 텐데. 내가 쓰던 카메라는 사용하기 어렵다. 실내에서 좋은 사진을 찍을 수도 없다. 그것을 살 때 판매원은 내게 카메라에 대해 많은 것을 알려 주지 않았다. 그가 물어봤다면 나는 어떤 종류의 사진을 찍고 싶은지 그에게 말했을 텐데. 이 카메라를 사기 전에 카메라 선택에 대해 공부했으면 좋았을 텐데. 시간을 되돌릴 수 있다면 나는 다시는 같은 카메라를 사지 않을 것이다. 우리 형의 말을 들었으면 좋을 텐데. 그는 내게 카메라를 골라 주겠다고 제안했다. 하지만, 나는 듣지 않았다. 우리 형은 늘 바쁘지만 내가 부탁하면 새 카메라를 사러 나와 함께 가주리라 믿는다.

(1) 현재 사실의 반대를 가정한 것이므로 가정법 과거가 적절
(2) 과거 사실의 반대를 가정한 것이므로 가정법 과거완료가 적절
(3) be동사가 가정법 과거에 사용될 때는 were가 적절
(4) 현재의 사실은 현재형으로 표현

B 1 과거 사실의 반대를 가정하므로 가정법 과거완료가 적절
3 의문사가 없는 의문문의 직접화법을 간접화법으로 나타낼 때는 whether나 if를 사용
4 '~이 없다면'이라는 의미의 가정법 과거 구문 if it were not for가 적절
5 불가능한 현실을 가정하는 가정법 과거가 적절

W WRAP-UP TEST

P.188

1 ⓑ 2 ⓓ 3 ⓑ 4 ⓐ
5 ⓐ 6 ⓑ 7 ⓒ
8 had handed in, wouldn't[would not] have failed
9 ⓒ 10 wouldn't you

1 너 올 여름에 이집트에 갈 거지, 그렇지 않니?
▶ 주절이 긍정이면 부가의문문은 부정

2 내가 너라면 그의 충고를 들을 텐데.
▶ 현재 사실에 대한 반대이므로 가정법 과거가 적절

3 경찰이 노부인에게 "무엇을 찾고 있으세요, 부인?"이라고 물었다.
▶ said to → asked, 〈의문사+주어+동사〉 어순

4 ⓐ 그 소년은 마치 지난밤에 아팠던 것처럼 행동한다.
ⓑ 그가 또 늦으면 선생님이 화를 낼 것이다.
ⓒ 그가 백만장자라면, 그는 어머니에게 큰 집을 사 줄 텐데.
ⓓ 그 책이 아니었다면, 나는 숙제를 마칠 수 없었을 것이다.
▶ ⓐ 과거 사실에 대한 반대를 가정한 것이므로 가정법 과거완료가 적절: → had been ⓑ 조건문 ⓒ 가정법 과거 ⓓ 가정법 과거완료

5 ⓐ 소풍 가기에 좋은 날이 아니다, 그렇지?
ⓑ 이 약을 먹으면, 더 나아질 거야.
ⓒ 그는 마치 큰 유산을 상속받은 것처럼 행동한다.
ⓓ 그때 그 일자리 제안을 수락했으면 좋을 텐데.
▶ ⓐ 주절이 부정이면 부가의문문은 긍정: isn't → is

6 내 친구가 나에게 "지금 무엇을 하고 있니?"라고 물었다.
▶ 간접화법은 〈의문사+주어+동사〉 어순이므로 if를 삭제

7 내가 그때 택시를 탔다면, 제시간에 공항에 도착했을 텐데.
ⓒ 나는 그때 택시를 타지 않아서, 공항에 제시간에 도착하지 못했다.
▶ 과거 사실에 대한 반대를 가정한 가정법 과거완료

8 나는 보고서를 제출하지 않아서 그 과목에서 낙제했다.
→ 보고서를 제출했다면 그 과목에서 낙제하지 않았을 텐데.
▶ 과거 사실에 대한 반대를 가정한 가정법 과거완료

9-10 만약 당신이 복권에 당첨된다면, 당신은 무엇을 하겠는가? 당신은 비싼 집을 살 것이다, 그렇지 않은가? 사람들은 당첨되기를 바라면서 복권을 산다. 그들은 당첨이 되었을 때 자신이 행복해 질 거라고 믿는다. 하지만, 이것은 항상 진실은 아니다. 당첨자 중 80퍼센트가 불행했다. 겨우 20퍼센트만이 행복한 삶을 살았다. 예를 들어 복권에 당첨되어 백만장자가 된 Philip Alcan은 자신의 집 소파에서 죽은 채로 발견되었다.

9 ▶ 현재 사실을 가정한 가정법 과거가 적절

10 ▶ 주절이 긍정이면 부가의문문은 부정, 조동사는 그대로 사용

Workbook 정답 ▸▸

Unit 01

1 be동사

P. 2

A

1 are 2 is
3 Are 4 is not
5 were 6 am
7 was 8 Were

B

1 Are 2 Is
3 Was 4 I am
5 they weren't [were not] 6 it is

C

1 The brown bear is a new animal in our zoo.
2 My history book was under the chair last night.
3 Ben and I are in the same music club.
4 They were not at the bus stop at that time.

내신 FOCUS

A 1 ⓓ 2 ⓑ
B 1 ⓒ 2 ⓐ
C 1 ⓐ 2 ⓑ
D 1 is my favorite flower
2 aren't[are not] students
3 was fat, is thin
4 Was, rainy and windy

2 일반동사

P. 4

A

1 sleeps 2 stays
3 comes 4 do
5 drive 6 flies
7 hold 8 has

B

1 cries 2 buys
3 buzzes 4 eats
5 dance 6 goes
7 wash 8 drinks

C

1 rides 2 enjoy
3 copies 4 makes
5 O 6 teaches

내신 FOCUS

A 1 ⓑ 2 ⓐ
B 1 ⓐ 2 ⓑ
C 1 ⓒ 2 ⓑ
D 1 gets up early
2 tries her best
3 starts at 3 o'clock
4 goes to a part-time job

3 일반동사의 부정문과 의문문

P. 6

A

1 (b) 2 (e) 3 (d)
4 (c) 5 (a)

B

1 Does 2 doesn't
3 Do 4 ride
5 Do 6 O
7 attend

C

1 He doesn't save $1
2 Does he have dinner at a Mexican restaurant
3 She doesn't ride the Number 7 bus
4 He visits his grandparents
5 Does the bakery sell
6 She doesn't throw trash

내신 FOCUS

A 1 does 2 do
B 1 ⓑ 2 ⓐ
C 1 ⓑ 2 ⓒ
D 1 does not live in Korea, lives in Spain with his family
2 Do they admire
3 Does this train go
4 My sister does not listen to

의문사 있는 의문문/There is [are]

P. 8

A

1 does　2 are
3 is　4 do
5 was　6 Was
7 arrive

B

1 Are　2 is
3 are　4 O
5 do　6 is
7 is

C

1 When do Lilly and Jerry walk
2 There aren't[are not] many fast cars
3 Why do Steve and Linda practice baseball
4 How many books are there
5 How much water was there

내신 FOCUS

A 1 What, Why　2 are, was
B 1 ⓐ　2 ⓓ
C 1 ⓑ　2 ⓐ
D 1 How much water is there
2 Who were you
3 There are old books
4 How does your brother go

Unit 02

현재시제/현재진행형

P. 10

A

1 goes　2 like
3 are playing　4 is carrying
5 arrive　6 talks

B

1 is throwing　2 learns
3 is flying　4 catches
5 am talking　6 is coming

C

1 counts　2 is practicing
3 sends　4 is having
5 gets

내신 FOCUS

A 1 ⓑ　2 ⓓ
B 1 ⓐ　2 ⓑ
C 1 ⓐ　2 ⓒ
D 1 goes to Tokyo
2 are building a sand castle
3 The last train leaves at 9 o'clock
4 is reaching

현재진행형 (부정문, 의문문, 불가동사)

P. 12

A

1 is driving　2 is talking
3 doesn't need　4 have
5 likes　6 feel
7 Are you going

B

1 doing　2 having
3 O　4 understands
5 isn't　6 Do you want

C

1 Are you checking　2 Is the clerk wrapping
3 doesn't go　4 orders
5 isn't[is not] walking　6 is running

내신 FOCUS

A 1 goes, is going　2 Is, standing, stands
B 1 ⓓ　2 ⓓ
C 1 ⓒ　2 ⓐ
D 1 like playing outside
2 are not watching TV
3 Are, peeling the oranges
4 She knows a lot

3 과거시제/과거진행형

P. 14

A

1 did　2 graduated
3 went　4 were they
5 flew　6 Wasn't
7 was paddling

B

1 presented 2 had
3 were building 4 put out
5 find 6 played

C

1 Were, eating 2 rumbled
3 called 4 clean up

내신 FOCUS

A 1 ⓐ read ⓑ made ⓒ thought ⓓ met
2 ⓐ bit ⓑ drank ⓒ went ⓓ sang
B 1 ⓑ 2 ⓒ
C 1 ⓑ 2 ⓑ
D 1 was playing hide-and-seek
2 didn't[did not] invite them to my birthday party
3 drove for 10 hours
4 What did you have for dinner

4 미래시제

P. 16

A

1 will travel 2 is going to drive
3 will not 4 are
5 finds 6 have

B

1 learn 2 return
3 snow 4 is going
5 will not 6 am
7 ignore

C

1 is leaving 2 will write
3 is going 4 will spend
5 are going to have

내신 FOCUS

A 1 will get up 2 will take off
B 1 ⓒ 2 ⓑ
C 1 ⓑ 2 ⓑ
D 1 will call you back
2 are going to be late
3 will not tell your secret
4 will go on a trip

Unit 03

1 현재완료(계속)

P. 18

A

1 has raised 2 graduated
3 have 4 passed
5 have heard 6 has prepared

B

1 won 2 has called
3 has celebrated 4 played
5 has taken 6 went
7 have studied

C

1 has worked 2 has taken
3 has snowed 4 have been
5 has read

내신 FOCUS

A 1 blew, has blown 2 for, since
B 1 ⓒ 2 ⓒ
C 1 ⓐ 2 ⓐ
D 1 Has, played baseball
2 How long have you worn
3 has dreamed
4 has been interested in

2 현재완료 (완료, 경험, 결과)

P. 20

A

1 has just caught 2 ever bought
3 has driven 4 has he asked
5 has never eaten 6 have already had
7 has left

B

1 have not visited 2 have made
3 has already changed 4 have not finished
5 have never taken 6 has just read

C

1 O 2 have not
3 has already 4 seen
5 read

내신 FOCUS

A 1 has gone 2 have been
B 1 ⓒ 2 ⓐ
C 1 ⓐ 2 ⓓ
D 1 How many times has Korea played
2 hasn't[has not] finished his homework
3 have ridden a roller coaster

과거완료와 미래완료

P. 22

A
1 will have 2 had been
3 will have 4 Had
5 had seen 6 had already changed
7 will have

B
1 will have reviewed
2 had already broken
3 will have started
4 hadn't[had not] looked
5 had lived
6 won't[will not] have finished
7 will have taught

C
1 had bought 2 will have driven
3 will have sold 4 had graduated

내신 FOCUS

A 1 had studied 2 will have stayed
B 1 ⓒ 2 ⓑ
C 1 ⓒ 2 ⓑ
D 1 had painted
2 will have completed
3 How many times had you read
4 I will have studied English

Unit 04

조동사(능력, 허가, 요청, 제안)

P. 24

A
1 make 2 is able to
3 catch 4 Could
5 sing 6 able to 7 Could

B
1 may leave 2 Shall, go
3 Will, send 4 cannot count
5 be able to play

C
1 he will be able to drive his own car
2 Can you come to my graduation on Thursday
3 is able to work for her father's company
4 Shall we introduce our speaker for this evening's event
5 Would/Could you hold the door for me

내신 FOCUS

A 1 is able to repair 2 Would/Could
B 1 ⓓ 2 ⓑ
C 1 ⓑ 2 ⓐ
D 1 can[is able to] run fast, he will win
2 Could/Would you say that again
3 may/can get up late
4 Shall, meet

조동사 (의무, 금지, 충고, 과거의 습관)

P. 26

A
1 would 2 must not
3 had better not 4 had to
5 used to 6 don't have to
7 will have to

B
1 had to 2 must
3 used to 4 don't have to
5 should not

C
1 should read 2 had better not call
3 used to go 4 will have to return
5 must not enter

내신 FOCUS

A 1 have to 2 would
B 1 ⓒ 2 ⓐ
C 1 ⓑ 2 ⓐ
D 1 had better go home
2 would[used to] climb up trees
3 should speak to your parents
4 don't have to write a report

3 조동사 (추측, 가능성)

P. 28

A
1 could have
2 should have
3 cannot be
4 must
5 must be
6 must have changed
7 shouldn't

B
1 must have eaten
2 might have washed
3 may not be
4 could be mowing
5 can't be

C
1 could have dropped
2 should have chosen
3 must have practiced
4 may have put

내신 FOCUS

A 1 can't　2 may
B 1 ⓑ　2 ⓐ
C 1 ⓒ　2 ⓐ
D 1 must be sick
2 should have attended
3 may/might have worn
4 should have told

Unit 05

1 to부정사의 역할

P. 30

A
1 Ad　2 N　3 A
4 Ad　5 A　6 N

B
1 (c)　2 (e)　3 (a)
4 (b)　5 (d)

C
1 to wear
2 to be
3 to become
4 To get on
5 to say

내신 FOCUS

A 1 To learn　2 to be
3 to help　4 to invite
B 1 ⓐ　2 ⓒ
C 1 ⓑ　2 ⓒ
D 1 practiced hard to get
2 decided to accept the offer
3 a chair to sit on
4 something to drink

2 to부정사의 의미상 주어/부정

P. 32

A
1 her
2 of them
3 him not to
4 of him
5 for her
6 him
7 not to

B
1 him
2 for them
3 you
4 for her
5 her son

C
1 me
2 of
3 for
4 him
5 not to prepare

내신 FOCUS

A 1 My uncle wants his son to be honest.
2 It is smart of him to hand in the paper in advance.
B 1 ⓐ　2 ⓑ
C 1 ⓒ　2 ⓐ
D 1 asked her to close the door
2 for children to play with
3 very kind of you to carry
4 told his daughter not to use the phone

3 부정사의 기타 쓰임

P. 34

A
1 too
2 enough
3 run
4 how to get
5 where to catch
6 to open
7 good enough

B
1 take
2 too heavy
3 burn/burning
4 how to wear
5 cautious enough
6 plan

7 where to put

C

1 so big, can hire 2 so slow, can't compete
3 strong enough to damage
4 too weak to win

내신 FOCUS

A 1 where I should put the broken vase
2 so interesting that it can attract over 10 million people
B 1 ⓑ 2 ⓓ
C 1 ⓑ 2 ⓓ
D 1 too young to ride
2 helped me (to) paint the fence
3 how to use this vending machine
4 hot enough to burn

Unit 06

Unit 1 동명사의 역할

P. 36

A

1	is	2	was beginning
3	sending	4	paying
5	Being	6	climbing
7	acquiring	8	transferring

B

1	P	2	G
3	P	4	G
5	G	6	P

C

1 Jumping into the pool
2 seeing her old boyfriend
3 calling his mother on weekends
4 preventing crime and keeping order
5 Cleaning up the city

내신 FOCUS

A 1 Having 2 going
3 memorizing 4 reading
B 1 ⓑ 2 ⓒ
C 1 ⓐ 2 ⓒ
D 1 building a big hospital
2 Keeping a diary every day is difficult

3 continued running after his dog

Unit 2 동명사의 의미상 주어/부정

P. 38

A

1	his	2	making
3	hiking	4	not answering
5	doing	6	not coming
7	was finding		

B

1	listening	2	fishing
3	sending	4	eating
5	touching		

C

1	O	2	his
3	not keeping	4	going
5	my	6	not doing

내신 FOCUS

A 1 singing[to sing] 2 singing
B 1 ⓐ 2 ⓒ
C 1 ⓓ 2 ⓐ
D 1 is looking forward to receiving
2 mind my using
3 I'll go swimming
4 are talking about not going to the party

Unit 3 동명사/to부정사를 쓰는 동사

P. 40

A

1	going	2	talking
3	to know	4	changing
5	to pick up	6	to pay
7	to explain		

B

1	meeting	2	to meet
3	watching	4	to ask
5	giving	6	to find

C

1 reading, to listen
2 eating, choosing[to choose]
3 to come, catching
4 to be, to break
5 smoking, running[to run]

내신 FOCUS

A 1 talking　　2 to talk
　3 crying　　4 to believe
B 1 ⓐ, ⓓ　　2 ⓐ, ⓒ
C 1 ⓓ　　2 ⓑ
D 1 are considering moving to
　2 remembered to buy, forgot to bring
　3 put off playing tennis
　4 expected him to come

Unit 07

Unit 1 분사의 종류 및 의미

P. 42

A
1 amazing　　2 confused
3 satisfying　　4 burnt
5 stolen　　6 spotted
7 touching

B
1 bored　　2 lit/lighted
3 spoiled　　4 broken
5 chosen　　6 embarrassed
7 surprising

C
1 P　　2 G
3 P　　4 P
5 G　　6 G
7 P

내신 FOCUS

A 1 singing
　2 lost
　3 shocked
　4 interesting
B 1 ⓑ　　2 ⓓ
C 1 ⓐ　　2 ⓒ
D 1 was really surprising
　2 boiled
　3 was very confusing
　4 scared to death

Unit 2 분사의 쓰임

P. 44

A
1 diving　　2 coughing
3 talking　　4 flying
5 missing　　6 screaming

B
1 taken　　2 standing
3 torn　　4 sliced
5 picked up　　6 interesting
7 encouraged

C
1 piled　　2 filled
3 playing　　4 used
5 dancing　　6 broken

내신 FOCUS

A 1 the puppy dozing off
　2 the book titled
B 1 ⓐ　　2 ⓓ
C 1 ⓑ　　2 ⓒ
D 1 barking
　2 the glasses lying by the bed
　3 pulling her shirt
　4 lost bag

Unit 3 수동태의 개념과 형태

P. 46

A
1 was fed　　2 were helped
3 complains　　4 be made
5 was broken　　6 Was
7 was delayed

B
1 was started　　2 are understood
3 received　　4 was startled
5 cleaned　　6 O

C
1 is ordered　　2 was developed
3 was welcomed　　4 was not held

내신 FOCUS

A 1 was built by　　2 Was, invented
B 1 ⓓ　　2 ⓐ

C 1 ⓒ 2 ⓐ
D 1 was decorated by a famous chef
2 are damaged by floods and fires
3 was solved by my brother
4 was the movie first shown

Unit 4 여러 가지 수동태

P. 48

A
1 of 2 with
3 about 4 of
5 at 6 with
7 with

B
1 for 2 O
3 in 4 for
5 to

C
1 is covered with the little grasshoppers
2 was asked of me
3 was shown to me
4 was given to me
5 were written to his grandparents

내신 FOCUS

A 1 to 2 for
3 with 4 about
B 1 ⓑ 2 ⓐ
C 1 ⓑ 2 ⓑ
D 1 was given an award by her teacher
2 was written by Billy
3 was satisfied with her math scores
4 are scared of injections

Unit 08

명사 (Ⅰ)

P. 50

A
1 coins 2 class
3 Korean history 4 Grace
5 babies 6 was
7 sheep

B
1 luck 2 car
3 news 4 pants
5 people 6 keys
7 men 8 mice

C
1 bushes 2 money
3 O 4 pianos
5 eggs 6 milk
7 cream and sugar

내신 FOCUS

A 1 ⓓ 2 ⓐ
B 1 ⓑ 2 ⓒ
C 1 ⓑ 2 ⓑ
D 1 our hope for the future
2 breathe in air
3 one orange and eight tomatoes
4 two wolves and five deer

명사 (Ⅱ)

P. 52

A
1 many 2 a slice of
3 juice 4 Ben's
5 of 6 dancers
7 any 8 a pair of

B
1 three boxes of 2 a piece of
3 a spoonful of 4 a carton of
5 many loaves of

C
1 pieces 2 a lot of/lots of
3 wine 4 slices
5 yesterday's 6 jars
7 much

내신 FOCUS

A 1 ⓓ 2 ⓒ
B 1 ⓓ 2 ⓒ
C 1 ⓑ 2 ⓒ
D 1 Bill's room is
2 two bottles of water
3 one pound of flour and three eggs
4 no fruit

Unit 3 관사

P. 54

A

1 a　　2 the
3 an　　4 The
5 an　　6 a
7 The

B

1 an　　2 the
3 a　　4 Ø
5 the　　6 Ø

C

1 (b)　　2 (a)
3 (d)　　4 (c)

내신 FOCUS

A 1 an　　2 the
3 Ø　　4 A
B 1 ⓑ　　2 ⓓ
C 1 ⓑ　　2 ⓐ
D 1 lots of stars in the sky
2 usually plays soccer
3 an old book in the black box
4 The man was

Unit 09

Unit 1 인칭/지시/의문대명사

P. 56

A

1 my　　2 We
3 him　　4 us
5 Whose　　6 this
7 It is　　8 Its
9 them　　10 who

B

1 She　　2 My
3 They　　4 His
5 He　　6 Her
7 It

C

1 Which　　2 What
3 Whose　　4 Which
5 What　　6 Who

내신 FOCUS

A ⓐ you　ⓑ its　ⓒ them　ⓓ whose　ⓔ whom
B 1 ⓐ　　2 ⓒ
C 1 ⓒ　　2 ⓐ
D 1 will prepare lunch for us
2 these pictures, those pictures
3 It rains a lot
4 Who(m) did you go

Unit 2 소유/재귀대명사

P. 58

A

1 Mine　　2 yours
3 Ours　　4 hers
5 his　　6 yours
7 theirs

B

1 herself　　2 himself
3 themselves　　4 yourself
5 ourselves　　6 myself

C

1 by myself　　2 of itself
3 for oneself　　4 beside himself
5 between ourselves

내신 FOCUS

A 1 ⓑ　　2 ⓑ
B 1 ⓓ　　2 ⓐ
C 1 ⓑ　　2 ⓐ
D 1 these pictures himself
2 hers or his
3 should love yourself
4 fixed his car by himself

Unit 3 부정대명사 (I)

P. 60

A

1 every　　2 Both
3 neither　　4 Some
5 all　　6 any
7 either

B

1 every　2 either
3 neither　4 some
5 any　6 All
7 both

C

1 O　2 some
3 any　4 either
5 friends　6 class

내신 FOCUS

A 1 some, any　2 All, Both
B 1 ⓓ　2 ⓓ
C 1 ⓒ　2 ⓐ
D 1 fail either math or English
2 each tree has a different name
3 articles about him were scrapped
4 Neither of the two boys was punished

4 부정대명사 (Ⅱ)

P. 62

A

1 One　2 no
3 the others　4 it
5 the others　6 another

B

1 most　2 One
3 no　4 another
5 each other　6 the others

C

1 Most, some　2 One, the others
3 Some, others　4 No

내신 FOCUS

A 1 One, the other　2 another, the other
B 1 ⓓ　2 ⓑ
C 1 ⓒ　2 ⓐ
D 1 bought a new one
2 No one complained about
3 Some people died, others were severely injured
4 Most of my books are

Unit 10

1 형용사

P. 64

A

1 a lot of　2 pretty
3 exciting　4 something fun
5 plastic　6 a little
7 favorite grandmother　8 careless

B

1 a lot of / lots of　2 some
3 boring　4 few
5 young boy　6 many
7 anything new

C

1 There is not much water in the pond.
2 A few stories from this book were interesting.
3 The good child gave flowers to her mother.
4 I want to buy something memorable in Paris.

내신 FOCUS

A 1 a lovely girl, beautiful
2 anything interesting, a lot of / lots of / much water
B 1 ⓐ　2 ⓓ
C 1 ⓑ　2 ⓑ
D 1 smell something sweet
2 My parents are friendly
3 few coins in my piggy bank

2 부사

P. 66

A

1 was always　2 very brave
3 rarely　4 well
5 severely　6 hard
7 Thankfully　8 usually plays

B

1 early　2 weakly
3 Finally　4 patiently
5 slowly　6 frequently

C

1 His mother is never worried about his grades.
2 She always talks to her family about her boyfriend.

3 My sister usually drives very fast everywhere she goes.
4 The young man makes mistakes too often.

내신 FOCUS

A 1 ⓐ 2 ⓓ
B 1 ⓐ 2 ⓒ
C 1 ⓒ 2 ⓓ
D 1 Why did you get up so early
2 Strangely, was deleted
3 kindly guided us to the concert hall
4 always plans future work carefully

Unit 3 비교급과 최상급(규칙, 불규칙)

P. 68

A
1 most 2 busiest
3 worse 4 better
5 oldest 6 greatest
7 more

B
1 worst 2 more quietly
3 longest 4 more clearly
5 busy 6 nicer
7 O

C
1 smallest 2 colder
3 latest 4 bigger
5 fastest 6 early
7 better

내신 FOCUS

A 1 most curious 2 is thinner
B 1 ⓓ 2 ⓐ
C 1 ⓑ 2 ⓐ
D 1 you speak more loudly
2 my worst habit
3 is more talented than
4 is the coldest month

비교급과 최상급(기타)

P. 70

A
1 twice as big as 2 much
3 hotter 4 as good as
5 friendliest 6 the more

B
1 than 2 closer
3 O 4 the more
5 richest 6 much/even/far/still/a lot

C
1 not as bad as 2 as soon as you can
3 most entertaining opera
4 three times as large as
5 The longer, the more

내신 FOCUS

A 1 is better than
2 as many letters as possible
B 1 ⓓ 2 ⓑ
C 1 ⓓ 2 ⓑ
D 1 is getting warmer and warmer
2 as successful as
3 is twice as expensive as
4 The faster you finish, the earlier you can

Unit 11

Unit 1 장소/방향 전치사

P. 72

A
1 behind 2 on 3 near
4 into 5 from 6 in front of

B
1 at 2 in 3 in
4 on 5 in 6 on

C
1 from 2 down 3 among
4 between 5 toward 6 under
7 from

내신 FOCUS

A 1 over 2 behind
3 out of 4 in
B 1 ⓓ 2 ⓒ
C 1 ⓐ 2 ⓑ
D 1 between the post office and the police station

2 under the bed
3 in front of City Hall
4 from Queens Mall to Meyer's Department Store

Unit 2 시간 전치사

P. 74

A

1 at	2 in	3 on
4 in	5 on	6 in
7 at		

B

1 in	2 around	3 until
4 by	5 since	6 during

C

1 at 6 o'clock	2 in a few minutes
3 for 30 minutes	4 on Tuesday morning
5 before the concert	6 by 1 o'clock tomorrow
7 from 7 to 10	

내신 FOCUS

A 1 until, by 2 for, during
B 1 ⓐ 2 ⓒ
C 1 ⓓ 2 ⓒ
D 1 were held in 1988
2 swims from 6 to 7
3 has lived with us since 2000
4 call me around/about 7

Unit 3 기타 전치사

P. 76

A

1 with	2 for
3 about	4 through
5 to	6 along
7 for	

B

1 with	2 by
3 through	4 around
5 along	6 on

C

1 with wood	2 around the pond
3 to the students	4 by bus
5 for $30	6 about the tallest buildings

내신 FOCUS

A 1 with 2 by
B 1 ⓐ 2 ⓒ
C 1 ⓑ 2 ⓐ
D 1 marched through downtown
2 was pleased with his math score
3 asking about my bike accident
4 is bad for your health

Unit 12

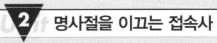

Unit 1 등위접속사

P. 78

A

1 or	2 but	3 so
4 so	5 but	6 or
7 and		

B

1 and	2 or	3 and
4 or		

C

1 not only	2 or	3 and
4 Both	5 not	6 Neither
7 but		

내신 FOCUS

A 1 and 2 or
3 but 4 so
B 1 ⓑ 2 ⓒ
C 1 ⓒ 2 ⓐ
D 1 not handsome, but cute
2 Neither Kevin nor Cathy repaired
3 the movie tickets now or the tickets will be sold out
4 gives us not only light, but also energy

Unit 2 명사절을 이끄는 접속사

P. 80

A

1 if	2 that	3 if
4 that	5 Whether	6 that
7 whether		

B

1 that Karen helped us
2 that Vickie didn't call us again
3 that you are going to college next year

C

1 what he is doing in the yard
2 how she found the name of the store
3 who the people by the door are
4 where she is going
5 why my parents grounded me for a week

내신 FOCUS

A 1 that 2 whether/if
B 1 ⓓ 2 ⓑ
C 1 ⓓ 2 ⓐ
D 1 know whether/if it is true
2 asked her whether/if he refused her offer
3 the fact (that) Mandy stole the wallet
4 that the little boy moved the big rock

Unit 3 부사절을 이끄는 접속사

P. 82

A

1 Unless 2 even though
3 because 4 since
5 because of 6 If
7 before 8 Until

B

1 After I had breakfast
2 Though they practiced hard yesterday
3 Unless they finish work quickly

C

1 Because/Since/As
2 because/since/as
3 while
4 Although/Even though/Though
5 when
6 before

내신 FOCUS

A 1 because 2 Though 3 until
B 1 ⓒ 2 ⓑ
C 1 ⓓ 2 ⓓ
D 1 Unless you do your homework
2 after we have a meal
3 Even though/Although/Though I was sick
4 Since/As/Because he didn't[did not] have enough money

Unit 4 부사절의 축약(분사구문)

P. 84

A

1 Hearing 2 Focusing
3 Being sad 4 Leaving
5 turn 6 Not saying

B

1 As 2 Although
3 When 4 Even though
5 Because

C

1 Breaking the vase
2 Not working hard
3 Walking his dog
4 Looking into the microscope

내신 FOCUS

A 1 Cleaning her room
2 Watching the weather forecast
B 1 ⓑ 2 ⓒ
C 1 ⓓ 2 ⓒ
D 1 Not knowing the reason
2 Seeing him, my dog started
3 Being late, I took a taxi
4 Opening the window, you can see

Unit 13

Unit 1 관계대명사

P. 86

A

1 which 2 that 3 who
4 that 5 that 6 who

B

1 which/that 2 which/that
3 who/that 4 which/that
5 who/that 6 who/that

C

1 Mary will buy something that we can eat
2 I waved at Frank who/that is my best friend at school
3 I don't know the woman who/that is standing by the cash register
4 The ring has a big stone which/that sparkles in the sunlight
5 I lost my phone which/that I bought last week

내신 FOCUS

A 1 who/that 2 which/that
B 1 ⓑ 2 ⓐ
C 1 ⓐ 2 ⓓ
D 1 the bag which/that his mother gave
2 is the biggest flower (that) I've[I have] ever seen
3 the Pyramids which/that are tombs for Pharaohs
4 bring something that can help poor people

Unit 2 관계대명사의 쓰임

P. 88

A

1	that	2	whom
3	that	4	which
5	for which	6	who
7	whose	8	who

B

1	that/which	2	whose
3	who(m)/who	4	whose
5	O	6	whose

C

1 I talked to his cousin who/that has a new car.
2 She tries to move the desk that/which is very heavy.
3 The man orders a sandwich which/that is healthy.
4 Mike is the only one that I can count on.

내신 FOCUS

A 1 who/that 2 whose
3 which/that 3 who(m)/that
B 1 ⓑ 2 ⓐ
C 1 ⓑ 2 ⓒ
D 1 raises the puppy that his friend gave
2 the person who made a presentation with me
3 the girl who I introduced to you
4 fixed the chair whose leg was broken

Unit 3 관계대명사의 특별 용법

P. 90

A

1 two wedding cakes
2 She bought a Korean mask
3 the picture
4 some ice cream
5 her sister's sweater
6 my sister's friend
7 milk
8 I traveled across the county by motorcycle

B

1	which/that	2	which
3	who	4	that

C

1	R	2	C	3	R
4	C	5	C	6	R

내신 FOCUS

A 1 나는 그녀에게 조언을 했는데, 그것이 그녀를 화나게 만들었다.
2 지난 일요일에 나는 James를 만났는데, 그는 정말 잘생겼고 귀여웠다.
B 1 ⓒ 2 ⓑ
C 1 ⓑ 2 ⓒ
D 1 I bought a watch, which cost $100
2 introduced Jake, who was bald
3 married a selfish man, which ruined her life
4 who invented the airplane, were born

Unit 4 관계부사

P. 92

A

1	why	2	the way
3	when	4	where
5	how	6	why
7	where	8	when

B

1	why	2	where
3	when	4	where
5	how	6	why

C

1 This is the coffee shop where I can have the best coffee.
2 This map tells me how I can find the airport.
3 The manual explains the reason why it made a noise.

내신 FOCUS

A 1 where　　2 when
3 why　　4 how
B 1 ⓑ　　2 ⓒ
C 1 ⓑ　　2 ⓐ
D 1 I remember the day when I drove a car
2 tell me how I can open the file
3 is the place where I used to play
4 I told him why I was

Unit 14

1 가정법

P. 94

A
1 tells　　2 were　　3 is not
4 invented　　5 stops　　6 drive
7 had

B
1 knew　　2 lend　　3 were
4 were　　5 do not fix　　6 were not
7 were

C
1 am not, can't do　　2 isn't, can't drive
3 isn't, can't get　　4 doesn't have, can't afford

내신 FOCUS

A 1 would call　　2 asked
B 1 ⓑ　　2 ⓐ
C 1 ⓐ　　2 ⓓ
D 1 is fine, will go on a picnic
2 had a big house, would invite
3 leaves early, will be very sad
4 knew the truth, would tell him

2 가정법(과거완료, 기타 가정법)

P. 96

A
1 were　　2 had　　3 had seen
4 had been　　5 Without　　6 had had
7 were

B
1 had, had had　　2 were, had been
3 saved, had saved　　4 talked, had talked

C
1 knew　　2 were not
3 would not have known　　4 had taken

내신 FOCUS

A 1 ⓒ　　2 ⓑ
B 1 ⓑ　　2 ⓐ
C 1 ⓑ　　2 ⓐ
D 1 I had a twin brother
2 as if he had seen a ghost
3 were not for, couldn't[could not] win the game

3 화법/부가의문문

P. 98

A
1 told, could　　2 to wait
3 asked, had made　　4 asked, would
5 said, he

B
1 are they　　2 won't he
3 isn't it　　4 does he
5 can she　　6 can't they
7 don't they

C
1 to eat all of her soup
2 if I am going to school now
3 not to behave so poorly around my parents
4 they were flying at 10,000 feet

내신 FOCUS

A 1 said, he was　　2 asked, if I wanted
B 1 ⓒ　　2 ⓐ
C 1 ⓒ　　2 ⓓ
D 1 I need some vitamins now
2 where she wanted to go
3 to do my homework
4 can she